Clemens Jobst / Hans Kernbauer
The Quest for Stable Money
Central Banking in Austria, 1816–2016

Clemens Jobst / Hans Kernbauer

The Quest for Stable Money

Central Banking in Austria, 1816–2016

Table of contents

Introduction

Milestone birthdays present an opportunity to reflect not just on one's own age but also to anticipate upcoming family birthdays of significance or recall past family anniversaries. Central banks are no different in this respect. Many central bank histories start with a reference to the oldest surviving member of the family, the Swedish Riksbank, founded in 1668. In the genealogical table of the oldest central banks in the world, drawn up by Forrest Capie, Charles Goodhart and Norbert Schnadt in their seminal contribution marking the tercentenary of the Bank of England, the privilegirte oesterreichische National-Bank (OeNB) comes in sixth.[1] Apart from the above-mentioned Sveriges Riksbank and the Bank of England (1694), the only central banks founded before the OeNB were the Banque de France (1800), the Bank of Finland (originally established as the Finnish Office for Exchange, Lending and Deposits in 1811) and De Nederlandsche Bank (1814). Finishing sixth was in fact close for the OeNB: Founded on June 1, 1816, it is just 13 days older than Norges Bank.

Yet this genealogy does not list defunct family members like the Banco di San Giorgio (1407–1805), the Bank of Amsterdam (1609–1820), or the Wiener Stadtbanco (1706–1816), precursors who would change the ranking had they survived.[2] Moreover, central banks' birth dates are frequently stated with the reservation that early on, these banks had few similarities with contemporary monetary authorities, evolving into central banks as we know them only in a slow process and over an extended time span. Passage to adulthood, to continue the analogy, is generally linked to the assumption of a lender-of-last-resort role, meaning the provision of sufficient central bank money during a financial crisis if required. To this end, the central bank must have "grown up" to be a neutral, nonprofit-oriented economic agent who acts in the general economic interest rather than competing with other commercial banks.[3]

Two recurring challenges

Now, if the OeNB was born in 1816, when did it reach adulthood? The eventful history of Austria's central bank does not lend itself easily to a teleological interpretation according to which early banks of issue developed into modern central banks at a determinable point in time. Thus, rather than judging at what point and to what degree the OeNB fulfilled modern-day criteria of central banking, a more appropriate approach is to view the bank as an institution that operates in a space that both in the past and today is defined by two dimensions: monetary stability and financial stability.[4]

Of course, the meaning of monetary and financial stability has changed during the past 200 years. Originally, money was considered to be stable if all coins were struck with consistent amounts of metal; later, the notion of monetary stability was linked with the convertibility of paper money against coins with a specified metal content. Not until the 20th century was monetary stability understood as the stability of a broadly defined index of consumer prices. Financial stability, on the other hand, has typically been a much broader concept, embracing the smooth operation of payment systems; last resort lending; the supervision of individual banks and other financial intermediaries; or the prevention of macroeconomic imbalances such as real estate price bubbles driven by excessive mortgage lending, which may jeopardize the stability of the entire financial system. The basic issue of monetary and financial stability has always been the same: Since money has been around, the sovereigns who exercised the right of coinage had an incentive to finance their expenditure by debasing the currency, either by reducing the weight of coins or by adding base metals to the alloy. Numerous instances of inflation from Classical antiquity to the modern age demonstrate this process; paper money, once it had been invented, made debasement only easier. As money and credit are closely related, financial crises have a long history as well.

Thus, upon its birth in 1816, the privilegirte oesterreichische National-Bank entered a well established area of politics in which it came up against a traditional player, the state, and the legacy of a municipal bank that was in some ways its predecessor and that used to be closely associated with the state: the Wiener Stadtbanco. The arrival of a "national bank" was a game changer insofar as the new bank was endowed with tasks and decision-making duties that had formerly been under the jurisdiction of the finance ministry. At the same time, the new bank received (at least some) independence from the state and some freedom from direct state control. Over time, the actual allocation of individual monetary policy responsibilities among the bank and other economic agents, especially the state, changed several times, as did the general economic and political setting within which monetary policy was run.

Looking at the 200-year history of the OeNB reveals that monetary policy again and again faced conflicting choices: *first*, the provision of a stable legal tender versus inflationary incentives to finance the state and boost the economy; *second*, the delegation of economic policy to an independent central bank versus the need to control this bank; *third*, transparency and accountability versus confidentiality; and *fourth*, a close versus a more arms-length relationship with the banking sector. Similarily, the issues that needed to be resolved against this backdrop of conflicting choices resurfaced time and again: Should exchange rates be flexible or fixed, and to which currency should fixed exchange rates be pegged? How should wars be financed? How should excess money in the aftermath of wars be handled? How should illiquid or insolvent banks be dealt with? How can the build-up of imbalances in the financial system be stopped? Should internal or external stability take precedence? Should capital movements be restricted? With regard to the broader institutional framework conditions, the latest game changer was the creation of the Eurosystem. In the Eurosystem, which comprises the European Central Bank (ECB) and the national central banks of the euro area countries, including the OeNB, central banking decision-making has largely shifted to the European level. Yet here, too, the same issues arise and the same decisions need to be taken as in previous decades and centuries.

Reading the past in the light of the present

These recurring themes are also reflected in the narratives of the OeNB's history. Of course, as a central actor in domestic and occasionally, like in 1857 or 1931, international economic policy, the bank deserves a prominent place in any account of Austria's political and economic history. Often, the questions and methods with which the history of the OeNB has been interpreted were influenced by big conceptual swings in historical science. An example of the significance of international trends for the historiography of Austria is the abundant literature on 19th century economic growth, which was produced at the same time as a similar literature on other European countries.[5] However, the regular resurfacing of the same issues and problems in monetary policy means that narratives of central bank history are likely to have been influenced more strongly by current issues than other areas of historiography. This is true even of the comprehensive chronology of OeNB history that historian Siegfried Pressburger compiled in the 1960s and 1970s: Although his narrative meticulously follows the sources he consulted, it at the same time echoes the themes that dominated the economic policy debate of the time–demand management and exchange rate policy–wherever he made reference to current themes.[6]

In the case of studies focusing on selected aspects of Austria's monetary history, the impact is to be felt to an even greater extent. Thus it comes as no surprise that a number of studies written during inflationary World War I and immediately afterward would closely examine the sovereign default and the currency reform following the inflation during the Napoleonic wars.[7] More recently, the dissolution of the Soviet Union and the breakup of Czechoslovakia revived interest in the collapse of the crown currency area after 1918. By the same token, the European unification process and the discussion surrounding the design of the Economic and Monetary Union in Europe prompted analyses of the operation of the partly similarly structured currency area in the dual monarchy before 1918.[8] The transition from the Austrian schilling to the euro in 1999 spawned a number of studies exploring the history of the schilling.[9] The discourse on the merits of fixed versus flexible exchange rate regimes is an evergreen in debates on economic policy.[10] Last but not least, the banking crisis of 2008 rekindled researchers' interest in the crises of 1873 and 1931, while the international financial support programs for Greece, Ireland and Portugal sparked a review of the League of Nations loans and related foreign control of Austrian fiscal policy in the 1920s and 1930s. These studies have either been published in recent years or are forthcoming.[11]

Partly, the choice of perspectives and topics is driven by the ambition to draw lessons from the past to help solve the urgent problems of the present. Yet it is just as important that current events lead us to question and redefine our understanding of the past. After all, the conventional wisdom no longer appears adequate in numerous cases, either because recent experience has cast doubts on the logic of old interpretations or because aspects and details of particular interest to us today have not been covered in the existing histiography. For instance, overview publications summarizing the OeNB's history in the 19th century largely neglected the role of the bank in the economic integration of the monarchy and barely scratched the surface in examining the relationship between the central bank and commercial banks. A closer look at these topics is relevant against the backdrop of the European integration process and of the new role of central banks and the EU today, and at the same time casts new light on the evolution of the OeNB from the treasury's banker to the banker's bank, a subject that was given short shrift in older publications.

This book is the first endeavor since Othmar Bachmayer and Siegfried Pressburger wrote their surveys of Austrian monetary history 50 years ago to provide a concise yet comprehensive overview of the history of the Oesterreichische Nationalbank. Since then, the collapse of the post-World-War-II monetary order under the Bretton Woods system, Austria's hard currency policy and the introduction of the euro have added important new chapters to the bank's history. Additionally, new works on the history of Austria's central bank published in the past 50 years have inspired us to reassess some of the older accounts. Finally, this history represents an opportunity to assign greater weight to the role of the OeNB in securing financial stability and to its role as the banker's bank than previous historical treatises did. To better meet the objective of delivering a compact overview, we have focused on selected developments in the two key areas of central bank policy: monetary stability and financial stability. Rather than providing an all-encompassing history of the OeNB, we favor overview descriptions over a chronological narrative wherever possible, omitting events that are not needed to understand the big picture. Issues not limited to a particular era or chapter, such as the definition of lender of last resort or monetary policy operations, are treated in boxes. For further reading, readers may turn to the ten-volume work heavily based on internal OeNB documents that Siegfried Pressburger began on the occasion of the 150th anniversary of the OeNB and that was completed with contributions by Hans Kernbauer and Fritz Weber in recent years. Pointers for further reference are provided in our exhaustive bibliography.

A first try at monetary autonomy—the Wiener Stadtbanco (1706–1816)

"The paper money scissors absolutely have to be taken out of the treasury's hands ... History and experience have invariably shown that if the power to cut out paper money lies with the public administration, it is as if a child had been handed a knife: It is impossible to prevent the treasury from damaging the country."

Count Zinzendorf in a petition
to the emperor submitted August 1, 1806[12]

On June 1, 1816, Emperor Francis I signed the decrees establishing the privilegirte oesterreichische National-Bank, almost exactly one year after the conclusion of the Congress of Vienna marking the end of a 20-odd-year period of wars in which Europe and Austria had been embroiled. Ultimately, the Austrian Empire emerged as one of the victorious powers, albeit with empty state coffers and a depreciated currency. The pressing tasks of the newly founded note-issuing bank thus consisted in supporting the state in restoring financial order and in reestablishing a sound currency.

The National-Bank was not the first bank Austria had created to shore up government finances. The first proposals to found banks based on Italian models were made in the first half of the 17th century, but they were never implemented.[13] Not until some 80 years later were financial institutions established that should assist in securing long-term financing for the public budget: the Banco del Giro, founded in Vienna in 1703, and the Wiener Stadtbanco, the Vienna City Bank, established in 1706.

Public banks in the 1600s and 1700s—innovative payment services and public debt management

On foundation, the Banco del Giro and the Wiener Stadtbanco joined the ranks of some 25 public banks already established across Europe.[14] These banks were operated by the treasury, by autonomous provincial or municipal entities, or by groups of people endowed with special rights and privileges by government.[15] The first public banks were set up in the late Middle Ages in the western Mediterranean area; banks in the Netherlands and Germany followed in the 16th century. Public banks were generally founded for one of two reasons, one being the need for an institution that would provide a stable means of payment. This was the case in Amsterdam, Genoa or Hamburg, which had suffered from the simultaneous circulation of different types of coins of varying qualities before the advent of public banks, whereas in Venice, cashless payment transactions had come to a standstill after the private banks that had handled them became insolvent. A second reason to found a public bank lay in the hope of facilitating the management and servicing of the public debt. To this end, national or municipal debt to individuals was–in simplified terms–converted into deposits with the public bank. These deposits were tradable through transfers and could be used as a means of payment for private transactions. Such arrangements providing for the transfer of debt into a form of money made holding public debt more attractive, so it became easier for the government to take out new debt. Ergo, these banks' common feature consisted in the creation of book money–deposit currency that had a more stable intrinsic value than coins or holdings with private banks and that was thus the preferred instrument for payments or could be traded more readily than other public debt instruments. Providing a stable means of payment and making government debt tradable are of course closely linked functions, as the Stadtbanco example will show below. At any rate, for all their differences, the public banks of the 15th to 18th century were the precursors of modern central banks, given their pivotal role of creating a liquid means of payment with a stable value.[16]

The banking models which evolved in the 15th and 16th centuries were further refined and adjusted over time. The mainspring of these developments were innovations that enhanced the quality of financial instruments–debt instruments and especially payment instruments. For such advances to catch on, their advantages had to accrue to issuers–the banks or the public administration–and to users of the instruments alike. Clearly, issuers had a vested interest in their instrument being used, which in the long run would happen only if people were willing to adopt it. Innovations could be technical, legal or institutional. Banknotes are an example of a technical innovation (pioneered by Sweden, France and England) that broadened the reach of money transfers because it freed businessmen from the need to hold an underlying bank account to make or receive payments. A legal innovation was the possibility of paying taxes without physically transferring coins, another winning feature of banknotes and bank deposits. Finally, an example of an institutional breakthrough was the removal of the bank of issue from the direct control of the state, preventing the government from covering its expenditure by putting too much money into circulation. The independence of the bank of issue protected monetary stability and increased the appeal of banknotes and ledger money alike.

A bankrupt sovereign in need of a public bank

The merits of public banks for a well-functioning economy and for a high credit standing of the state did not go unnoticed in Austria. Indeed, a number of blueprints were developed in the 17th century for banks that would facilitate payments and support trade.[17] Yet the first public bank to be actually established in Austria in the early 18th century was clearly created for another key reason: out of the need to improve public debt management.

Public finances in Austria around 1700

The driving force behind the foundation of the Banco del Giro in 1703 was the looming insolvency of the state following the death of the merchant and banker who had played a central role in public finance, Samuel Oppenheimer. The very fact that a single individual could be a linchpin is indicative of how public finances were organized during the reign of Leopold I: They were inextricably bound up with the identity of the reigning monarch. Revenues and expenditure as well as debt were connected to the monarch ad personam.[18] Technically, the national budget was dependent on two revenue streams, which theoretically fed two expenditure streams. One stream of revenue was the income that arose from royal prerogatives, like monopolies, returns from mining rights and the rights to levy tariffs, customs and excise duties. This revenue–the *camerale* revenue, i.e., income administered by the court treasury *(Hofkammer)*–was mainly channeled into civil spending. The funds for the military budget resulted from tax income, called *contributionale*[19] income, the collection of which had to be authorized by the diet in which the nobility, the clergy and the municipal administration were represented. Above all during wartime, the authorized expenditure was often less than needed, and the representatives of the estates wielded their power of assent to elicit concessions from their sovereign in other matters. Not surprisingly, the negotiations often proved arduous.[20] Time and again, the sovereign was forced to bankroll gaps in the military budget by drawing on the *camerale* budget or by borrowing, even more so as Austria was in a state of almost permanent warfare.

Just like all state revenue went to the sovereign ad personam, all debt incurred was his personal responsibility, not that of the state.[21] Debt was generally collateralized by pledging earmarked revenue to which the sovereign was entitled, like customs or tolls. Binding debt ad personam to the sovereign subjected such transactions to high risk. The rule of law was not fully developed, and the sovereign's dealings with his creditors were autocratic and arbitrary. If the coffers were empty, creditors could face unilateral extensions of payment deadlines or see short-term claims rolled over into long-term debt. Creditors with less clout could be turned away; major creditors could be charged as criminals or jailed.[22] Many of the government's business partners were, moreover, at a disadvantage in transactions with the erratic authorities because they were members of a religious minority. Jews were especially vulnerable: All Jews had been expelled from Vienna within recent memory, in 1670, and the few families that had been permitted to settle in Vienna since were subject to tough restrictions.[23] As timely payments by government depended on the negotiation skills of individual creditors, government promises of payment were virtually untradable. Thus it was that around 1700, only few creditors were willing or able to lend the sovereign money. For the government, the lack of attractiveness of its debt securities meant that it had to pay high interest of between 6% and 12% or temporarily even 20% on long-term debt; short-term and thus more pressing loans commanded even steeper rates.[24]

To effectively wage war and to meet all other official expenses in this system, the sovereign depended on wealthy private-sector financiers for buying weapons, keeping the troops supplied, procuring goods and, of course, funding the related transactions. In Vienna, this money came from a group of warehousers and court suppliers, who served as both brokers of goods and brokers of money:[25] merchants were bankers and vice versa. The business model drew extensively on international family networks that facilitated trading and banking. Most of all, the networks also gave merchants and bankers access to their business partners' considerable financial resources for onward lending to the sovereign. These merchant families were by no means all Jewish; Protestants also played an important role.[26] In addition to providing their own capital, the court agents also negotiated loans from the nobility and high officials to the sovereign. For these lenders, engaging the services of a court agent had bene-fits: The court agent was sufficiently indispensable to the emperor to enforce his claims–and thus indirectly those of his suppliers and creditors–against the emperor. But the mutual dependency of the sovereign and the financiers as well as the powerful role of individuals made this system highly vulnerable to disruptions.

In Western Europe the state emancipated itself progressively from the reigning monarch during the 17th and 18th centuries. This dissociation was the prerequisite for a modern market for government debt.[27] The Habsburg monar-chy embarked on this process later than other countries: It did tap the existing Western European markets to issue bonds from the late 17th century onward, collateralizing the bonds with revenues from copper and mercury mining.[28] Domestically, though, the government broadly retained its funding habits. Yet by the beginning of the 18th century, the decision makers had realized that the framework of public finance governance, in particular public debt manage-ment, had to be improved on the pattern of foreign models. Oppenheimer's death in 1703 very dramatically exposed the system's weak spots.[29]

Oppenheimer had been truly essential in keeping Austria's public finances afloat.[30] On his decease, scores of creditors turned to the government for sat-isfaction with the argument that Oppenheimer had merely brokered their busi-ness and that their claims on Oppenheimer ultimately represented claims on the state. As the state did not have the funds to service its debts with Oppen-heimer, it imposed a moratorium, thus precipitating a general financial crisis. The need to mitigate the immediate impact of the bankruptcy and the foresight to address the basic problems of state debt management at the same time led to the creation of the Banco del Giro, a bank that was not only named after its Venetian namesake created in 1619 but also copied its business model: making claims on the state, notably those from the Oppenheimer bankruptcy, transfer-able in the form of bank accounts.[31] The respective claims would thus no longer be assertable directly for payment in cash from the state, but instead be kept in circulation as book money. If accountholders found that book money was useful for facilitating payments, the state even stood the chance of attracting additional deposits from individuals in the medium term–provided the liabilities of the Banco del Giro were credibly backed. That was to be achieved by assigning selected state revenues as collateral. And this is the very point at which the project failed: The provinces and the court treasury, the body in charge of administering the *camerale* budget and thus the precursor of the finance ministry, insisted that tax revenues were earmarked and could not be reallocated at a whim. Hence, the Banco del Giro did not obtain the funds it needed and was unable to fulfill the role it had been assigned. While it continued to exist as part of the Stadtbanco founded in 1706, it no longer played a role as an independent institution.[32]

Benefiting from Vienna's credit score—the Wiener Stadtbanco

In the meantime, Count Gundaker Thomas von Starhemberg, head of the court treasury since 1703 and hostile to the Banco del Giro, was promoting banking projects of his own, which were crowned with success after the death of Leopold I and the accession to the throne of Joseph I in 1705. Like the masterminds of previous bank plans for Austria, Starhemberg was well aware of the achilles heel of any public bank in an absolut monarchy: The ability to build public trust hinged on independence from the state, and building trust was a prerequisite for getting citizens to make deposits and accept money issued by the bank in payment. To build trust in the independence of his initial banking project, Starhemberg intended to give a prominent role to the estates of the Austrian and Bohemian crown lands. His rationale was as follows: being representative bodies, the estates had the right to levy taxes and enjoyed autonomy from the emperor and were thus in a position to lend financial support to the bank.[33] The scenario that was actually implemented in 1705 accorded this role to the City of Vienna, which was an integral part of the Lower Austrian estates. Starhemberg thus copied a system that had worked well in France, where the king exploited the good credit score of the municipality of Paris to raise new debt more easily and at a lower cost.[34]

The bank thus created started to operate in 1706 under the name of Wiener Stadtbanco.[35] Unlike the business model proposed earlier, which intended the bank to use its deposit base in support of trade and industry, the sole purpose of the Stadtbanco was to fill the state's war coffer. To this effect, the state transferred part of its debt to the municipality, which assumed responsibility for the payment of interest and capital on the debt and received earmarked tax revenues in return. To secure the public's trust, the bank was run by municipal government officials, and the municipality of Vienna also provided guarantees for the bank's liabilities. The Stadtbanco's independence from influence was meant to ensure that the bank accepted government debt only if it was appropriately covered by tax revenues.[36] Depositors were promised exemption from taxation and protection against seizure of property, especially during wartime. This was a material advantage particularly for foreign creditors. In return, the Stadtbanco had to cede any profits from its more efficient administration of the pledged taxes or from lower interest on debt to the state. In other words, like the Banco del Giro, the Stadtbanco was not a bank in the modern sense, but a special agency administering the public debt. It generated advantages for the state's creditors and thus made holding state debt more attractive, which in turn made it easier to finance the public debt at a lower interest rate.

In reality, the role of the Vienna municipality in administering the bank was far weaker than the public was led to believe, and it was curtailed more and more over time. As a case in point, the *Ministerial-Bancodeputation*–the supervisory body first installed to represent the finance ministry at the Stadtbanco– was given the right to intervene directly in operations as early as in 1706.[37] In 1716, the magistrate lost the right to appoint the bank's officials. In retaliation, the municipal authorities in 1717 announced that they would be liable for the Stadtbanco's debt only to the extent of the anticipated income on the revenue assigned to the bank.[38] Increasingly, the separation between the bank and the treasury existed only on paper.

Despite the close association between the Wiener Stadtbanco and the court treasury, the new institution nevertheless succeeded in gaining the trust of the public over time. At the outset, the bank was mainly engaged in setting up and managing interest payments on the claims on the predecessor bank, Banco del Giro, and in rolling them over into longer-term debt of the Stadtbanco. It also succeeded in increasing profits by managing the taxes and duties transferred to it more efficiently. From 1712, the bank received growing volumes of deposits that could be withdrawn anytime subject to a period of notice that was contingent on the amount withdrawn. By 1724, some 90,000 investors had made deposits with the Stadtbanco, bringing the total volume to several million florins.[39] No small part of the Stadtbanco's success was due to the scarcity of interest-bearing, liquid investment alternatives in the early 18th century. The Stadtbanco was particularly attractive for small investors. The estates of deceased craftsmen, for instance, frequently contained deposits of 100 to 1,000 florins, sometimes also more.[40] The circle of government creditors expanded, marking another key step toward reducing the dependence of government on a single creditor.[41] The great appeal to investors was reflected by the drop in the interest rate on government debt from between 9% and 20% at the start of the century to just 5% to 6% in the late 1720s. Consequently, all 6% government bonds were converted into 5% bonds in 1732 and into bonds carrying only 4% interest in 1766.[42] At the same time, the Stadtbanco's high credibility made it possible to raise large volumes of funds for the state at short notice if required.[43] From the finance administration perspective, the Stadtbanco was thus a tremendous success.

The further biography of the Stadtbanco was conditional on the development of the fiscal deficit. The government tried to take advantage of the Stadtbanco's favorable financing conditions without going so far as to endanger the bank's credibility and the confidence in its liabilities. It is hardly surprising that differences of opinion often arose between the bank's management and government officials about defining the limits of government borrowing. Moreover, the different perceptions were compounded by political conflicts. Emperor Charles VI, for example, was less well disposed toward the bank than his predecessor, Joseph I, and attempted to establish a new bank that was directly answerable to the state. This institution, *Universal-Bankalität*, operated from 1715, but with little success. It had to be taken over by the Stadtbanco in 1721 to prevent its insolvency.[44] The Stadtbanco, though, proved to be an effective support in financing the numerous and, on occasion, long drawn-out wars against the Ottoman Empire and France. A comparison of the public debt at the beginning and at the end of Charles VI's reign illustrates the Stadtbanco's importance: The volume of direct government debt financing–money the state received directly from creditors–barely changed from 1711 to 1740 and came to just under 50 million florins. Conversely, during the same period, the government debt held by the Stadtbanco rose from 12 million to nearly 55 million florins, meaning that all new government borrowing during Charles VI's thirty-year reign was handled by the Stadtbanco.[45]

Municipal bank in name only: turning into a general government authority

Maria Theresa's accession to the throne in 1740 did not result in any immediate changes in the Stadtbanco's management. Providing cash advances to the state and issuing Stadtbanco debt certificates for government use as payment or collateral remained the bank's most important operations.[46] 1745 marked the death of Count Starhemberg, on whose initiative the bank had been founded in 1706 and who had decisively influenced the bank's policy as the president of the Bancodeputation since 1711. After the Austrian war of succession (1740–1748) had ended, Empress Maria Theresa introduced a number of reforms to transform Austria from a loose association of estates-based states to a uniform, centrally administered state. The reforms concerned the military, educational and legal systems and especially the administration of public finance. In the next decades, the power of the estates was gradually curtailed and at least the Bohemian and Austrian lands were combined into a centrally administered state.[47]

Against the backdrop of these reforms, the organization of the Stadtbanco was an anachronism with its co-management by the Vienna municipal authorities and its authority to levy various duties, depriving the sovereign of his direct claim to this revenue. In an era of absolutist centralization, policy makers clearly favored a purely state-operated credit institution. Accordingly, from 1749, the influence of the Vienna municipal authorities was limited to appointing the chief tax collector and cashier, whereas the bank was run exclusively by the civil servants seconded from the finance ministry. A Prussian diplomat in Vienna aptly described this change when remarking that the Bancodeputation, originally simply charged with supervising that the management appointed by the municipal authority complied with regulations, had "gradually taken full management control of the Stadtbanco, reducing the role of the municipal administration to that of lending its name."[48] But the reforms launched in 1749 by Count Friedrich Wilhelm Haugwitz, Maria Theresa's chief financial counselor, left the statutory organization of the Stadtbanco and of the Bancodeputation unchanged, at least on the surface.[49] Nobody wished to damage the bank's creditworthiness by moving it closer to government control. In the public eye, the president of the Bancodeputation now personified the guarantee that the bank would retain a certain degree of independence from the treasury and would thus secure its public standing and its success. This strategy continued to work for the time being when Count Rudolf Chotek was elected president of the Bancodeputation in 1749.[50]

Yet the treasury's appetite was by no means sated. When a government reform was launched in 1761, Chancellor Wenzel Anton von Kaunitz criticized the lack of state control of the tax revenue earmarked for the Stadtbanco. Kaunitz did not have a high opinion of the Stadtbanco's independence and designed a scheme for a state bank fully integrating the Stadtbanco as well as the Bancodeputation into the treasury.[51] Another plan, masterminded by a counselor to Empress Maria Theresa, Count Karl von Zinzendorf, envisaged upgrading the Stadtbanco into a bank of issue, based on the model practiced in England.[52] Zinzendorf proposed converting government debt into bond debt, his intention being that government funding needs would no longer be met by the Stadtbanco but directly by investors. However, both plans proved unfeasible. Zinzendorf at least succeeded in founding the Vienna Stock Exchange in 1771, a public, regulated market that made trading in government securities more transparent and thus more attractive to investors.[53] In a political environment with increased absolutist and centralization tendencies, the forces in favor of putting a single agency in charge of government revenue prevailed in the end. Further reforms incorporated the Bancodeputation into the court treasury in 1764/65. Nevertheless, the appearance of independence was kept up, and even Joseph II was aware that the autonomy of public debt management, for the very purpose of which the Stadtbanco had been launched in 1706, had to be preserved on paper so as not to compromise the attractiveness of the Stadtbanco's bonds.[54] Ultimately, although its independence was increasingly curtailed, the Stadtbanco existed for more than 100 years, to be superseded only by the Oesterreichische Nationalbank in 1816.[55]

Paper money and inflation

Next to the foundation of the Stadtbanco, the issue of paper money was the second great financial innovation in Austria in the 18th century. Paper money–an interest-free, readily transferable means of payment–was the endpoint of a development begun in 1706 to devise more liquid and thus lower-interest forms of government debt. The introduction of paper money marked a significant structural break in Austria's monetary history. Once again, the government's pressing need for funds gave rise to this innovation. In 1762, Austria was in the throes of the final stage of the Seven Years' War (1756–1763) and urgently required additional money that it was unlikely to obtain from either taxes or loans. The Stadtbanco was instructed to issue 12 million florins of paper money, called *Bancozettel*. The paper florins carried neither interest nor a compulsory conversion rate; nobody could be forced to accept them. But they came with the convenience of being legal tender at par for up to half of tax payments due. The new notes could be paid for only with coins and could be redeemed for coins at the Stadtbanco at any time.[56] As it was assumed that part of the notes would remain in circulation, the Stadtbanco could lend the government the cash equivalent. To make the paper florins attractive for use in payments, they were issued in fairly small denominations: Some 4.5 million of 12 million florins were notes with a face value of 5 florins. The issue was intended as a temporary measure to tide over the government until it could return to floating government bonds. Therefore, holders of at least 200 paper florins were entitled to exchange these for Stadtbanco obligations bearing 5% interest,[57] and the law called for the destruction of redeemed paper florins. 7.8 million paper florins were returned until 1766 and were burned in a high-profile operation just outside the city walls, "on the glacis left of Schotten-Thor."[58]

Despite these returns, paper florins had remained in circulation for a notable period. Their appeal showed among other things in their premium of 1% to 2% on coins in the market: The public was obviously willing to pay extra for the ease of handling paper florins.[59] Their success story made paper money issues a keystone of government strategy for future wars.[60] While paper money issuing was still looked upon mainly as an extraordinary measure, issues on a small scale even during peacetime were heralded as a way to economize on coin metal and to accustom the public to paper notes.[61] When the bulk of the paper florins launched originally had been redeemed by 1770, a second 12 million paper florin tranche was issued in 1771. Again, the issuing volume was officially announced, but this time, there were two important changes compared to 1762: The notes could no longer be exchanged for interest-bearing bonds, but they could now be used to pay taxes to the full extent. In fact, half of all tax debts over 10 florins had to be settled in paper money. This forced the general public to use paper money, resulting in the spread of paper florins to peripheral areas previously unfamiliar with paper money. When more paper money was issued in 1785, geographical coverage was extended to Galicia, Hungary and Transylvania.[62] The value of the paper money issued thus reached 20 million florins throughout the Habsburg monarchy.

Paper money finances the Napoleonic wars

In 1792, a long series of wars between France and varying European coalitions began during the French Revolution and continued throughout Napoleon's reign. With some interruptions, the military conflict went on for more than 20 years, until 1815. Austria participated in nearly all wars in the coalitions against France, so until 1814, it was invariably among the losers. The wars and the reparation payments to the victors were expensive, and issuing new paper money was a quick fix to finance the required expenditure, driving a powerful rise in the volume of paper florins in circulation from 1797 onward (chart 2.1). As a result, the government increasingly had to resort to coercion to keep paper florins in circulation. *First,* new issues were no longer officially announced, as the public became apprehensive about the growing amounts of paper money and more and more frequently presented paper money for exchange into coins. *Second,* the government decreed in 1796 that paper money had to be accepted for government payments to individuals. In early April 1797, the government restricted paper florin redemptions for coins to 25 florins and extended compulsory acceptance to transactions between individuals. Once the unlimited convertibility of paper florins had ended and acceptance for private-sector transactions had been made mandatory, the last two hurdles to an unfettered issue of further paper money had been removed. The path to inflation had been cleared.

From now on, not only did the circulation of paper money swell rapidly, but the remaining metal currency also began to disappear from circulation. At the stock exchange, the premium of paper money over silver reversed into a rising premium of silver over paper money (chart 2.1). The dwindling volume of silver coins in circulation made payment transactions more cumbersome. People hoarded not just the largest coins, like the 1-florin coin, but also the smaller coins–they, too, were made fully of silver. The silver content of the florin had been standardized in the coin reform of 1753 that defined 20 florins to equate 1 Cologne fine mark, which contained about 234 grams of silver. Agreements with Bavaria and most imperial estates made this "Convention standard" the general coinage standard in Germany, too. Austrian coins were thus also referred to as "Convention standard florins," as expressed by the abbreviation "CM" for Conventionsmünze used after the abbreviation "fl" for florin. The Convention standard was also applied to smaller coins down to the 3-kreutzer coin, 20 of which contained the same amount of silver as a florin coin (in the predecimal system, 1 florin equaled 60 kreutzer).[63] People therefore hoarded low- and high-denomination coins alike. This represented a problem for payments: Large amounts could be settled with paper money, but there was no paper substitute for small amounts, as the lowest paper money face value was 5 florins. Low and mid-value coins were already in short supply during the winter of 1794/95. The government responded by issuing smaller coins with a markedly lower silver content. In the next few years, a debasement race between silver coins and paper money ensued, where the declining value of paper money made it attractive to hoard even the newer coins with a lower silver content. Whereas the silver content of the 1-florin coin remained intact in mint runs after 1796, the silver content of the 6-kreutzer and 12-kreutzer coins was diluted to less than half. After 1799, all pretense was dropped and coins were minted only in copper; after 1807, even the 30-kreutzer coin (½ florin) was struck in copper.[64] In this fashion, no less than 150 million florins worth of silver coins and 10 million florins worth of copper coins were put into circulation–only to disappear again in no time.[65] In 1799, the first paper money with face values of

1 florin and 2 florins was issued.[66] In June 1800, about 190 million paper florins were in circulation, and by the time Austria had been defeated in the War of the Second Coalition at the end of 1801, the circulation had ballooned to nearly 320 million florins.[67]

Chart 2.1: **Paper money in circulation, silver price of paper money at the Vienna Stock Exchange and food prices in Vienna** (logarithmic scale)[68]

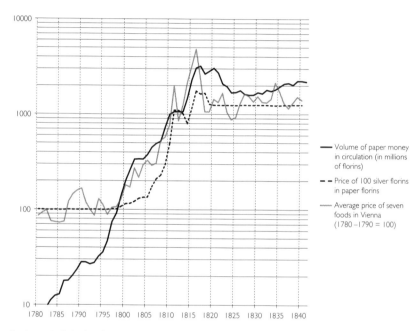

In the period displayed, currency reforms were implemented in 1811 and again in 1816. Data comparability over time was ensured by converting all nominal values into paper florins as used before 1811.[69] From the beginning of wars against France in 1792 until 1816, the volume of paper money in circulation grew a hundredfold in Austria. During these years, brief peacetime periods in which the circulation volume was stable from 1803 to 1805 and 1810 to 1813 alternated with phases in which the money volume surged, in particular from 1809 to 1810 and 1813 to 1816. Until 1796, the rising amount of notes in circulation had no effect on the price of paper money in silver or the general price level. Even after silver traded at a premium over paper money, the devaluation of paper money at the stock exchange trailed money supply growth for a long time. In 1806, paper money inflation finally accelerated. In 1818, the price of silver and the general price level stabilized at about 12 times the prewar level.

After 1801, the government tried several times to stabilize the volume of paper money in circulation but was instead repeatedly forced to issue substantial volumes of new money. Partly, the stabilization measures were pursued only half-heartedly and with ulterior motives. In 1804, a portion of the notes was incinerated, which was effectively communicated and widely reported in the official gazette.[70] In fact, however, this measure was intended above all to improve the silver price of paper money, clearing the path to possible additional issues in the future. During this period, the government also founded national printing works to print paper money itself and nationalized several paper factories. The resolve to reestablish monetary order appeared to be altogether perfunctory. Printing more and more paper money simply proved a facile way to raise funds, even during the brief interim periods of peace.[71] Arbitrary issuing of paper money by parts of the government administration and by the military compounded the disorder. The lack of monetary control becomes evident in the fact that reliable records were kept only on print runs after September 1808 but not on the volume of paper money in circulation.[72]

The drawbacks of monetary financing get the upper hand

After its defeat in the war of 1809, Austria had to cede lands with a population of about 3.5 million and a size of around 100,000 km²–nearly 17% of its former surface area. Paper florins were declared null and void in the ceded territory and returned to circulation in the smaller monetary area, causing the devaluation of paper money to accelerate dramatically. Stopping inflation and restoring monetary order once again moved to the top of the political agenda.

During the first inflationary phase from 1797 to 1805, the loss in the silver price of paper money on the stock exchange was steady but slower than the expansion of the paper money supply (chart 2.1). Evidence also indicates that prices of goods reacted faster to the higher money supply than the price of silver. Measuring overall inflation during this period is very difficult. The most readily available prices are food prices. Food has the benefit that it represented the bulk of average household spending during the era, so that its prices are representative. Yet food prices could fluctuate sharply from year to year in line with harvest output and as a result of war. Conservative estimates would nonetheless support evidence of a rising trend in food prices toward the end of the 1790s beyond annual fluctuations, i.e., the data signal a persistent rise in the price level. In the following years, the price of goods increased faster than paper money lost value at the stock exchange.[73] Most likely, this was due to a general belief that government would reestablish convertibility after the end of the war, i.e., bring the price of 100 silver florins expressed in paper money back to 100. The pattern shifted after the War of the Third Coalition in 1805. In June 1806, first rumors surfaced of plans to overprint, i.e., devalue paper florins, in order to drastically cut their circulation volume. These rumors speeded up the decline of the silver price of paper money at the stock exchange, as a result of which paper money inflation soon outpaced the rise in food prices.[74] New issues and repatriated paper florins after the defeat in 1809 further accelerated the loss of value compared to silver; at the same time, the price of silver became more volatile and less reliable. The general insecurity in payment transactions had reached a stage at which stabilization was imperative. What was even more serious from the government's perspective, though, was the impact of the devaluation on the budget. Under the prevailing taxation system, taxes were assessed at nominal values and could not, or not easily, be adjusted to inflation. So, while taxes were being paid in increasingly worthless paper money, the nominal value of government expenditure (except interest payments on the government debt, which were also calculated in inflated paper money) rose unremittingly. As long as the silver premium had remained manageable–under 30% until 1805–the losses had been bearable. However, a silver premium of close to 500%, as happened in early 1810, resulted in real fiscal revenue shortfalls that were no longer sustainable.[75]

There were two alternatives to address this problem: Either paper money could be devalued, a scenario developed by state and conference minister Zinzendorf as early as 1806. However, the emperor viewed this measure as a breach of promise and was highly averse to it. Or the amount of money in circulation could be reduced. In agreement with the emperor's preference, the president of the court treasury, Count Joseph O'Donell, proceeded with this scenario: It was published as the silver decree in February 1810. The key component of the decree was the creation of the *Vereinigte Einlösungs- und*

Tilgungsdeputation, a government agency in charge of controlling the volume of paper money in circulation and handling the voluntary exchange of paper money issued so far for a new paper money series called redemption certificates (*Einlösungsscheine*). Other than the indication that the redemption certificates would not be issued at a rate of 1:1, the plan did not foresee a fixed exchange ratio, so that the conversion in fact implied devaluation.[76] This approach was meant to reduce the costs for the state, but it was deemed to be unproblematic, as conversion was voluntary. However, many details of the plan remained unclear. Above all, it was unclear what value the redemption certificates should have. They would not be exchangeable for coins, at least not from the outset, and they would not be listed at an official rate. And, unlike the original paper money that they replaced, they would not qualify as legal tender.[77] Thus the promise that the certificates would be redeemed step by step in silver with tax revenues, in particular a long-term wealth tax, served as the only indication of the value of the redemption certificates.[78] This was rather vague. In the end, the plan was never actually implemented. O'Donell died the day the silver decree was issued, and while his successor, Count Josef Wallis, continued preparations, he worked on the other option, devaluation, in parallel.[79] After the silver price of paper money had recovered briefly following the announcement of the silver decree, the silver premium started to climb again because the measures outlined in the silver decree were not pursued further and because yet more paper money was issued. That, and the failure of efforts to place bonds abroad, convinced the emperor of the need to take radical action. March 15, 1811, marked the issuance of the momentous imperial devaluation decree dated February 20–in effect a declaration of default.[80]

Sovereign default and currency reform in 1811

The decree of 1811 centered on the compulsory devaluation of paper florins to 20% of their face value and their exchange for a new paper currency referred to as redemption certificates, as envisaged in the silver decree of 1810. Given an outstanding volume of government paper money of slightly more than 1 billion florins as stated in the decree, the supply of redemption certificates was fixed at just over 200 million florins, which was defined as an upper threshold.

Gradual backing of the redemption certificates with underlying assets or their gradual redemption were to be the next steps.[81] The new paper currency based on the redemption certificates was called "Vienna standard florins." Redemption certificates were declared the only legal tender with immediate effect, but to ease the transition, old (Convention standard) paper florins would also be acceptable at one-fifth of their face value for a limited period. For national finances, it was important that taxes and duties now had to be paid in redemption certificates, and all payments by the state treasury were in redemption certificates, which drove up spending in real terms. To relieve the strain on the budget, government bond yields were halved while leaving the nominal value of the bonds unchanged. For holders of government bonds, these measures nevertheless represented an improvement, as despite the halving of the original nominal yield, at least payments were in redemption certificates, which were worth five times as much as the old paper florins they replaced. The wealth tax planned in 1810 was never introduced.

A substantial portion of the devaluation decree concerned the conversion of liabilities in the form of old paper florins incurred between January 1799 and March 1811 into new Vienna standard florins. Across-the-board devaluation to 20% was considered discriminatory, as it would have disproportionately devalued the liabilities agreed when the paper florins had still been valued at close to par. Thus the decree fixed the conversion rate to the price of silver on the stock exchange at the time of the respective business transaction. The only exception was the period of extremely strong devaluation between October and December 1810, when the price of 100 silver coins expressed in paper money surged from just under 500 to over 1,000. For this period, the conversion was set at 500 old florins = 100 new florins.[82]

The idea behind the devaluation decree was to dry up the paper money supply so much that the value of paper money would be on a par with that of silver again. This required an estimate of the paper money supply consistent with a stable silver par value without–as stated in the decree–restraining the amount in circulation too much and "depriving our subjects of the recognized benefits of paper money, which is so important for industry and which becomes harmful only if it is too abundant."[83] Drawing on the experience with the paper florins in circulation between 1801 and 1809, the amount chosen was just over 200 million florins, one-fifth of the amount of paper money in circulation when the devaluation decree was issued.[84] However, this was only a rough guess. If the silver premium should persist despite the contraction of the paper money supply to one-fifth, the authors of the decree provided for a further reduction of the circulating paper money through redemptions.

The decree of 1811, in particular the devaluation of the currency, remained etched in the minds of Austrian citizens for decades. Given the censorship practiced at the time, few negative comments by contemporaries have been passed down, but most 19th century treatises and economic essays were critical of the measures.[85] Later governments also considered the decree a "cautionary example of a brutal and wrongful method of debt relief that shook financial and legal relationships to the core and that must never be adopted again, if only on political grounds."[86] As explained below, the determination to avoid similar coercion was elementary in the approach to restoring the currency in 1816. The impact of the decree on the economy is difficult to assess.[87] Some authors consider 1811 to have been the turning point between the long growth period that began in the 1770s and the long period of stagnation that lasted at least until 1825, for which they at least partly blame the devaluation of 1811. The role of the monetary reform is hard to view in isolation, though, as other factors also weighed on economic developments after the end of the Napoleonic wars. When the continental blockade imposed by Napoleon had been lifted, Austrian products once again had to compete with British imports; at the same time, fiscal and monetary policy became more restrictive.[88] Likewise, it is hard to gauge whether the reduction of government debt also had a positive impact. Like Austria, England and Prussia had amassed significant debt during the war, but they repaid their debts in the next decades. Before Austria declared insolvency, it had amassed debt in the order of some 80% of GDP, which was well below the debt ratio of England (close to 260%) but significantly above the debt ratio of Prussia (some 40% in 1815).[89] That the haircut provided less relief than thought was partly because Austria did not stick to its plan rigorously: As a token of amends to its creditors, Austria began to reverse the haircuts made in 1811 by gradually lifting the interest rate to the originally agreed level after 1818.[90]

Inflation returns

Ultimately, the devaluation decree had little support–mainly because despite all the sacrifices, it could not accomplish the goal of stabilizing the currency. The decree actually did redistribute wealth to the state and to creditors with senior claims. But that was about all–otherwise, all it managed to do was to replace one paper currency with another without addressing the deeper causes of devaluation. Moreover, the architects of the decree did not take into account the expectations of the public and so ignored a key determinant in the demand for paper money. Without the prospect of exchanging paper money for coins, there was no orientation for the price of the new redemption certificates. Immediately after enforcement of the decree, the price of 100 silver florins expressed in new (Vienna standard) paper money settled at 160 florins, only to surge to 250 florins in June 1811.

People were right to be suspicious. The government did not reduce its deficit, the main driver of past inflation. Even though the interest rate on government debt had been halved, debt expenditure did not fall, as redemption certificates were used to pay interest. Salaries also had to be paid in redemption certificates, an added expense that the cancellation of inflation adjustment allowances could not offset.[91] Finally, expensive new wars soon weighed on the national budget again. Austria managed to finance its war expenses as an ally of France in the French invasion of Russia in 1812 without printing more paper money. After the French retreat from Russia, Austria mediated between the belligerents, but military outlays were needed even to maintain a neutral position. To prevent breaking the explicit commitment in the decree of February 1811 not to increase the supply of redemption certificates, the government decided in April 1813 to create yet another category of paper money, called anticipation certificates (*Antizipationsscheine*), which represented a claim on future tax revenues and which were to be redeemed over a period of 12 years. Like the redemption certificates, anticipation certificates were issued at a compulsory exchange rate and were therefore equivalent to redemption certificates in nearly every respect. After Austria had declared war on France in August 1813, the volume of anticipation certificate issues swelled rapidly, bringing the total to 195 million (Vienna standard) florins by the conclusion of peace in May 1814: The volume of paper money in circulation in the monarchy had nearly doubled within a year. One reason to fire up the printing presses may have been that the war went quickly and favorably for Austria, giving rise to the hope–the anticipation–that the freshly issued anticipation certificates would soon be redeemed with taxes and French reparation payments after the war. But in fact, paper money issues continued even after the peace agreement in May 1814 and increased considerably in the short war after Napoleon's return from exile in 1815. Yet paper money and hence the Wiener Stadtbanco certainly helped Austria win the war–at the cost of a dysfunctional currency and at the cost of a sharp increase in the supply of paper money. In June 1816, the volume of outstanding redemption certificates and anticipation certificates reached almost 640 million (Vienna standard) florins, equivalent to almost 3.2 billion old paper florins.[92] Since the outbreak of the War of the First Coalition in 1792, paper money in circulation had thus burgeoned to 120 times the original volume. That was the situation on foundation of the Oesterreichische Nationalbank.

Fragile stability during the Nationalbank's formative years (1816–1848)

"The history of the privilegirte oester-reichische National-Bank is just a continuation of the history of government paper money. While being different in appearance and name, the banknotes issued by this bank are not that much different in n a t u r e from the old government paper money. ... The malady basically stems from when the Nationalbank retired the old (Vienna standard) paper money in exchange for its own banknotes, which were convertible into silver on demand. These operations dating from the early years of the Nationalbank sowed the seeds for its later misery."

Wagner, *Kritik*, p. 577; emphasis in original

The reason for the creation of a new note-issuing bank in 1816 was the fact that just a few years after Austria had witnessed sovereign default, its monetary system was back in a state which the shock therapy of 1811 had meant to remedy: Paper money was circulating in large quantities, and silver coins commanded a high premium. Restoring the stability of the currency and putting it on a sustainable basis had become a matter of urgency. Emperor Francis therefore issued instructions to draft a reform bill even before the war against France ended with the abdication of Napoleon in April 1814. The new finance minister appointed in the fall of 1814, Count Johann Philipp Stadion, believed that a currency reform needed to come second to putting public finances in order, as the currency reform would not be feasible otherwise. Credible fiscal consolidation, however, would not be possible until after the end of the war, which had become a moving target as the hostilities with France reemerged in March 1815. Hence, the process dragged on. Another year went by until the financial reform bill was finally endorsed by Emperor Francis in March 1816, based on the blueprint proposed earlier by Baron Franz Xaver von Pillersdorf. June 1, 1816, saw the publication of a monetary reform decree and a decree that provided for the incorporation of a private note-issuing bank–i.e., the birth of the privilegirte oesterreichische National-Bank.

A private stock corporation as a guardian of Austria's currency

All things considered, the preconditions for monetary reform were far better in 1816 than five years earlier. Unlike in 1811, when Austria was in constant danger of being drawn–at substantial cost–into the ongoing hostilities between France and England, the conclusion of the Congress of Vienna had upped the chance of a prolonged period of peace. This in turn promised to eliminate the need to once again turn on the monetary tap to finance costly warfare. Moreover, inflation, which had flared up again soon after 1811, had not progressed to the peaks measured before the latest reform. While the price of silver coin expressed in paper money had overshot the 1,000 florin mark for 100 silver coins by the end of 1810, it stood at a comparatively low rate of 350 florins in redemption certificates in early 1816. Hence, compared with 1811, less radical measures would do in 1816.

Not only did the preconditions differ, but policy makers had also learned their lessons following the failed reform of 1811. The goal in 1816 was the same as it had been in 1811, namely to bring silver coins back into circulation as soon as possible, and to keep them circulating in parallel with paper money. This, of course, would work only if the note-issuing bank managed to keep the rate of paper florins at silver parity. Informed by the simple logic of quantity theory, the reform attempts of 1811 had hinged on reducing the supply of paper money. Yet while reducing the supply of paper money was a prerequisite for improving the silver price of paper money, in hindsight, such a reduction by itself had not been sufficient as long as trust in the stability of paper florins was lacking. This was the lesson from 1811.

Pillars of currency reform

The best recipe for building trust was to allow holders of paper money to exchange such money for silver coins one-to-one on demand. Hence, the immediate return to silver convertibility was the first and most important pillar of reform. At the same time, expectations would be instrumental in getting holders of paper money to hold on to it rather than exchanging it for silver coins right away. In other words, anchoring *expectations* about the future development of the supply of money was even more important than rapidly reducing the money supply. Hence it would be of the essence, as finance minister Stadion underlined, to convince the general public that adequate backstops were in place to keep the supply of paper money from rising to excessive levels ever again. In 1815, after the end of the Napoleonic wars, the government was in a position to make such a promise in a convincing manner, even more so as the state coffers had been refilled with a sizeable amount of silver from the reparation payments following the peace agreement.[93] Thus, credibly consolidating the budget constituted the second pillar of the reform.

The third pillar consisted in establishing a new note-issuing institution that would be accountable for converting paper money into silver. Having repeatedly breached its promise in recent years, the state had discredited itself for good as an issuer of paper money in the eyes of the general public. The central innovation of Pillersdorf's reform plan, and also of other reform plans launched between 1812 and 1814, was to transfer the right to issue paper money to a banking institution that would be independent from the finance ministry or, to cite Pillersdorf, "an autonomous institution whose primary concern is the currency and which is built on the quality of its own credit."[94] Unlike the agency installed in 1810 to retire government paper money and unlike the Stadtbanco, which started to operate in 1706 and was labeled as independent but had been so in name only, the new bank was to be a stock corporation under private ownership. According to this plan, the strength of the banking institution was built on three elements: a stock of silver coins that the bank had to keep in its vaults for a percentage of all banknotes issued, the paid-in share capital, and the autonomous management of the bank's operations on behalf of its stockholders. Specifically, the day-to-day business was to be managed by a governing board, headed by a governor. To underline the independence of the new institution, the decree issued by the emperor in 1816 entrusted a select group of merchants, bankers, factory owners and Viennese tradesmen with the job of selecting the first governing board. The governor was appointed by the emperor, but on the proposal of the stockholders. This ensured to "buy-in" the Viennese merchant bankers, who, as state creditors and key players on the foreign exchange and silver markets, would be instrumental in determining the market price of the new paper money and hence in ensuring the success of the monetary reform. Moreover, this framework had the merit of making it easier for the new institution to also serve as a bank for the private sector and to act as a catalyst for trade and industrial activities in Austria.

While there was consensus on those three fundamental issues, the government and the commission working out the reform bill were at odds about the sequencing of the reforms and the timing of the measures. Pillersdorf's reform plan provided for converting the existing government paper money into interest-bearing debt obligations and thus for retiring it from circulation immediately and completely. Another member of the commission, Karl Friedrich Kübeck, feared that such an approach would stoke sharp deflation and trigger payment systems problems, since it would take time for the new paper money to be issued by a yet-to-be-established bank to gain broader acceptance. He therefore argued in favor of reducing the outstanding government paper money only gradually. The solution adopted was to go for a parallel circulation, i.e., to launch new banknotes into circulation that would be convertible into silver without withdrawing the inconvertible old (Vienna standard) government paper money at the same time. While the value of the banknotes for which the monetary reform reinstated the Convention standard was fixed given their convertibility into silver, the old (Vienna standard) paper money would trade at market prices. The old paper money was to be retired from circulation gradually over time.

This line of action restored currency stability right away, thus enhancing trust, facilitating the settlement of economic transactions and, last but not least, shoring up public finances, as it provided for the payment of taxes in banknotes or silver coins rather than in depreciated Vienna standard paper money. At the same time, the reform did without coercive measures, an aspect that policy makers considered to be particularly important given the shock of sovereign default in 1811: Holders of old paper money were under no obligation to convert it but were free to trade it in the market or to use it in payment, as before. The latter was true on paper at least; in effect the market price of florins based on the Vienna standard soon stabilized at a rate of 2.5 to 1 against florins based on the Convention standard. Thus the reforms of 1816 in fact devalued the Vienna standard florin, which had initially been meant to equal the silver florin, by 60%.

Innovations compared with the Stadtbanco era

With its key task of reducing the burden on public finances that resulted from the retirement of government paper money, the Nationalbank had taken over the role of the Stadtbanco. At the same time, the establishment of the Nationalbank brought a number of innovations and also entailed a modernization of the institution. As with the Stadtbanco, independence from the state was meant to enhance trust in the institution and in the paper money it issued. Yet while the independence of the Stadtbanco had been built on a premodern concept of the state, in which the central government had only limited control over the autonomous city of Vienna–which was at the same time a certain anachronism in an absolute monarchy (as outlined in the previous chapter)–the new Nationalbank was designed to operate under private ownership as part of a larger framework of separation of powers. In other words, the state had learned its lesson following the failed attempts of establishing independent control of note issuance *within* the framework of public administration, examples being the Stadtbanco and the agency that had been set up in 1810 to retire government paper money. The independence and autonomy of the Nationalbank's governing board, which was accountable only to the shareholders, was spelled out repeatedly in the decree incorporating the bank in 1816. Under the new regime, the role of the state, which was represented by the state commissioner, was limited to monitoring compliance with the bank's charter.

A second difference between the Stadtbanco and the Nationalbank was with regard to the bank's claims on the state. This aspect, too, reflects a more modern take on the powers of the state and on the nature of government debt. The Stadtbanco's receivables from the state had been linked to dedicated parts of future public revenue, which were pledged to the bank and which it administered directly. The direct involvement in tax collection is well illustrated by the number of employees, which, according to an estimate by Dickson, amounted to as many as 2,000 to 2,700 in 1762, most of whom were tax officials.[95] The new Nationalbank, in contrast, was no longer involved in the tax administration; much rather, its claims were directed against the entirety of the public finances managed by the treasury. Accordingly, it only had a headcount of 45 in 1818.[96]

The most important change with regard to how the role of the Nationalbank would evolve, though, referred to the right of the Nationalbank to engage in regular banking operations beyond the redemption of government paper money. The Stadtbanco had restricted its business to taking in deposits and lending on to the treasury. The Nationalbank, in contrast, was now free to lend to businesses and individuals, to maintain current accounts and to conduct cashless payments. Supporting trade and industry was in the express interest of the state, and the lending business moreover promised to improve the bank's earnings, which would make Nationalbank stocks more attractive for potential investors. In the pre-revolution period, i.e., before 1848, many such loans went to private Viennese bankers, which paved the way, at least in the long run, for the adoption of a role as the banker's bank.

The bank's management between the state and the Viennese haute finance

The independence of the new Nationalbank that was considered so important for the credibility of currency stability was built on including non-state representatives in the bank's management. The state led the way by appointing the provisional governing board, which was tasked with running the bank until the share capital had been subscribed, until the bank's charter had been defined and until the permanent governing board had been installed.[97] As a sign of its willingness to subject the new bank to broader public control, the government invited a number of interest groups such as representatives of trade and industry, merchants and factory owners, to draw up a shortlist from which the emperor appointed six executive directors. Two other executive directors came from the state agency that had been charged with retiring government paper money and thus represented the state. In other words, the governing board was dominated by trade and banking representatives. The governor heading the provisional governing board was a high official, though, namely Count Adam Nemes.[98]

With the adoption of the charter in July 1817, the permanent governing board stood ready to become operational. The new charter provided for the executive directors to be elected by the 100 biggest shareholders of the Nationalbank. The governor and the vice governor, in contrast, were appointed by the emperor. The first governor and successor to Nemes was Count Josef Dietrichstein, who had played a key role in the drafting of the charter. A top official, Dietrichstein had been a direct representative of the Crown as former Marshal of Lower Austria. In the words of Stadion, he was "agreeable and reliable, which would make him a submissive agent in support of the interests of public administration," evidently a major criterion in the view of the government. The first vice governor at his side was Heinrich Ritter von Geymüller, director of one of Vienna's most important banking houses. Baron Pillersdorf, who had drafted the decrees of 1816, served as state commissioner. In the end, the governing board, with the exception of the governor, was made up entirely of members of the Viennese haute finance.[99]

This setup, with the governor representing the government and the vice governor the Vienna-based banks, would be kept up for decades to come. Following the passing of Dietrichstein in 1825 and an interim period in which Vice Governor Steiner was the acting governor, the next two governors were Baron Adrian Nikolaus von Barbier (appointed in 1830), former vice president of the court treasury, and Carl Ritter von Lederer (1837–1847), former state councillor.[100] The next vice governors, in turn, were Johann Heinrich Geymüller, the Elder (1817–1820), Melchior Ritter von Steiner (1820–1837), Baron Bernhard von Eskeles (1837–1839) and Johann Heinrich Ritter von Geymüller, the Younger (1839–1841), all of whom were members of the Viennese haute finance.[101]

While the balance between representatives of the state and of private Viennese bankers in the governing board remained broadly unchanged until 1848, the state made an effort to increase its influence in the bank's management once it had managed to consolidate its finances somewhat. The first opportunity presented itself during the negotiations between the state and the shareholders about the bank's initial charter. The starting point of the negotiations was a blueprint drafted by the state commissioner, Baron Pillersdorf. While the representatives of the bank's shareholders were expressly allowed free reign in their deliberations, the draft that they eventually submitted to the finance ministry in the spring of 1817 after lengthy negotiations came up against resistance. Finance minister Count Stadion fully rejected the amendments the shareholders had proposed for Pillersdorf's draft, which all had aimed at increasing the bank's independence and autonomy. Evidently, the state had in the meantime regained sufficient authority so that it was not prepared to make any further concessions to the Viennese haute finance. In fact, the charter adopted on July 15, 1817, even removed some of the explicit lines of defense for the bank's independence that had been enshrined in the incorporation decree of 1816. The provision that the government would "instal only the first governing board" was dropped. While in 1816 the state commissioner had been expressly prohibited from "exerting any advisory or decisive influence on the bank's management or on any of its business areas," he was now explicitly given such a role and in particular the responsibility of monitoring adequate coverage of banknotes in circulation by specie, a task that effectively gave him widespread influence on the bank's management.[102]

The founding charter expired in 1841 after 25 years. The renewed charter, which became effective in 1841, provided for a further expansion of state influence on the bank, reflecting the concerns of the finance ministry about the adequacy of silver stocks and the maintenance of silver convertibility, which had been jeopardized in 1830 and then again in 1840. One way to limit the leeway of the governing board would have been to impose rules that prescribe a certain ratio between the volume of banknotes in circulation and the stock of silver reserves. While such rules were integrated in the charter in 1863, in 1841, policy makers opted for a more direct form of intervention. Evidently, stringent rules did not appear feasible given the weak financial position of the bank, and stringent rules would, moreover, have restricted the flexibility of the bank, which did have its merits for the government, too.[103] Instead, the state wielded its influence through the state commissioner. Unlike in the charter of 1817, which had limited the commissioner's right of intervention to a violation of charter provisions, the commissioner was now in a position to veto any measure that he considered to "clash with state interests" and refer matters to the finance ministry for final decision.[104] Moreover, the charter included a long list of items on which the bank had to liaise with the finance ministry. These items included setting the amount of precious metal reserves, changing the interest rates for discounts and advances, setting dividend payments and appropriating money from the reserve fund; in other words, all matters of relevance on the decision-making agenda of the governing board.[105] With a view to keeping an eye on the loan portfolio, an issue that repeatedly gave rise to conflicts in the 1820s and 1830s in light of the high share of firms with close links to executive directors, a second state commissioner was installed. He was put in charge of monitoring the eligibility of the bills of exchange and securities put up as collateral for discounting and secured lending transactions and of ensuring the "impartiality of the procedures."[106] The role of the state was strengthened further by the fact that the executive directors, while nominated by the banking committee, were henceforth appointed by the emperor.[107] With hindsight it is difficult to say to what extent the finance ministry actually availed itself of the new possibilities and to what extent new charter provisions merely codified established practice. At any rate, the staffing of the governing board was left unchanged, and the discounting volume tended to rise after 1841, contrary to what more stringent control of the discount operations might have suggested.

Distributing seigniorage income

The legal form of a private stock corporation that had been adopted for the Nationalbank also had an impact on how the bank operated. The state was intent on maximizing the seigniorage income from issuing paper money (see box p. 77), as it had done at the time of the Stadtbanco, under the condition that the paper money remained stable in value compared with silver. Yet while the state used to be the only beneficiary of the seigniorage income gained by the Stadtbanco, it was now confronted with a private player that pursued its own economic interests. Now the size of the seigniorage income as well as its distribution among the state and the bank's shareholders required an explicit agreement. Indeed, among the shareholders it was the big private Viennese bankers who had the real say, whereas smaller investors lacked both access to the relevant information and the power to make a difference. Hence, the bargains that the bank and the state agreed on need to be seen in a wider context, in which the chronically underfunded state relied on the bond market for raising money as well as on the Viennese banks to act as intermediaries in this process. At the same time, these Viennese banks accounted for the majority of the executive directors sitting on the Nationalbank's governing board.[108] In the bank's formative decades, the compromises reached against this backdrop had a major impact on the bank's business operations.

Under the incorporation decree of 1816 the state did not participate directly in the balance sheet profit of the bank. Instead, seigniorage income was redistributed through loans that the central bank granted to the state at a preferential rate of interest, i.e., below the rate at which the state was able to raise money in the bond market. The low interest charged on government debt reduced the bank's profit at the benefit of the state. In the 1820s, when the yield on government bonds was between 6% and 7%, the average rate of interest that the bank charged on its loans to the state stood close to 4% (chart 3.1). In other words, in the absence of monetary financing, the state would have had to pay an interest rate that would have been 2 to 3 percentage points higher. The following years saw a constant decline in the yield of government bonds in the market, and the state also negotiated more favorable conditions with the bank. The debt instruments assigned to the bank in turn for retiring old (Vienna standard) paper florins after 1826 were unremunerated and the short-term rate for discounting treasury notes was lowered in several steps. Thus, the average interest payable on the bank's receivables from the state dropped to 2%. At the same time, lending by the Nationalbank to the state increased, which is why the seigniorage income available for distribution to the shareholders rose as well. Until 1847, shareholders who had acquired their stocks in 1818 received annual dividends which were never below 10% and ultimately above 12%, and generally very stable. One reason for the high dividends was the limitation of the share capital. According to the plans of 1816, the bank was to be endowed with a share capital of 60 million florins. Yet when more than half of the envisaged share capital had been paid in by March 1820, the governing board suspended the further issuance of shares, acting on the concern that it might not be possible to put additional funds to profitable use.[109] The combination of business with the state financed through the issuance of paper money and a lower share capital enhanced the Nationalbank's net returns. As the general level of interest declined at the same time, the high profits caused the stock price of the Nationalbank shares to soar. Close to 1848, Nationalbank stocks were traded at a rate of 1,500 florins, i.e., three times the price at which the stocks had been issued between 1816 and 1818.

A further group with privileged access to central bank credit were a few Viennese bankers who were the only ones to meet the criteria for discount and lending operations. The rates for discounts and advances were also mostly below market rates, or were at least judged to have been so by a number of contemporaries.[110] Having access to central bank refinancing was thus tantamount to receiving a subsidy. Even in the absence of details on bank lending, it is safe to assume that the Nationalbank's managers were the key beneficiaries themselves, as they were both the main clients of the bank as well as the ones who took the decisions on accepting bills of exchange for discounting.

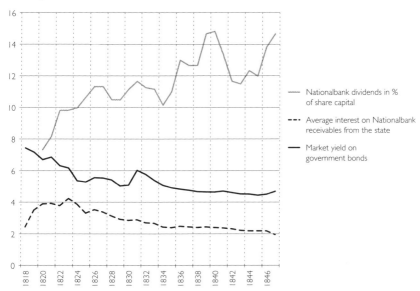

The state received its share of the seigniorage income in the form of loans at preferential rates. Thanks to a rising volume of business operations, the bank was able to pay increasingly higher dividends in most years. Investors who had bought Nationalbank stocks in 1818 were able to make substantial profits until 1847.

The state, the bank's executive directors and its shareholders had a common interest in maximizing the volume of banknotes in circulation, as higher circulation figures increased the amount of interest-bearing claims in the bank's books. However, the downside of a large amount of interest-bearing assets was a small stock of unremunerated silver coins, which the bank needed in case holders of banknotes requested payment in silver. In other words, the obligation to guarantee the redemption of banknotes lowered the seigniorage income that the bank was able to achieve. Yet as will be seen below, the silver reserves of the Nationalbank were in effect very small in its formative decades compared to later years.[112] To secure banknote redemption, the state acted as a backstop by furnishing the bank with coins on demand from its own treasury or from the state mint offices, or by supporting the purchase of silver abroad. This allowed the bank to hold smaller reserves and achieve higher profits, which it was able to channel back to the state and to distribute to its shareholders. In sum, the fundamental harmony of interests between the state and the Nationalbank's governing board meant that receivables from the state were the main counterpart to banknotes in circulation, that receivables from discounts and advances played a minor role, and that the bank held only a very limited amount of silver. At the same time, the bank operated on a lower volume of share capital than had initially been envisaged. While this twin leverage had the merit of enhancing the profits of stockholders and lowering the burden on public finances, it rendered the Nationalbank vulnerable to crises of confidence, just like the Stadtbanco had been.

Note-issuing bank of an economically and politically heterogeneous empire

The decree of 1816 granted the Nationalbank the right "to print and issue banknotes in the entirety of the Austrian monarchy."[113] Based on the boundaries drawn at the Congress of Vienna in 1815, the Austrian monarchy was about 700,000 km² in size, which made it the second-largest state in Europe after Russia. The monarchy comprised a large number of territories that differed heavily in terms of their economies and the structure of public administration. Together with later enlargements like Galicia (now part of Ukraine), the German-Bohemian core countries had been integrated into a relatively uniform administrative area under the reign of Maria Theresa and Joseph II.[114] At the same time, Austria had failed to integrate the Hungarian Kingdom, which retained its relative sovereignty and had a pre-absolutistic governance structure, with the local nobility playing a relatively strong role in the field of tax collection in particular.[115] A third unit was the Kingdom of Lombardo-Venetia, which had been established in 1815 by merging older Habsburg domains with the Venetian Republic and was largely centrally organized, very much like the German-Bohemian lands.[116]

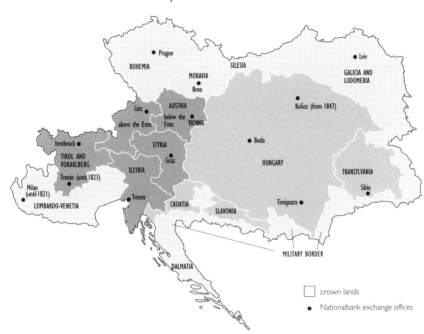

BOHEMIA
Prague
SILESIA
MORAVIA
Brno
Lviv
GALICIA AND
LODOMERIA
Linz
AUSTRIA
below the
above the Enns Enns VIENNA
Košice (from 1847)
Innsbruck
TIROL AND
VORARLBERG
STYRIA
Graz
Buda
ILLYRIA
HUNGARY
Trento (until 1823)
Milan
(until 1821)
Trieste
LOMBARDO-VENETIA
CROATIA
SLAVONIA
Timişoara
TRANSYLVANIA
Sibiu
MILITARY BORDER
DALMATIA

☐ crown lands
● Nationalbank exchange offices

The note-issuing monopoly of the Nationalbank extended across the Habsburg monarchy, which was the largest state in size in Europe after Russia in 1815. The wide distribution of paper money was one legacy of paper money inflation. With a view to facilitating the exchange of state paper money for banknotes issued by the Nationalbank, the latter opened numerous exchange offices in the major cities of the monarchy. In due course, those exchange offices also exchanged banknotes for silver coins and vice versa. However, the credit business of the Nationalbank remained restricted to Vienna until 1847.

The differences in governance regimes across the monarchy were overshadowed by different levels in economic development.[118] Most of the industrial centers were located in the western parts of the monarchy. Bohemia and Moravia were strongholds of a dynamic textile industry, which employed an army of homeworkers. In the Alpine regions, mining and metallurgy firms had a long-standing tradition and continued to outperform their European peers up to the middle of the 18th century and beyond even though they had lost in competitiveness during the Napoleonic wars.[119] Lower Austria, too, had a strong industrial base, which was increasingly organized in a factory style. The other lands of the monarchy, though, were largely dominated by agriculture, apart from some mining areas and major cities.

The robust economic performance of the western parts of the monarchy, which was strong even in an international comparison, was the result of an economic upswing that had started in the middle of the 18th century.[120] This upswing was driven by the above-mentioned reforms of Maria Theresa and Joseph II.[121] The elimination of customs barriers between Bohemia, Moravia and the other Austrian lands in 1775 had led to the creation of one of the biggest free-trade areas within Europe at the time.[122] Contrary to what the reactionary political attitude of the state after 1815 would suggest, numerous institutional obstacles to sustained economic growth had in fact already been eliminated in the period preceding the revolution of 1848.[123] Between 1817 and 1845 the Austrian population grew at an annual growth rate of 1%, without triggering a Malthusian overpopulation crisis as had been the case in the 18th century.[124] Driven by new technologies in the food and textile industries and for producing and processing iron, manufacturing output grew by 2.5% per annum in Austria and by 1.7% in Hungary and thus significantly faster than the size of the population.[125] In the area of infrastructure, the network of overland roads, which the state had started to develop in the second half of the 18th century, continued to grow.[126] From the mid-1830s onward, the infrastructure was developed further by rolling out a railway and a telegraph network.

Few banks and many banknotes—money and credit before 1848

While the economy was thriving, the financial system remained underdeveloped. With the exception of the Wiener Kommerzial-, Leih- und Wechselbank, which had been founded in 1786 and whose charter expired in 1812, the Nationalbank was the only Austrian banking institution to have been established as a stock corporation.[127] In itself, this pattern was quite common in early 19th century Europe. In England, France and Germany, too, it was merchants turned private bankers which served as pillars of the banking system. Their Viennese counterparts were the banks of Arnstein & Eskeles, Fries, Geymüller, Sina and Steiner, which engaged above all in the lucrative business of trading in government bonds and of intermediating loans to the high nobility, while re-maining active in industrial production as well.[128] A new line of financing busi-ness opened up in the 1830s with the capital-intensive construction of the first railways. Moreover, short-term trade loans, as extended by the private Vien-nese bankers and a range of larger and smaller discounters, were the main source of debt funding for industrial companies.[129] What was entirely lacking in Austria, however, were local banks, which, like country banks in England, would have bundled savings from local investors and channeled them into loans for agricultural and industrial investments. Beyond Vienna and Trieste, larger numbers of discounting firms existed only in Lombardo-Venetia.[130] Fi-nancing was also difficult for farmers. Smaller farmers did not have access to long-term loans, but even big landowners other than a few aristocratic families had difficulties raising money for their investment projects. While Galicia fi-nally received a mortgage lending institution in 1841, after twenty years of ne-gotiations, similar efforts of the Lower Austrian and Bohemian estates failed on account of the opposition of the central government. The central govern-ment was suspicious about the initiative of the estates and feared the compe-tition for its own bonds.[131]

In the decades preceding the revolution of 1848, the gap that had formed on account of the lack of private bankers outside Vienna was filled in part by a new type of financial institution, namely savings banks, which targeted a broader public. Originally designed as a safe form of investment for small and very small savings, the savings account soon evolved into the instrument of choice for the middle class of small tradesmen and individuals of small private means. The savings banks, in turn, invested the deposits they received in bills of exchange and government bonds, later also in mortgage loans. Following the establish-ment of the first savings bank in Vienna in 1819, the concept gradually spread to other cities. Notwithstanding their merits, savings banks dealt with sums that remained moderate and of little importance from a macroeconomic point of view. For instance, in 1847 the aggregate savings deposits totaled slightly more than 60 million florins, at a time when the government debt exceeded 500 mil-lion florins. By 1847, savings banks had been established in a mere 17 cities, most of them in Bohemia and in the Alpine lands.[132]

Most probably, the same east-west divide existed when it came to the role that money played in the economy. The use of cash is notoriously difficult to measure, even for the monarchy in its entirety. The reason is that the lines between individual currency areas were still blurred at the time under review. In border regions and in major trading places in particular, foreign coins and foreign paper money circulated on a par with domestic notes and coins.[133] Above all full-bodied silver coins were welcome beyond domestic borders, notwithstanding the numerous bans on exporting silver coins. Given these cross-border flows, mint office records on the amounts of coins struck per year do not warrant conclusions about domestic volumes of cash circulation. However, episodes of significant inflation can give some indication of the amount of cash in circulation. Until 1799, the volume of government paper money rose continually without driving up the exchange rate of the Austrian florin against foreign currencies or without causing paper florins to be traded at a discount to silver. Yet in 1799, government paper money started to trade at a discount to silver, which implies that paper money must have crowded out the bulk of coins by that time. Since we know that the state had issued some 140 million paper florins by 1799, the volume of coins in circulation must have reached some 150 million florins, or 5 florins per capita, before the market was flooded with government paper money. For 1847, estimates based on a similar method yield some 100 to 120 million florin coins in circulation, plus another 220 million paper florins, which translates into some 8.8 florins per capita.[134] This average roughly equaled the monthly wage of unskilled workers in Vienna. At the same time, this figure offers little insight into the daily use of cash, as this average was calculated for all crown lands taken together and thus masks the strong economic heterogeneity of those areas. Moreover, banknotes also played a significant role not only in daily transactions but also in wholesale trade alongside bills of exchange.[135] However, the per capita figures do give an indication of the use of money in the economy and its composition. Compared with Western economies such as England, France or Prussia, the volume of cash in circulation was rather low, which implies less economic output and a less monetized economy above all in the eastern parts of the economy, where peasant-landlord relationships such as robot obligations continued to persist, where wages were paid in kind and where the need for cash, be it coins or notes, was limited.[136]

Notwithstanding the low degree of monetization in the Austrian economy, the banknotes issued by the Nationalbank played a prominent role in the Austrian economic system (chart 3.3). This was because of the high share of paper money in the volume of cash circulating in Austria, which–at more than two-thirds–was well above the share of banknotes in circulation in France and Germany, where paper money accounted for less than 25% of cash. One of the reasons is that unlike in France, where the banknotes of the Banque de France were for a long time limited to the Greater Paris area, the banknotes of the Nationalbank circulated throughout the monarchy.[137] This dominance of paper money in Austria goes back to the era of government paper money. Of the 450 million (Vienna standard) florins which were retired between 1816 and 1847, one-third was redeemed in Vienna, but another third in Prague and Brno as well as more than 10% in Budapest and Lviv respectively, which was a clear sign of the widespread use of paper money in the monarchy. With the early standardization and distribution of paper money in its entire territory, the Habsburg monarchy was decades ahead of other European countries.[138]

Chart 3.3: **Cash in circulation in Austria, Germany and England** (in florins)[139]

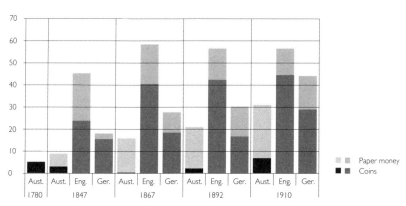

The rise in per capita cash in circulation was largely driven by the growing monetization of the economy and the rising national income.[140] In Austria, paper money accounted for the bulk of cash in circulation as early as in the first half of the 19th century. In periods of inflationary monetary financing of the state, such as 1848/49 or 1866/67, paper money crowded out coins almost entirely. Coins returned into circulation in 1878 and especially after the currency reform of 1892.

The tasks of the Nationalbank

According to the charter, lending to the private sector was supposed to be the main line of business of the new bank, and discount operations were intended to account for the bulk of lending (see box on page 60). Indeed, the low degree of development of the Austrian banking system provided the newly established Nationalbank with many opportunities for doing business as a commercial bank, nourishing expectations and hopes in the government and in the business world alike. The decree of 1816 and the charter of 1817 gave the bank a wide range of tasks alongside issuing banknotes: discounting bills of exchange and securities, lending against the provision of collateral, taking in deposits, accepting precious metals and securities for safe deposit, and maintaining bank accounts. Subject to the availability of adequate funds, the bank was even allowed to grant long-term mortgage loans.[141] In practice, however, transactions with the state dominated from the very start. This does not really come as a surprise, since retiring government paper money and replacing it with banknotes convertible into silver was the primary objective of the authors of the decree of 1816. However, the state and the bank soon went beyond the redemption of the government paper money and developed a close relationship, where the state again and again took recourse to bank money whereas the bank derived a significant part of its income from doing business with the state.

Retirement of government paper money

The number-one task of the new Nationalbank was to retire the old (Vienna standard) paper money that had been issued in the form of redemption and anticipation certificates. In line with the decrees of 1816, this was to be done in two ways. *First*, the Nationalbank would accept such paper money in payment for its stocks. The idea was for the Nationalbank to issue 50,000 stocks for the equivalent of 2,000 Vienna standard paper florins and 200 silver florins per share.[142] In return for the paper money paid in, which was to be destroyed, the Nationalbank would receive government debt obligations remunerated with an interest rate of 2½% in silver. Together with the silver subscription payments, the yield on the government debt obligations was supposed to create the bedrock of funding for the numerous bank operations which the Nationalbank was licensed to carry out. *Second*, the bank was to be put in charge of exchanging the larger part of the government paper money on behalf and for the account of the treasury. For 140 Vienna standard florins, holders of paper money would receive 40 Convention standard florins (that is two-sevenths) in the form of banknotes issued by the Nationalbank and 100 Convention standard florins (that is five-sevenths) in the form of government debt instruments with a 1% yield in silver. The banknotes would be convertible into silver coins at the Nationalbank on demand. To ensure the convertibility of the banknotes, the bank was meant to receive silver coins worth about one-third of the newly issued banknotes from the state. As envisaged by its drafters, this concept made paper money redeemable in its entirety with the use of relatively little silver, as the bulk of the government paper money was going to be exchanged for long-term debt instruments subject to a small rate of interest. Furthermore, the plan relied on the credibility of the new bank, as a result of which a small amount of silver should suffice to keep a large amount of banknotes afloat at parity with silver.

This plan needed to be modified after a short time. Given the prices at which old (Vienna standard) paper money and government bonds traded at the stock exchange in mid-1816, the exchange relations defined in the decrees of 1816 were most favorable for holders of government paper money. Pillersdorf had argued for a less favorable price in the run-up, but he had been overruled by Stadion, whose rationale was to signal the honest effort of the public administration. The option to trade in government paper money for banknotes and government bonds was particularly attractive. For the first time in decades it was now possible to exchange an unlimited number of government paper money for banknotes which were, in turn, convertible into silver coins. The treasury underestimated the attractiveness of its offer and above all the incentive to rapidly convert the banknotes into coins. Already on July 3, 1816, a mere two days after the start of redemption, the bank was forced to limit the opening hours of its cash counters and to man fewer counters with a view to slowing down the exchange process. These restrictions sent the wrong signal, though, undermining trust in the new banknotes from the outset. Backfiring, this move merely attracted larger crowds.

When even the imposition of an upper exchange amount and the requirement to seek advance written approval remained without effect, the Nationalbank stopped the redemption altogether in August 1816. Instead, the bank purchased paper money at the stock exchange, i.e., at the prevailing market price, and thus at a rate that was more favorable for the treasury. Even those purchases were stopped in January 1817 and never resumed. The first attempt at retiring government paper money had thus failed. In sum, little more than 50 million florins out of the circulating 550 million (Vienna standard) florins had been withdrawn from circulation.[143]

In 1819, the treasury resumed the plan of having the Nationalbank retire the government paper money.[144] Rather than giving holders of paper money the opportunity to exchange their old (Vienna standard) paper florins for banknotes and government bonds, the new approach was based on an agreement made between the bank and the state in 1820 that enabled the bank to control the exchange process. In turn, the state assigned a particular amount of silver coins and state debt obligations with an interest rate of 4% to the bank. This new process worked. The price of old (Vienna standard) paper money stabilized soon at the exchange ratio adopted by the bank, namely 250 Vienna standard florins to 100 Convention standard florins. Since old government paper money and the new banknotes were circulating throughout the monarchy, as outlined above, the Nationalbank opened exchange offices in all major provincial cities, which handled the exchange of the old paper money for banknotes, the supply of banknotes in various denominations, and the exchange of banknotes for coins and vice versa.[145] The exchange spanned several years, with slowly dropping volumes. As the state continued to need Vienna standard paper money to redeem outstanding debt that had to be serviced in Vienna standard florins, the last of the notes were not withdrawn until 1858. Even so, banknotes issued by the Nationalbank accounted for 90% of the paper money circulating in the monarchy by 1832 (chart 3.4).

Advances to the treasury

In addition to retiring old (Vienna standard) paper florins, the Nationalbank assisted the treasury also in a number of other ways, in particular by providing short-term financing. As was the case in other countries, the Austrian finance

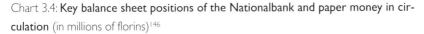

Chart 3.4: **Key balance sheet positions of the Nationalbank and paper money in circulation** (in millions of florins)[146]

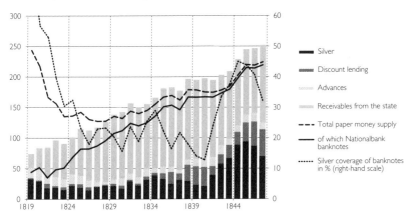

▬	Silver
▬	Discount lending
▭	Advances
▭	Receivables from the state
---	Total paper money supply
—	of which Nationalbank banknotes
⋯⋯	Silver coverage of banknotes in % (right-hand scale)

The volume of banknotes in circulation increased continually from 1818 to 1848. Up to 1830, the new banknotes merely replaced old (Vienna standard) government paper money as the latter was being retired, with the volume of paper money actually going down up to that date. Only after that date did it rise again. Up to 1848, receivables from the state were the main counterpart to banknotes in circulation on the asset side. Despite the rapid rise in banknotes in circulation, silver reserves hardly rose until 1840, but were markedly increased thereafter. Starting in the mid-1830s, the bank also became more active in discount lending.

ministry was looking for ways to reduce the cash working balances it kept because of the mismatch in time and location in terms of the inflow of tax revenue and the outflow of payments. A common instrument for bridging inflows and outflows was to issue short-term treasury bills. Given the apparent difficulty of establishing a private market for treasury bills in Austria, the finance ministry opted for discounting state money orders at the Nationalbank. Initially designed as a temporary form of credit, discount loans for short-term money orders soon developed into a permanent facility to which the state took recourse for increasingly higher amounts. In parallel, the interest rate payable by the state was lowered to 4%, and then to 3%. The favorable interest rate, which was 1 percentage point below the official discount rate of the Nationalbank and most probably also below prevailing market interest rates, made this instrument even more attractive for the state. For the bank, in turn, discount loans constituted a simple and relatively risk-free form of investment. In 1847, the government used short-term Nationalbank loans in order to cushion the meltdown of railway stock prices, which was threatening to jeopardize the creditworthiness of the state.[147] Another form of emergency measures were collateralized loans that the bank, in 1838, granted Hungarian cities that had been badly devastated by flooding. This action too was clearly a fiscal measure, which is why the loans were also guaranteed by the respective municipal and state governments.

Doing commercial bank business

As the bulk of the new banknotes were issued in exchange for government bonds and as the bulk of the paid-in share capital was used to provide advances to the state, little money remained for discounting and for granting advances other than to the state in the first few years. The conditions for taking recourse to discount loans were most restrictive. Little information exists about the identity of the submitters of bills of exchange, but the low number of submissions, the high average amounts and the low overall volume of discount lending would imply that only a select few Viennese businessmen met the Nationalbank's eligibility criteria. A list dated 1836 shows that the bulk of the bills probably related to international trade.[148] Another sign for the restrictive discounting practice is the dearth of information on rates paid for discounting bills of exchange by institutions other than the Nationalbank in the Viennese market. In the first half of the 19th century, the contemporary press was not yet systematically reporting market rates. The existing indicators would imply, though, that market interest rates, while sometimes lying below the official discount rate of the Nationalbank, would tend to exceed it.[149] This means that the Nationalbank must have effectively limited recourse to discount loans, as otherwise holders of bills of exchange would have discounted them at the bank offering more favorable conditions rather than on the market. Systematic restrictions on discount lending would also explain why the official discount rate remained stable at 5% for years rather than responding to economic and political events. This policy was no doubt facilitated by the way discount lending was organized. Discount transactions were effectively handled by a small group of Viennese merchants and bankers, who found themselves on both sides of the transaction as submitters of bills of exchange and as members of the governing board and the discount committee.[150] Hence, the discount volume of the first two decades was rather low. The year-end figures were mostly well below 10 million florins and paled in comparison to the size of state debt, which surged from 30 million florins in 1820 to 130 million florins in 1835. From the mid-1830s discount lending picked up, though, which may reflect the fact that the lion's share of the old paper money had been retired by then and that lending to the state had stabilized, so that the bank had more leeway for expanding private credit. In 1847, the bank, which had previously restricted its credit business to Vienna, opened a branch office in Prague, which started to discount local bills of exchange.

The second form of private credit consisted in the provision of advances. In these operations, the bank would provide funding in turn for the provision of collateral rather than–in the case of discount loans–through the purchase of short-term debt instruments. In practice, most secured lending would involve government bonds, by far the most important category of securities at the Vienna Stock Exchange, after the highly dysfunctional market for government bonds following sovereign default in 1811 had been rebuilt with bond conversions and new issues.[151] Accordingly, demand for advances was high, with its volume exceeding the discounting volume for 20 years. At the same time, the possibility of short-term refinancing against the provision of collateral also supported liquidity, thus shoring up the price for government bonds. As a result, those transactions were highly welcome from the perspective of the state. Later, advances stagnated and were overtaken in 1835 by the growing discounting business.

Discounts and advances proceeded smoothly most of the time, and the terms and conditions were seldom adjusted. On occasion, there would be sharp spikes in demand for refinancing, for instance because concerns about the solvency of a bank or a large bond issuance increased the demand for payment means and cash reserves. Then a situation might arise where sound firms and banks lacked sufficient eligible collateral for taking recourse to discounts and advances. In those instances the bank repeatedly responded by expanding the list of eligible collateral. As a case in point, in September 1820 the bank was confronted with what it deemed a "veritable crisis," in which it was instructed by the finance ministry to assemble 12 leading banks and put up a joint guarantee for discounting additional bills of exchange and providing new loans. This move made it possible to discount bills of exchange that would otherwise not have met the eligibility criteria of the Nationalbank.[152] This model of joint liability, pioneered in this particular case, was reactivated numerous times during the 19th century, in particular in 1848 and 1873. Another type of nonstandard monetary policy measures was adopted in 1823 when the bank also started to accept, following lengthy debates, its own stocks as collateral for advances. The same procedure was adopted in February 1826, when the death of the Russian Czar and an uprising in Saint Petersburg sparked panic in the Viennese financial market. The insolvency of Bankhaus Geymüller in 1841, in contrast, is not evident from the monthly data of banking transactions.[153]

Maintaining convertibility: confidentiality, silver purchases and discount rate policy

In its role as bank of issue, as the treasury's banker and as a provider of discount and lending facilities for the private sector, the Nationalbank pursued a number of strategies in parallel, i.e., a mix that would not necessarily be labeled monetary policy today. In all business areas the bank was subject to one important constraint, though, which ultimately had to guide its action: keeping banknotes convertible in silver specie.

Between 1820 and 1847, the volume of banknotes issued by the Nationalbank increased from 50 to 220 million florins. In the early years, most of the new banknotes were mere replacements for Vienna standard government paper currency (chart 3.4). As the Nationalbank did not exchange all Vienna standard government paper that it retired for its own banknotes, the supply of paper money dwindled until the end of the 1820s, and rather significantly initially. In the early 1830s the supply of paper money started to rise again. The economy was growing and in need of increasing amounts of cash. To be able to exchange banknotes for silver on demand, the bank theoretically also had to hold more silver. In actual fact, though, the silver reserves hardly increased until the end of the 1830s, and specie coverage for the banknotes was often only one-fifth, at times even less. The low silver reserves enabled the bank to earn higher profits. There is no clear yardstick for judging whether the coverage ratio was too low, however. Common practice in the late 19th century suggests a lower limit of 40%. The plan to retire Vienna standard paper florins as designed in 1816 had implied a ratio of one-third, even though the charter itself did not contain any explicit provisions on this point. Yet even one-third need not necessarily be enough, as evidenced by the revolution of 1848, when the bank, within just a few weeks, had to suspend the redemption of banknotes although its coverage ratio had reached 32% at the end of 1847.

The fact that the bank managed to operate for 30 years holding occasionally much lower reserves without provoking a bank run was largely due to the fact that many relevant details were simply kept secret. This was common practice in pre-revolutionary Austria, and applied to all areas of government policy, such as the level of government revenue and spending or the size of government debt. In the case of the bank, the only evidence that was publicly available were the accounts that the governor shared with the bank's stockholders in his speech at their annual general meeting. However, the bank did not disclose the full balance sheet; it only provided scant information, in little detail, about income and expenditure figures–on the basis of which dividends were calculated. Shareholders were not given any information on the silver reserves or the volume of banknotes in circulation, though. Access to information about the full balance sheet was limited to the closed group of the state commissioners and the governing board.

Such secrecy enabled the bank to let the silver reserves drop to a very low level, if necessary, without provoking a run. Even so, coverage would on several occasions drop so sharply that the bank had to take action. Given the lack of monthly financial statements for the pre-revolutionary era, we must largely rely on the account Governor Baron Carl von Lederer (1772–1860) gave in 1847. Lederer cited three episodes–namely in 1830, 1836 and 1840–with a particularly low coverage ratio. There were only two things the bank could do in such an event: either raise the silver reserves or reduce the volume of banknotes in circulation through limiting credit volumes or increasing the discount rate.

Discounts and advances

For many years, rediscounting bills of exchange represented the Nationalbank's main monetary policy operation in domestic currency; at the same time, bill discounts were also commercial banks' main source of central bank funding until World War I. Starting in the 1920s, discount operations began to lose importance. Yet banks seeking to bridge short-term liquidity bottlenecks resorted to discount operations up until the 1990s. It was not until the introduction of the euro in 1999 that the OeNB terminated its discount operations.

Discounting bills of exchange

Bills of exchange contain an instruction to a third party to pay a given sum of money at a designated future date or on demand and thus serve to either transfer money or to take out a loan that is to be repaid by a third party in a different location. Their ready transferability made bills highly attractive for international and later also domestic trade and lending transactions. When a bill is discounted, i.e., transferred, its owner sells it to a business partner at a discount from the face value of the bill. The discount is calculated as the interest payable for a given period at a specified discount rate. Discounting allows bill owners to transfer a bill received in payment as payment for their own liabilities or to cash it, i.e., to receive payment before the bill was actually due.

For commercial banks and especially note-issuing banks, bill discounting was attractive for several reasons.[154] First, discount operations are short-term, meaning that payment can be expected quickly. Second, bill transactions enjoy strong legal protection and therefore came with little risk. A bill not only obliges the drawee (the person to whom the bill is addressed as an order to pay) to honor the bill, i.e., to pay the full amount on the due date, but also represents an obligation for every single person who has signed the bill: Whenever a bill is transferred–discounted–an additional signature is added to the bill, and each signature reduces the risk of default.[155]

The Nationalbank set up the framework for its discount operations accordingly. Initially, access to discounting was not limited to banks: the Nationalbank would accept bills for discounting from "any man, regardless of social standing, if he is known to the bank as law-abiding."[156] In reality, however, access was strictly limited. Bills presented for rediscount had to bear the signatures of at least three "good and reliable persons."[157] The "reliability" of the parties to a bill of exchange was established in two stages. The bank's management regularly updated credit lists of persons and companies eligible to take out discount loans and of their discount credit limits. Additionally, every bill presented was examined by a discount committee staffed by bank officials and by renowned local entrepreneurs who could be expected to be well informed about the financial solvency of the presenters of bills. The bank always had the right to reject bills submitted for rediscount without stating any reasons. Other provisions determined a maximum maturity of three months and originally a minimum amount of 300 florins; this threshold was successively reduced and finally abolished in 1887. The place of payment of bills of exchange was also important. As the Nationalbank had to cash the bill at maturity, it could only accept bills payable at locations at which it had an office or a representative. Before the office in Prague was established, only bills payable in Vienna were eligible for rediscounting. The geographical scope of eligibility was later widened as the bank opened additional branch offices.

Whereas the bank determined the rediscounting conditions and the effective discount rates and publicly announced them, actual utilization of the rediscount facility was at the discretion the bank's counterparties; in today's terminology, discount operations would be considered a "standing facility."[158] As a consequence, the bank was able to control the discount volume only indirectly via the price (the discount rate) or by setting individual limits. Such volume limits were commonly used until the 1870s and after 1945 in the form of rediscount limits.

Providing advances against collateral

In addition to discounting bills of exchange, the Nationalbank also provided advances against marketable securities pledged as collateral (these operations were also known as lombard loans).[159] As in discount operations, the initiative for the granting of an advance lay with the counterparty; the central bank only determined the general conditions and set the interest rate. Maturity was agreed upon individually subject to a three-month maximum. At the outset, only government bonds were eligible as collateral. Over time, the list of eligible securities was expanded. The maximum amount of the loan was calculated as the price of the pledged securities on the stock exchange minus a haircut. If the price of the collateralized securities dropped below a specific threshold during the term, the debtors had to provide additional securities or repay the loan. The concept of lending against collateral was later also adopted by the Eurosystem and in fact constitutes the most important tool in its toolbox. The main difference is that lending against collateral is no longer organized as a standing facility. Instead, the Eurosystem sets a total refinancing volume and then uses a tender procedure to allot liquidity among individual bidders.[160]

Mostly silver purchases were the measure of choice, for instance in 1830, when the July revolution in France had siphoned off silver from Austria. The same measure was adopted in 1840, when tensions between France and other European states on the Egyptian-Ottoman issue in tandem with rising key interest rates in France and England caused the demand for Nationalbank discounts and advances to mount, triggered silver exports and pushed the coverage ratio down to an unprecedented 9%.[161] This time, in addition to purchasing silver, the bank's management also tried to reduce the amount of banknotes in circulation. The debate on the required action aptly reflects the thinking of the time.[162] Increasing the discount rate was considered to be inadequate, as borrowers would put up with higher interest rates rather than discounting smaller sums. Quantitative restrictions were considered to be more fitting but also more dangerous, as they might trigger the costly winding-up of outstanding operations, which could lead to high losses. Ultimately, gentle pressure on the large discounters and a wait-and-see attitude sufficed in both 1836 and 1840; the discount volume dropped again, and silver flowed to the bank.[163]

As a result of this view, which accorded the interest rate only little influence on demand for discounts and advances and hence on the volume of banknotes in circulation and the coverage ratio, the discount rate played only a limited role as a policy instrument in the pre-revolutionary era. From the establishment of the bank until October 1829, the discount rate remained constant at 5%, apart from a short spike in the first half of 1818, and mostly at 4% in the period from 1829 to 1848. Time and again, the low volume of discount lending proved to be the key argument in the interest rate debates–until 1829 the governing board was frequently considering lowering the rate to 4%. Advocates of a lower discount rate argued that the rate in private discount operations lay below 5% and that the conditions offered by the bank were thus unattractive. The opponents of lowering the discount rate put the small size of the business down to the state of the economy and the subdued demand for credit, and they were concerned that, in the event of an interest rate reduction, nonresident investors might sell Austrian bonds, thereby draining the silver reserves of the bank.[164] Against the backdrop of these recurring arguments it is interesting to note that most changes in official interest rates were urged by the government.

The reductions of 1829 and 1833 were related to major capital market operations of the state, the hope being that lower interest rates would facilitate those operations.[165] In other words, the modern-day role of the discount rate as a monetary policy instrument had not yet developed.

Taking stock of the first 30 years

When Governor Lederer drafted his account of the first 30 years of the Nationalbank, he had a success story to share. Inconvertible government paper money had been replaced by silver-backed banknotes, and the bank had supported the state in a number of ways: Advances provided against government bonds had stabilized the market for government debt; the possibility of placing money orders with the Nationalbank's offices throughout the monarchy enabled cashless money transfers, which facilitated treasury operations; and "finally there was an institution that stood ready to lend short-term to the public administration on demand without jeopardizing its own existence by doing so."[166] But the government was not the only beneficiary; trade and industry had benefited as well: being able to discount bills of exchange had made it easier to raise short-term funds and indirectly also supported investment in real assets. In moments of panic, the Nationalbank was like a beacon of calm.

Yet this apparent stability depended on a combination of intransparency and inaccountability to the general public and a fragile business model that paired low reserves with high, illiquid credit to the government. When the reserves dwindled menacingly in 1830 and 1840, the bank was able to secure convertibility only with the help of the state in purchasing additional silver and transferring silver reserves from the treasury to the bank. Yet what would happen if holders of banknotes were to request redemption for silver specie at a time when the bank could not rely on the state to tide it over? What would happen when the precarious state of the Nationalbank's assets became general knowledge? Then convertibility would be in acute danger. This moment of truth came in March 1848.

Turning from the treasury's banker to the banker's bank (1848–1878)

"In a season of pervading gloom [after the stock market crisis in 1873] there was one unfailing anchor of trust: even if it was deeply mired in crisis, Austria could not possibly be on the brink of collapse if a central credit institution like the Oester-reichische Nationalbank was standing firm on solid ground–in fact on foundations that were more stable and sturdy than ever."

Neuwirth, *Bankacte*, p. 372

When the Metternich regime was coming under ever heavier fire in the 1840s, criticism was also leveled at the Nationalbank, which was, quite correctly, perceived as a public institution. As the bank did not publish its financial statements, observers could all but speculate about the state of affairs. A good measure of the degree of uncertainty and distrust is the range of figures on the volume of outstanding banknotes that circulated among the public. Two widely read publications from 1845 put this volume at 150 million florins and more than four times that much, 647 million florins, respectively–when in actual fact some 215 million florins were circulating at the end of 1845.[167]

1848—the revolution accelerates long-term change

In February 1848, news of the toppling of the King of France and of emerging uprisings in Italy spread to Austria. These news surfaced at a time when the general public was cut off from reliable information of any kind. Against this backdrop, the veil of secrecy that had in the past saved the bank from a run on its counters in similar situations, was sparking concern and, very soon, even panic. Before the end of the month, customers had pulled out a sizeable sum of money from savings banks and had exchanged a significant amount of banknotes against specie.[168] In response, the Nationalbank resorted to a measure that was a small revolution in itself. To restore confidence, the governing board decided to start publishing end-of-month financial statements.[169] The first monthly financial statement, referring to February 29, was published on March 6.[170] On this date, banknotes in circulation were disclosed as totaling 214 million florins, the stock of silver coins was given as 65 million florins, and the government was shown to have borrowed 81 million florins from the bank. This meant that the ratio of banknotes in circulation to silver reserves was, in fact, considerably better than it had been throughout the 1830s (chart 3.4 in the previous chapter). At the same time however, and even though the bank did not indicate that half of its discount loans consisted in loans to the government, which implies that receivables from the state totaled 131 million florins rather than the disclosed 81 millions, the financial statements clearly showed that claims on the sovereign were the main counterpart of banknotes in circulation; in other words, that large-scale redemption of banknotes for specie would require state support. Rather than calming holders of banknotes, the publication of the bank's financial statements hence sent even larger crowds to the tellers of the Nationalbank. On top of that, the political crisis was escalating. On March 13, Metternich resigned, and on March 15, Emperor Ferdinand I promised the drafting of a constitution. Meanwhile, during the month of March, the bank's silver reserves dwindled by 12 million florins, and the amount of banknotes in circulation contracted by 16 million florins. By the end of April, the stock of silver reserves and the amount of banknotes in circulation were 30 million florins below the levels recorded at the end of February (chart 4.2). The ensuing countermeasures brought a sense of déjà vu from the times of the Napoleonic wars: Exports of Austrian silver coins were banned and the redemption of banknotes against coins was first restricted and then suspended, followed by measures to enforce the acceptance of banknotes at par value. This inevitably resulted in the re-emergence of a premium on silver coins (chart 4.3). Next, the smaller coin denominations were disappearing from circulation, just like during the Napoleonic wars. The bank responded by issuing smaller banknotes, worth 1 and 2 florins, in late May; and even smaller banknotes and underweight coins would follow in 1849. Before then, the general public resorted to self-help, such as cutting up 1-florin and 2-florin notes into smaller units.[171]

Suspending the redemption of banknotes for silver stopped the depletion of the silver reserves, and purchases of silver from abroad helped reverse some of the decline.[172] Enforcing par acceptance of banknotes allowed the bank to re-increase the amount of circulating banknotes. This move came at the eleventh hour, because the government was in need of additional loans to be able to finance the suppression of the uprisings in Italy and Hungary. Following a drop to 177 million florins until May 1848, the volume of banknotes in circulation thus went soon up again to more than 250 million florins.

In the fall of 1849, the last of the rebels were capitulating in Hungary and Venice. The revolution in Austria was officially over. Yet, the events of 1848 ushered in a new era for the Nationalbank. Two major themes were to occupy the bank in the years ahead: The bank would have to stabilize the currency in view of the state's requests for monetary financing; and it would have to reinvent itself in the context of dynamic economic growth and the gradual evolution of a modern financial system. While these issues were by no means new, 1848 and its repercussions added extra emphasis and accelerated change.

For the time being, the most dramatic change was the suspension of silver redemption, which the bank had kept up since 1818. Initially, this measure was conceived as temporary, but the massive depletion of the silver reserves and massive lending to the state prohibited a rapid return to convertibility. These problems were compounded by the fact that the state issued inconvertible paper money of its own. Reinstating silver convertibility presupposed that those quantities would also have to be adequately backed by silver reserves, or else withdrawn from circulation. Ultimately, regaining convertibility remained a moving target that the central bank continued to invoke yet pursue in vain for decades.

Furthermore, the revolution also brought a number of fundamental changes to the way the bank operated. The regular publication of monthly and later also weekly financial statements was retained despite the return to public censure under the neo-absolutist regime. Unlike before 1848, the bank was now acting under the watchful eyes of the general public and drawing heavy criticism. Over the medium term, the publication of financial statements marked the first steps toward a broader definition of central bank accountability to the public, which was cast into law with the new charter of 1863 and reflected in the publication of increasingly voluminous annual reports. Not by coincidence did this process evolve in parallel with the development of parliamentary rights after 1860, and increasing demands for accountability by the state.

However, the most important catalyst for change in the long run is likely to have been the support that the Nationalbank had provided to businesses and savings banks during the revolution: Against the backdrop of a gradually emerging banking system, the Nationalbank had, for the very first time, accepted the role of a central banking institution throughout the monarchy. While the emergency loans it had extended amid the turmoil of 1848 soon expired, the bank made sure to increase its presence in the provinces rather than pulling out again and refocusing on business in Vienna. More and more, the

Lender of last resort

In very general terms, a lender of last resort is an institution which may halt the flight from less liquid assets to cash and equivalents by providing adequate amounts of liquidity.[173] A classic example would be a bank run. A bank facing a run might be unable to meet this sudden demand for cash, since most of its deposits are tied up in loans with longer maturities. In such a situation, the central bank can tide over the distressed bank by purchasing loans outstanding from the bank or by lending central bank money as required. The ability to supply central bank money, one of the most liquid types of assets, makes the central bank the natural lender of last resort. Of course, other institutions, such as governments or groups of private banks, might play a similar role.[174]

There is no consensus among economists as to what the scope and design of last resort lending should be. For example, should lenders of last resort support only individual banks or even entire asset markets, such as stock markets or sovereign bond markets? Should access to liquidity assistance be restricted to illiquid institutions or should insolvent institutions be eligible as well? And, for that matter, is it at all possible to draw a clear line between illiquidity and insolvency? Should additional liquidity be provided through direct loans or via open market operations? Which assets are adequate for purchase by the central bank, or for use as collateral for central bank credit? How high a price should be paid or interest rate charged? Some authors question the need for a lender of last

resort altogether, voicing concerns about moral hazard: Presuming that they will be bailed out by the lender of last resort, institutions may take on more risks than they would in the absence of a lender of last resort, which may thus create the very crisis it is supposed to remedy.

The Oesterreichische Nationalbank as a lender of last resort

Definitions of the lender of last resort differ in the literature, depending on the answers to the aforementioned questions.[175] To put the actions taken by Austria's central bank into perspective, it is useful to distinguish between standard measures and specific crisis management operations. Depending on their design, standard monetary policy instruments provide for a number of mechanisms counterbalancing a sudden increase in the demand for liquidity.[176] In this context, discounts and advances served as a natural backstop, as these facilities were available to banks on a daily basis and at their own initiative, thus facilitating timely as well as easy access to central bank money. In the first decades of the Nationalbank's existence, however, both facilities were limited in their ability to respond to crises: Access was granted to a small number of individuals based in Vienna only, collateral policies were quite restrictive and operations were limited in amount, making it impossible to count on the facilities' availability. In the course of the 19th century, though, restrictions were eased gradually. Most importantly, the Nationalbank abandoned upper limits for discounts and advances, which was possible for two reasons: On the one hand, the bank increasingly used interest rates to regulate demand in its operations and on the other, restrictions on the amount of banknotes in circulation, valid until 1888, were suspended. These developments were reflected in short-term market interest rates which exceeded the official discount rate time and again until the 1870s, indicating a restrictive approach to discount operations (chart 4.4). Later on, however, interest rates were above the official rate only once in a while, lying below it continuously from 1888.[177]

In crisis episodes, the Nationalbank repeatedly adopted nonstandard measures, too, for example by extending its list of eligible collateral for policy operations. As a case in point, in 1823 the bank started to accept, following lengthy debates, its own stocks as collateral for advances. Another measure the Nationalbank resorted to repeatedly was the creation of joint liability support committees consisting of banks and merchant banks. The committees were able to sign and thus guarantee bills which would not have met quality requirements otherwise, and thus turn them into eligible assets. After having called on the services of support committees for the first time in 1820, the bank particularly relied on them during the crises of 1848 and 1873.

There were various reasons for taking extraordinary rescue measures. Quite often it was the finance ministry which asked for interventions and relied on the bank's financial resources, sometimes also providing guarantees. Cases in point are rescue operations to prevent the meltdown of railway stock prices in 1847 and the provision of special loans during the revolution of 1848. The reason why the bank intervened in favor of the great merchant banks in Vienna, Arnstein & Eskeles, the rescue of which ultimately failed at great cost, probably lay in the fact that Arnstein & Eskeles had close ties with the Nationalbank.[178] Furthermore, there are several early cases where the governing board clearly perceived the Nationalbank to be responsible for the stability of the banking system.[179] Concerns about individual institutions of systemic relevance are therefore likely to have played a significant role when the government supported, e.g., the Bodencreditanstalt in 1873 and in 1929, the Creditanstalt in 1931 as well as the BAWAG in 2006. In all of these instances, lending of last resort by the central bank was supported by government guarantees.

bank was taking on the role of providing emergency liquidity to banks, i.e., assuming a lender of last resort function. Step by step, a bank designed to serve the needs of the treasury was turning into the banker's bank.

The return to silver convertibility proves to be a moving target

The post-1848 era saw a lively public debate about ways to improve monetary and financial arrangements. As far as the bank was concerned, proposals ranged from reorganization to outright dissolution.[180] These considerations were all motivated by the aspiration to restore the convertibility of the currency. Most observers considered the suspension of the redemption of banknotes to have been due to fundamental structural problems rather than by the political crisis of 1848: The underlying problem, which the events of 1848 had merely exposed, was the high level of public debt in the books of the Nationalbank. Moreover, while the bank had been criticized even before 1848 for a bias in the provision of loans–restricting access to its services to residents of Vienna and allegedly giving privileged access to a small group of Viennese merchant banks–this criticism was now voiced much more vehemently. Reaching out to other geographic areas was also in the interest of public policy: The government in fact expected the Nationalbank to lend financial support to its ambitious plans for advancing infrastructure, industry and agriculture. However, increasing lending and limiting the volume of banknotes in circulation, as a necessary precondition for restoring the currency's convertibility, were two conflicting goals, as the coming years would show time and again.

Between 1848 and 1866, the public authorities developed a number of plans to reinstate silver convertibility of banknotes. The measures adopted, subject to repeated revisions on account of new funding needs on the part of the state, were based on varied combinations of the following pillars: *First,* the government would have to pay down its debt with the bank, except for some limited and fixed amount, which would be retained. The corresponding inflow of funds would allow the bank to reduce the amount of banknotes in circulation, to acquire additional silver reserves and to finance new lending to the private sector. In the process, silver and short-term private credit rather than claims on the public sector would evolve as the main counterpart of banknotes in circulation. *Second,* the shares of the OeNB that had been retained in the initial public offering in 1816–1818 could be sold to further improve the bank's balance sheet structure, by either increasing the amount of silver reserves or funding additional credit to the private sector.[181] *Third,* most reform plans included an amendment to the charter that would explicitly limit the amount of banknotes in circulation and regulate its coverage. *Fourth,* the government paper money, circulating in parallel with banknotes issued by the Nationalbank since 1849, would have to be redeemed.

However, until the year 1867, all attempts at stabilizing the currency and restoring its convertibility failed because of the precarious state of public finance. Following the suppression of the revolution and the handover of the crown to Francis Joseph I in late 1848, the Austrian government turned its back on the notion of a constitutional state and parliamentary democracy. Given the presumed necessity to centralize the empire, the government took action to enforce this goal with military and administrative means, and to support the modernization of the economy by investing in public works and by acting as a catalyst for private-sector initiatives.[182] Even though the reforms were reasonably successful, the failure to generate the necessary financial basis for its ambitious external and domestic policies would eventually lead to the collapse of the neo-absolutist state. The precarious state of Austrian public finance was partly a legacy of the pre-revolutionary period, when the government had managed to balance the annual budgets only by issuing new bonds to be able to finance servicing the interest rate payments for the debt inherited from the Napoleonic wars.[183] After 1848, administrative and judicial reforms, the agrarian reform legislation adopted in 1848 that compensated landlords for the abolition of remaining feudal rights, and investments into railroad construction drove up expenditure sharply, without offsetting increases in revenue.[184] Therefore, the government remained highly dependent on issuing bonds in the capital market–and on stopgap funding from the central bank. The three reform cycles observed until 1867, which will be discussed below, invariably followed the same pattern: The state made an effort to pay down its liabilities with the

Nationalbank either by issuing bonds or by assigning assets to the bank, thus helping to improve the silver coverage ratio of banknotes. These attempts worked fine until another war broke out, which drove up public funding needs, which were met either by borrowing from the bank directly or by issuing state paper money in circumvention of the note-issuing bank. Hence the silver coverage ratio deteriorated again, which caused the currency to depreciate vis-à-vis silver, which in turn sent all players back to square one.

Success and failure of currency stabilization until 1859

By the time the war against Piedmont-Sardinia was over and the revolution in Hungary had been suppressed in September 1849, the Nationalbank's receivables from the state had jumped from 125 million florins to 225 million florins. In an attempt to repay its debt, the state used war reparations payable by Piedmont and consolidated the remaining part, which consisted of numerous small positions, into a new block of debt with a uniform coupon of 2%. Several rounds of repayment indeed brought down the debt to 122 million florins by the end of 1853.[185] However, since the government continued to run deficits, it was only able to make those downpayments by issuing paper money of its own, in parallel to banknotes proper issued by the bank, and by enforcing par acceptance of the state paper money. In sum, these measures initially continued to drive up the total circulation of paper money sharply, before a slight drop in the run-up to 1853 (chart 4.1).[186] In other words, these transactions did nothing but move the currency problems from the central bank's to the government's balance sheet.

In 1854, the government decided to put an end to the parallel circulation of government and central bank paper money. The Nationalbank exchanged the state paper money for banknotes proper, which was reflected by a sharp rise in the value of banknotes in circulation and of course also in the bank's receivables from the state. To raise the funds needed to pay down these liabilities, the government issued bonds, called the *Nationalanlehen,* on a large scale in the domestic market.[187] Thanks to significant pressure, the bonds were in fact forced loans, investors ultimately subscribed to 512 million florins, or some 50% of the government debt outstanding in 1853.[188] While the proceeds of the bond sale were duly used to pay down the liabilities stemming from the conversion

Chart 4.1: **Paper money in circulation** (in millions of florins)[189]

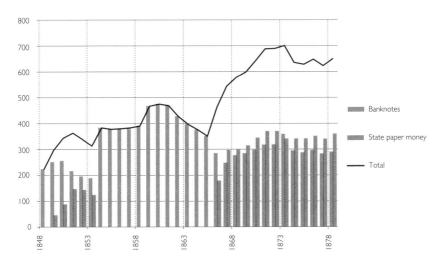

To finance public expenditure, the state repeatedly turned on the monetary tap between 1848 and 1866, either by taking recourse to monetary financing through the central bank or by issuing paper money directly.[190]

of paper money, the Crimean war starting in mid-1853–for which Austria, while remaining neutral, nonetheless kept troops mobilized in large numbers–tied up such large amounts that the bank had to advance another 80 million florins to the state in 1855.[191] In short, harmonizing paper money circulation had worked, but it had failed to bring down the receivables from the treasury in the bank's books.

In a next attempt, dated 1855, finance minister Baron Karl Ludwig von Bruck assigned a portfolio of public real estate holdings to the bank, the idea being that the gradual sale of this portfolio would generate money to pay down the public debt.[192] To facilitate the process, the government instructed the Nationalbank to establish a mortgage loan division.[193] In other words, the bank was meant to help fund the sale of the public property by issuing mortgage loans to potential buyers. Even so, the large-scale transfer of landed property to capitalist entrepreneurs met political resistance and sales were slow. Ultimately, the state had to take back the bulk of the real estate holdings from the bank in

1866.[194] Another element in Bruck's plan promised more immediate remedy. By 1853 the bank had already issued the 49,379 shares reserved in 1818 for later issuance and had brought the sum total to the statutory amount of 100,000 stocks.[195] Now Bruck wanted the bank to increase capital once again, not least to fund the newly created mortgage loan division. In 1855 the bank issued 50,000 shares requiring subscribers to pay in silver, with a view to increasing its precious metal reserves.[196] As a result of the two corporate actions, the paid-in capital of the Nationalbank jumped from 30 million florins to 103 million florins. At the same time the bank's precious metal reserves almost doubled by the end of 1857.

By early 1854, the ratio of banknotes in circulation to the bank's silver reserves had improved to such an extent that restoring convertibility appeared to be a feasible target. Restoring convertibility moreover coincided with the intentions of foreign policy. In the early 1850s, the then trade minister Bruck had been seeking a rapprochement with the Zollverein created by some members of the German Confederation in 1834, in order to regain some of the influence Austria had lost in the Confederation. While Austria failed to secure full membership, it did achieve the conclusion of a trade agreement with the Zollverein in 1854. Among other things, the agreement provided for the medium-term harmonization of the coinage system, with a view to reducing transaction costs in cross-border trade. The coinage agreement signed in Vienna in 1857 standardized the silver content of the three silver currencies used by German Confederation members such that 1.5 Austrian florins corresponded to 1 Prussian thaler.[197] To align the Austrian florin with the Prussian thaler, Austria had to reduce the silver content of the (Convention standard) florin by about 5%. The new florin, now called "Austrian standard florin," was also decimalized in the process of the changeover. Hence, 100 Convention standard florins à 60 kreutzer were replaced by 105 Austrian standard florins à 100 (new) kreutzer.

For the Nationalbank, the coinage agreement was of the essence in as much as it committed all signatory countries to ensure that their paper money would be convertible at all times by January 1, 1859. Following issuance and ready convertibility of the new (Austrian standard) florin banknotes, which started on September 6, 1858, the silver premium disappeared. Apparently, monetary re-

Chart 4.2: **Nationalbank assets and banknotes in circulation** (in millions of florins)[198]

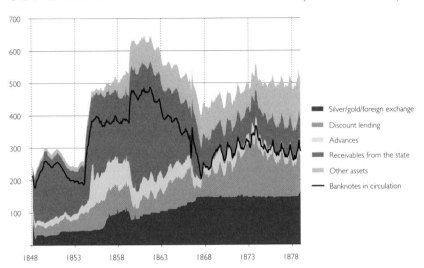

The legend reads:
- Silver/gold/foreign exchange
- Discount lending
- Advances
- Receivables from the state
- Other assets
- Banknotes in circulation

The volume of banknotes in circulation rose sharply in 1854, reflecting the conversion of state paper money into banknotes, and in 1859, given monetary financing of the war against Italy. The war of 1866 is all but inconspicuous in the data as the government circumvented the central bank by issuing paper money of its own (chart 4.1). Consequently, receivables from the state were the main counterpart on the asset side for a long time. The reform plan masterminded by finance minister Plener in the early 1860s was a success in as much as it ensured coverage of banknotes in circulation exclusively by precious metal reserves and lending to the private sector after 1867. The receivables from the state that remained on the books were roughly on a par with the bank's stock of share capital.

form had been a success (chart 4.3). In actual fact, however, convertibility was a close call from the very start. While silver specie accounted for as much as 44% of the volume of banknotes in circulation by the end of June 1858, it did so only subject to an imperial decree that exempted smaller denomination banknotes (5, 2 and 1 florins) from silver coverage requirements. The smaller denominations were, however, fully convertible into larger denominations at all times and thus constituted a potential claim on the bank's silver reserves as well.[199] Adjusted for the smaller denominations, the silver coverage amounted to just above 25%. Moreover, the bank suffered considerable inroads into its stock of silver in the initial months after convertibility took effect, requiring the

Chart 4.3: **Price of 100 silver florins at the Vienna Stock Exchange**[200]

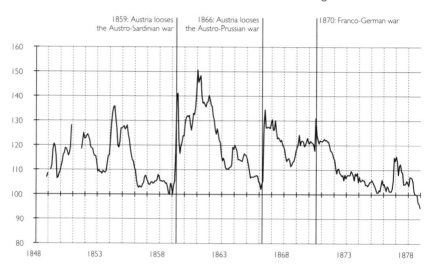

The attempts to stabilize the currency were invariably linked with the state of public finances and hence with the regime's internal and external position. Following the suspension of the redemption of banknotes for specie in 1848, the prices at which silver florins traded at the Vienna Stock Exchange became an indicator of the state of Austrian politics. Price meltdowns reflected not only war times; the peak of the silver premium in 1860 coincided with a domestic crisis, which only calmed down once a parliamentary assembly was convened in 1861.

support of the state, which immediately provided the bank with 10 million silver florins and committed to further transfers of silver and a reduction of the volume of the smaller denominations.[201] In the end, convertibility was never put to the test, as the convertibility of banknotes for silver was suspended when the war against Piedmont-Sardinia broke out on April 29, 1859.[202] The state heavily resorted to monetary financing right at the start of the war. At least, the bank managed to prevent a large-scale run on its silverholdings–and thus a repeat of 1848–by rapidly suspending convertibility. The issuance of new banknotes and uncertainty about the further development of the currency caused the silver premium to reach new heights, peaking at 40% in 1859.

Seigniorage and the central bank's balance sheet

Originally, seigniorage referred to the profit resulting from the difference between the face value of coins and the lower cost of coin metal and production. Historically, minting coins was typically the privilege of princes or lords ("seigneurs" in French), which also made them the beneficiaries of the related profits, the seigniorage. Translated to money creation today, seigniorage has come to mean the profit accruing to the central bank because it does not pay interest on its banknote liabilities but receives interest on its assets.

The determinants of seigniorage are best illustrated using a simplified central bank balance sheet.[203] Looking at the assets and liabilities of the Oesterreichische Nationalbank, we find banknotes to have typically been the main liability, plus in later years also current account deposits by the private sector and banks. Assets essentially fall into three categories: precious metals as well as assets in foreign currencies, loans to the non-government sector, and loans to the government sector. Originally, precious metals–minted or unminted silver and gold–guaranteed the convertibility of banknotes; later, the value of the domestic currency against foreign currencies like Deutsche Mark. Foreign currency reserve assets basically fulfill the same purpose. The other major asset category is loans to banks and enterprises. Here, discounts and advances (see box on page 60) used to be the National-bank's main types of operation. Finally, the Nationalbank had claims on government resulting from market purchases of government securities or, historically, also from direct lending.

Assets	Liabilities
Gold, silver	Banknotes
Foreign currency	Current accounts
reserve assets	Capital and reserves
Discounts and advances	
Claims on government	

In this simplified balance sheet, seigniorage income corresponds to the income on the assets held against (unremunerated) bank-note liabilities. For lending to the private sector, the central bank usually receives interest according to the official discount or lombard rate. The precious metal reserves do not earn interest, and on foreign assets interest is generally lower than on domestic currency assets. Thus, reserve holdings entail forgone earnings. Claims on government can earn market yields; if they involve direct lending, they may earn low yields or none at all.

Until 1878, the government received its share of seigniorage in the form of subsidized loans and services that the National-bank provided free of charge.[204] The bank's statutes of 1878 first introduced a direct profit-sharing mechanism. Over time, the share of profit transferred to the state gradually expanded; in parallel, the central bank's scope to build up reserves was curtailed. Nowadays, the Austrian government receives its share of seigniorage first in the form of corporate income tax. The profit remaining after tax is appropriated as follows: an amount equivalent to 6% of the capital stock goes to the owner, nowadays the Republic of Austria, which is also the statutory beneficiary of 90% of the remaining profit (on bank ownership see box on page 252). The funds left over after statutory allocations are used to fund nonprofit foundations established by the OeNB.

A new charter modeled on the Peel's Act and another war in 1866

Austria's defeat in 1859 and its loss of Lombardy undermined government plans to swiftly redeem the advances it had received from the central bank.[205] The next attempt at restoring the currency was made under a new constitutional framework. Defeat against Italy had prompted the Emperor to reassess the stabilizing role of a parliament invested with budgetary powers. A first step was to convene a parliament in 1861, which was given jurisdiction over money and credit matters. The new finance minister, Baron Ignaz von Plener, combined the stabilization of the currency with a renewal of the Nationalbank's charter, which would have expired in 1866. The new charter and the agreement governing the mutual debts of the government and the bank, which both took effect at the start of 1863, were in fact the first regulations that were negotiated and adopted in a parliamentary process, subject to the involvement of broader circles. The new rules represented a break with the previous organization and policies of the bank in a number of ways.

The bank was granted a larger degree of independence from the state than in all previous charters. Above all the chambers of commerce representing industry and trade and thus playing an important role in public opinion, had blamed the high and changing silver premium on the lack of certainty about the prospective volume of banknotes in circulation. According to the chambers, it was the lack of constitutional restrictions on the issuance of banknotes that made it impossible to anchor expectations.[206] Here, the new charter was meant to protect the bank against demands from the treasury. The influence of the public authorities was reduced to a minimum: Now, the state commissioner only monitored compliance with the charter, and the bank was forbidden to do business with the state other than in a few clearly defined areas.[207] Moreover, the charter strengthened the role of the stockholders, larger numbers of whom were now allowed to join the annual general meetings, and elected representatives of whom also joined the governing board meetings at which the key interest rates were fixed.

Public supervision of the bank was replaced by rules about the issuance and redemption of banknotes. The volume of banknotes the bank was allowed to issue and the type of assets that were eligible as counterparts had first been defined in 1858. Since then, the bank had been required to back one-third of its banknotes with silver reserves and the remainder with discounted trade bills, subject to the respective statutory provisions, or receivables from secured lending operations.[208] The biggest concern of the drafters of the new charter was a sharp expansion of banknotes in circulation that might endanger their convertibility for specie.

Considerations of how to best prevent a sharp expansion triggered a lengthy and intensive debate mirroring the controversy between the banking school and the currency school observed earlier in England.[209] Members of the currency school were strong advocates of strictly aligning the volume of banknotes in circulation with the bank's precious metal reserves, taking a leaf out of Peel's Act. Under the latter, the Bank of England was only allowed to issue notes up to a statutory amount above which every additional note had to be fully covered by precious metal. As a result, at least in the argument of the currency school, the amount of currency in circulation would be governed by the in- and outflow of precious metal reserves, thus being beyond the (potentially calamitous political) control of the central bank.[210]

The critics of Peel's Act, known as the banking school, argued that the inherent lack of flexibility was bound to generate crises and instead supported a system of proportional reserve asset coverage, such as had been in place in Austria since 1858.[211] Such a system of proportional coverage required only a certain ratio of any additional note issued, like one-third, to be backed by additional reserve assets. This made it easier than under Peel's system to increase the circulation of banknotes whenever necessary. To keep the volume of banknotes in circulation from expanding too much, the advocates of the banking school relied on the quality of the assets backing the banknotes other than precious metal. As long as the central bank accepted only short-term and liquid instruments, such as trade bills, thus their opinion, there was no danger of excess issuance. In Austria, and against the opposition of the representatives of the Nationalbank, the balance of opinion ultimately tilted toward a modified version of Peel's Act, as favored by finance minister Plener.[212] By analogy to Peel's Act, the statutes from 1863 allowed the bank to issue banknotes up to the amount of 200 million florins without silver coverage; beyond this threshold, every single note had to be fully backed with silver. The 200 million florins would have to be backed through the bank's discount and secured lending operations. The statutes became known as the *Plenersche Bank Akte.*

Yet in 1863, the volume of banknotes in circulation backed neither by metal reserves nor by receivables from discounting and secured lending–and instead by state debt–vastly exceeded the 200 million florin threshold (chart 4.2). Therefore, downpayment of the sums with which the government was indebted to the bank and increasing the silver reserves was a central precondition for implementing the new Bank Act. In order to do so, the state committed to fully redeem its liabilities against the bank, by the end of 1866, in an agreement adopted in 1862 in parallel with the charter. Exempted from this requirement was an unremunerated block of 80 million florins that the bank put at the disposal of the state until the charter was due to expire in 1878, in turn for having been granted the monopoly right to issue banknotes.[213] In the following years, the government duly redeemed its outstanding debt in the form of silver, thus increasing the Nationalbank's silver reserves. However, unlike under the regime of finance minister Bruck, the receipts from the state and the revenues from the sale of the bank's securities portfolio were above all used to fund the gradual reduction of the volume of banknotes in circulation. Only moderate amounts were used to conduct discount and lending operations. From early 1863 until the end of April 1866, the value of banknotes in circulation dropped by close to 90 million florins or 20%.

The shrinking value of banknotes in circulation coincided with a period of a sharp decline and, ultimately, stagnation of industrial production in Austria, blamed by numerous contemporaries and historians on the deflationary monetary policy and the associated appreciation of the Austrian currency.[214] More recent evidence challenges this notion, explaining the weak economic activity with factors in the real economy, such as crop failures, the decline in the output of the textile industry triggered by the American civil war and reduced public spending on the railway system.[215] Judging from the low level of market interest rates (chart 4.4), the increasing volume of discount lending and the fact that the branch offices were unable to place all the funds put at their disposal for lack of adequate demand, the Nationalbank appears to have pursued a relative accommodative credit policy in those years.[216] In this view, the decline in the supply of money reflected low demand rather than restrictive monetary policy.

The adjustment program was well on track to be implemented as planned until the end of 1866. However, the plans were thwarted yet again by a military dispute, repeating the pattern of 1859 with a new set of opponents, namely Prussia and Italy. As a result of the war that started in May 1866, the state was again in need of direct borrowing from the bank, in the form of banknotes and silver specie.[217] After the end of the war, the state did repay the advances received, causing its liabilities with the Nationalbank to indeed reach the level of 80 million florins targeted in 1862 by 1866. At the same time, however, the state again resorted to issuing paper money of its own in massive proportions, thus driving up the aggregate amount of paper money in circulation by more than half (chart 4.1). This left the bank in a rather ambiguous situation at the end of 1866: The finances of the central bank had indeed been restored; its banknotes were now adequately backed by silver reserves. Yet the other side of the coin was an enormous amount of state paper money in circulation, which had blown up the silver premium to such proportions that a swift return to the silver convertibility of banknotes seemed out of reach.

Taking on a new role in the financial system

While the narrative of the years between 1848 and 1866 is characterized by continuity with regard to the close ties the Nationalbank retained with the government, it reflects substantial changes with regard to the bank's role in the financial system, triggered by the broad support the Nationalbank had given to businesses and savings banks during the revolution. Having originally stepped in with short-term loans that were temporary by design, the bank became permanently established in the provinces and gradually evolved into a central institution for the briskly expanding banking sector.

Reaching out across the monarchy—the branch network of the Nationalbank

During the revolution of 1848 and 1849, the Nationalbank financed not only the government to a substantial degree, but also–and frequently upon the pressure of the ministries of finance and the interior–cities, credit institutions, industry and trade hard hit by upheaval and war. In doing so, the bank repeatedly breached its tight statutes: it discounted bills whose term exceeded three months, that did not feature the required three signatures or that were redeemable in places other than Vienna or Prague. Moreover, in its lending operations it accepted collateral other than the stipulated bonds (see the box on p. 60). Such breaches of the statutes went unpunished, given that the only potential plaintiffs–the state commissioner and the ministry of finance–had in fact instructed the bank to provide the required funding. The Nationalbank proved rather resourceful in designing such loans. To ensure that the loans were extended exclusively to illiquid, yet solvent businesses, the bank tapped support committees formed by local companies based in Vienna, Brno, Budapest and Trieste. These support committees distributed the funds at the local level and assumed joint liability of the bills they rediscounted at the Nationalbank.[218] Add to this direct loans to large businesses, such as spinning and weaving mills, the shipping company Lloyd in Trieste and numerous savings banks.[219] At the height of the revolution in 1849, extraordinary loans amounted to more than 6 million florins.

The bulk of this amount was repaid in the years that followed. However, in the process the bank had acquired experience in lending outside Vienna and Prague and, in this context, had established many business contacts.[220] So, when some local credit institutions again encountered liquidity problems in the subsequent years, they once more turned to the Nationalbank for help. And even though the directors of the bank were more cautious now–in contrast to 1848/49 the monarchy was not really in jeopardy–, the bank granted new extraordinary loans. The state commissioner again played a key role as he had to approve any loans that did not comply with the statutes. Being torn between the contradictory aims of limiting lending to restore convertibility and supporting economically or politically relevant credit institutions and cities, he did not pursue a clear strategy, though. In the end, between 1850 and 1859 the Nationalbank granted extraordinary loans worth 37 million florins.[221]

Most loans extended outside Vienna were not granted on an individual basis; instead such lending was quickly institutionalized as the Nationalbank started to set up branch offices. This brought a fundamental change to policy. Up to 1847, the bank had had hardly any representation outside of Vienna. It is true that the bank had, right at the beginning of its existence, established a dozen of smaller exchange offices in the provincial capitals. Yet these offices basically only withdrew the old government-issued (Vienna standard florin) paper money from circulation and put new banknotes issued by the National-bank into circulation.[222] Later, they also exchanged banknotes of various denominations, changed banknotes into coins and offered an early form of cash-less money transfer to and from Vienna. These small outlets were based in all politically important locations and were run in close cooperation with the local fiscal administration, or frequently by civil servants.[223] The exchange offices, no doubt, played an essential role for distributing banknotes and for standard-izing money in circulation in the monarchy, but they were hardly able to influ-ence local economic conditions because they did not extend loans.

The main reason why the bank had not made use of its statutory right to es-tablish discount offices across the monarchy was that the bank hesitated to di-vide the already low stock of silver coins among several locations. At the same time, given its brisk business with the government, the bank management had had little incentive to pursue additional, potentially risky and cost-intensive business areas.[224] Following the significant increase in the silver stock after 1841, the situation changed. In 1847, the bank responded to the government-en-dorsed request made by Prague's tradesmen and business owners. The office in Prague, opened in 1847, was the first branch office of the bank to offer the same discount facilities as the Vienna headquarters.[225] A similar office was set up in Budapest in 1851.[226]

By 1855, the bank had already established 14 branch offices in the main cities of all important crown lands. Credit for the rapid setting-up of the network, was, however, hardly due to the bank management, which was reluctant to grant the numerous requests submitted by cities and trade chambers.[227] Instead, this de-velopment was driven by the government, which sought to counteract the defla-tionary pressures emanating from public-sector debt reduction by stepping up lending. In addition, the government hoped that the branch offices would help improve the economic structure and boost local business.[228] Against this backdrop, discounting was simplified further. For instance, the minimum amount was reduced and it became possible to discount bills due in Vienna in the branch offices and vice versa.[229]

Moreover, as from 1854, most branch offices were entitled to engage in secured lending, an activity hitherto limited to the Vienna headquarters.[230] The impetus once again came from the government, which sought support for a large-scale bond issue, the 1854 *Nationalanlehen*. Even though individuals, municipalities and foundations were allowed to stretch out payment for bond purchases over an extended period of time, they frequently lacked the necessary funds to fulfil the quotas imposed under governmental pressure. To prevent a failure of the bond issue, the bank had to order its branch offices to grant loans in turn for taking in government securities as collateral. Furthermore, it opened additional branch offices.[231] As a result, secured loans, which up to 1854 had averaged about 15 to 20 million florins, jumped to over 130 million florins in February 1855. The *Nationalanlehen* was, however, not the only factor driving secured lending. In addition to the temporary problem of accommodating the government bond issue, the markets faced a structural burden stemming from agrarian reform legislation.[232] One of the measures of 1848 that the neo-absolutist regime did not repeal concerned the abolition of the remaining feudal liabilities which the landlords had in part been compensated for by means of long-term agrarian debt obligations, the *Grundentlastungsobligationen*. Landlords seeking to sell these obligations to receive working capital or to make investments faced weak demand for such securities and low prices, in particular in the case of obligations issued by the peripheral provinces of Galicia and Hungary. Much rather, once the bank's branch offices started to provide secured lending, agrarian debt obligations were soon used in large quantities as collateral for refinancing at the Nationalbank. In the peak year of 1858, more than 10% of all agrarian debt obligations were pledged with the Nationalbank as collateral for loans.[233] Even though secured lending was limited to three months according to the bank's statutes, such loans were, in fact, frequently rolled over, up to several years. Moreover, a small number of debtors accounted for a large share of the outstanding amounts.[234] The volume of outstanding advances subsequently declined after 1855, but nevertheless stabilized at a level that was markedly above that persisting in the early 1850s.

The establishment of a mortgage lending division in 1855, as mentioned above, must also be seen within the context of agrarian reform. The new division was meant to support not only the sale of property transferred from the government to the bank, but also to promote agricultural loans, which up to then had been underdeveloped in Austria. In spite of the great hopes put into it, the bank opted to tread very cautiously, focusing on larger properties in Vienna and Hungary. For Hungary, the lack of a land register proved to be problematic.[235] The lending volume edged up gradually in the first few years, reaching no more than a good 65 million florins in 1870. By that time, new players had started to dominate the market, including specialized mortgage banks, which were organized as stock corporations. The amount of mortgage loans outstanding vis-à-vis incorporated banks and savings banks already totaled some 450 million florins in 1870. This notwithstanding, the Nationalbank appeared to have supported, above all in the initial years when it still held a de facto monopoly in mortgage loans, large landowners in adjusting to the changed conditions resulting from agrarian reforms.[236] Mortgage lending operations were run as a separate business within the bank and did not generally impact monetary policy or money supply. Rather than being paid out in cash or credited to an account held with the Nationalbank, loans were paid out in the form of mortgage bonds which debtors were allowed to sell in the stock exchange for their own account. Monetary aggregates hence remained unchanged.[237]

The rise of a modern banking system

In the 1860s, the environment for monetary policy changed fundamentally. Up to 1853, Vienna was not home to a single stock corporation that had been set up specifically to do business in banking in the strict sense of the word. Apart from just a few selected firms which were allowed to discount bills directly at the Nationalbank, the bulk of industrial enterprises depended entirely on Vienna's private bankers for short-term loans. The latter were again able to refinance themselves with the Nationalbank. In light of an expansionary economy, rising exports and imports resulting from a series of free trade agreements and the ambitious investment policy pursued by the neo-absolutist government, the lack of credit institutions was increasingly perceived as a problem. The establishment of the Niederösterreichische Escomptegesellschaft in 1853, which specialized in short-term trade credits, paved the way for modern incorporated banks in Austria. The Escomptegesellschaft targeted those smaller clients which did not have direct access to the Nationalbank. The bills acquired by it averaged out at some 700 florins in the early years of its existence.[238] While this amount still equaled a bricklayer's annual earnings in Vienna, it nevertheless was only half of the average amount of the bills discounted at the Nationalbank. In 1856, the Creditanstalt für Handel and Gewerbe was founded on the model of a universal bank: apart from granting short-term loans, this "credit institution for trade and industry" served as an investment bank, providing funding for the establishment of companies and long-term financing of industrial and railway construction projects.[239] Given its sizeable capitalization, the new credit institution played a central role for the Austrian economy. At 60 million florins, its nominal capital was twelve times as high as the capital of the Escomptegesellschaft and twice as high as the capital the Nationalbank had disposed of before 1853.[240] Both the Creditanstalt and the Escomptegesellschaft were supported by the Nationalbank during the setting-up and in their ongoing business operations. For instance, the Escomptegesellschaft received a large part of its funds from rediscounting, i.e., selling the bills it discounted to the Nationalbank. In 1855, it rediscounted bills worth 15 million florins–or one-quarter of its entire stock of bills–with the Nationalbank. The Escomptegesellschaft also proved to be an important business partner of the Nationalbank: its rediscounted bills (15 million florins) accounted for one-third of the Nationalbank's bills portfolio.[241] Moreover, the Nationalbank also backed these new institutions during times of crisis. When the financial crisis of 1857 hitting, above all, England and Germany spilled over to Vienna, the Creditanstalt–threatened by a sharp decline in stock prices–was granted a special line of credit collateralized by bills, which it was able to pay back not long thereafter. Amid numerous bankruptcies in Austria, the Nationalbank was nonetheless capable of preventing large-scale losses in 1857, given that the other signatories of the bills came to the rescue whenever acceptors faced a liquidity shortage.[242] The rescue initiative on behalf of the Hamburger Bank, an early example of cooperation among central banks, likewise turned a profit.[243] In contrast, the support provided to the renowned bank Arnstein & Eskeles resulted in substantial losses.[244]

By 1865, 11 incorporated banks had been established in Austria, and 4 in Hungary. The number of savings banks likewise rose perceptibly. In other words, from the Nationalbank's perspective, more and more intermediaries were able to buy bills from borrowers who did not meet the eligibility criteria for central bank credit and stood ready to accept such bills with a view to re-discounting them at the Nationalbank. At the same time, the structure and functioning of the money market were evolving as well, with increasing breadth and transparency in evidence. Similarly to the Nationalbank, both the Escomptegesellschaft and the Creditanstalt disclosed their standard discounting conditions. Starting from 1860, not only stock prices, but also prevailing market interest rates were regularly published in the press. Around this time, the Nationalbank started to register a seasonal pattern in banknote circulation and in the demand for discount and secured loans (chart 4.2). Demand for means of payment fluctuated also back then in sync with economic agents' payment behavior. In fact, agriculture was a key factor in the 19th century: as crops were harvested and shipped in the fall, the related payments drove up the demand for means of payment.[245] In contrast to the 1850s–no monthly data are available for the years before 1848–such fluctuations were increasingly reflected in the balance sheet of the Nationalbank from 1860 onward. In other words, a larger share of the increased demand was passed on to the Nationalbank's discount offices, which was most likely a consequence of the widened network of branch offices, the setup of local credit institutions and the closer financial links between Vienna and peripheral areas. Moreover, amid economic growth and the increasing use of bills of exchange as a payment instrument, more bills were in circulation, which their owners were able to have discounted at the Nationalbank, either directly or indirectly. The Nationalbank, which was free at any given time to raise banknotes in circulation via discounts and advances, accommodated the seasonal uptick in the demand for liquidity. In case the demand was so strong that it jeopardized compliance with coverage rules, the Nationalbank would hike the discount rate. As a result, a seasonal pattern emerged in the 1880s; the central bank would increase the discount rate by 0.5 or 1 percentage point in October and then lower the rate again in February.

As discounting gained in importance, the Nationalbank was able to gradually scale down the outstanding amounts of secured loans. Apart from two peaks recorded in 1869 and 1873, which are discussed below, collateralized lending declined from over 80 million florins in the 1850s to less than 30 million florins in the 1870s. In parallel, the average term of secured loans shrank from more than a year to less than three months. In part this was doubtlessly due to the fact that the capital market had in the meantime managed to digest the large issues of agrarian debt obligations and government bonds. At the same time, however, the Nationalbank actively sought to cut back collateralized lending. Its motivation for this step was less the associated risk–the bank only accepted marketable government debt and applied a hair cut of 30%–but rather liquidity, i.e., the leeway to reduce the volume of such transactions whenever necessary. Customers borrowing on collateral frequently did not dispose of regular sources of income, which, in contrast, allowed drawees of bills to pay up their debt in cash when due without having to rely on the central bank to prolong their loan.[246] The Nationalbank directors therefore thought that secured loans should never tie up too large a share of the bank's resources.[247] As from 1862, they always set the rate for secured loans above the discount rate, mostly by 1 percentage point, which was clearly indicative of the new policy.[248]

Monetary policy after 1866: from fiscal to monetary dominance against all odds

On the back of the 1863 Bank Act and given the sizeable redemption of the state's liabilities by 1866, the Nationalbank had come a long way metamorphosing from its initial role as the treasury's banker to a more modern-type bank of issue: For the first time in its history, the Nationalbank not only had a well-defined goal but also the necessary operational framework to achieve its objectives.

The goal that the bank pursued was to keep the silver equivalent of the domestic currency at a fixed level. To this end, the bank was obligated, by a statutory provision, to buy and sell silver at a fixed rate at all times.[249] As long as the bank kept up this obligation, the price of silver provided as expressed in banknotes could not deviate materially from mint parity. As most other European countries also had silver currencies at the time and as the relative price of silver and gold in the international markets remained rather stable, subject to low volatility, at a rate of 1:15.5, the exchange rate between the Austrian florin and all relevant foreign currencies, be they silver, gold or bimetallic, was virtually fixed. In other words, the silver convertibility of banknotes implied that the bank also pursued an exchange rate target. This objective was not new per se, but what was different was that now, i.e., after 1866, the bank also had the necessary toolbox to enforce the convertibility of its banknotes and the stability of its currency. The bank was independent in setting its key interest rates; unlike under the charter of 1841, it was neither restricted by interest rate maxima nor dependent on the government's approval. Due to the large amounts paid back by the state, the residual public debt was below the amount of paid-in share capital. As a result, banknotes in circulation were backed entirely by silver and gold holdings as well as short-term credit to the private sector–which could be reduced promptly if meeting the convertibility objective so required– rather than by receivables from the treasury, over which the bank had little control (chart 4.2). As the bank was now actually able to control its balance sheet, it was capable, for the very first time, to also enforce its interest rate decisions on the market. In modern parlance, Austria had switched from a system of fiscal dominance, in which monetary policy and the price level are governed by public sector deficits, to a system of monetary dominance, under which monetary policy and the price level are within the bank's own power. From now on until 1914, interest rate policies and balance sheet control were the cornerstones of the bank's business operations.

This notwithstanding, the bank had to face up to challenges after 1866. Given the massive parallel issuance of government paper money following the war against Prussia, more than half of the circulating paper money had not been issued by the Nationalbank. Acceptance of the state paper money was enforced, and the redemption of banknotes in silver specie remained suspended. In the following years these conditions in fact undermined the mechanism that would have forced the central bank to pursue a monetary policy compatible with the convertibility of its banknotes. The bank time and again rejected accountability for the exchange rate, on account of the amount of state paper money in circulation. From a medium-term perspective, however, the constraints created by the state paper money should not be overrated. Unlike in earlier episodes, the amount of government liabilities with the bank was fixed, and the same was true for the amount of state paper money. Thus, it was the bank rather than the state that determined the availability of additional money, as well as its marginal value, i.e., the interest rate. In principle, the bank was therefore in a position to conduct monetary policy in an autonomous fashion.

The "Gründerzeit" boom and bust

For the time being, however, monetary policy-making was driven by the repercussions of the lost war against Prussia. The excess liquidity created by the issuance of government paper money sharply dented demand for central bank discount and lending operations. Dividends, which had suffered already in the 1850s from the near quadrupling of paid-in capital without a corresponding increase in revenues, came under severe pressure. Following an average yield of 11.9% in the 1830s and 10.5% in the 1850s, the dividends paid by the Nationalbank dropped below a level of 7% in 1867 for the first time ever.[250] The governing board of the Nationalbank responded by investing parts of the bank's silver reserves that were no longer required to back banknotes in circulation into foreign bills of exchange. These foreign exchange assets had the merit of being easily convertible back into silver and generating interest at the same time. On top of this, the bank further eased its credit conditions and pushed discount lending by the branch offices.[251] Finally, the share capital was reduced from 110 to 90 million florins, which improved earnings per share.[252]

Anyway, this period of low yields was surprisingly short lived. 1868 marked the start of an economic boom driving a stock exchange bubble that would

Chart 4.4: **Official and open market interest rates**[253]

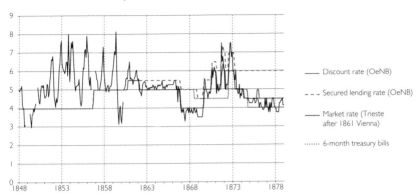

——	Discount rate (OeNB)
- - -	Secured lending rate (OeNB)
——	Market rate (Trieste after 1861 Vienna)
······	6-month treasury bills

In the 1850s and the 1860s, the interest rates paid in financial markets typically lay above the Nationalbank's official interest rates, reflecting restrictions on access to discount lending. This pattern began to change after 1873. Now the market interest rates typically hovered below the official discount rate, while the rate for secured lending was always set at a level above the discount rate. The early years of the industrial boom after 1867 coincided with a period of historically low interest rates. While the Nationalbank significantly raised its key rates after 1870, the yields on treasury bills remained low, thus fueling stock exchange activity.

bust dramatically on May 9, 1873, a day that entered history books as Black Friday.[254] The boom was driven by a combination of factors. The traumatic defeat against Prussia in 1866 had seriously undermined any political ambitions Austria may have had in Germany and Italy. It also accelerated the long overdue settlement with Hungary, giving Hungary a parliament of its own and an extended degree of autonomy; and consolidated the parliamentary regime also in the remaining parts of the monarchy. From a long-term perspective, the Compromise between Austria and Hungary had serious consequences for the Nationalbank, which will be discussed in the next chapter. For the economy, though, the elimination of external and internal uncertainty and the improvement in the fiscal situation paved the way for an upswing, which was carried by a building boom–epitomized by the grand buildings lining the Ringstrasse boulevard in Vienna–and investment in railroad construction and the upstream iron and engineering industry.[255] This boom was supported by a number of "miracle harvests," which promoted exports abroad and fueled railroad revenues. Between 1866 and 1873 the Austro-Hungarian railway network grew from 6,125 km to 15,597 km.[256] Investments were to a large extent funded by stock corporations, which were by now springing up in droves. The stocks in the new transportation, construction and industrial corporations were issued by an increasing number of banks that made big profits as underwriters while at the same time offering investors generous loans to finance the stock purchases. This resulted in an increasingly fragile credit-financed boom of stock market speculation.

The upturn was further fueled by excess liquidity and low interest rates. The 1863 Bank Act principally established, if in a crude way, a limit for the degree of monetary policy accommodation, by restricting the volume of banknotes in circulation other than those backed by silver to 200 million florins. As the Nationalbank was under no obligation to consider the outstanding government paper money in calculating the amount of eligible banknote issuance, the volume of paper money in circulation in Austria continued to rise considerably in 1866/67. While the total money stock consisting of banknotes and government paper money well exceeded the sum targeted by the 1863 statutes, the 200 million florin constraint did not become binding for a long time, as a result of which the central bank did not see any need to tighten monetary policy. In December 1866, the bank in fact lowered the discount rate from 5% to 4% in response to declining demand for discount and lending operations. Market interest rates now moved markedly below the level prevailing in the previous years (chart 4.4), stimulating new investment and stock issuance. These conditions were quick to refuel demand for central bank credit. Yet concerned about its profits, the bank retained its aggressive credit policy, lowering the rate for secured lending in 1868, and even accepting stocks as collateral in secured lending from 1869 as well as investing directly in repo loans at the stock exchange.[257] From October 1868 to June 1869, secured lending, including repos, tripled from 20 million florins to more than 60 million florins. Whether these expansionary policies may have driven the concomitant price rally at the stock exchange or only accompanied it, the Nationalbank hit the brakes in July, terminating all loans to the stock exchange and increasing the interest rates in discount and lending operations. This was followed by a minor price crash at the stock exchange in early September 1869–a harbinger of the stock exchange meltdown that was to occur in 1873.[258]

With the benefit of hindsight the bank now proceeded with greater caution. Yet it was neither able nor ready to stop the creation of another speculative bubble that was soon fueled by the emergence of new banks and stock corporations. In a speech before the Hungarian parliament, the long-term secretary general of the bank and one of the most brilliant economic policy makers of the time, Wilhelm Lucam, argued that keeping a lid on the emergence of speculative bubbles was neither the job of the bank nor a feasible option. Much rather, what the bank could and should do in the event of a crisis was to contribute to a soft landing by ensuring an adequate supply of credit.[259] To be able to provide such credit in the first place, the bank needed to have a sufficiently large buffer within its issuance limit of 200 million florins. Such reasoning turned this buffer into the key indicator for monetary policy. As long as the buffer was sufficiently large, the governing board did not see any reason to restrict lending, considering measures that increased liquidity and had an accommodative effect while leaving the buffer unaffected as being essentially unproblematic.[260]

In the early 1870s, the confluence of several factors facilitated further increases in the supply of money without the constraints imposed by the 200 million florin limit becoming binding. Reparation payments that France was required to make to Germany following the peace agreement of 1871 triggered sizeable inflows of capital to Austria, among other countries. In addition, liquidity conditions were eased further by government policies. As mentioned above, the volume of government paper money had been made subject to a statutory limit of 400 million florins, as a result of which the amount of government paper money could not increase on a sustained basis. However, the upper threshold of 400 million florins related both to government paper money proper as well as to short-term treasury bills, which had been first floated in 1848.[261] When yields were low on these treasury bills relative to market level interest rates, the holders of those bills opted to let the bills expire and reinvest the proceeds in the market at a higher yield, rather than rolling over the treasury bills. Market interest rates exceeded the yield on treasury bills from mid-1869 onward (chart 4.4). This was mirrored by a corresponding decline in the outstanding volume of treasury bills and an offsetting rise in the volume of government paper money. While as much as 55% of the sharp rise in the supply of money observed in the period from 1865 to 1873 occurred in 1866 and 1867, thus reflecting operations to finance the war against Prussia, another 45% were accounted for by the accommodative policies of the finance ministry and the central bank *after* the end of the war (chart 4.1).

Thus the stock exchange boom continued in this context of accommodative monetary policy. In the period from 1866 und 1873, the number of stocks listed at the Vienna Stock Exchange rose from 31 to 347,[262] with banks accounting for more than 100 of the new listings. At the end of 1873, the paid-in nominal capital of Austrian and Hungarian banks totaled more than 450 million florins, compared with close to 90 millions six years earlier.[263] The large crash occurred in early May 1873. Within just a few months, the market value of the stocks traded in Vienna dropped from 2,714 million florins to 1,546 million. With losses of 58% and 74%, respectively, banks and building corporations suffered the most.[264] The Nationalbank considered the losses at the stock exchange as the necessary correction of a speculative bubble that needed to run its course. Therefore it limited its support for the stock exchange to loans to a fund established by Viennese banks, which was supposed to lend against collateral in order to put an end to fire sales and halt a further meltdown of prices. These loans were settled already in July 1873, though. Much rather, the Nationalbank saw its basic role as providing generous credit for solvent firms to help them overcome the consequences of the ensuing panic. This line of action was facilitated by two sets of measures. *First,* on May 13, 1873, the finance ministry suspended the upper threshold of 200 million florins established for the volume of banknotes in circulation.[265] This move enabled the bank to enter into higher discount and lending operations should the need arise. *Second,* the Nationalbank encouraged the establishment of support committees such as had been in place already during the crisis of 1848. Unlike the Nationalbank itself, the support committees were in a position to discount bills with longer maturities and to refinance goods or securities that were not eligible for central bank refinancing. Committee members were liable through capital contributions and thus had a vested interest in monitoring the bills they discounted for rediscount by the Nationalbank. By agency of support committees and large banks with outlets in regions in which the bank did not operate any branch offices, it was thus possible to offer credit also in smaller towns, which was particularly important in the Hungarian part of the empire.[266] In Vienna and Budapest, the Nationalbank also contributed directly to the funding of the support committees.[267] On top of that, the bank extended extraordinary loans to town municipalities and to individual industrial corporations.[268] At least two cases also involved the bail-out of banks which lacked adequate collateral to participate in the bank's regular refinancing operations.[269] As a result of increased lending, banknotes in circulation rose from 330 million florins on the eve of the crisis to 373 million florins by November 1873. By that time, banknotes in circulation lay 28 million florins above the (suspended) statutory limit.[270]

For a long time, the years following 1873 were termed "the Great Depression" in Austrian economic history.[271] This negative view was strongly influenced by the decline in price levels. A more broad-based reading of economic output indicators has since led to a re-assessment of this finding.[272] Above all the Hungarian economy was quick to rebound, benefiting from the inflow of Austrian capital, with investors who had been burnt on the stock exchange seeking a safe haven in the form of bonds issued or guaranteed by the Hungarian state.[273] This dichotomy was also evident in the banking sector. While in Austria the number of banks had dropped to 43 by 1878, following a sharp rise from 11 in 1865 to more than 120 in early 1873, Hungary, while having witnessed an equally spectacular expansion, barely suffered a decline.[274]

For the Nationalbank, the receding price level meant that the demand for cash stagnated despite real economic growth. This was mirrored by weak demand for discount and lending operations, with average refinancing amounts declining from more than 200 million florins in 1873 to a range of 130 to 140 million florins in the late 1870s. The only segment registering a rise where mortgage loans, where the bank evidently managed to regain ground against joint-stock banks. The stockholders of the Nationalbank benefited greatly from the boom and the crisis of 1873. The dividend issued for 1873 was as high as 11.2%. Now followed some lean years; by 1878 the dividend was back at 7.3%.

200 years of monetary policy in pictures

The new Nationalbank's job: mopping up inflationary paper money

1762 marked the first issuance of paper money, called Bancozettel, in Austria. During the Napoleonic wars, the volume of Bancozettel paper florins (1) and later redemption certificates (2) and anticipation certificates (3) in circulation increased sharply, causing paper money to lose 87.5% of its value. The need to reform the currency gave rise to the decision to establish the privilegirte oesterreichische National-Bank in 1816.

1

2

3

The Nationalbank as a stock corporation

The Nationalbank was established as a stock corporation with the aim of mobilizing private capital for the currency reform and emphasizing its independence from the state. New shares were issued in 1853 and 1855 and capital was repaid in 1868, as recorded on share (4). After 1955 (5), the Nationalbank's shareholders comprised the Republic of Austria, banks and the social partners. Since 2010, the Republic of Austria has been the OeNB's sole shareholder.

4

5

Parity in bank management

The composition of the Nationalbank's management was a mirror image of the different monetary policy stakeholders. In the first decades, the position of governor was always staffed with high officials, while the vice governor usually represented private Viennese bankers. Baron Carl Joseph Alois von Lederer (6), for example, had already pursued a successful career as state councillor before he was appointed governor of the Nationalbank in 1837. Banker and vice governor Baron Melchior Ritter von Steiner (7) on the other hand had played a major role in raising the money necessary to facilitate the early withdrawal of French troops from Vienna in 1809. After 1878, the position of governor was staffed alternately with Austrian and Hungarian nationals, among them high officials as well as a number of university professors such as Gyula Kautz (8, governor 1892-1900) and Leon Ritter von Biliński (9, governor 1900-1909). Biliński also epitomizes the close connection between the central bank and the state: before and after serving his term as governor, he headed the Austrian finance ministry.

6

7

8

9

The state in need of money

In crisis situations, the state kept requesting inexpensive credit from the bank. On two occasions, in 1848/49 and 1866, it went so far as to issue its own paper money. In the revolutionary years 1848/49, the two opposing sides both turned on the monetary tap, with Hungary issuing large volumes of so-called "Kossuth notes" (10). The state paper money issued in 1866 remained in circulation until 1903. The 5-florin note (state paper money) of 1881 (11) shows a profile view of Emperor Francis Joseph I. Banknotes issued by the Nationalbank never featured the emperor – this was an expression of the bank's "self-confident distance to the state."

10

11

The note-issuing bank as a catalyst of integration

For a long time, the Nationalbank's main business was in Vienna. After 1848, the bank gradually established a network of branch offices, which in 1913 comprised offices in more than 100 locations such as Lviv (12, Lemberg, L'viv, L'vov, today: Ukraine), Sarajevo (13, today: Bosnia and Herzegovina) and Timișoara (14, Temesvár, today: Romania). The branch offices granted loans to local banks and enterprises. Uniform credit standards and uniform interest rates throughout the empire contributed to the economic integration of the Habsburg monarchy.

12

Temesvár — Osztrák—Magyar Bank

13

14

Banknotes as a symbol of national conflict

After the transformation of the Nationalbank into the Austro-Hungarian Bank in 1878, the Hungarian government demanded that banknotes should have two matching sides–one in German and the other one in Hungarian (15, 18)–as a symbol of the equality of the two halves of the empire. This meant that banknote text in the many other languages of the monarchy disappeared from the banknotes, which triggered violent protests. Activists began to overprint or stamp the banknotes, using various techniques ranging from simple marks (18) to complicated prints featuring symbols like the Crown of Saint Wenceslas and the coat of arms of the Lands of the Bohemian Crown (15). While Czech activism was most pronounced in this respect, there were also overprints in Polish, Italian (17), Romanian, Serbian and Ukrainian (16). In the end, the bank had to replace 400,000 banknotes.

16

15

17

18

World War I

To promote the sale of war bonds during World War I, the Anglo-Austrian Bank pointed to the robust economic growth Austria-Hungary had experienced since 1870 (19). In fact, however, the monarchy was hardly prepared to cope with the enormous burden resulting from the war. Apart from war bonds, loans from the central bank were the major source of capital for the state. As a consequence, the volume of money in circulation increased substantially and inflation was high.

19

Currency separation

The collapse of the monarchy in 1918 marked the end of the currency area, with the monarchy's successor states introducing new currencies. In a first step, the banknotes circulating in the respective state territories were stamped. Only stamped banknotes were recognized as official means of payment. The banknotes shown here feature the stamp of the Serbs, Croats and Slovenes (20) and the Hungarian stamp (21).

20

21

The central bank of a small country

Before World War I, the central bank had planned to build vast office premises off Alser Strasse to merge its various offices which, until then, had been located in different buildings in Vienna's first district. The crowning highlight of the new premises would have been an 85 meter high tower– Vienna's first highrise (22, 24). After the collapse of the monarchy, however, the central bank was no longer responsible for the currency of 50 million people but only for that of 6 million. So the only building that was actually finished was the original printing facility at the rear end of the premises (23, 24), which has housed the Oesterreichische Nationalbank to this day.

22

23

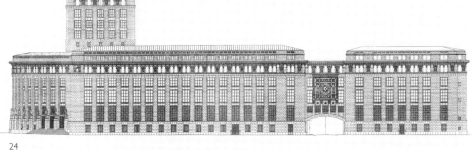

24

Hyperinflation

In the fall of 1921, hyperinflation set in, driving up prices by more than 40% per month and requiring the issue of banknotes in increasingly higher denominations. In 1922, banknotes with a nominal value of 500,000 crowns (26) were issued alongside 1-crown banknotes (25). The depreciation of the crown came to an end in October 1922, when the League of Nations agreed to guarantee the issuance of international bonds by Austria. This means that the 1,000,000-crown banknote (27), which was already in the pipeline, was never put into circulation.

25

26

27

League of Nations loan and introduction of the schilling

To finance its budget deficits and stabilize the currency, Austria issued international bonds on a large scale in 1923. The bonds, which were guaranteed by members of the League of Nations, were tied to very strict conditions and required Austria to provide government receipts as collateral for loan servicing and redemption. The bonds were issued in eleven countries, including Austria (28). In 1925, the crown was replaced by the schilling or, to be precise, 1 schilling replaced 10,000 crowns, which prompted numerous caricatures in the press: "This will make you laugh–10,000 crowns are now called 1 schilling" (29).

29

28

Creditanstalt crisis

The day after it became known that the Creditanstalt, Austria's biggest bank, had lost 85% of its capital, the leading Viennese daily ran the headline "a crisis averted" (30). Yet the true loss was much higher, triggering a run on the Austrian schilling, which cost the Nationalbank the bigger part of its reserve assets. The following years saw an acceleration of the demise of banks and of the concentration process that had started in the banking sector in the 1920s. Here an ad tendering furniture und fixtures from dissolved banks for sale (31).

31

30

Preis in Wien: 32 Groschen.

Fliegen Sie in 8 STUNDEN von **Wien** nach **Paris** zur Kolonialausstellung. CIDNA. WIEN I., KÄRNTNERRING Nr. 7. TELEPHON R 20-3-93.

Empress of Britain 42,500 Tonnen — nach **AMERIKA** — Kürzeste Überfahrt 3½ Tage auf offener See. 5 Tage insgesamt. **CANADIAN PACIFIC.**

Neue Freie Presse.
Morgenblatt.

Nr. 23944. — Wien, Dienstag, den 12. Mai — 1931.

Eine abgewendete Finanzkatastrophe.

Verluste der Credit-Anstalt von hundertvierzig Millionen. Intervention von Regierung, Nationalbank und Hans Rothschild. Die Rettung gesichert.

Wien, 12. Mai.

Gutes Material für Genf. Ein herrlicher Beweis für das Wohlergehen in Oesterreich, das manchen Parlamentariern des Auslandes noch immer bemerkenswert erscheint. Die Credit-Anstalt, die bisher mächtigste und stärkste Bank von Oesterreich mit vertrauenswürdiger Führung, sie muß Verluste von hundertvierzig Millionen Schilling im Jahre 1930 verzeichnen. Die offenen Reserven und ein großer Teil des Aktienkapitals, das hundertfünfundzwanzig Millionen beträgt, sind aufgezehrt und Staat, Nationalbank und das Haus Rothschild müssen in die Bresche springen, um die Situation zu retten. Die Rettung, dies sei vorweg betont, ist gelungen, das Kapital der Credit-Anstalt wird um ein Viertel verkleinert, dann werden einundzwanzig Millionen neue Aktien ausgegeben, die zu einem erhöhten Kurse vom Staate, von der Nationalbank und vom Hause Rothschild übernommen werden. Das letzte Resultat dieser Transaktion ist also keine Schwächung, sondern eine Stärkung der vorhandenen Mittel der Bank. Wir glauben, daß das beinahe grausame Zerreißen des Schleiers vor der ganzen Oeffentlichkeit sicher letzten Endes als die einzig vorhandene Möglichkeit anzusehen war. Trotzdem, manchmal ergibt sich in solchen unglücklichen Verwicklungen die Alternative: soll man das Publikum vorbereiten, soll man langsam die Kulissen stellen für das kommende Drama oder ist es besser, durch ein Unglück ex machina, durch einen Donnerschlag, der plötzlich hereinbricht, die Erregungen zu konzentrieren und deswegen auch ihre Zeitdauer zu verkürzen?

Es wäre heute gänzlich sinnlos, wollte man in dieser Beziehung etwa Kritik üben. Wir stehen vor einer Situation, die mit scharfen Umrissen unabänderlich gegeben ist, wir können nur unter der Wirkung einer so nervenerschütternden Krise und mit dem schmerzlichen Anteil an dem Schicksal eines so ehrwürdigen Unternehmens, wir können heute nur die Genugtuung äußern, daß es in dreitägigen Verhandlungen geglückt ist, einer unnennbaren, gar nicht zu schildernden Katastrophe beizukommen und drei Viertel der österreichischen Arbeiterschaft vor der Arbeitslosigkeit zu bewahren.

Mußte es dazu kommen, war das schmerzliche Resultat des vorigen Jahres unvermeidlich? Es ist nicht unsere Sache, zu entscheiden, ob nicht Irrtümer geschehen sind. Aber im wesentlichen ist es doch der einfache Ausdruck der Weltkrise und der österreichischen Krise im besonderen, der in diesem Verlust von hundertvierzig Millionen zutage tritt. Es ist ferner die Uebernahme der Bodenkreditanstalt, deren Wirkung sich schwerer zu tragen mag, als man am Anfang glauben konnte; damals, in jenen Oktobertagen vor anderthalb Jahren, als die Credit-Anstalt mit Aufopferung zum Teil auch aus politischen Gründen sich entschlossen hat, die stürzenden Mauern einer Schwesterunternehmung zu stützen. Mindestens sechzig Millionen sind im letzten Jahre an den Werten der Bodenkreditanstalt verloren gegangen, nicht nur durch Effektenverluste, sondern insbesondere auch durch Abschreibung von Zinsen, die als uneinbringlich betrachtet

Der Grönlandforscher Wegener verloren?

Berlin, 11. Mai.

Zu den Vermutungen, die in der Presse über das Schicksal Professor Alfred Wegeners aufgetaucht sind, hat Professor Baschin vom Geographischen Institut der Berliner Universität, der auf Grund seiner praktischen Arbeiten als einer der besten Kenner der arktischen Probleme gilt, erklärt, er müsse es leider nach der Lage der Verhältnisse für ausgeschlossen halten, daß Professor Wegener noch am Leben ist.

Currency reform and economic miracle

In December 1947 the liquidity overhang in Austria, which essentially stemmed from financing the military expenditure of the Third Reich, was reduced by means of a currency reform: One new schilling replaced three old schillings (32). The political parties and the social partners had agreed on this measure to ward off a return of hyperinflation, which had plagued the country after 1918. After World War II, the United States supported European reconstruction through "Marshall Plan" loans and donations (33). Under the U.S. European Recovery Program, as the Marshall Plan was officially known, Austria received free-of-charge deliveries of food, agricultural equipment and machinery. These deliveries were urgently needed, but Austria lacked the foreign exchange and foreign credits to procure them.

32

33

Hard currency policy

Having experienced hyperinflation after World War I, the Austrian population was acutely aware of the importance of a stable currency. During elections, the two major parties–the Social Democratic Party and the Austrian People's Party–both repeatedly advertised the continuation of the hard currency policy (here 1995: 34 and 1983: 35), which was seen as the equivalent of monetary stability.

The exchange rate of the schilling was pegged to the Deutsche mark, which helped making imports cheaper. The credibility of this policy relied on broadly parallel developments in inflation, productivity, the current account and public finances both in the Federal Republic of Germany and in Austria. Keeping pace with Germany required huge economic policy efforts, unlike the implicit message delivered by some cartoonists (37), with Austrian chancellor Kreisky free-riding on German chancellor Schmidt's bicycle in 1981 (36).

Für einen harten Schilling.

34

35

Damit unser Schilling hart bleibt am 24. April

SPÖ ⊗ Liste 1

36

37

From the schilling to the euro

Austria joined the euro area as a founding member in 1999. Whereas many an Austrian was looking forward to the cash changeover (38), others saw the loss of the schilling with mixed feelings; after all a trusted currency was being replaced by a new and yet unfamiliar currency (39). For the Nationalbank, joining the Eurosystem essentially boiled down to continuing the stability-oriented it had pursued in the previous decades. At the same time, its role changed and it also assumed new responsibilities within the framework of the single monetary policy and with a view to ensuring financial stability.

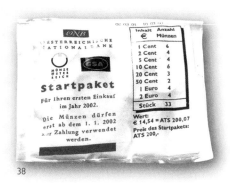

38

39

Two governments, one bank—the Austro-Hungarian monetary union (1878–1914)

"The monarchy's best-functioning
joint institution"

Tibor Kállay, Hungarian minister of finance, 1918[275]

As we have seen, the remnants of the war of 1866 included a blown-up circulation of state paper money, which significantly affected monetary policy-making and made it impossible to restore banknote convertibility any time soon. Yet large quantities of state paper money were not the only difficult legacy of the events of 1866. The loss of the war against Prussia had also precipitated a reorganization of the monarchy: The Compromise of 1867 turned the centralized *Austrian Empire* into a dual monarchy, consisting of two multinational states run from Vienna and Budapest, respectively, that operated autonomously in major policy areas while pursuing common *Austro-Hungarian* policies in matters of war, finance and foreign relations. Hungary had been ruled centrally from Vienna after the collapse of the revolution in 1849 and had refused to send representatives to the parliamentary assembly created in 1860, and so the new setup reintegrated Hungary into the political system. However, the decentralization of the empire did not bring about a permanent stabilization; the conflicts existing between Austria and Hungary and within the two halves of the empire persisted.

The new setup created a precarious situation for the Nationalbank. Mirroring the concept of the dual monarchy, the *privilegirte oesterreichische National-Bank* was transformed into the *Oesterreichisch-ungarische Bank*, the Austro-Hungarian Bank, in 1878. Instead of one government and one parliament, the bank was now dealing with two governments and two parliaments. Having thought to have emancipated itself from direct state influence with the 1863 charter, the bank now found itself confronted with new political demands. The key concern was no longer closing the gaps in the state budget, since this was prevented by the political deadlock between Austria and Hungary and did not become relevant again until World War I. Instead, the bank was above all confronted with Hungary's quest for a bank of issue in its own right, got bogged down in credit policy issues and found itself challenged by rising demands from national stakeholder groups across the monarchy who asked for more adequate representation of ethnic interests in the day-to-day management of the bank. The new challenges appeared all the more acute given that the bank's charter would no longer be renewed for 25 years as in the past, but only for 10. This put the bank in a state of nearly permanent negotiations with the two governments and the two parliaments.[276]

Although in theory the politization of the bank question meant less leeway in setting monetary policy, the specific constellation of having one bank of issue facing two governments ultimately gave the bank a rather substantial degree of autonomy. Not only were the Austrian and Hungarian governments rarely able to agree, they also had domestic crises to contend with in each of their territories. When in 1892, the fundamental decision was made to retire the government paper money and to switch from a silver currency to a gold-backed standard. implementation became blocked politically. In the end, the bank was given de facto–if not explicit–responsibility for monetary policy as an autonomous entity acting in the interests of Austria-Hungary as a whole. The result was two decades of successful stabilization policy, probably the most satisfying time in the first 100 years of the bank's history.

A separate note-issuing bank for Hungary?

In many European countries, it was already common by the mid-19th century to have only one bank authorized to issue banknotes. Other countries such as England, Scotland, France (before 1848) and the German Empire (after 1871) however permitted more than one bank to print money, subject to more or less strict state regulation. The idea of having multiple banks of issue went along with the prevailing liberal distrust of both state and private monopolies and the belief that competition among note-issuing banks would lead to a higher quality of the paper money in circulation. Under this line of thinking, the non-convertible notes issued in Austria were a good example of low-quality money that could only be kept in circulation by virtue of the Nationalbank's monopoly position and the status of the notes as legal tender.

Accordingly, there were also fractions in Austria in the mid-19th century calling for an end to the privileged position of the Nationalbank and more competition.[277] In the case of Austria, however, the argument that was more frequently raised related to the positive impact of additional note-issuing banks on regional economic development. As discussed above, the Nationalbank was criticized for focusing too much on Vienna and neglecting the rest of the empire.

In 1848, Hungarian and Croatian revolutionaries added their voices to those demanding the establishment of *national* banks of issue. They were successful in the case of Hungary, at least for some time, where the Hungarian Commercial Bank issued notes during the revolutionary period.[278] National banks of issue, such was the reasoning, would utilize their right to issue currency for the purpose of extending credit to local businesses and much better so than the Nationalbank in Vienna could ever do. To understand the movement towards decentralization, it should be recalled that in the period around 1850 and even later, it was not unusual for note-issuing banks to grant credit to private individuals. Since savings accounts were still relatively uncommon at the time, issuing banknotes was one of the few possibilities to mobilize funds for lending in economically weak regions. Decentralization was moreover a way to cope with the significant challenges of obtaining the necessary information across the vast expanse of the Austrian Empire.[279] It is thus hardly surprising that–despite his centralistic views–finance minister Bruck seconded the views of representatives of the Hungarian aristocracy such as Emil Graf Dessewffy in the 1850s, as he believed that the economy would benefit from setting up regional (note-issuing) banks in Prague, Trieste and Budapest. In the end, however, the idea of issuing notes decentrally was neither compatible with the state's funding requirements nor the need to strictly control circulation of the banknotes to enable a return to currency convertibility, the most important goal of monetary policy in the 1850s. The plans were not pursued any further. Instead, the government's request that credit be extended on a regional basis was met via the Nationalbank's new branches.[280]

However, this solution did not fulfill the function that Hungarian and Croatian nationalists would have attributed to their national banks, which was to actively contribute to the formation of a modern Hungarian, Croatian, etc. nation state by supporting the creation of an internal market, promoting financial integration and presenting the nation and the currency as a single entity to the rest of the world, both economically and symbolically.[281] The *joint* Nationalbank did all of that, but at the level of the empire and not at the regional level as desired by the nationalists pushing for autonomy. It would have taken *national* banks of issue to achieve that goal. Thus control over extending credit and national symbols remained points of contention in banking policy until the collapse of the monarchy.

Compromise of 1867: no agreement on bank of issue

The Compromise of 1867 between Austria and Hungary addressed the long-disputed legal position of Hungary and offered a framework for resolving the aforementioned conflicts. It awarded the Lands of the Hungarian Crown, which included Croatia and Transylvania in addition to the Kingdom of Hungary, a large degree of independence. Those Lands, together with the remaining countries of the former Austrian Empire–officially designated as the Kingdoms and Lands represented in the Imperial Council–formed the dual monarchy of Austria-Hungary. The two halves of the empire were able to set policy autonomously for the most part, and fiscal policy was entirely in the hands of the respective empire half. The Compromise stipulated certain areas in which decisions would continue to be made jointly.[282] Similar to EU procedures today, different decision-making processes were applicable depending on the matter at hand. The only issues still subject to joint decision making were the so-called pragmatic affairs: foreign policy, and warfare and related funding, and, after 1878, the administration of Bosnia-Herzegovina. Those areas were governed by joint institutions, one government and one committee comprised of representatives of both parliaments. All other areas in which practical considerations made it appear expedient to coordinate policy-making had to be regulated in individual agreements concluded by the two states at ten-year intervals. These matters of common concern, or dualistic affairs, included foreign trade and customs duties, indirect taxes and cross-border railway lines.[283] Although the necessity of renewing the Compromise at regular intervals made it possible to adapt it to changed circumstances, the fact that there was no clause providing for the continuation of the previous arrangements if no agreement could be reached brought the monarchy (and the bank) to the verge of collapse every ten years (in 1877, 1887, 1897 and 1907).

When the Compromise of 1867 was negotiated, the question of the bank of issue was omitted in the final version to ensure that agreement would at least be reached in political matters. The Compromise therefore contained no provisions relating to the Nationalbank itself. It merely stipulated that the issuance of coins would be jointly regulated and that the Austrian currency would continue to be used as the single currency in both halves of the empire for the time being.[284] Hungary was reluctant to recognize the 1863 Bank Act–which gave the Nationalbank monopoly rights until the end of 1876–for both practical reasons and as a matter of principle since from a Hungarian perspective, the legislation had been approved by an unauthorized parliament. By contrast, Austria considered itself bound to the Bank Act enacted by the Reichsrat. This put the Austrian government in a difficult position vis-à-vis the bank, which was demanding financial compensation for the losses it had incurred from the issue of government paper money in 1866, which had been in violation of the statutes. At the same time, Austria was extremely interested in coming to a quick agreement, because if the bank's charter was not extended before it expired in 1876, Austria would be required to repay the loan of 80 million florins granted to it by the bank in 1863 for the duration of the bank's charter. The temporary solution was for the Austrian and Hungarian governments to conclude a separate agreement in which Hungary declared its willingness to acknowledge the rights of the Nationalbank and agreed to refrain from establishing a note-issuing bank in Hungary as long as the Nationalbank considered Hungary's interests in its lending policies.[285]

Monetary union up for renewal every ten years

The solution set forth in the Compromise of separating fiscal policy while maintaining, at least for the time being, a joint central bank and a common monetary policy meant that the Habsburg monarchy had become a de facto monetary union[286]–albeit one on a shaky footing. The necessity of renewing the Compromise every ten years resulted in both sides regularly debating the pros and cons of continuing the union. Hungary–the smaller of the two states and traditionally underrepresented among both bank shareholders and governing board members–had to weigh the benefits of the better control over decision-making processes that a Hungarian central bank would bring against the costs of leaving the union.[287] Back then, being able to affect exchange rates did not have the same bearing on the decision for or against an autonomous monetary policy that it does today, because in the economic logic of the time, the natural objective for both Hungary and Austria was to ensure that its currency was backed by gold (or silver). From the perspective of macroeconomic policy there was no reason to leave the union. A much greater factor in the deliberations was the concept of the central bank as an instrument to aid in the creation of a modern nation state, both in economic and symbolic terms. The key concept for Hungary was "parity," i.e., full equality of the Hungarian half of the empire with the Austrian half.[288] The establishment of a Hungarian central bank would have brought full parity. But on the cost side the new bank would have required either gold or silver reserves plus a significant amount of capital (since central banks were often highly capitalized in the 19th century, as shown by the example of the Oesterreichische Nationalbank). In the required scope such capital could only have been procured abroad. Immediately after 1867, however, confidence in the new Hungarian state was still low and the cost of capital very high, which made Hungary dependent on Austrian funds.[289] Another complicating factor was that the creation of a Hungarian currency would have increased uncertainty among potential foreign investors. From the Austrian government's perspective, the main consideration was preserving the internal market and even the empire itself. The outcome of the regular re-negotiation of the Compromise and the resulting changes in the bank's statutes was a gradual increase in influence for Hungary. This could indicate that Hungary had the better negotiating position.[290]

The first difficulties emerged directly after conclusion of the preliminary agreement between the Austrian and Hungarian governments in 1867. Since the Austrian government had no official control over the private Nationalbank, the agreement was not submitted to either parliament, nor was it even published until the conflict between the three parties–the central bank and the Hungarian and Austrian governments–had escalated. What followed was years of public debate, a parliamentary enquête in Budapest and negotiations between the two governments. The central bank used the size of the credit facilities granted to the branches located in Hungary as a negotiating tool, while the Hungarian government threatened to establish a well-capitalized commercial bank that could have formed the nucleus of a later note-issuing bank. The stock market crash of 1873 prevented implementation of that plan while at the same time highlighting the positive aspects of a strong, joint central bank to many in Hungary.[291] A solution to the bank issue was still lacking, however. Either the bank's charter would have to be renewed before the end of 1876 or an alternative found. Since the timing of the charter renewal coincided with the initial renewal of the customs union, the matter of the central bank became one point of negotiation among many. The negotiation process was highly complex. The main turn of events for the central bank was when the Hungarian government under Kálmán Tisza switched from demanding a separate note-issuing bank for Hungary to calling for a cartel bank model. According to this model, one bank in Vienna and one in Budapest, each endowed with its own equity capital, would be linked by contractual agreement and by a joint board consisting of representatives sent by the two directorates–a constellation not unlike that of today's Eurosystem. Such a Hungarian bank would have been autonomous in its credit policies within the territory of Hungary while being able to transfer the stability and credibility of the Austrian currency–such as it was–onto the now common currency, thus avoiding the risks of going alone. However, the implied full-fledged equality for Austria and Hungary and weaker powers for the joint board were unacceptable for the representatives of the Nationalbank as well as the Austrian government. After all, the population of Austria was 30% larger than that of Hungary, and the difference in economic weight was even greater. In response, Wilhelm Ritter von Lucam, secretary general of the Nationalbank, prepared a counterproposal that would have left all decision-making power in Vienna and relegated Budapest more or less to the status of a glorified branch office.[292] This was of course not acceptable to Hungary. The negotiations stalled.

How Hungarian was the Austro-Hungarian Bank?

After a one-year delay, in 1877 Austria and Hungary finally agreed on a compromise between two cartel banks and a single joint bank. The new design comprised two directorates, one in Vienna and one in Budapest. The directorates were made up of Austrian and Hungarian nationals respectively and were responsible for establishing the size and allocation of central bank credit at the level of their respective branches. In a further expression of parity between the two halves of the empire, the bank was named the Austro-Hungarian Bank and its banknotes had identical designs in German and Hungarian on each side. A separate agreement stipulated a minimum funding level for the Hungarian branches. Parity was also evident in the appointment of the governor. From 1878 onward, the Austrian and the Hungarian finance ministers alternated between nominating Austrian and Hungarian nationals for the position.[293] At the same time, key decision-making powers were left at the central level. Specifically, a General Council was given authority over the two directorates and entrusted with a wide range of powers, in particular the authority to set terms and conditions of business operations, to manage the bank's assets, to decide on the establishment of branches and to set a uniform interest rate for the entire empire. The General Council was composed of the governor, the two chairmen of the Vienna and Budapest directorates acting as vice governors, two additional members from each of the two directorates and eight members elected directly by the shareholder assembly. This meant that within the General Council the members sent by the directorates were in the minority. Given that the great majority of voting shareholders in the General Meeting were Austrian nationals, the citizens of Austria enjoyed a majority on the General Council. Another concession made by Hungary was to take responsibility for a portion of the 80 million florins owed by the state to the bank based on the provisions of the charter of 1863.

The subsequent renewals of the Austro-Hungarian Bank's charter in 1887, 1899 and 1910 kept within these general terms agreed in the Compromise of 1878. The fact that the statutes were renewed in 1887 with no major modifications showed that Hungary was by and large satisfied with the bank's policies. With each renewal, the bank agreed to establish additional branches. Since the bank always opened the same number of branches in Austria and in Hungary, Hungary's share in the branch network gradually increased from 20% in 1878 to more than 40% in 1913. In 1899, however, Hungary again demanded a cartel bank and used the threat to establish its own bank of issue to achieve a significant extension of parity. Now the General Council and all of its sub-committees consisted of equal numbers of Austrian and Hungarian nationals and–more of symbolic importance–the General Council meetings were held in both Vienna and Budapest on a rotating basis. The transfer of some of the General Council's powers to the directorates could also be viewed as a Hungarian success, although the reasons were more of a pragmatic nature.[294] In fact, however, Hungary's increasing influence in the General Council should be seen in the context of the general increase in state involvement in the bank resulting from Austria-Hungary's move to gold in 1892. As described below in more detail, the two states transferred large quantities of gold to the bank as part of the reform and demanded greater supervisory authority in return. Since under dualism the Austrian and the Hungarian government were on an equal footing, the increase in state influence on the bank automatically represented an additional step towards parity. The campaign for a separate Hungarian central bank was renewed with vehemence in 1905 when the independence party took over power from the liberals, who had governed for many years. The campaign ultimately failed due to resistance in Hungary itself, and in 1911 the previous statutes were renewed with no significant changes to the dualistic structure of the bank.[295]

Czech, Polish and Slovenian politicians also brought forth nationalistic arguments, although to much less success than Hungary. Their demands were also concerned with political symbols, representation on the General Council and lending conditions. One key issue was the languages printed on the banknotes. For practical reasons, up to ten different monarchy languages had been included on both paper money issued by the state and banknotes issued by the National-bank.[296] This changed under the statutes of the Austro-Hungarian Bank, which designed its banknotes to have two matching sides–one in German and the other one in Hungarian–as an expression of parity. At the urging of the Hungarian government, which wished to bolster the role of the Hungarian language in the Kingdom of Hungary, none of the other languages of the monarchy were included. It is therefore not surprising that the new notes, which were issued in 1881 during a period of serious dispute between the Czechs and the Germans, quickly became a symbol of discrimination against the non-German and non-Magyar population. Activists overprinted the notes with Czech as well as Polish and Italian wording, forcing the Austro-Hungarian Bank in 1881 to either exchange or remove from circulation a total of 400,000 10-florin notes, corresponding to 3.3%

of the total notes in circulation. It was not until 1901 that all of the languages of the Austrian half of the Empire were again included on the Austrian side of the banknotes. Another point of contention was the role of the Prague branch, the composition of the General Council and the use of the Czech language in bank transactions. The Czech side repeatedly demanded that Prague be elevated to a position similar to that of Budapest and that local chambers of trade and commerce be able to participate in the election of the local directors. It is difficult to say whether the repeated complaints of discrimination against non-German and non-Magyar firms with regard to their eligibility for discount transactions and the allocation of credit lines were true or not. One reason is that the issue of national discrimination was in practice interwoven with differing ideas about how a central bank should be run. Many critics wanted the bank to become an instrument of regional policy and demanded that inexpensive credit be granted to agricultural cooperatives, for example. By contrast, the Austro-Hungarian Bank's management wanted to keep investments as liquid and secure as possible, which by definition excluded many of the new credit institutions–some of which were also pursuing a national agenda–from central bank access.

To give voice to their complaints, Czech-Bohemian savings banks began buying up shares in the Austro-Hungarian Bank on a large scale after 1900 to allow them to send representatives to the General Meeting. The German-Bohemian savings banks proceeded to apply the same tactic. As the years went by, the General Meetings began to resemble the chaotic meetings of the Austrian parliament more and more. Vociferous disputes were commonplace, although the criticism was directed more at Hungary's perceived disproportionately large role than at preferential treatment for German interests. Such criticism was shared by German political parties such as the Christian Social Party. However, the Austro-Hungarian Bank rejected all attempts to encroach upon its territory. In its view, the dualistic nature of the bank reflected the constitutional structure of Austria-Hungary, not national affiliations. This response was not entirely unjustified given the fact that between 1900 and 1910, for example, then governor Leon Biliński, although a citizen of Austria, was a prominent representative of the Polish Club in the Austrian parliament. In the end, the Czechs failed to obtain their own national representation in the directorates and in the General Council prior to 1918.

Thus it ensued that on the eve of World War I, Hungary was able to influence banking policy to a much greater degree than would have been warranted based on its importance for the economy of the dual monarchy. It is rather surprising that Hungary's repeated threats to withdraw from monetary union were as effective as they were. The majority of contemporaries as well as the secondary literature purported that Hungarian demands for its own central bank were politically motivated and that Hungary would have been the economic loser in the event of separation.[297] This perspective did not afford Hungary a particularly strong negotiating position. By contrast, more recent works have downplayed the disadvantages that Hungary would have incurred from leaving the monetary union. Hungary's threat to establish its own central bank can therefore be seen as credible, which would explain why Austria repeatedly gave way to Hungarian demands. The reason is that international capital markets already treated Hungarian bonds as though Hungary were an independent state. Thus Hungarian state financing did not depend on continuation of the monetary union, and since Austria was greatly interested in preserving the union, it made major concessions in the two areas of most importance to Hungary: acknowledgement of Hungary's equal standing with Austria through increased parity and access to inexpensive, short-term financing in all regions of Hungary.[298] At the same time, Austria's position is more readily comprehensible when one considers that the disadvantages for Austria in making the concessions were minimal. Increased lending by the Austro-Hungarian Bank in Hungary did not remove funds from Austria given the ease in obtaining short-term capital in Austria, in part thanks to the widespread branch network of the commercial banks.[299] In Galicia, which like Hungary had little local capital at its disposal, the Austro-Hungarian Bank branches enjoyed a similar significance as in Hungary. In any case, the bank's model of maintaining branches in peripheral regions brought good returns for the (often Austrian) shareholders as the bank was compensated for its intermediating between high- and low-interest-rate regions.[300] The extent to which economic advantages for the one side were associated with disadvantages for the other is therefore unclear. Ultimately, political symbols seem to have been the main point of contention.[301]

Return to a stable external value

In addition to the unresolved question of the constitutional structure of the monarchy, the second burden inherited from the neo-absolutist regime was the large quantities of non-convertible government paper money in circulation. As in previous foreign policy crises and military engagements, the outbreak of war against Prussia in May 1866 led to a sharp rise in the silver premium. Within just a few weeks the florin lost one-third of its value on the foreign exchange market. As opposed to the situation after 1853 and 1859, however, the Austrian and Hungarian governments made no new attempts in the subsequent years to prop up the currency and reestablish banknote convertibility. The volume of state paper money in circulation was too large, and it was too difficult for Austria and Hungary to agree on how to divide up responsibility. In the 1870s and 1880s, the exchange rate between the Austrian florin and the German, French and British currencies—all of which were gold- or silver-backed—fluctuated between 10% and 30% below parity.

From silver to gold

The year 1873 saw a major development for the international monetary system and with it, the Austrian florin. Ever since 1800, the ratio of gold to silver had remained nearly constant on the international market at 15.5, i.e., the price of 15.5 grams of silver was equivalent to the price of 1 gram of gold. This ensured a stable ratio between silver-backed currencies (such as in the German states, the Netherlands, Russia and, at least legally, Austria), the few gold-backed currencies (the British pound sterling and the Portuguese milreis) and those on a bimetallic standard (such as the French and Belgian francs). However, when the new German Empire decided in 1873 to introduce a gold-backed common currency (the mark), France suspended the minting of the silver franc. This resulted in such a decline in demand for silver for monetary purposes that the relative price between silver and gold started shifting to the detriment of silver.[302] Efforts to retain silver as a monetary metal persisted for some time, for which reason the decline in the value of silver was not abrupt.[303] In the end, however, those endeavors came to naught and the ratio of silver to gold

Chart 5.1: **Price of 100-florin silver and gold coins** (in florin banknotes)[304]

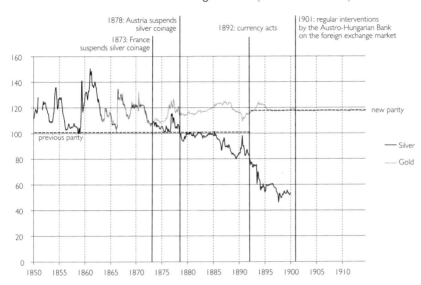

Although the florin nearly reached parity in 1866 thanks to the Plener reforms, the war with Prussia led to renewed devaluation. No further attempts were made to stabilize the currency until the early 1890s, and the florin exchange rate fluctuated quite heavily. In 1873, the value of silver in relation to gold began decreasing on the international markets. In this chart, this is evidenced by the divergence of the price for silver and gold in Vienna.[305] In 1892, the crown was introduced as the new Austrian currency and a fixed gold-crown ratio was established. After 1896, the exchange rate remained very close to the new parity.

dropped from 15.5:1 to approximately 20:1 in 1885 and 40:1 in 1900. Most countries switched to the gold standard.[306]

Austria had traditionally been on the silver standard, and the Austrian florin had been aligned with the silver currencies of the German states under the coinage treaties of 1753 and 1857. After losing the war against Prussia in 1866, Austria withdrew from the Coinage Treaty of 1857. At the time, at an international level efforts were being made to unify the various coinage systems in order to promote world trade, which was benefiting already from the growing global economy and declining transport costs.[307] A 25-franc gold coin–broadly equivalent to 5 U.S. dollars or 1 pound sterling–was to serve as the basis for the global currency. This was an attractive option for Austria, which was interested in forming new alliances, including trade alliances, after its exclusion from the process of economic unification in Germany.[308] In 1870, Austria began minting 4-florin and 8-florin gold coins, which were the equivalent of 10-franc and 20-franc coins in terms of their weight and fineness.[309] However, the alignment with the franc had virtually no practical effect given that the paper money in circulation in Austria continued to trade at a discount compared with both the silver and the gold florin. The gradual loss in the value of silver after 1873 thus at first had no impact on the Austrian currency.

By 1878, however, the value of silver had dropped so sharply that parity was established, i.e., the value of one paper florin was again nearly equivalent to the value of one silver florin coin. For the first time since 1848, it was again an attractive option for private individuals to import silver to Austria and have florin silver coins minted on their own account at the national mint. The Austrian government became concerned about being overrun with silver and tying the Austrian florin to the (falling) price of the commodity. It suspended free coinage of silver as well as the Nationalbank's obligation to buy up silver at a fixed price in banknotes. From that point onward, the Austrian currency was essentially no longer linked to any metal. As with currencies today, its value was determined solely on the basis of demand and the supply itself influenced by monetary policy. Silver nonetheless continued to play an important role for the market price of the florin. In 1878, governments resumed coining silver on a large scale at their own account—irrespective of the suspension of *private* silver coinage—in order to generate seigniorage, or the difference between the face value of the coins and their production cost (see the "seigniorage" box on page 77). Most of those coins were not needed for transaction purposes, where people preferred state paper money and banknotes. Therefore, of the 100 million florins coined between 1878 and 1890, some 85 million were exchanged for banknotes and relegated to the vaults of the Nationalbank, as shown in chart 5.3, which depicts the steady increase its metal reserves. Pricing of the florin on the foreign exchange markets and the currency's high volatility was very likely impacted by the ever-present possibility of new silver coins being minted, which would effect a loss in value of the florin due to the increase in money supply.[310] One indication of the uncertainty that ensued was the fact that investors were demanding higher returns on government bonds denominated in Austrian florins (i.e., silver) at an average of 5.3% in the 1880s than on government bonds denominated in gold florins (average of 4.7%).[311] It would therefore appear that rather than protecting the economy of Austria-Hungary from external shocks, the flexible exchange rate was more a source of added uncertainty.

Currency reform in a stalemate between Austria and Hungary

By the end of the 1870s, most European countries and the USA had moved to gold-backed currencies. That was also the logical option for Austria-Hungary if it wanted to return to a precious metal-backed currency, as generally desired, with the possible exception of parts of the export sector. However, there were three primary obstacles to transitioning to the gold standard: the unbacked government paper money would have to be taken out of circulation, a substantial volume of gold would be required, and a formula would have to be found for dividing up the costs between Austria and Hungary. Tax reforms in Austria and Hungary in 1889 brought prospects of a considerable period of budget surpluses for the first time in a long while, making it easier for both states to cover the costs of retiring government paper money. Moreover, the gold premium declined significantly between 1887 and 1891, i.e., the florin appreciated, which was perceived as a disadvantage by Hungarian agricultural operations in particular. Hence unlike in the decades before, the planned stabilization of the currency became an expansionary measure rather than a restrictive one, which broadened support for reform and facilitated its implementation.

After discussing the key reform issues for both countries in parliamentary enquêtes, the parliaments passed a series of currency laws in 1892. However, the reforms took so long to implement that the ultimate goal of convertibility of the banknotes to gold coins was not achieved before the monarchy collapsed. This was mainly due to the fact that any legal steps involving the currency had to be approved jointly by Austria and Hungary and thus formed part of the complex negotiation process associated with the regular renewal of the Compromise. Paradoxically, both sides were pursuing the goal of a stable, gold-backed currency but were unable to agree on execution. The Austrians largely regarded external stability as the primary factor, and were not as concerned with the statutory requirement for the gold convertibility of banknotes. For a major part of the Hungarian contingent, however, convertibility was not only an objective in and of itself but a prerequisite for formation of a Hungarian note-issuing bank whose credibility would be based on the obligation of both the Austrian and the Hungarian central bank to redeem their banknotes for gold at any time. Yet for the Austrians it was unacceptable that a statutory redemption obligation could further the Hungarian cause. Add to that concerns in Austria that convertibility would require restrictive monetary policies. This basically blocked the legal implementation of convertibility despite the fundamental consensus on a stable currency.[312] At the political level, the stalemate led to the Austro-Hungarian Bank having to make the actual policy decisions. Although the statutes of 1899 had increased state influence, the bank now had maneuvering room that it would never have had in a unitary state. As described below, the bank used its leeway to enforce strict fixation of the exchange rate on the market in line with the consensus in both Hungary and Austria. The result for Austria-Hungary was a currency that was effectively convertible to gold without convertibility being legally regulated.

This pragmatism, which had evolved in part as a consequence of the domestic political situation, colored all aspects of reform, also when it came to deciding on the gold content of the new currency. Since most experts found the florin to be an impractically large unit of currency, the crown–subdivided into 100 hellers–was introduced as a new unit of currency in order to facilitate monetary transactions, with one crown equal to one-half florin.[313] However, it was decided that the gold content of the crown would not be equivalent to half that of one gold florin but would equal the average exchange rate in recent years, which resulted in depreciation of approximately 19% against the gold florin (chart 5.1). This meant that by contrast with previous attempts to restore currency convertibility in 1853, 1859 and 1866, no appreciation and thus no deflationary monetary policies were necessary.

The Austrian and Hungarian governments also took a pragmatic stance regarding procurement of the gold backing needed for the new currency. At the

end of 1891, 455 million florin banknotes plus government paper money totaling 365 million florins were in circulation, i.e., paper money valued at a total of
820 million florins. If 200 million florins were left without metal backing, as had
been provided for in the central bank's statutes since 1863, then the Austro-
Hungarian Bank needed approximately 620 million florins in gold. In 1892, the
Austro-Hungarian Bank had 80 million florins in gold and foreign currencies
convertible to gold. The bank had acquired the gold between 1871 and 1874, i.e.,
before the price of silver began dropping, in preparation for potentially moving
to the gold standard. Despite that foresighted transaction, a considerable gap
thus remained to be filled. To reduce the costs involved, the two governments
decided against demonetizing the silver florin. The silver florin retained its status as legal tender for an unlimited period of time and could be used by the
central bank to back banknotes in the same way as gold. However, to protect
the value of the crown it was not permitted to mint any new silver florins.[314]
Keeping the silver florin reduced the quantity of gold needed, the majority of
which came from gold bonds issued by Austria and Hungary in 1892 and 1893.
The governments transferred the receipts from the bonds to the Austro-Hungarian Bank and in turn received banknotes and silver that they used to retire
the government paper money. By 1901, all government paper money had been
withdrawn, and the costs were split between Austria and Hungary in a 70:30
ratio.[315]

The central bank takes over exchange rate policy

   The adoption of new currency laws in 1892 did not immediately stabilize the
exchange rates. The gold premium went back up to 6.5% (relative to the new
parity) in November 1893, and until the end of 1895 was consistently over 1%
(chart 5.1). The Austrian and Hungarian governments felt themselves cheated
out of the fruits of their labor and put pressure on the Austro-Hungarian Bank
to bolster the exchange rate by selling gold. Initially skeptical due to fears for
its only recently acquired gold reserves, the bank in 1896 began to regularly
buy and sell foreign exchange on the open market–a policy that soon proved
successful.[316] Regardless of the lack of an explicit commitment to its convertibility into gold, the exchange rate of the crown against the major international

gold-backed currencies fluctuated in a range similar to that of the rates between the gold currencies themselves after 1896.[317]

As opposed to what a simplified idea of the gold standard might indicate,
the buying and selling of gold by the Austro-Hungarian Bank was not of prime
importance in stabilizing the external value of the crown. The bank did not wait
until the export of gold became profitable before selling foreign exchange in
the market. Rather, after 1896 the Austro-Hungarian Bank became a regular
player on the foreign exchange market and actively managed exchange rates.[318]
This was made possible by the dominant position achieved by the Austro-Hungarian Bank in 1901, when the governments transferred their substantial gold
and foreign exchange holdings to the bank and entrusted the bank with managing all public payments in foreign exchange, mainly to service foreign debt.
As a result the bank became both a regular buyer and seller in the market. Its
constant presence on both sides of the market and its innovative use of forward contracts and temporary exchange of foreign currencies for crowns (an
early form of foreign currency swaps) allowed the Austro-Hungarian Bank to
make up for near-term discrepancies between the supply of and demand for
foreign exchange and thus minimizing exchange rate fluctuations. The resulting confidence in a stable medium-term exchange rate facilitated policy-making for the Austro-Hungarian Bank. As a result, it did not have to raise interest
rates as much as other Western central banks in response to international financial crises such as the crisis of 1907, thus creating less of a burden on the
domestic economy.[319] When the bank began issuing gold coins in 1903, confidence in the bank's notes was so high that the public gave preference to the ac-
customed banknotes and re-deposited the majority of the coins with the bank.

The policy of indirect gold backing at a time in which most central banks,
with the exception of the Belgian National Bank, held only minimal foreign exchange assets and relied primarily on their gold reserves plus changes in the
discount rate, represented an innovation that garnered international attention
from both economists and monetary policy makers alike.[320] Domestically, de-
facto stabilization of the currency settled the political stalemate between Austria and Hungary regarding the question of effective redeemability of the
crown notes in gold. Once the continuance of the joint central bank had found

some level of acceptance among the majority of Hungarians, de facto convertibility was a compromise found acceptable by all parties. In a concession to the Hungarian side, convertibility as an objective was retained in the statutes, but the choice of timing was left to the Austro-Hungarian Bank and hence removed from the reach of policy makers.[321] In return, the Austro-Hungarian Bank agreed in the statutes of 1911 to "hold the value of the crown stable in foreign currency." However, this was nothing other than what the bank had already been doing in the preceding years. The legal obligation for the banknotes to be redeemable in gold was no longer of significance.

Conducting business in a large empire

The transformation of the Nationalbank to the Austro-Hungarian Bank in 1878 did not immediately bring any major changes in the bank's main areas of activity, namely discount lending and granting advances and mortgage loans. As the years passed, however, expansion of the branch network, increasing importance of money transfers and the substitution of banknotes for government paper money gradually strengthened the role of the Austro-Hungarian Bank in the banking system.

Growing branch network and deepening financial integration

With respect to the branch network, the reorganization of the bank and creation of a head office in Budapest in 1878 presented an opportunity to improve its administrative structures. In 1876, the bank had 24 branch offices–far fewer than smaller countries such as France (76) and Prussia (59). While one reason for this was the delayed economic development and minimal use of bills of exchange in many regions of the monarchy, the bank itself explained its hesitation by citing, among other things, the lack of control over the branches provided by its organizational structure.[322] For example, the branches were not headed by an official sent from Vienna but by a board elected by the local chamber of trade and commerce.[323] Implementation of the statutes of 1878 put the branch offices under the supervision of the respective directorate in

Vienna or Budapest. Management of the branches was now assigned to a bank official who also had a veto right at the meetings of the discount committee, which assessed the quality of the bills of exchange presented for discounting. That committee, which consisted of local dignitaries, merchants and tradesmen who provided valuable information but had also opened up a possible channel for inside trading, was thus subjected to direct control by bank employees. In 1880, the bank began keeping a central register of all companies registered in the monarchy. The bank officials themselves received regular visits from inspectors who reported to the General Council in Vienna.[324] Frequent reassignments, including cross-postings between Austria and Hungary, were an additional instrument for preventing ties with local interests from becoming too close and thus ensuring uniform management.

The improved structure of the branch network made it possible for the bank to considerably expand its scope of operations and harmonize its conditions of business. The discount rate–which had in some cases varied between branches–was standardized after 1878 and the bank stopped differentiating between bills of exchange payable at the location of submission and those that the bank had to send to another branch for collection. Previously, access to discounted bills of exchange was a privilege reserved for inhabitants of cities with branch offices. Now, after the territory of the monarchy was divided up into banking districts and one branch assigned to each district, anyone was able to do business with the central bank. The bank availed itself of two instruments to make it even easier to residents outside of cities with branch offices to access the bank. *Korrespondenzkredite,* correspondence loans, enabled financial institutions and industrial firms to submit bills of exchange and receive cash by mail and were agreed on an individual basis. Such correspondence loans were an extension of the credit lines granted by the bank outside of Vienna during the crisis of 1848/49 and which had remained in existence afterwards. In 1878, the procedure was standardized and the number of correspondents rose sharply.[325] The second possibility for extending credit outside of the cities with branch offices was created by setting up *Nebenstellen,* contract offices. Contract offices were banks–in Austria nearly always savings banks–that discounted bills from local businesses on account of the Austro-Hungarian Bank as well as cashed bills when due. Every contract office was subordinated to a branch office that was responsible for evaluating the bills presented, while the presenter of the bill had to bear the costs of using the contract office in the form of a commission over and above the discount rate.[326] The cashing of bills that had been submitted to other branches or to the head offices in Vienna or Budapest soon became more important in the day-to-day operations of the contract offices than actual lending. The system proved so effective that the bank in 1886 began actively seeking out financial institutions that could serve as contract offices. Within two years, the number of contract offices had risen to nearly 150.

Chart 5.2: **The branch network of the Austro-Hungarian Bank**[327]

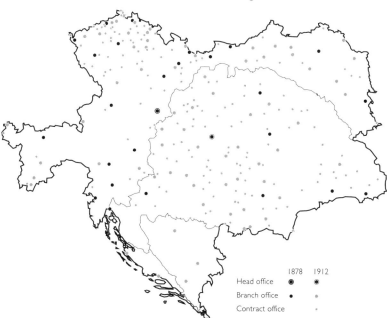

	1878	1912
Head office	◉	◉
Branch office	●	●
Contract office		·

After 1878, the bank expanded its branch network on a large scale. This map from 1912 shows the relatively equal distribution of the branch offices and contract offices in Hungary and the extreme regional differences in Austria, where the branches and contract offices were concentrated primarily in the northern Bohemian and Silesian industrial areas. There were hardly any contract offices in the Alpine regions or the lands on the Adriatic Sea. Worthy of note are the three branches in Bosnia-Herzegovina, which the bank opened after the annexation in 1908.

The new organizational structure allowed the branch network to expand quickly between 1878 and 1913, and the number of branches increased from 24 to 101 (chart 5.2). Since the regular renewal of the statutes always provided for opening up new branch offices, the bank did not establish any new branches on its own initiative. However, the bank was responsible for setting up contract offices. The number of contract offices remained near the figure of 150 reached in the 1880s until 1900, after which it rose continually until reaching 250. In terms of regional distribution, Hungary–which until 1878 had only a few branches–caught up quickly, and by 1913 accounted for 40% of all branch offices. That figure exceeded Hungary's share in the economic output and the population of the monarchy as a whole and reflected the success of Hungary in the renegotiations of the charters, although it was also due to Hungary's greater territorial expanse.

The share of the different regions and nationalities in the discount business of the Austro-Hungarian Bank–which as described above was being closely watched by the various national groups–differs greatly depending on the indicators used. Turnover was higher in Vienna owing to the large number of bills of exchange presented. However, those bills remained in the portfolio for shorter periods of time since most of them had a significantly shorter remaining maturity than bills discounted outside Vienna. This is why a comparison based on average portfolio holdings yields a very different result, showing a much bigger share of provincial offices in discount operations. Whether a bill was allocated to its place of submission or the place of payment also made a substantial difference. A comparison of the two methods illustrates the central position of Vienna in the payment and credit system of the monarchy. In 1910, for example, 35% of all bills of exchange were presented in Vienna, but only half of those were actually payable in Vienna. Most of the bills not payable in Vienna originated in Hungary (excluding Budapest), although some came from Galicia as well. Those figures were a politically charged issue, and it is certainly no coincidence that the Austro-Hungarian Bank changed the format of its annual report in 1906, i.e., at a time when the independence party heading the Hungarian government was again calling strongly for bank separation. Under the new format, discount volumes were no longer reported by place of presentation but by place of payment in order to more clearly demonstrate the high volume of Hungarian business. Regardless of the specific indicator chosen, however, all measures point to gradually increasing business volumes in Budapest relative to Vienna and at the Hungarian branches relative to the Austrian ones after 1878.

There were various reasons for the high weighting of the peripheral, economically weaker regions such as Hungary and Galicia in the bank's discount portfolio. One factor already mentioned was public pressure from Bohemia, Galicia and above all Hungary, which could have made it appear politically expedient for the bank, in view of the necessity of regularly reviewing the statutes, to actively promote those regions, Hungary in particular. From the shareholders' point of view, the peripheral regions offered attractive conditions given that discounting bills with longer remaining maturites was more profitable: while the discount rate was the same, the longer terms meant that the fixed costs for discounting and collection were offset by higher interest income. Moreover, persons submitting bills in Vienna had more discounting alternatives than were available in Transylvania or Bucovina, plus the standard market interest rates were higher in the peripheral regions than in Vienna or Budapest. This made the Austro-Hungarian Bank–which was obligated under its statutes to charge a uniform interest rate for the entire empire–an attractive business partner in the peripheral regions, and it accordingly received a large portion of that discount business. This way the Austro-Hungarian Bank most likely played an important role in the process of economic integration in the last third of the 19th century, when the monarchy developed into a large single market and interest rates converged significantly, including regional rates.[328]

By contrast with the well-documented geographic allocation of discount transactions, there is little information on the identity of the Austro-Hungarian Bank's business partners. The high amount of the average discounted bill would indicate that discounting remained an exclusive business, despite the expansion of the branch network and the reduction in the minimum transaction amount. Although the average sum declined from more than 2,000 florins before 1878 to just under 1,000 florins in 1913, that amount is still more than one year's income for a low-level public servant or tradesman in Vienna.[329] The high average was not the result of the figures being skewed by a few large transactions either. In 1913, 70% of all bills were submitted in an amount of 150 florins or more. The little information that is available on the bank's business partners also supports the idea of exclusivity. Even though discount and lending facilities were also available to non-financial firms and private individuals, the majority of the transactions came from banks. A list for Austria from 1910 shows that banks had a share of nearly 95% in bill discounting, and the rest was accounted for by savings banks, credit cooperatives and other companies. In Hungary, the economically important milling industry was a major player, but even so remained far behind the banks among the major discounters.[330] This is further evidence that despite all efforts to democratize lending, the Austro-Hungarian Bank essentially played the role of the banker's bank.

Money demand and discounting policy

Whereas the transformation of the Nationalbank to the Austro-Hungarian Bank brought extensive changes in terms of the bank's structure and microeconomic aspects of lending, the processes for controlling the supply of money and setting interest rates did not change at first. The statutes of 1878 retained the system, in place since 1863, of having a fixed quota of fiduciary notes. This allowed the bank to initially issue 200 million florins in notes covered by discounts and advances, but required 100% silver backing for each additional note issued beyond 200 millions. Initially, the figure of 200 million florins stipulated somewhat randomly in the Bank Act of 1863 did not represent an effective restriction despite a rising demand for currency in the context of a growing and increasingly monetized economy. The height of the boom of 1873 and the subsequent crash were a temporary exception, after which notes in circulation decreased until 1878 in a climate of falling prices. After 1878, the Austrian and Hungarian governments took advantage of the decrease in the price of silver to begin minting silver coins again, most of which went to the Austro-Hungarian Bank, thus enabling it to increase the volume of banknotes in circulation (chart 5.3).

Although the growing silver reserves eased the restrictions associated with the 200 million florin quota, the volume of banknotes in circulation approached the legal threshold more and more frequently in the 1880s. This was regarded as increasingly detrimental to implementing a rational monetary pol-

Chart 5.3: **Key central bank balance sheet positions** (in millions of florins)[331]

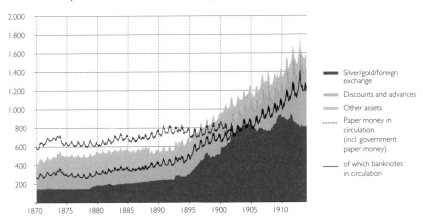

The volume of paper money in circulation rose until 1873, after which it stabilized and did not experience any more substantial growth until it was finally redeemed after 1900. The rules of the 1863 Bank Act required that any sustained increase in the volume of notes in circulation be supplemented by an increase in the metal reserves. The reserves began increasing in 1878 due to the inflow of silver coins and after 1892, when the proceeds of the gold bonds flowed in and favorable exchange rates facilitated private gold imports. Even though the coverage ratio decreased again in the years prior to 1914, the Austro-Hungarian Bank nonetheless held much higher metal reserves than it ever had in most previous years.

icy. A solution was found when the statutes were renewed in 1888. The new system followed the example of the Reichsbank by combining proportional coverage with a fixed quota. Proportional coverage meant that the bank had to hold at least 40% of the banknotes in circulation in gold or silver, which it had always done in any case. The decisive factor was that the bank was now permitted to exceed the quota of 200 million florins in uncovered notes as long as it paid a tax of 5% on the excess amount. This regulation ensured that the volumes not backed by metal did not rise too far above the figure of 200 million florins, which was considered to be a reasonable estimate of the normal cash requirements of the economy. The possibility to increase the note issue beyond the 200 million threshold if need be, however, relieved the bank of the necessity of either having to maintain a buffer over the maximum amount to guard against a sudden rise in demand for cash or, as in 1873, having to ask the government to suspend the Bank Act. The average level of banknote reserves, i.e., the unused portion of the quota, declined accordingly from nearly 40 million florins between 1884 and 1887 to just 1 million florins between 1888 and 1891.

The new regulation made liquidity management much easier not only for the Austro-Hungarian Bank but also for commercial banks and savings banks, which could now rely on obtaining cash from the Austro-Hungarian Bank if needed. It was also no longer necessary for them to prepare for a possible future rationing of access to central bank loans. The share of cash in total assets shrank accordingly from 2% to 3% in the 1870s to 1% to 2% in the 1880s.[332] The easing of the previous quantitative restrictions on central bank money also facilitated faster growth in deposits with banks and savings banks.[333]

In general, the banking system was regaining momentum around 1880 after a phase of stagnation resulting from the bank collapses of 1873. Existing institutions expanded their branch networks, and new institutions were created. The development was supported by the fact that around 1890 a new generation of executives came into power at the banks that had not been in positions of responsibility during the traumatic events of 1873 and therefore acted with less restraint than their predecessors. The new risk-taking culture directly benefited Austro-Hungarian industry, which received both direct loans and assistance in going public.[334] Thus began a second phase of industrial expansion. Between 1885 and 1914, the number of companies listed on the Vienna Stock Exchange rose from 114 to 262.[335] An additional factor in this expansion was the improvement in financial technologies. For instance, the new coverage rules finally permitted the Austro-Hungarian Bank to expand cashless payment transactions. While the original statutes of 1817 had provided for the establishment of current accounts and the option to make bank transfers, this met with little interest in the business world at the time.[336] For the Nationalbank, current account holdings represented a risk under the 1863 coverage framework since the accountholders could demand payment in cash at any time, meaning that current account balances had to be taken into consideration when calculating the safety buffer for the banknote reserves. This complication was eliminated under the new system in which any unexpected withdrawals could, if necessary, be paid by exceeding the quota, subject to taxation. Hence from the perspective of the bank, the current accounts were left with only the beneficial aspect of not requiring any metal backing. The possibility of increasing the use of current account balances to reduce the need for cash also appealed to the Austrian and Hungarian governments, which hoped to decrease thereby the costs of returning to banknote convertibility. From the 1900s onward, the local offices of the two treasuries were integrated into the cashless money transfer system of the bank, as were the Austrian and the Hungarian Postsparkasse institutions, which themselves handled extensive check traffic between their thousands of outlets.[337] In spite of this, cash retained its key role among both large and small banks until 1914. As late as 1895, even at the Creditanstalt, Austria's leading bank, more than half of all incoming payments were made in cash and not by check or money transfer.[338]

Chart 5.4: **Official discount rates in Austria-Hungary and selected countries** (in %)[339]

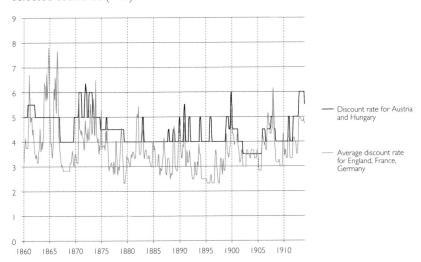

Discount rate for Austria and Hungary

Average discount rate for England, France, Germany

Before 1860, the Nationalbank did not change its discount rate for long periods at a time. Apart from a brief episode during the financial crisis of 1873, the bank remained true to this practice until the end of the 1880s. The chart also shows that interest rate levels in Austria were largely uncoupled from those in other countries. This changed upon stabilization of the exchange rate in 1896, from which point onward the Austrian interest rate broadly followed the international trend.

However, it was the currency reform of 1892 that brought the biggest change in the monetary policy of the Austro Hungarian Bank. Once the state paper money had been retired, the entire volume of paper money in circulation was under the direct control of the Austro-Hungarian Bank. This necessitated stricter management of money in circulation, as the bank was now required not only to adhere to the coverage provision in the charter but in addition to maintain the external value of the crown near legal parity by buying or selling gold or foreign exchange. In an era of unrestricted capital movement, it was the level of the domestic interest rate compared with foreign interest rates that was the main determinant for the movement of short- and long-term capital. Domestic and foreign interest rates did not have to coincide at all times since exchange rates were permitted to fluctuate in a small range around parity. Given a range of ±0.4%, the interest rate differential for a three-month bill of exchange could equal 1.6%.[340] Nevertheless, adherence to the gold standard made Austria-Hungary much more susceptible to medium-term trends on foreign capital markets and in the international economy, as can be seen from the fluctuation in the Austro-Hungarian Bank's discount rate. In the decade between 1878 and 1888, the Austro-Hungarian Bank changed its discount rate only three times. After 1888, a pattern emerged in which the discount rate generally amounted to 4%, but in the fall of each year was raised by either 0.5 or 1 percentage point, depending on utilization of the banknote reserve, and in the spring was lowered back to 4% after the high cash requirements of the previous fall had subsided. The counterpart to a stable discount rate was upward and downward revaluation of the florin on the foreign exchange markets. After 1892, and in particular after 1898, the pattern in interest rate trends changed. Cycles of higher and then lower interest rates now lasted for several years and followed similar trends in Germany or in England (chart 5.4). The Austro-Hungarian Bank had to adapt its policies to international interest rate changes if it wanted to maintain a fixed exchange rate. In addition to its foreign exchange policies, which could help absorb short-term imbalances, the high level of gold reserves acted as a buffer and enabled a certain degree of flexibility. Large quantities of gold flowed into Austria in the initial phase after currency reform, for which reason in 1901–1903, the banknotes at times had a metal reserve

backing of more than 100% (chart 5.3). In 1909, a slow erosion of the gold reserves commenced while the volume of banknotes in circulation continued to
expand rapidly. In 1910, the bank negotiated an increase in the amount of the
tax-free banknote quota but unlike in the past, was not able to prevent the volume of notes in circulation from exceeding the sum of the reserves and the
quota on a sustained basis. The bank's growing difficulties can also be explained by the tensions in the Balkans, which put pressure on state budgets,
impeded the inflow of foreign capital and, at times, increased demand for cash.
The situation relaxed in early 1914, and heighted optimism was evident at the
meetings of the General Council. No one suspected that the last chapter in the
history of the Austro-Hungarian Bank would commence in the summer of 1914.

World War I and the collapse of monetary union (1914–1919)

"Never in the entire history of money has the global monetary situation seen an upheaval as fundamental as that which occurred during and after the World War."

Gustav Cassel, *Post-war stabilization*, p. 1

W orld War I began in the summer of 1914. In addition to costing millions of lives, the four years of war necessitated the mobilization of vast material resources. The Austro-Hungarian Bank had to issue banknotes to help finance the war, just as the Stadtbanco had done with its paper money during the Napoleonic wars. The end of the war in 1918 signified the end of the monarchy and with it, the demise of the bank of issue, which had served the monarchy for more than 100 years.

War preparations and the initial weeks of conflict

T he outbreak of war in 1914 did not come as a full surprise to the bank. Certainly by the time of the crisis surrounding the Austrian annexation of Bosnia-Herzegovina in 1908 and the two Balkan wars in 1912 and 1913, a military engagement of the monarchy on the Balkans became more and more likely. Discussions of financial preparations for war had also been one of the components of the European armament race preceding World War I. For instance, the Austrian and Hungarian governments had negotiated war scenarios with the bank back in 1908 and again in 1912.[341] However, the agreements concluded were confined to some vague promises. The governments pledged to take recourse to monetary financing only in emergencies and after exhausting all other resources; to refrain from amending or suspending currency laws and bank statutes if possible, and to restore normal conditions as soon as possible after the war. In contrast, no tangible results such as an increase in the state's cash reserves were achieved. The calculations left almost no margin for error, as could be seen in 1912 when the ratio of gold to banknotes decreased markedly and nearly reached the statutory minimum of 40%. This left the bank little leeway to extend advances to the state in the event of war or even to cover private funding requirements, which were likewise expected to rise. Even a limited military engagement of three months–estimated by the army to cost 2.5 billion crowns, two-thirds of which was to come from central bank loans–would necessitate suspending the coverage regulations and thus entail a massive intervention in the structures that had been painstakingly established after the currency reform of 1892. The warning issued by the bank's governor, Sandór Popovics, to the two governments met with no response, however, and his concerned questions as to how the war would be financed if it lasted longer than the estimated three months went unanswered as well.[342]

Although the bank's management had in fact considered the issue of an impending war, the actual outbreak of hostilities thus found the bank largely unprepared. Francis Ferdinand, successor to the Austro-Hungarian throne, was assassinated on June 28, 1914. While this did not lead to any particular unrest at first, once the ultimatum was issued to the Serbian government on July 23 the central bank was immediately forced to part with large quantities of cash, foreign exchange assets and gold. Within a single week, the bank lost 170 million crowns in gold and foreign exchange while discounts and advances more than doubled, rising from 954 million to 2,046 million crowns. The value of the banknotes in circulation increased by nearly 1 billion crowns to 3.1 billion crowns.[343] Demand came primarily from banks making preparations for possible runs on their institutions. In response to the decreasing ratio of gold to banknotes in circulation and rising interest rates abroad, the central bank increased its key interest rate from 4% to 8% in several steps. However, the rate hikes failed to curb demand for gold, foreign currency and banknotes, and emergency measures had to be implemented. On July 31, 1914, the government ordered a payment moratorium on the majority of private claims at the same time as it called for general mobilization. Originally planned to last only two weeks, the moratorium was extended several times and was not lifted until the end of July 1915. The payment moratorium in combination with high military expenditures, which were financed by central bank loans, increased money in circulation to such an extent that the original liquidity shortage turned into a liquidity surplus by August 1914. The financial crisis was over; now the focus was on financing the state's war expenditures.

State financing and central bank policy during the war

The financial cost of war is normally calculated to include not only direct military expenditure but also related costs such as expenses for disabled veterans, surviving family members and refugees as well as for rebuilding after the war. Estimates of the total costs incurred by Austria-Hungary as a result of World War I range between 21 billion and 25 billion crowns, calculated at 1913 prices–a figure corresponding to approximately 80%–90% of GDP in the last year of peace.[344] While this sum does appear enormous, it is significantly less than the amounts incurred by other nations involved in the war. Even before 1914, the military budget of Austria-Hungary was small compared with military spending by other European countries.[345] During the war, the monarchy experienced great difficulties in mobilizing its economy for war. Some countries were able to increase their GDP during the conflict, while the economic output of the monarchy decreased by 10% in the first year alone. By 1918, Austria-Hungary's GDP had dropped to less than two-thirds of the pre-war figure.[346] The decrease was due to the intermittent occupation of parts of the monarchy by Entente forces in addition to the growing scarcity of both workers and raw materials.[347] Furthermore, the monarchy was less and less able to redirect the economic output, which was decreasing in any case, to fund the war. Seen over the entire four years of World War I, Austria-Hungary expended 25% of its economic output for the war. In France and Germany this figure stood at 50%.[348]

From intermittent loans to ongoing war funding

There were basically three ways to mobilize the necessary resources: levying new taxes, issuing paper money and issuing loans. As far as taxes were concerned, neither Austria nor Hungary found it prudent to take drastic action. Austria had not had a parliament since 1914, and the government did not want to endanger the country's precarious political equilibrium by imposing new charges.[349] In Hungary, the political situation was similar. The majority of funding therefore came from paper money and loans, with a system of issuing war bonds in combination with direct loans from the central bank becoming entrenched over the years.

In the end, some two-thirds of the war funding came from bonds that Hungary and Austria issued every six months from the fall of 1914 onward. The two states did not hesitate to use all means at their disposal, including appeals to patriotism and citizens' own financial interests, to encourage broad swaths of the population to subscribe to the high-interest war bonds. The central bank supported these efforts by opening up its branches to bond subscribers. Within four years, the bond liabilities of the two countries had risen from just under 20 billion crowns to nearly 95 billion crowns.[350] In addition to funding military expenses, the war bond launches were designed to remove some of the money from circulation that had been put into the economy via direct central bank loans.[351] However, in reality the proceeds from the war bonds were not used to repay central bank loans. Much rather, the Austrian and Hungarian governments kept taking out new loans.

The Austro-Hungarian Bank was a key player right from the start. In the initial weeks of the war, the commercial banks feared massive withdrawals by account-holders and were neither inclined nor able to assist the Austrian and Hungarian governments to any great degree. The first loan for mobilization of the army—which the two governments received from one Austrian and one Hungarian banking syndicate in August 1914—was only possible because the banks had been able to use the treasury bonds to obtain advances from the Austro-Hungarian Bank at a favorable rate. This meant that the army was being funded using central bank loans even before the actual outbreak of hostilities. The two governments also attempted to borrow from the Austro-Hungarian Bank directly. On August 17, 1914, major elements of the Austro-Hungarian Bank's statutes were rescinded, weekly publication of the financial statements was discontinued and both the requirement that at least 40% of all banknotes be backed by gold and the prohibition on extending loans to the state were lifted. Despite the bank's repeated references to its independence and the need to protect the currency to the greatest extent possible, the resolutions of August 17 paved the way for monetary financing and inflation alike.

By the summer of 1915, it was clear that the war would not be over anytime soon, upon which the Austrian and Hungarian governments endeavored to come to a permanent agreement with the central bank rather than continuing to obtain funding on an ad hoc basis. The governments gave weight to their request by threatening to issue paper money themselves. Although the bank underpinned its reluctance to agree to such funding with arguments of currency stability, in the end it capitulated.[352] The result was a new model for central bank loans, essentially a standing facility that could be accessed quickly and easily at the discretion of the treasury. The Austro-Hungarian Bank approved a credit facility of 1.5 billion crowns, 954 million crowns of which were earmarked for Austria and 546 million crowns for Hungary based on the ratio established in the Compromise. The interest rate was originally set at 1% and later lowered to 0.5%. Two loans were disbursed in 1915, four in 1916 and 1917 each, and eleven in 1918.[353] By the end of the war and adding the various credit transactions concluded, Austria had incurred a debt of 25.1 billion crowns and Hungary 9.9 billion crowns (or 35.0 billion crowns in sum) with the Austro-Hungarian Bank.

The natural outcome of providing increasingly higher loans to the state was rapid growth in the supply of money. By the end of 1914, the sum of all banknotes in circulation and bank balances had already reached 6.5 billion crowns, or more than double the figure of 2.7 billion crowns recorded in December 1913. During the first phase of the hostilities, the rise in prices lagged behind the increase in the money supply (see chart 7.1 in the next chapter). However, as inflation began accelerating in the second half of 1916, this situation was soon reversed. Inflation rose again sharply in the final months of the war as essential goods became increasingly scarce and people were suffering from starvation, even in Vienna. Ultimately, prices, like the money supply, rose to twelvefold the level of mid-1914. In other words, Austria-Hungary suffered much higher levels of inflation than most other war-faring countries, reflecting the struggles of the monarchy to mobilize a shrinking supply of goods for the purposes of the war.[354]

Discount and lending transactions dry up, gold reserves vanish

Owing to the rapidly growing supply of money from the loans extended to the two governments, private demand for central bank loans decreased. Discount transactions began declining in the fall of 1914 following a brief spike at the start of the war. In September, the bank lowered its discount rate from 8% to 6%. October saw a further reduction to 5.5%, and in April 1915 the rate was again lowered to 5%, where it remained until the end of the war. However, demand for discount loans from the central bank was sparse even at that low rate given that the oversupply of liquidity had pushed down rates on the open market to between 1.5% and 2.0%.[355] The discount portfolio decreased from 863 million crowns at the end of 1914 to 177 million crowns in 1915 and 22 million crowns in 1917. Secured loans fared somewhat better, fluctuating between 580 and 670 million crowns during the war. However, this still fell far short of the growth in the bank's total assets and in the money supply (chart 6.1). As a result, the official discount rate and the secured lending rate lost all significance in steering liquidity. The question of whether the interest rate had been set too low in view of accelerating inflation is an academic one, since it was loans to the two states that were driving inflation rather than private-sector loans.[356] Governor Popovics also found the interest rate to be of little use in regulating the money supply. His idea was to issue certificates of deposit to absorb the excess liquidity.[357] However, the Austrian finance minister was opposed to this plan since it would mean paying interest on the certificates, and the bank did not in fact begin issuing certificates of deposit until April 1918. By the end of October 1918, certificates worth approximately 3 billion crowns had been issued. That amount was too low, however, to have any substantial impact on the level of market interest rates and thus inflation.

Although the bank had built up a large supply of gold and foreign exchange assets after 1892, its holdings rapidly diminished as the war progressed. Losses were especially significant in the days following the declaration of war. The losses started slowing in early August 1914 when the bank began reserving payments in gold and foreign exchange for the military administration, for servicing public debt and for essential imports. Mutual payment embargoes were soon enacted, meaning that private individuals no longer had to service their debts payable in gold or foreign currency in other warring states. In Austria-Hungary, it was permitted to use paper money to service payment obligations denominated in gold crowns for the duration of the war.

The monarchy required high volumes of foreign exchange. Not only were key pre-war Hungarian agricultural exports now blocked by the trade embargo imposed on the Central powers, but demand for imports had increased due to the need to supply the military and later the general population with food. There were nonetheless no corresponding restrictions on foreign trade until the end of 1916. It was not until the start of 1916 that two *Devisenzentralen*, central offices for payments to and from foreign countries, were established in Vienna and Budapest as per the German example. Along with the Austro-Hungarian Bank, the major banks in those central offices joined forces and agreed to offer all of the foreign exchange assets they received for sale. A major weakness in this concept, however, was that membership in the central offices was voluntary and there was absolutely no legal obligation to turn over foreign exchange holdings and incoming foreign exchange assets to the centers. It is hardly surprising that the outgoing payments soon surpassed the incoming amounts, and the Austro-Hungarian Bank was forced to make up the difference. Moreover, the rates offered by the central offices did not always reflect market conditions. For example, the crown was kept at an artificially high level–especially against the Deutsche mark–for political reasons. Although currency controls were tightened in the following years, this could not solve the basic problem of a lack of foreign means of payment. By October 1918, the Austro-Hungarian Bank was left with only 268 million crowns in gold.[358]

Chart 6.1: **Key balance sheet positions of the Austro-Hungarian Bank** (in billions of crowns)[359]

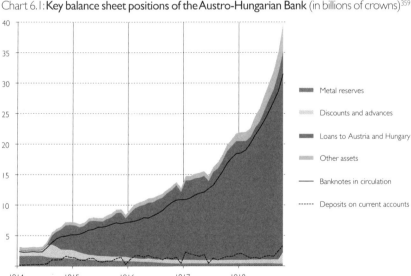

Metal reserves

Discounts and advances

Loans to Austria and Hungary

Other assets

Banknotes in circulation

Deposits on current accounts

While the demand of commercial banks for discounts and advances had risen significantly in the first few weeks of the war, the following expansion of the balance sheet of the Austro-Hungarian Bank was driven almost entirely by the credit requirements of the Austrian and the Hungarian governments. At the same time, the volume of banknotes in circulation also increased sharply. Deposits on current accounts, on the other hand, after having increased sharply in the early war months, remained broadly stable at a level of 1½ million crowns i.e., at a rather insignificant level compared to that of cash in circulation.

The charter of the Austro-Hungarian Bank came up for renewal during the war. By contrast with previous charter negotiations, this time the Austrian and Hungarian governments quickly came to an agreement. The most significant change was the introduction of a quota of subsidized loans for small farmers and tradesmen. In addition, the two governments agreed to repay their debts to the bank within five years of the end of the war. However, the statutes could not be adopted because no agreement could be reached in the parallel negotiations on the Compromise of 1917. The interim solution was to renew the previous statutes until the end of 1919. The end of the monarchy in 1918 made it unnecessary to resume negotiations, and the charter of the joint central bank expired for good on December 31, 1919.

The end of the monarchy and the joint currency

In the fall of 1918, the monarchy collapsed. This resulted in the creation of three new countries–Czechoslovakia, Hungary and (German) Austria. Other parts of the former monarchy joined the existing countries of Romania, Italy and Serbia,[360] and Galicia became part of the restored Poland. The former joint economic and currency zone dissolved rapidly.[361] The first act of currency separation occurred in January 1919 with the overprinting of the banknotes circulating in the Kingdom of Serbs, Croats and Slovenes (Yugoslavia), which could be exchanged for Serbian dinars at a rate of 4:1.[362] Although the Austro-Hungarian Bank protested against the violation of its charter, it was powerless to prevent the collapse of the currency zone. In February 1919, the banknotes circulating in Czechoslovakia were stamped, and only those banknotes could be used for payment from March 10, 1919 onward.[363] Alois Rašin, the Czech minister of finance, had on January 17, 1919, already prohibited the Austro-Hungarian Bank's head office in Prague to lend against Austrian or Hungarian bonds as collateral arguing that secured lending by the Austro-Hungarian Bank would only serve financial speculation.

To prevent large quantities of unstamped banknotes from overrunning the country, increasing the money supply and accelerating currency depreciation even further, the Republic of Austria was left with no choice but to follow the example of its neighboring states. On February 27, 1919, finance minister Otto Steinwender enacted an Overstamping Directive stipulating that all banknotes in circulation in the Republic of German-Austria that had been issued by the Austro-Hungarian Bank were to be overprinted with "German-Austria" in the period between March 12–19, 1919. However, the public feared that some of the stamped notes would have to be used for mandatory bond purchases, as had occurred in Czechoslovakia. Thus only some of the banknotes in circulation were presented for overstamping, and much of the population's cash was deposited in savings accounts. From March 25, 1919 onward, the stamped banknotes were the only legal tender in Austria.[364] The notes in circulation in Italy were overstamped in April 1919, those in Romania in June and July, and Hungary and Poland followed suit in March and April 1920, respectively. The Treaty of Saint-Germain, which was signed on September 10, 1919, served to sanction the dissolution of the joint currency zone that had already taken place. Liquidation of the Austro-Hungarian Bank was governed by Article 206 of that Treaty.[365] However, since the provisions of Article 206 were virtually impossible to implement, the successor states finally agreed at conferences held in Vienna in February and March of 1922 to directly distribute the bank's assets and liabilities. Austria was ultimately allocated a share of 13.8% in the net assets of the Austro-Hungarian Bank, which translated into approximately 29 million gold crowns.[366]

Hyperinflation and a new currency (1919–1931)

"To the extent that the League provided the technical and moral support to an economic program, this necessarily involved costs for a government in terms of loss of sovereignty and decision-making power."

Juan Flores and Yann Decorzant, Going multilateral

Once the "long 19th century"[367] had drawn to a close as World War I ended in 1918, a new political order emerged in Europe as its map was essentially redrawn by the Paris Peace Treaties. These political changes came on top of fundamental changes in the structure of the European economy and, in fact, of the world economy, that had occurred by the end of World War I. After having become the world's largest economic power in the latter half of the 19th century, the United States of America had since also replaced the United Kingdom as the largest international creditor nation. The creditor-borrower relationships established by war loans and commitments to reparation payments would have a tremendous impact on the course of economic (and political) developments in the period up to World War II.

Hyperinflation and stabilization

The economic consequences of the new political reality of Europe were particularly severe for the Republic of Austria, which rose from the ashes of the Habsburg Empire alongside newly emerging countries that sought to cement their political independence with economic independence. Until 1918, Vienna—then the imperial residence and capital of an empire of 52 million inhabitants—and the Alpine lands, which formed the new Austria after the war, had been part of an integrated economic area that thrived on a strong division of labor. In the Alpine regions of Austria, agriculture was underdeveloped; Austria's production conditions were not as good as those of other parts of the former monarchy; and Austria largely sourced its commodities and energy (coal) from the successor countries, which were at the same time the major markets for its industry. Furthermore, Vienna's major banks had been active in the entire area of the monarchy, the currency area of the crown. And Vienna had been the administrative and commercial center of the Habsburg monarchy—a function that became obsolete with the disintegration of the empire.

In terms of central banking matters, the Austro-Hungarian Bank remained the central bank of the Republic of Austria until the end of 1922. However, from January 1920 on, a separate set of books was maintained for the transactions of

the Austrian entity of the Austro-Hungarian Bank. In the last years of its existence, the central bank essentially played the part of a printing press to finance
the budgetary needs of the country, as it had done during World War I. In doing
so, it contributed to hyperinflation, the runaway inflationary process in 1921.

The last governor of the Austro-Hungarian Bank, Alexander Spitzmüller, did
not see any alternative to turning on the monetary tap during the first post-war
years to finance the federal budget deficit. In a letter from March 1920 to his
Dutch counterpart, Simon Vissering, Spitzmüller stressed that Austria would
not be able to balance the deficit on its own nor finance it with domestic bonds.
"It is out of the question," he wrote, "that we would be able to limit our spending
to our tax receipts without provoking riots, anarchy and social chaos in Austria
and, in consequence, in Central Europe." The governor's assessment of the
seemingly hopeless state of financial and monetary conditions in Austria is also
reflected in a letter addressed to the president of the German Reichsbank,
Rudolf Havenstein, written in April 1920: "Your Excellency may empathize
when I say that it fills me with unspeakable bitterness to be forced to end my
career in money and banking by having to keep using the printing press. And
yet I see no other way out, knowing that even this way may lead to chaos and
monetary anarchy."[368]

The deficit of the Austrian federal budget was growing unrelentingly in the
years after World War I. While tax receipts still offset 84% of monthly spending
in the period from November 1918 to June 1919, budgetary revenues had
dropped to 36% of spending by the second half of 1921.[369] The main budgetary
items were food subsidies, interest on national debt and unemployment benefits and therefore items where cuts were considered out of the question by
the government. Newly issued government bonds helped to broadly offset excess spending in the first budgetary period, but the subsequent budget deficits
were mainly financed with loans from the central bank. When the bank finally
stopped discounting treasury notes on November 18, 1922, the state owed the
Austrian entity of the Austro-Hungarian Bank a total of 2,561 billion crowns.[370]
This hefty sum was equal to 75% of all budgetary deficits accrued since the
founding of the Republic. Turning on the monetary tap had been a practical
necessity because the issuance of bonds would have increased the debt pile

inherited from the monarchy even further, thus exacerbating the debt service requirements that many banking sector representatives and other experts considered too heavy a burden for the young Austrian Republic.[371] Doubts about the viability of Austria were widespread, prompting many banks, enterprises and wealthy individuals to transfer liquid assets abroad. The Innsbruck branch office of the central bank, for example, reported to Vienna that the local banks were violating the regulations regarding the smuggling of crowns: "They openly admit that they cannot afford to comply with the corresponding regulations, because illegal transfers are the only way to generate a sizeable profit."[372] Since the suggestions to service the war debt inherited from the empire by means of a wealth tax could not be implemented, there was no alternative to printing money.[373] At the same time, the state benefited from the growing supply of money, since the ensuing inflation made it possible to pay down the national debt in cheaper crowns because the finance ministry invoked the principle of "a crown is a crown."[374] This de facto expropriation of war bond holders, which led to the impoverishment of the middle class, was one of the factors that contributed to the polarization of Austrian society in the interwar period.

Some figures may illustrate the extent by which monetary financing of the budget deficit stoked inflation: The first weekly financial statements of the Austro-Hungarian Bank after the armistice show a total stock of banknotes of 32.6 billion crowns and short-term liabilities of the central bank of 5.1 billion crowns, i.e., a total of 37.7 billion crowns in circulation. By the end of 1919, the total amount of currency in circulation had increased by some 60% to 60.4 billion crowns. On January 31, 1920, the Austrian entity of the Austro-Hungarian Bank disclosed a total amount of 14.9 billion crowns in circulation. By November 30, 1922, this amount had increased 243-fold, to a total of 3.6 trillion crowns.[375] Between these two dates, prices kept surging, and there was even a period of hyperinflation, from September 1921 to September 1922 (chart 7.1). Going back even further, to the start of World War I, we find the level of prices in Austria to have increased more than 14,000-fold in the period from July 1914 to September 1922.[376] During World War I, foreign exchange restrictions had kept the fall in the external value of the crown to "a mere" ±2% per month. While 1 U.S. dollar cost 4.95 crowns in July 1914, it traded at 83,600 on August 25, 1922–which corresponds to a 16,889-fold increase.[377] Thereafter, the exchange rate of the crown recovered slightly over the following weeks and was finally stabilized at 14,400 times the pre-war rate.

Chart 7.1: Depreciation of the crown during and after the war (July 1914 = 1; logarithmic scale)[378]

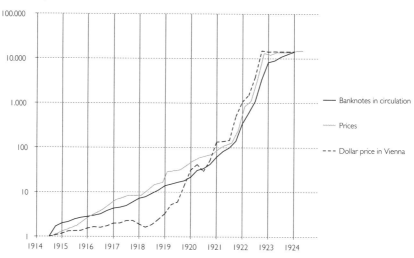

The number of banknotes in circulation rose exponentially during the war. Similar to the inflation of paper money after 1796 (chart 2.1), the cost of living did not increase as quickly as the number of banknotes in circulation until the second inflationary phase occurring in the second half of the war, when it more than made up for the difference. Thanks to strict capital and currency controls, however, the crown did relatively well in retaining its external value. Not until the end of the war did the depreciation process start accelerating. In the period of hyperinflation, domestic inflation (+44% per month) was more closely aligned with the increases in the U.S. dollar exchange rate to the crown (+41%) and lay above the monthly increase in the money supply ("only" +32% due to the higher velocity of circulation).

The League of Nations loan

The depreciation of the crown came to a sudden halt in autumn 1922 when it became known that the League of Nations would guarantee the issuance of international bonds by Austria.[379] Federal Chancellor Seipel, who had taken office in May 1922, had initially appealed to the Supreme Council of the Allied

Powers for financial assistance, but had been referred to the League of Nations instead.[380] After talks in Prague, Berlin and Verona, where Seipel had managed to convince the powers striving for dominance in the Danube region[381] to preserve the status quo in the face of the imminent "collapse of Austria," he appealed to the League of Nations Council on September 6, 1922, to provide fast and effective help for Austria. The Protocols on the financial reconstruction of Austria, which formed the basis for issuing international bonds in the amount of 650 million gold crowns, were signed in Geneva on October 4, 1922.[382]

While the League of Nations had no capital of its own for supporting states in financial difficulties, it organized support from creditor countries and financial institutions and made it possible for countries like Austria to consolidate their public finances by raising funds abroad. The financial assistance of the League of Nations was tied to strict conditions for monetary and financial policy, since it was granted to states that had evidently failed to manage their public finances on their own.[383]

As indicated above, the intervention of the League of Nations was motivated by geostrategic considerations, since it was aimed at maintaining the balance of powers in Central Europe that had been created by the treaties concluded at the Paris Peace Conference. Financial assistance for Austria was designed to restore the economic conditions that had prevailed before World War I, which many considered a "lost ideal." This was also the goal of similar League of Nations interventions in Hungary, Bulgaria, Estonia, Greece and Gdansk. In his book about the leading bankers of the 1920s, Liaquat Ahamed writes: "After the war, there was a universal consensus among bankers that the world must return to the gold standard as quickly as possible. The almost theological belief in gold as the foundation for money was so embedded in their thinking, so much a part of their mental equipment for framing the world, that few could see any other way to organize the international monetary system. Leading that quest were Montagu Norman and Benjamin Strong"[384]–the governor of the Bank of England and the president of the Federal Reserve Bank of New York.

The Geneva Protocols on the financial reconstruction of Austria of October 1922 stipulated the appointment of a commissioner-general and a supervisory commission by the League of Nations to monitor the reform of Austria's public finances ("Protocol II"). "Protocol III" regulated the financial policy measures Austria had committed to implement and required Austria to provide the gross receipts of the tobacco monopoly and customs as collateral for servicing the guaranteed bonds. The protocols stated that the commissioner-general would monitor the appropriate use of the funds from the League of Nations loan and the consolidation of public finances. For the position of commissioner-general, the choice fell on Alfred Zimmermann, a former mayor of Rotterdam with important credentials, in Montagu Norman's opinion: he was an uncompromising opponent of socialism and a supporter of radical Manchester Liberalism, who opposed any form of "social legislation, public welfare spending, capital taxation and trade unions categorically."[385]

The international bonds guaranteed by the League of Nations were issued in June 1923 in eleven tranches in ten different currencies.[386] The net proceeds of 631 million gold crowns were credited to a bond account at the Austrian central bank of which the commissioner-general had sole control. Funds that were not cleared by the commissioner-general for use for fiscal purposes had to be invested with foreign banks or, with those banks acting as intermediaries, in short-term financial instruments of the countries in which bond tranches had been issued. Yet the interest rates on these transactions were unfavorable for Austria as they were 6 to 7 percentage points below the yield of the international bonds at the time of issue.[387] Owing to this large differential, the finance minister and central bank representatives were able to convince the commissioner-general and the advisor of the central bank to agree to investing the remaining funds with Austrian banks for a higher yield. Yet the upshot was that there was in fact little demand for such foreign currency deposits among Viennese banks. As outlined in a letter from the central bank to the finance minister: "This can be explained by the already considerable foreign currency reserves of the domestic banks as well as by the fact that industry and trade plowed back large profits during the periods of economic upturn in foreign currency, which they have not yet fully liquidated in crowns."[388] This argument is in line with the aforementioned reports from branch offices of the central bank stating that banks and companies had transferred large amounts of capital abroad, contributing to the plummeting exchange rate of the crown.

Reestablishment of the Oesterreichische Nationalbank

The adjustment program agreed upon in Geneva also provided for the reestablishment of the Austrian central bank. The legislative act paving the way for the creation of a central bank was adopted in July 1922[389] after Vienna's major banks had agreed to subscribe for 24 millions of the capital stock of 100 million Swiss francs and to guarantee the subscription of an equivalent of 36 million Swiss francs.[390] The Anglo-Austrian Bank and Länderbank, which had been under British and French ownership, respectively, since 1921, retracted their commitment to subscribe when the governor of the Bank of England, Montagu Norman, declared that the creation of a central bank would be ineffectual unless it was accompanied by measures to balance the budget and to issue international bonds with a view to stabilizing the Austrian currency.[391] Moreover, the League of Nations requested amendments to the Nationalbank Act of July 1922, which were adopted by the national parliament in November 1922.[392] December 22, 1922, marked the inaugural general meeting of the Oesterreichische Nationalbank (OeNB),[393] chaired by the Postsparkasse president, and the bank became fully operational on January 1, 1923.[394]

In the words of Article 1 of the Nationalbank Act, "The Oesterreichische Nationalbank is a stock corporation which, within the framework of these statutes, is responsible for regulating the circulation of money in the Republic of Austria, facilitating the settlement of payments and maintaining the flow of credit to the economy. In particular, however, it is tasked with preparing the resumption of gold payments (exchange of banknotes for metal) by acquiring precious metals and stable foreign currency reserves and maintaining gold payments after their legal resumption. It must use all means at its disposal to ensure that the value of its banknotes with respect to the value of currencies of countries with the gold standard or a stable currency at least not depreciate until the exchange of banknotes to gold is legally regulated."

The primary task of the monetary policy of the OeNB was to create the conditions required for a return to the gold standard of the pre-war years. Until the resumption of gold payments, which was to occur when the federal debt with the Oesterreichische Nationalbank had sunk to 30 million gold crowns (= the amount of its equity), 20% of the total amount of money in circulation minus the loan payable by the federal state had to be backed by precious metal reserves[395] for the first five years. In the subsequent five-year periods, the amount of banknotes backed by gold and/or foreign exchange reserves was to be increased to 24%, then 28% and 33.33%. In case of underfunding, the OeNB would have to pay a "banknote tax" for any banknotes in circulation above those ratios. The OeNB's note-issuing privilege in Austria was designed to end on December 31, 1942. The central bank's independence from the state was reflected in regulations that prohibited the recourse to monetary financing by the federal, provincial and municipal authorities and that provided for the election of the General Council members by the General Meeting, in which the Austrian government held a minority position. Only the president of the OeNB was to be appointed by the president of Austria upon recommendation by the federal government.[396]

The first president in the history of the Oesterreichische Nationalbank was Richard Reisch, a former short-time finance minister who was sitting on the board of *Bodencreditanstalt*, a leading Viennese bank.[397] His appointment was controversial, as the League of Nations, and Montagu Norman in particular, had wanted to see a foreigner in this position.[398] Norman even meant to question Britain's participation in the League of Nations loan when he heard of Reisch's appointment.[399] Britain remained on board, however, because Federal Chancellor Seipel informed the League of Nations commissioner-general of the government's intention to "assign a first-rate foreign advisor with special authority to assist" the president of the OeNB.[400] This plan was implemented in spring 1923, when finance minister Viktor Kienböck informed Reisch on March 14, 1923, that he had agreed on an amendment to the OeNB's statutes during loan negotiations in London with banking representatives, determining the appointment and competences of this advisor. Kienböck wrote that "our friends at the League of Nations and in the City," meaning London, "set great store in the prompt resolution of the matter."[401] The amendment to the statutes was passed by the General Council at its next meeting on March 23, 1923, and then by the General Meeting on April 17, 1923. The national parliament subsequently endorsed the respective amendment to the statutes of the Oesterreichische Nationalbank on April 28, 1923.[402] As an agent of the Financial Committee of the

League of Nations and, ultimately, the Bank of England, the advisor had the rank of a co-president of OeNB. His agreement was required for any measures related to central bank policy, be it a motion to change interest rates, to invest reserves of the bank or agreements with the federal state or local authorities. Before making a decision, the advisor regularly consulted the Bank of England and the commissioner-general. Charles Schnyder von Wartensee, vice president of the Swiss National Bank, acted as advisor from June to December 1923. He was followed by Anton von Gijn, a former minister of finance of the Netherlands (May 1924 to January 1926) and Robert Ch. Kay (January 1926 to June 1929), a confidant of Montagu Norman.

Central bank policy under foreign control, 1923–1929

The Oesterreichische Nationalbank began its work on January 1, 1923, under difficult conditions. The bank's foreign exchange reserves, listed as 93 million gold crowns in the first weekly financial statements published on January 7, 1923,[403] sank by 16% from January 4 to January 24. The challenge for the bank was whether it would be able to maintain a stable exchange rate if the depletion of its foreign reserves were to continue. State commissioner Schwarzwald, a high-ranking official in the ministry of finance, insisted on measures to ensure a stable exchange rate out of concern for the country's credit standing. He suspected "strange obstructions by speculating groups" in Zurich and Geneva and called for more restrictive discounting policies "to highlight the scarcity of money, make it harder to plow back profits in foreign currencies, and perhaps encourage businesses to sell their foreign currency holdings."[404] Speculation against the crown let up after a few weeks, in March 1923, when Austria was able to place short-term bonds totaling 3.5 million pounds sterling (78.6 million gold crowns) in six countries to tide the country over until the proceeds of the League of Nations loan became available.[405] From March to December 1923, the supply of foreign currency exceeded demand, causing the foreign exchange reserves to be 86% higher at year-end than at the outset of the year.[406]

Had the crown been devaluated too much?

The acquisition of foreign exchange and increased discounting of trade bills resulted in an enormous increase of the money supply: the amount of bank-notes in circulation and short-term liabilities of the OeNB increased by approximately 74% in 1923, prompting concerns about the stability of the currency, as wholesale prices increased by 12.6% and the cost of living rose by 20% in the same time frame.[407] President Reisch, however, was of the opinion that in a long-term comparison in U.S. dollar terms, the amount of money per capita had increased less in Austria than in other countries and that the high interest rates in Austria showed that there was no undue increase in money supply. Spitzmüller, the last governor of the Austro-Hungarian Bank, had blamed the increase in the money supply on too low an exchange rate of the crown and was in favor of its revaluation.[408] As was to be expected, industry representatives[409] rejected the deflation policy Spitzmüller advocated, but renowned economists like Joseph Schumpeter and Ludwig von Mises also opposed it. Schumpeter[410] cautioned against adjusting the exchange rate, as this could precipitate a crisis of confidence, and Mises rightly argued that a deflation policy would not be able to reverse the redistribution that had occurred during the period of inflation: "Those who will profit from the increase of the value of money are not those who were hit by the depreciation during the inflation, and the ones who will have to bear the costs of this policy are not the same people who profited from the depreciation. Deflationary policies do not reverse the consequences of inflation."[411] The growth of money supply and the increase of the price level in 1923 can indeed be viewed as a reaction to the lower but stable external value of the crown. While the index of the U.S. dollar exchange rate averaged 14,681 in the last quarter of 1922 (July 1914 = 100), the domestic price index (same basis) totaled 9,803, and the volume of banknotes in circulation totaled 6,415.[412] Adjusted for price changes, the real increase in the money supply since before World War I considerably lagged behind the depreciation of the crown because the velocity of circulation had increased drastically during the period of inflation.

With regard to interest rate policy, the OeNB initially maintained a discount rate of 9%, the level at which it had been first set in September 1922. The chief executive director was of the opinion that the interest level was severely exaggerated as a result of speculative frenzy during the period of inflation,[413] putting excessive pressures on borrowers now that the currency had been stabilized. A member of the General Council suggested monitoring the use of central bank credit as he suspected that such funding was being used to finance cross-border investments. The president opposed this, as he considered controlling the use of central bank credits to be irreconcilable with the "private sector-focused structure of the Austrian economy."[414] The governing board, however, instructed all branch offices in an internal circular to report on the use of discount loans wherever possible.[415] The advisor of the OeNB, incidentally, also believed that Austrian banks were funding foreign borrowers, which he considered a "luxury" in light of the lack of capital in the country.[416]

Bull market and speculation against the franc

Interest rates in 1923 were also driven by the bull market at the Vienna Stock Exchange. In December 1922, the stock index for Austrian companies listed on the Vienna Stock Exchange stood at 719 (first half of 1914 = 1),[417] thus substantially trailing the increases in the price index or in the U.S. dollar exchange rate. The net asset value of companies appeared to be considerably higher than their market value, making it profitable to buy stocks. The increase of stock prices by 648% in 1922 and 261% in 1923 resulted in scores of foundations and flotations of enterprises. In 1922, 265 stock corporations were founded and another 236 corporations increased their capital, and the figures were not that different in 1923, which saw 250 new stock corporations founded and 151 instances of capital increases.[418] A total of 475.6 million shares switched hands at the Vienna Stock Exchange in 1923, compared to 7.2 million shares traded in 1913.[419]

A large share of the money being invested in the stock market consisted of repatriated flight capital and of funds of foreign speculators. This also explains the massive influx of foreign currency to OeNB accounts from March 1923 on. But, as the president of the Vienna Merchants' Guild, Cornel Spitzer, pointed out in an OeNB General Council meeting, many merchants preferred to gamble on the stock exchange and to try to make money by granting overnight loans rather than pay their suppliers. This was indeed tempting, as the yearly average interest rate on secured loans in 1923 was approximately 66%.[420] At the same time, the rising level of interest rates led to a decline in investments in real assets. Chief Executive Director Brauneis wrote: "It was becoming increasingly harder to raise affordable funds for legitimate production needs, because investors on the stock exchange stood ready to pay virtually any interest rate, in anticipation of making high capital gains within a matter of days."[421]

The boom at the Vienna Stock Exchange reached its peak in late 1923/early 1924. Foreign investors started withdrawing from the market, which was reflected in an increased demand for foreign exchange.[422] The speculators now began targeting the French franc, which had lost much of its value against the U.S. dollar since the end of the war because of France's high budget deficits.[423] International speculation against the French franc came to a sudden end in March 1924, when J.P. Morgan & Co. granted the French government a loan of 100 million U.S. dollars.[424] In Vienna, too, speculators had bought U.S. dollars forward against francs, taken out franc-denominated loans or ordered French goods on credit. The sharp rise of the franc exchange rate by some 86%[425] from March to April 1924 generated losses estimated at around 10 to 15 million U.S. dollars.[426] The failed speculations brought down a number of small banks and sharply drove up the supply of stocks. A group of banks rapidly set up a support committee with a view to pooling funds for intervention. The OeNB and the finance ministry also contributed to this fund, out of concern that a complete collapse of rates stock prices destabilize the currency.

To prop up prices, the Wiener Giro- und Cassenverein intervened on the stock market on behalf of 12 Viennese banks. With the agreement of the commissioner-general, the OeNB supported the cause with 300 billion crowns of government money. Following repayment of these funds in June 1924, the OeNB granted the support committee a loan of 5 million U.S. dollars (= some 70 million schillings),[427] of which 14 million schillings remained outstanding at the end of 1925. The OeNB credited this amount to a trust company holding the unsold shares of the support committee.[428] While failing to prevent the fall of share prices, this initiative is likely to have attenuated it somewhat. Between January and October 1924, the stock index on the Vienna Stock Exchange sank by 64%.[429]

OeNB policies meet with Bank of England criticism

The end of the period of speculation also marked the beginning of a consolidation process in the Austrian banking sector which would take a decade and cause great losses for the economy. Between January and August 1924, 8 small and medium-sized Viennese banks defaulted, and out of 19 banks established in the other federal provinces, 12 banks had to close.[430] The largest bank to default in 1924 was the Allgemeine Depositenbank, which had been controlled by the "undisputed king of the nouveau riche,"[431] Camillo Castiglioni, since 1918.

To prevent the collapse of further banks, the OeNB pursued a "liberal" refinancing policy which led to an increase in trade bill discounts by approximately 90% from mid-April to early August 1924.[432] These developments called for an increase of the discount rate, but the bank "sought to delay such a step in the interest of easing pressure on production and given the predominant character of our lending as lending of last resort," as stated in the annual report for 1924.[433] At the advisor's suggestion, the OeNB had already introduced a 2% add-on to the discount rate in February 1924 for trade bills submitted for discounting with only two signatures and a term of more than 30 days.[434] Upon urging of "influential members of the international community"–the Bank of England, the Financial Committee of the League of Nations, the commissioner-general appointed by League of Nations–the discount rate was raised to 15% by August 1924 in two steps.[435] The call for a change of the statutes to transfer the competence for interest-rate setting to the governing board because the General Council, in particular the representatives of banks, opposed an increase of interest rates, went unheeded. Instead, the OeNB installed an executive committee as requested by the League of Nations, to be able to speed up decision-making when fast action was required. This executive committee was made up of the president, the two vice presidents, the chief executive director and his deputy.[436]

"Influential members of the international community" also criticized the OeNB's involvement in the support committee that had been set up after the collapse of speculation against the franc.[437] OeNB President Reisch, however, expressly considered it "one of the greater tasks of a modern central bank, particularly in times of crisis" to provide liquidity, as he explained in a talk in Budapest. Indeed, interventions by the central bank were "informed by deeper insight and in the bank's intrinsic interest" because "crises have a tendency to snowball; chances are that they will spill over also to sound institutions, causing major havoc unless countermeasures are taken in a timely manner." A policy of non-intervention, he argued, was fraught with danger. "Given the choice," Reisch said, "of supporting an undeserving individual and thereby securing the livelihoods of thousands of his victims or at least making their lives a bit easier or of condoning the economic downfall of this undeserving individual but also of his victims, the choice must surely fall on the first option."[438]

The bankers in London did not share Reisch's opinion, though. The Bank of England also considered the interest and refinancing policy of the OeNB too lax and inadequate for Austria's economic situation. Consequently, the Austrian government was urged at the meeting of the League of Nations in September 1924 to "demand a discount policy from the central bank that is suited to maintaining the stability of the crown not just in relation to gold but also in relation to goods."[439] President Reisch interpreted this criticism of the Oesterreichische Nationalbank as a vote of no confidence against him personally and offered his resignation to Federal Chancellor Seipel, who refused it.[440] The differences of opinion between the president of the Austrian central bank and Bank of England Governor Norman persisted. They came into the open in December 1924 during a visit of Reisch to the Bank of England. During his three-day stay in London from December 9 to 12, 1924, Reisch failed to convince his contacts at the Bank of England and the British treasury of the adequacy of the OeNB's policy, as he had hoped. He reported on the discussions in a lengthy presentation at a General Council meeting on December 18, 1924, according to which fundamental differences of opinion prevailed on almost every aspect of the debate.[441] Reporting on the talks, the "Times," the mouthpiece of the City of London, wrote that the OeNB had created inflationary conditions in Austria and that Reisch had expressed doubts about the validity of the quantity theory, the theoretical framework on which the monetary reconstruction of Austria had been built. It added a warning: "The Austrian people would be unwise to ignore the consequences that must follow if the policy pursued is not approved in countries where Austria desires to borrow."[442]

The schilling replaces the crown

At the meeting of the League of Nations Council in September 1924, it was indicated that it would be desirable to establish, as soon as possible, a "statutory ratio between the Austrian crown and a fixed gold weight."[443] The state commissioner had already announced at a meeting of the governing board of the OeNB in August 1924 that the finance minister was about to submit a new currency bill to parliament,[444] which was why he opposed the issuing of new 1-million and 10-million crown banknotes. Evenually, the so-called Schilling Conversion Act was passed by parliament on December 20, 1924.[445] It provided for the conversion to a new currency, the schilling, at a rate of 10,000 (paper) crowns to the schilling (1 schilling = 10,000 paper crowns = 0.694 gold crowns; 1 gold crown = 14,400 paper crowns = 1.44 schilling). The fine gold weight of the schilling was fixed at 0.21172086 g, which was approximately 30% less than the weight of the gold crown.

The schilling was introduced in stages. The federal, provincial and municipal administrations had to use the new unit of account no later than June 30, 1925, i.e., one year ahead of the accounting conversion deadline that applied for non-public organizations (July 1, 1926).[446] The OeNB had lobbied in favor of combining the switch to schilling-denominated business accounting with requirements for current cost accounting.[447] The provisions for the revaluation of assets and liabilities were laid down in the Gold Accounting Act of June 4, 1925.[448] This act did not apply to the OeNB, however, as the finance minister had supported the OeNB's view that the special statutory accounting provisions in the bank's charter overrode general law provisions. Hence, the OeNB switched to the schilling as its unit of account on March 1, 1925.

The first weekly financial statements in schilling of March 7, 1925, showed a gold and foreign exchange reserve of 485.5 million schillings. Thereof, repurchase agreements on U.S. dollars and pound sterling transactions accounted for 154 million schillings.[449] Discount loans and secured lending made up 122 million schillings, and advances to the government totaled 214.5 million schillings. The value of banknotes in circulation was 757.1 million schillings, that of the overall money supply 822 million schillings. Under statuory provisions,

20% of banknotes in circulation would have been required to be backed by currency reserves; the actual ratio worked out at 43%, well above the benchmark.

The financial statements of Austrian banks based on gold accounting standards as at January 1, 1925, were published in the second quarter of 1926. A comparison with the 1913 balance sheet illustrates the depletion of assets caused by warfare and inflation–or rather the depletion of capital and total assets that the banks considered tolerable so as not to unsettle their Western European counterparties. In other words, the balance sheets only indicated what they were meant to indicate.[450] The aggregated gold balance sheets of Austria's seven largest banks showed a decline in total assets by 70% and a decline in capital and reserves by over 76% compared to 1913.[451] But even these figures appear to have been based on an overly optimistic valuation of assets. The banks overstated the value of their securities in order to avoid–as the minutes of a Bodencreditanstalt board meeting reveal–disclosing too little equity, which they feared would make a bad impression abroad.[452] As London banks expected a yield of 8% to 10% for their stakes in Austrian banks–a yield that could not be generated as the capital figures had been overstated–the banks' reserves were depleted over the following years to fund dividend payment.[453] This was one of the reasons that brought on the collapse of a number of banks in the decade that followed, developments which would of course have a significant impact on Austrian financial and monetary policy.

Economic developments after the stabilization of the currency

In the post-war inflation years, prices in Austria did not grow as fast as the crown exchange rates against the currencies of low-inflation countries. The ensuing "export bonus" helped boost exports and employment. Industrial production and exports moreover benefited from the reduction in real wages that was achieved through rent control measures and food subsidies. This advantage later disappeared with the stabilization of the exchange rate of the crown. The Ruhr Crisis in Germany in 1923 temporarily generated additional work for the Austrian iron and steel industry,[454] but the reduction of the budget deficit, the low investment activity caused by the high interest rates and the increase in prices decreased real output by 1.1% in 1923.[455] From 1924 to 1929, the real gross national product grew by an annual average of 3.5% to 105% of the volume of 1913. Despite real economic growth, employment figures sank by approximately 200,000 from 1922 to 1929, while the number of unemployed increased to over 280,000. In 1929, before the start of the Great Depression, the unemployment rate stood at 12.2%.[456]

The conditions for the issuing of bonds guaranteed by the League of Nations were aimed at balancing the Austrian budget. While this goal was met, it was essentially met through measures that increased revenue rather than cut spending–as urged by the Financial Committee of the League of Nations–although the dismissal of over 80,000 public officials did reduce public personnel costs. The budgets from 1924 to 1929 generated a cumulative surplus of 87 million schillings. The primary goal of fiscal policy was to balance the budget in order to guarantee monetary stability. Stimulating growth was not on the agenda, in consensus with the prevalent economic opinions at the time.[457]

Less than 50% of the proceeds of the League of Nations loan were used to finance budget deficits. In sum, 73 million schillings were used to reduce the state's debts with the OeNB. Such repayment had been requested by the League of Nations in June 1926 when it partially ceded financial control of Austria, following a study commissioned by the Council of the League of Nations that had shown that Austria was financially stable.[458] In mid-1926, Commissioner-General Zimmermann left Austria. However, Rost van Tonningen, who had worked under him, remained in Vienna until the end of June 1928 to monitor whether the remaining parts of the League loan were being used according to the agreed-upon terms.

The activity of the OeNB advisor was also extended in 1926. The General Council of the OeNB had agreed to a corresponding change of the statutes in October 1925 against its convictions, as ultimately the wishes of the "influential members of the international community" were binding for Austria.[459] In January 1926, Robert Ch. Kay, a confidant of the governor of the Bank of England, was appointed as advisor of the OeNB. The Austrian President Hainisch let him know at his inaugural visit that he had full confidence in the OeNB and that Austria needed no foreign advisor.[460] This surely did nothing to improve the relationship between the OeNB and the Bank of England.[461]

The relationship between the OeNB and the Bank of England remained tense in the following years due to ongoing differences of opinion regarding interest and monetary policy, on the issue of investing foreign exchange reserves and with regard to granting loans to the banks' support committee. The demand of the Bank of England to end foreign exchange control, however, was implemented in two phases, in March 1925 and December 1926.[462] The OeNB withdrew its foreign exchange deposits from Austrian banks in 1925[463] and moved its deposits with London banks to the Bank of England. In return for the OeNB concentrating its foreign exchange investments at the Bank of England, the latter indicated it would provide support loans should monetary conditions in Austria require such intervention.[464]

The risks of high short-term foreign debt

Following an increase to 15% in August 1924 as mentioned above, the OeNB's discount rate still remained at 10% in July 1925. The high interest rates in Austria brought an influx of short-term loans and, as a result of the foreign exchange assets acquired by the OeNB, also increased the central bank money supply. Short-term loans in pounds sterling commanded an interest rate of 8% in Vienna in late 1924/early 1925, compared with some 4% in London.[465] The annual report of the OeNB for 1926 welcomes the large increase of foreign exchange reserves to 76% of the overall central bank money supply, as it "fully guarantees that the economy can provide the necessary foreign currency to repay short-term loans if needed."

"However," the report noted, "a further considerable increase in Austrian short-term external debt is not desirable, as it would lead to too strong a dependence of our domestic economy on the development of money markets abroad and would seriously hinder the OeNB's monetary and lending policies."[466] A survey of the external debt of individual banks initiated by the chief executive director, however, came to nothing: banks were not willing to provide the desired information to the OeNB, and the General Council rejected the proposal of the chief executive director.[467] Yet the short-term external debt of Austria continued to rise until 1930. In 1930, the OeNB estimated the total to be 1.75 billion schillings.[468] At the end of 1930, the OeNB had foreign exchange reserves worth 1,081 million schillings, or 91% of the total money supply.[469] The OeNB's gold and foreign exchange assets grew stronger than the central bank money supply, while the bank's holdings of bills of exchange and its advances to the government were declining.[470]

The concern expressed in the 1926 annual report that an increase in short-term foreign debt could "seriously hinder" the bank's monetary and lending policies proved correct over the following years. The OeNB was faced with increased demand for foreign exchange when interest rates rose abroad or other profitable investment opportunities appeared, or when domestic political tensions prompted international creditors not to renew their portfolios with Austrian banks. For example, the political controversy about a change of the Austrian constitution in autumn 1929, when the conservative parties and their paramilitary "Heimwehr" groups sought to limit the competences of the parliament in favor of expanding the power of an authoritarian presidential regime,[471] worried both Austrian depositors and foreign creditors. The withdrawal of deposits from the Bodencreditanstalt, one of the financial backers of the Heimwehr organizations, spelled the end of this financial institute, Austria's second-largest bank. To prevent its imminent bankruptcy, the Bodencreditanstalt was merged with the Creditanstalt in September 1929 with OeNB support.[472]

Structural problems of the Austrian banking sector

In its 1929 annual report, the OeNB lists some of the most severe mistakes of banking policy that sealed the fate of Bodencreditanstalt. Thus, the bank had neglected "to adapt its business model to the dramatic downsizing of Austria in a timely manner. Instead, it sought to hold onto higher dividends and share prices, maintaining a policy of prestige that was ill suited to the so difficult new conditions. Above all, however, it maintained–on advice of its industrial experts–the hope of being able to preserve its affiliated industries, which were among the largest in Austria, in their previous dimensions. Time and again, it advanced considerable funds as needed, immobilizing itself increasingly, hoping to be able to recoup these funds through industrial debt and equity issues once the situation on the stock market recovered."[473]

This characterization of the business policies of Bodencreditanstalt can, to some extent, also be applied to other Austrian banks. The bank managers had "fundamentally misinterpreted or underestimated"[474] the consequences of the structural changes brought about by the end of the Habsburg empire. The banking sector was far too large for the new Republic of Austria. In 1913, it had accounted for more than two-thirds of the own funds of all banks in the region of Cisleithania, while the economic potential of the Republic was hardly more than a quarter of the Austrian part of the monarchy.[475] The Viennese banks made every effort to retain their pre-war business model, supported by banks elsewhere in Europe, "for whom the Viennese banks continued to be the major players when it came to lending to the Central European market."[476] Foreign banks granted short-term loans, which the Viennese banks often used to maintain and expand their business in other parts of the former empire in the form of longer-term loans. It was not until the latter half of the 1920s that the Austrian banking sector was forced by the ongoing crises to resize itself to adapt to the new domestic conditions. Banks had already started to collapse after the end of speculation against the French franc in spring 1924, when the banks that had been founded for the purpose of participating in this wave of speculation were the first to close. But even well-established banks, like the Allgemeine Depositenbank, which had been founded in 1871, went bankrupt.[477] The OeNB contributed to an effort to save the Depositenbank,[478] but this failed, as did the support efforts for Biedermannbank and Centralbank der deutschen Sparkassen.[479]

The Postsparkasse also had to be refinanced in 1926 after incurring total losses of 319 million schillings (3.1% of the nominal gross national product of 1926) due to mismanagement and business policy mistakes, loss-making transactions with the speculator Sigmund Bosel, and the embroilment of politics and business.[480] Even the Bank of England, the majority shareholder of Anglobank, had to accept that it was difficult to manage a bank profitably in Austria. The Anglo-Austrian Bank, or Anglobank for short, had been founded in 1863 and converted into a British banking institute in 1921 by special legislation. After World War I, it was intended to act as a facilitator between the Western European capital markets and the Austrian economy, but it was not able to achieve its business policy goals. In 1926, Creditanstalt took over the Austrian business of Anglobank, making the former the largest bank in Austria by far.[481]

The merger of Creditanstalt with Bodencreditanstalt in the fall of 1929 expanded this dominant position further. The OeNB supported the merger of Austria's two largest banks in two ways: on the one hand, Creditanstalt was granted a three-year deadline to settle part of the bill of exchange debt of 70 million inherited from Bodencreditanstalt, and on the other hand, the OeNB invested more than 15 million U.S. dollars of its foreign exchange reserves in banks that held deposits with Creditanstalt.[482] The expectation of the OeNB's chief executive director that "the merger brings great profit opportunities for Creditanstalt and it will not regret taking this step"[483] did not materialize. Had the economy developed more favorably, this optimistic expectation might have been fulfilled. However, the Great Depression hit banks with close ties to industry, as was the case with Creditanstalt, particularly hard. Only 20 months after the merger, the losses incurred in the acquisition of Bodencreditanstalt were counted among the main factors that contributed to the collapse of Creditanstalt.

The Creditanstalt crisis, the Great Depression and World War II (1931–1945)

"The gold standard itself was the principal threat to financial stability and economic prosperity between the wars."

Barry Eichengreen, *Golden fetters*, p. 4

When the news about the troubles of Creditanstalt reached the Bank of England on May 11, 1931, as the Austrian government disclosed the bank's massive losses in 1930, Harry Siepmann, a close advisor of Bank of England Governor Montagu Norman, said: "This, I think, is it, and it may well bring down the whole house of cards in which we have been living."[484] The Bank of England was apparently fully aware of the fragility of the international financial system that had emerged after World War I. The wake-up call for larger circles came just a few weeks later, on July 13, 1931, when the Macmillan Report on Britain's banking and financial system was published, shaking public confidence in financial stability with the information that the short-term debts of London's banks amounted to 2 billion U.S. dollars. Even this amount may have been understated, though: the actual figure was likely closer to 3 billion U.S. dollars.[485]

Throughout the 1920s, London's banks had continued to finance foreign governments and businesses as they had before the war, even though the capital outflows had ceased to be offset by surpluses of the current account of the British economy.[486] Already during World War I, the United States had become the largest creditor country in the world. The total debt of war loans granted to England, France etc. amounted to 11.8 billion U.S. dollars. The United States insisted on direct repayment of the inter-Allied war debts rather than accepting reparations owed by Germany to its European World War I opponents in their stead.[487] From 1924 to 1930, Germany paid 10.1 billion reichsmark in reparations and moreover ran up a cumulative foreign deficit (excluding reparations) of 5.1 billion reichsmark. To finance those outlays, Germany relied heavily on foreign loans.[488] Yet when rising U.S. interest rates and the bull market on Wall Street made capital investments abroad less attractive for U.S. creditors in the late 1920s, this source of financing dried up. When capital inflows came to a halt, Germany adopted deflationary economic policies, as the rules of the gold standard implied. This aggravated the crisis in Germany and on the global markets.

In the U.S. industry, declining export turnover had brought on the economic downturn already in summer 1929. This downturn was further aggravated by the Wall Street crash in October 1929. What initially seemed like a periodically occurring cyclical downturn turned into the most severe economic crisis since the onset of industrialization due to the contractionary policy that the U.S. Federal Reserve adopted: by 1933, the U.S. real gross national product was about 30% lower than in 1928, industrial output was down nearly 50%, investments 88%, and exports 70%. In parallel, the U.S. unemployment rate had climbed to 25%.[489] Naturally, a setback of such proportions in a country whose industry accounted for some 46% of all industrial products of the world's 24 largest industrialized countries in 1929 was bound to have catastrophic consequences for the global economy, particularly once the United States switched to a highly protectionist customs policy under the 1930 Smoot-Hawley Tariff Act.[490]

The asymmetric monetary effects that emanated from the gold standard also contributed to transferring and reinforcing economic effects in the 1920s. Gold flows going into the United States and France were sterilized to some extent rather than increasing the money supply and fueling demand in these countries. At the same time, countries with balance of payments deficits, which were experiencing an outflow of gold, were forced to implement more restrictive economic policies. This is why the conferences in Brussels (1920) and Geneva (1922), whose goals included restoring the pre-war monetary system, ultimately reconstructed but the façade of the gold standard, to put it in the words of economic historian Barry Eichengreen.[491]

The Creditanstalt crisis

The global economy had entered its second year of downturn when Austria's largest bank announced in May 1931 that it had made a loss of 140 million schillings in 1930.[492] The Creditanstalt, founded in 1855 by the Rothschild family and wealthy aristocrats, was among the finest banks in Central Europe and had excellent ties with the Western European banking community–not least because Louis Rothschild was the president of its board. Its board included prestigious banking experts: Otto Niemeyer (Bank of England) and Henry Strakosch (Union Corporation, London), members of the Financial Committee of the League of Nations, Peter Bark (Anglo-International Bank, London), Max Warburg (Bankhaus Warburg, Hamburg) and Eugène Schneider-Creuzot (Paris).[493] Apparently, neither the board of the bank nor its management were aware of how bad the bank's finances actually were until spring 1931. Yet if the news of the losses of the Creditanstalt escalated the financial crisis, as has often been argued,[494] it did so because of the surprise factor rather than the amount of debt that the bank had incurred abroad. The Creditanstalt crisis was the trigger, not the cause, of the ensuing financial turmoil. In 1931, the Creditanstalt had 76 million U.S. dollars in foreign loans,[495] which was approximately 0.5% of the total short-term cross-border liabilities of European and U.S. banks and enterprises as estimated by the BIS.[496]

The OeNB was involved in the negotiations for the bail-out package made public on May 11, 1931. It contributed 12.4 million schillings to help cover the losses and subscribed for new (preferential) shares worth 17.6 million schillings. Its share in the capital increase of 177.5 million schillings was 9.9%, compared with a share of 33% taken up by the state, whereas the share of Rothschild diminished to 7.4%.[497] Although the disclosed losses equaled 85% of the bank's equity, the existing share capital was reduced by only 25%. Finance minister Otto Juch's argument for sparing the existing stockholders in this way was that a further reduction of the share capital would have created the impression that the Creditanstalt had collapsed! In addition, further cuts would have brought the bank under majority public ownership, which would have shaken the confidence of the foreign patrons of the bank.[498]

As the president of the OeNB told Governor Norman, he was convinced that the bail-out program had eliminated all losses and that the recapitalization had stabilized the Creditanstalt.[499] However, before long, rumors were circulating which spread the claim that the bank's losses were considerably higher than had been made public, causing a run on the Creditanstalt. The funds withdrawn from Creditanstalt accounts were exchanged to foreign currency, hoarded[500] or deposited at other banks. In order to be able to make payments in schilling and foreign currencies, the Creditanstalt turned to the OeNB to discount bills with a total value of over 400 million schillings in May 1931. By the end of May, its liabilities with the central bank had grown to 471 million schillings, which corresponded to 78.2% of the aggregate bill portfolio of the OeNB.[501] Consequently, the money supply at the end of May 1931 was more than 25% higher than it had been at the beginning of the month.[502]

Foreign creditors withdrew some 120 million schillings from the Creditanstalt in the first two weeks after the loss of the bank had been made public.[503] Negotiations with the "Austrian Credit Anstalt International Committee" in London about a moratorium began immediately after May 11. But only after the national parliament and government had, following pressure from abroad, decided to issue a state guarantee for deposits placed with the Creditanstalt, did the committee of foreign creditors agree on June 16, 1931, to leave its remaining deposits of 71 million U.S. dollars at the bank for another two years.[504]

Mirroring the assessment of the Austrian government and of foreign stockholders and creditors, the prevailing opinion of the OeNB was that Austria's largest bank must not be allowed to fail. Chief Executive Director Brauneis argued that the bankruptcy of the bank, which had ties to over 60% of the Austrian industry, would cause an "incalculable catastrophe" for Austria, not least because of the high deposits other Austrian banks had at the Creditanstalt and its many international credit relationships.[505] The OeNB and the Austrian government hoped to receive support from the Bank of England in saving the Creditanstalt, but the Bank of England advised the Austrian authorities to turn to the BIS, because coordinating joint efforts of central banks was one of the reasons for which the BIS had been created in 1930.[506]

From banking crisis to monetary crisis

The consequences of the rising volume of bills submitted for discounting by the Creditanstalt were a fixture on the OeNB's policy-making agenda from mid-May 1931 onwards and caused deep-rooted disagreements about how to proceed. On May 23, 1931, the OeNB stood ready to halt the further discounting of Creditanstalt bills and hoped to convince the government to set a moratorium so as not to jeopardize the currency, as is evident from the draft of a letter to the ministry of finance, which was never sent in the end. The government strictly opposed declaring a moratorium, though, because of pressure from abroad and put its hope on mastering the critical situation with the support of "considerable foreign loans."[507] Yet three days later the government adopted a moratorium nonetheless, which was due to take effect on May 27, because the OeNB would only continue financing the Creditanstalt with government backing. In a further turn of events, this decision was reversed upon urgent request of the BIS,[508] and the discounting of Creditanstalt bills was resumed on May 29, this time with a government guarantee.[509] The next day, the OeNB received a loan of 100 million schillings that had been arranged by the BIS.[510] Along with this loan, a BIS representative–Gijsbert Bruins–was sent to the OeNB.[511] To quote economic historian Kindleberger, "The niggardliness of the sum and the delay together proved disastrous."[512] Evidently, the minor support that the OeNB received from fellow central banks also reflected the precarious situation in which many central banks were finding themselves in the spring of 1931.

In the meantime, the OeNB's portfolio of discounted trade bills continued to grow. In an effort to reduce the volume of discounting requests, the bank increased its discount rate in June 1931 in two steps, from 5% to 7.5%.[513] Because its foreign exchange holdings had already dwindled to a critical level, the OeNB once again urged the finance minister to issue an immediate moratorium in a letter dated June 13.[514] Again, the minister of finance denied the request with reference to the firm opposition of foreign interests. A motion by OeNB Vice President Thaa to restrict discount operations did not receive the support of President Reisch because he was of the opinion that such a move would "cripple the economy and drive it to the brink of ruin."[515] When Thaa resigned in reaction to this, the General Council decided to limit further loans to the Creditanstalt to 30 million schillings, only to reverse this decision a few days later. The reasons for this reversal, as invoked by Reisch, were the formation of a new government and a slowdown of the flight from the schilling. Chief Executive Director Brauneis, meanwhile, was not willing to support this turnaround in the policy of the central bank. While not formally resigning so as not to alarm the general public, he vacated his position for several months "for health reasons."[516]

Foreign exchange control, OeNB under new management

The financial assistance from the Bank of England, the agreement with the foreign creditors and the end of the government crisis had a temporary reassuring effect on the Austrian savers. However, when Germany declared July 14 and 15, 1931, bank holidays in reaction to the banking crisis and introduced foreign exchange control, withdrawals from Austrian banks, in particular from savings banks, increased rapidly. In response, the OeNB's executive committee increased the discount rate to 10% on July 22, but judging from the ongoing drain of foreign exchange reserves, this measure was ineffective in halting the flight from the schilling. On October 9, 1931, Austria finally introduced foreign exchange control measures, too.[517] The OeNB had, in effect, already been most restrictive in releasing foreign currency ever since the Bank of England had abandoned the gold standard on September 20, 1931.[518]

Between April 30 and October 7, 1931, the OeNB's foreign exchange reserves had dwindled by the equivalent of 848 million schillings. Put differently, only the equivalent of 204 million schillings remained at its disposal by October 7, 1931, including the short-term advances of 100 million schillings that the Bank of England had made to the Austrian government, which might, however, be called in at any moment.[519] With the decision to make foreign exchange transactions subject to control by the OeNB and to de facto remove the prevailing currency peg to gold, Austria joined the ranks of countries that had been pushed to similar measures since mid-July 1931: Germany, Hungary, the United Kingdom, Norway, Sweden, Greece, Denmark, Italy, Czechoslovakia, Finland, Yugoslavia, and Latvia.

Controlling foreign exchange transactions was ineffective in preventing the flight from the schilling, though, as a black market for foreign currency was quick to emerge. In the public opinion, foreign exchange control was considered "unnecessary and immoral" and the prevailing sentiment was that "nobody can be expected to adhere to such regulations,"[520] as Chief Executive Director Brauneis, who had since returned to his post, reported to the General Council. The rate of the schilling on the black market was considerably lower than the official rate; by the second week in November 1931, this discount had risen to over 34%.[521]

Policy makers did not, in actual fact, truly consider reinstating the gold parity of the schilling. A return to gold parity would have meant a steep appreciation of the schilling, as many countries had already abandoned their gold peg. It would have also required the OeNB to drastically restrict the volume of its refinancing operations, which was out of the question if the liquidity of the Creditanstalt was to be preserved. As a result, the discount portfolio of the OeNB continued to grow, rising to 1,051 million schillings by the end of 1931. This was an increase by 982 million schillings from the onset of the Creditanstalt crisis on May 7. The OeNB's receivables from the Creditanstalt under discount operations amounted to 679 million schillings at the end of 1931 (65% of the OeNB's total discount portfolio). The total money supply at the end of 1931 was 1,311 million schillings, almost 12% more than at the end of 1930.[522]

Throughout November and December 1931, the General Council and the executive committee of the OeNB repeatedly debated whether to keep up lending to the Creditanstalt, without being able to agree on a decision.[523] In a meeting with the finance minister, the representative of the Financial Committee of the League of Nations, Rost van Tonningen, who had been observing the developments in Vienna since August 1931, although not officially appointed until November 6, 1931,[524] was adamant that the central bank would need to put an end to funding the Creditanstalt. He believed that suspending central bank funding was the only measure that would force the government to finally begin restructuring the bank.[525] On January 25, 1932, a majority of the General Council against the vote of the president of the OeNB finally passed the decision to stop discounting Creditanstalt bills unless the management of the Creditanstalt was replaced within two weeks. President Reisch offered the Federal Chancellor his resignation on February 2, 1932, which was accepted on February 5.[526]

The Austrian president appointed Viktor Kienböck as successor. Kienböck was a Member of Parliament for the conservative party and had twice served as finance minister, from 1922 to 1924 and from 1926 to 1929. In a meeting of the General Council on February 9, 1932, Kienböck stressed that he would seek to foster close cooperation with the government, as indeed mandated by the OeNB's role as a "public institution." While opposing bilateral clearing agreements and any reduction of the discount rate, he was in favor of retaining foreign exchange control.[527] Thus was the scene set for the following years. Beyond these fundamental issues of central bank policy, the number-one item on the agenda of OeNB policy makers would be the reorganization of the Austrian banking sector, particularly the Creditanstalt.

Transfer moratorium, Lausanne loan and devaluation of the schilling

The most urgent problem facing the OeNB when Kienböck took office was the hemorrhaging of foreign reserves, which had dwindled to such levels that it was impossible to keep servicing the foreign debt. For the whole of 1932, the Austrian authorities would require 240 million schillings to be able to meet interest and loan repayment obligations. In sum, requirements for cross-border transfers were estimated to total 280 million schillings[528]–when the equivalent of 144 million schillings in foreign exchange reserves were at the OeNB's disposal by the end of 1931.[529] Already on February 4, 1932, Vice President Thaa had argued in favor of urging the government to take swift action to introduce a transfer moratorium.[530] A moratorium was of the essence for the OeNB also for another reason: cash in circulation and currency reserves had sunk below the legally required minimum coverage ratio of 24% of banknotes in circulation, requiring the OeNB to pay the statutory banknote tax.[531] In agreement with the government, the OeNB stopped providing foreign exchange assets for debt servicing on outstanding cross-border loans on June 23, 1932.[532] The reasons for this step were outlined in a federal government note to the League of Nations.[533] As long as the exchange embargo was in place, Austrian debtors would have to pay their debt servicing fees as they became due into a "foreign debt fund" maintained by the OeNB in schillings at the exchange rates set by the OeNB. While these payments did not discharge the debtor, no Austrian court would be able to sentence debtors to further payments for the duration of the transfer moratorium.[534] After foreign exchange control was lifted, the funds accumulated in the foreign debt fund were transferred to the respective foreign creditors by mid-1935.

In August 1931, the Austrian government had requested the League of Nations to examine the economic and financial situation of Austria and to recommend suitable measures for overcoming the crisis. On September 21, 1931, following a report drafted by League of Nations experts Avenol and Loveday,[535] Chancellor Karl Buresch agreed to a set of measures as a precondition for issuance of bonds guaranteed by the League of Nations: balancing the budget, cutting spending, reducing short-term debts, reducing bank costs, legal regulations for banks, appointment of an advisor to the OeNB, abolition of foreign exchange control, harmonization of the exchange rate and settlement of the foreign debts of the Creditanstalt.[536] The budget consolidation program promised by Chancellor Buresch, which included drastic cuts to personnel and material costs as well as tax increases, was passed by the Austrian parliament on October 3, 1931.[537] The "Lausanne Protocol" of July 15, 1932, established the conditions for bond issuance. The internationally guaranteed "Lausanne bonds" were issued by the Austrian government in the second half of 1933 with a maturity of 20 years. The net proceeds of 309 million schillings were mainly used to settle short-term debts of the state and the state railways, with 8.5 million schillings being used to repay the state's debt with the OeNB.[538] Neither the League of Nations nor the Austrian policy makers considered using the proceeds from the loan to stimulate the Austrian economy.

The return to a single, uniform exchange rate on the external and domestic markets was gradually achieved through a generalization of "private clearing." The OeNB initially allowed individual exporters to sell their foreign exchange proceeds to importers for more than the official exchange rate. Later, "sector clearing" was permitted,[539] and by May 1933, nearly the entire foreign exchange transactions in external trade operations were settled at free exchange rates. Under the Gold Clause Ordinance[540] adopted by the federal government on March 23, 1933, all liabilities in gold or foreign exchange had to be settled at the intrinsic value prevailing at the contract date. In other words, the government had acknowledged the fact that the schilling had been devalued.

Restructuring of banks

In the Lausanne Protocol, the Austrian government had committed itself to quickly finding a solution for the debts of Creditanstalt with the OeNB and foreign creditors. The Creditanstalt owed the OeNB approximately 700 million schillings for trade bills, 571 million of which the state assumed as primary debtor as of July 1, 1932.[541] The interest rate agreement on OeNB advances to the state, which now amounted to 663 million schillings, took into consideration the "financial capability of the Federal Republic." This resulted in a considerable reduction in the revenue of the OeNB, as a part of the federal debt was interest-free and another part was remunerated at a rate of 3%, well below the discount rate. The OeNB therefore had to cut personnel and material costs considerably. The salary of the chief executive director was cut by 20%, those of the governing board members and their deputies by 14%, and the wages of regular employees by 8.5%.[542]

Having paid off its debts to foreign creditors and following other balance sheet adjustments,[543] the Creditanstalt's total assets, as disclosed in July 1933, had shrunk to 635 million schillings, i.e., to one-third of the 1930 level. The valuation adjustments and operating losses for 1931 and 1932 totaled 987 million schillings, which corresponded to over 51% of public spending in 1931.[544] In hindsight, the adjustments made to the balance sheet of Creditanstalt were apparently overly conservative, given the recognition of assets at their liquidation value. In the following years, the bank was very solvent, cautious in its credit policy and needed no more refinancing aid from the OeNB. Moreover, the response to interest policy measures adopted by the OeNB was very limited in the following years, as the Creditanstalt had gained a near-monopoly position in Austria after its 1934 merger with the Wiener Bankverein.[545]

Concentration of the banking sector

Apart from the Creditanstalt, other Viennese banks had run into trouble as well, including the Niederösterreichische Escomptegesellschaft and the Wiener Bankverein. The Wiener Bankverein, which had been founded in 1869 by the Bodencreditanstalt and had been controlled by a German-Belgian group of banks since the 1920s, was one of the largest banks in Vienna. In its financial statements for 1932, it made year-end loan loss provisions amounting of 45.7 million schillings, which turned out to be insufficient. Having analyzed the situation of the Bankverein and another large Viennese bank, the Escomptegesellschaft, the OeNB concluded in October 1932 that their own funds were not nearly sufficient to make the necessary write-offs. The president of the OeNB duly informed the Ministerial Council but saw no way of intervening "while conditions were not under control at the Creditanstalt, ... because our immediate priority was to save Creditanstalt, for fear of risking knock-on effects."[546]

When President Kienböck considered the bankruptcy of the Escomptege-sellschaft to be unavoidable based on end-March 1933 figures, the outcome of a three-day session of the Ministerial Council from March 18 to 20 was to adopt a bail-out plan for these banks in order to "avert the national disaster that would result from a bankruptcy."[547] The OeNB-owned auditing and trust company "Gesellschaft für Revision und treuhändige Verwaltung" was capitalized with 140 million schillings with a view to acquiring hard to realize assets from Bankverein and Escomptegesellschaft and with a view to injecting new capital. The OeNB contributed 40 million schillings[548] from its pensions reserve fund.

Via the auditing company, the OeNB now owned the majority of both banks, and the auditing company itself had become the resolution authority or bad bank for "frozen" balance sheet items of Bankverein and Escomptegesellschaft. Despite cutting personnel costs,[549] neither bank was in a position to balance its accounts for the following fiscal year 1933 without outside help.[550] Yet as the reserves of the OeNB had been nearly exhausted and as the federal budget was in dire straits itself, neither the central bank nor the state had the necessary means to capitalize a new bank that would have integrated the viable parts of Bankverein and the Escomptegesellschaft. Thus, the only feasible option with a view to solving the banking crisis was to go for a merger with Creditanstalt.[551] OeNB President Kienböck and Adrianus van Hengel, the Director General of Creditanstalt, agreed on a number of measures that would be the last act in the concentration of the Austrian banking sector in the interwar period: The OeNB would support the merger of Creditanstalt and Bankverein by transferring shares at no cost and by canceling bills submitted by the Bankverein for discounting, and it would subscribe for new shares of the merged institute (Öster-reichische Creditanstalt-Wiener Bankverein, CA-BV) in the amount of 25 million schillings. The CA-BV would assume the equivalent of 70 million schillings in deposits and liquid assets of the Escomptegesellschaft. The Escomptegesellschaft would be renamed "Österreichische Industrie-Aktiengesellschaft" and henceforth serve as a holding company; its assets would be adjusted and it would be recapitalized (9.9 million schillings), with the OeNB serving as the sole shareholder.[552] The CA-BV was now under majority public ownership: the Federal Republic held 71 millions of the 167 million schillings share capital, the OeNB 25 millions. In the words of the economics journal *Der Österreichische Volkswirt*, a "mammoth bank" had been created, which had the power to decide "which enterprises would exist, merge or be liquidated in Austria."[553] The restructuring of the Austrian banking sector had cost the Federal Republic and the OeNB approximately 1.1 billion schillings, which corresponded to about 11.6% of the average nominal GNP for the years 1931 to 1934. The use of public funds had been considered necessary by the government and the central bank in order to avert the dramatic consequences of the collapse of a bank that was deemed too big to fail.

Stable exchange rate, stagnating economy

After these crises, the business model of the CA-BV, now the largest Austrian bank by far, was primarily aimed at steering clear of risks. The bank's volume of loans outstanding sank by 25% between 1934 and 1937, which the bank explained with the "creditunworthiness" of potential clients.[554] In its annual report for 1936, the bank, in a complete reversal of the business policy it had pursued since its founding in 1855, described itself as a merchant bank that did not see its mission in immobilizing itself with long-term investment loans. Much rather, it was committed to supporting trade, industry and business first and foremost with self-liquidating loans, i.e., with loans that would be repaid through the underlying business operations, through consolidation into long-term loans or through the company's own equity.[555] With deposits by customers rising again after 1934,[556] the solvency of the banking system increased step by step, gradually reducing the need to take recourse to central bank refinancing. The number of bills discounted at the OeNB in 1937 was 92.5% lower than in 1929. In terms of volume, the reduction was not as marked (−52%), but approximately 90% of the entire bill volume were financial bills from the OeNB-owned Industriekredit AG.[557] The gradual reduction of the discount rate from 8% at the beginning of Kienböck's OeNB presidency to 3.5% on July 10, 1935, did not stimulate the lending of Austrian banks, as interest rates in 1933 were over 13% even for prime debtors, against the backdrop of a general decline in prices.[558]

A balanced budget as the ne plus ultra

The Austrian government and the OeNB agreed with the representative of the Financial Committee of the League of Nations and the OeNB advisor that balancing the budget and maintaining the stability of the currency should be the priorities of economic policy. As Bachinger and Matis note, "there were hardly any supporters of an expansionary policy."[559] Stephan Koren, president of the OeNB from 1978 to 1988, writes about the years after 1933: "In addition to an overly cautious, ultraconservative economic policy, the main reason for the slow and hesitant development in the few remaining years until the occupation of Austria, which lagged behind that of other countries, was likely the difficult political situation both in Austria and internationally."[560] Between 1932 and 1937, a mere 365 million schillings were spent for investment out of the federal budget, less than 3% of total federal spending or just under 0.7% of the nominal gross national product.[561]

The primacy of currency stability is also reflected in the 1936 decision of the government and the OeNB to maintain the exchange rate of the schilling when the countries of the "gold bloc"–France, Belgium, the Netherlands, Switzerland, Italy and Poland, which had stuck to the gold standard until that year–devalued their currencies by 14% to 33%. In a joint communiqué, the Austrian government and the Oesterreichische Nationalbank explained that the efforts to keep the currency stable were meant to keep a lid on prices. As Chief Executive Director Brauneis argued in a meeting of the General Council, price increases were bound to trigger wage increases, "creating conditions which would have been highly detrimental for Austria economically or politically."[562] The Federal Republic provided a total of 10 million schillings in financial aid for exporters who found themselves in dire straits due to the de facto appreciation of the schilling.[563] This was approximately the amount by which the appreciation decreased the debt servicing burden for Austria's foreign debt.[564] The high foreign currency debt of Austria was yet another key argument for keeping the exchange rate stable, in addition to the fear of price increases caused by depreciation. The total external debts in 1932 were estimated at 4.7 billion schillings, or approximately 50% of GNP, those of the public sector at 2.3 billion schillings (24% of GNP).

The conversion of bonds, particularly of bonds issued with the help of League of Nations guarantees, to which the League's supervisory committee agreed in September 1934, also eased the burden on the balance of payments. The average nominal interest rate of 4.7% of the guaranteed Austrian converted bonds with a maturity from 1934 to 1959 was considerably lower than that of the "Geneva bonds" (6.3%) and the issuing prices of the individual tranches were generally higher than for the League of Nations bonds.[565] The representative of the League of Nations estimated in his report to the League's Financial Committee of December 1934 that the conversion would save Austria 60 million in the first three years and 45 million each following year.[566]

A lower foreign debt servicing burden, the repatriation of money invested in safe havens and the narrowing deficit in the current account–according to estimates of the Austrian Institute of Economic Research, 1937 was the first year in the interwar period to see a current account surplus (35 million schillings[567])– increased the OeNB's foreign exchange holdings considerably. At the end of 1932, it had had the equivalent of a mere 90 million schillings at its disposal. By the end of 1937, these foreign exchange reserves had risen to 445 millions, an increase of 355 million schillings.[568] Between 1932 and 1937, buying gold and foreign exchange was the only source of money creation for the central bank. The volume of banknotes in circulation in 1937 totaled 944 million schillings, which was an increase by 30 millions over 1932. Over the same period, the OeNB's short-term liabilities increased by 34 million schillings, whereas its bill portfolio decreased by 191 millions to 188 million schilings, its receivables from secured loans dropped by 24 million schillings (1937: 0.7 million schillings) and its receivables from the treasury shrank by 51 millions to 612 million schillings.[569]

In the final years of the First Austrian Republic, the country had a stable currency and its central bank had comparatively high amounts of foreign exchange reserves, but a large part of Austria's productive resources lay untapped. The real gross national product in 1937 was 9% lower than before World War I,[570] the unemployment rate was 22%, the number of gainfully employed people was 355,000 lower than in 1929.[571] The underutilization of productive capacity and the OeNB's considerable gold and foreign exchange reserves were a big asset for fascist Germany, which significantly stepped up political pressure on Austria in the mid-1930s, and a welcome reinforcement of its military strength, to quote a report on the military-economic situation dated March 15, 1938.[572] Germany's economy had been operating without any slack since 1936 because of the rearmament efforts, and unemployment had been eliminated, as the National Socialist propaganda kept emphasizing time and again. Many Austrians believed the propaganda that the policy of the National Socialists would bring jobs and wealth and did not see or did not want to see that the course of the "Third Reich" policies was set for war.

Liquidation of the OeNB, the reichsmark replaces the schilling

In early 1938, German government agencies were seeking to create a monetary union between National Socialist Germany and Austria. The Oesterreichische Nationalbank would maintain a fixed schilling exchange rate to the reichsmark under the influence of the German Reichsbank, and German foreign exchange provisions would be rolled out to Austria. The economic integration of Austria with Germany was part of Hitler's "evolutionary strategy": he was convinced that Austria would "fall into Germany's lap like a ripe fruit before too long if the Berchtesgaden agreement[573] was implemented."[574]

A few days after the annexation of Austria, on March 17, the German Reichsbank was commissioned to liquidate the OeNB. Henceforth, the OeNB's governing board would act on behalf of the Reichsbank, which replaced the OeNB as the new monetary authority. The employees were transferred into the employ of the Reichsbank. As outlined by historians Rathkolb and Venus, 26 of the around 800 employees were immediately dismissed for political or "racial" reasons, and 54 were sent into retirement or demoted.[575] The reichsmark became legal tender in Austria alongside the schilling. The German Monetary and Banking Act entered into force in Austria on April 23, 1938, and OeNB banknotes lost their status as legal tender within a matter of two days.[576]

The conversion rate was set at 1.5 schillings to 1 reichsmark, representing an increase of over 30% beyond the official exchange rate in Berlin, which was fixed for the rather small part of reichsmark holdings that were not limited by foreign exchange control. Given the extensive range of foreign exchange control in Germany, it is not possible to determine a "true" exchange rate that would adequately reflect the prevailing economic conditions. However, judging from the development of prices in the months following the Anschluss, an exchange rate of 1.5:1 amounted to an appreciation of the schilling.[577]

The German Reichsbank, which had argued in favor of an exchange rate of 2:1, seized the OeNB's gold reserves (approximately 78 tons) and its foreign exchange reserves (worth approximately 538 million schillings)–which was a considerable amount compared to its own foreign exchange reserves, which had totaled 77 million reichsmark at the end of 1937. Moreover, private individuals were forced to sell any gold and foreign assets they owned (estimated at 1,200 million schillings)[578] and Austria's balances from bilateral clearing agreements yielded another 94 million schillings.[579]

Beyond Austria's gold and foreign exchange reserves, Austria's workforce and material resources were also a great asset for the ongoing rearmament policy of the National Socialist regime. Food, strategic commodities and semi-manufactured goods were especially sought after. In 1938, the volume of Austrian exports to Germany tripled from the previous year. Production in Austria grew noticeably due to investments in road construction, hydroelectric plants, the mining industry, oil extraction and iron production. Private consumer demand also picked up in 1938, because the long-term unemployed received unemployment benefits again and because the payroll increased by nearly 400,000 people, a 23% increase from the previous year. The growth of Austria's real GNP (excluding agriculture) in 1938 is estimated at approximately 15%.[580]

Despite the massive growth of production after the Anschluss, the general price level actually went down in 1938. Wholesale prices and the cost of living were 2.3% to 2.5% lower in December 1938 than at the end of 1937. The appreciation of the schilling, the adoption of the German price regulation system and the introduction of the lower German rates for railways, postal services and turnover tax contributed to the drop.[581] The continued strong increase of the real GNP by some 16% in 1939 increased the official cost of living index only marginally because of the price and wage freeze and the wartime economic steering measures from fall 1939 onwards.

The Reichsbank's policy during the war

Under the National Socialist regime, the German Reichsbank did not put its monetary policy toolbox to the use of reducing or eliminating the discrepancies between economic supply and potential demand. Monetary policy served the Nazi regime as a tool for quietly financing Germany's rearmament effort and war costs: In its administrative report for 1936, the Reichsbank indicated the "military readiness" of the German Reich as its primary economic policy goal, and Reichsbank President Hjalmar Schacht "saw the role of the Reichsbank as purely political."[582] This also becomes evident in Schacht's functions: He served as president of the Reichsbank from March 1933 to January 1939. At the same time, he was minister for economics from August 1934 to November 1937 and general plenipotentiary for the war economy from May 1935 to November 1937.[583] The German Reichsbank itself had been demoted to a public authority that was under direct control of the government through a number of legislative changes once the National Socialists had come to power. This development culminated in the German Reichsbank Law of June 1939, which provided that the German Reichsbank would be "directed and administered ... in accordance with instructions from the Führer and Chancellor of the Reich and under his supervision."[584] When Reichsbank President Schacht and the members of the Board of Directors wrote to Hitler in early January 1939 warning him of the danger of inflation resulting particularly from the "unrestrained public spending," all signatories of the letter were promptly dismissed.[585] Under Schacht's successor as president of the Reichsbank, Walther Funk, who also served as economic minister at the same time, the Reichsbank lost more of its relevance, becoming "a kind of 'cash office' of the government with no autonomy whatsoever."[586]

The Reichsbank's main function under the National Socialist regime was to ensure the unobstructed financing of rearmament and war costs of the Third Reich. In 1938/39, armament costs already amounted to a quarter of the gross social product (GSP), and they increased to 70% of the GSP by 1943/44. Only a third of the total expenditure of the Third Reich from 1939 to 1945 was covered by regular domestic revenue. 12% was met with contributions requested from the occupied territories and 55% was financed through domestic debt. Unlike the efforts to finance World War I, no war bonds were issued, as the obligation to subscribe for bonds was considered psychologically disruptive. "Instead," a study on monetary policy during the National Socialist regime finds, "they attempted to absorb the increasing liquidity in the banking system caused by the ongoing public spending by using the Reichsbank as an intermediary who provided suitable securities. The banks were more or less forced to invest in these securities."[587] When confidence in the reichsmark began to wane in 1943 and people started hoarding their savings at home or spending them on the black market rather than depositing them with banks and savings banks at previous levels, the direct financing of the budget by the Reichsbank snowballed. The final monthly financial statements published by the Reichsbank, referring to February 1945, showed that 98% of all bills of exchange listed under discount transactions were treasury bills and bonds. The amount of cash in circulation increased greatly in the final phase of the war. At the end of the war, it is estimated to have been 73 billion reichsmark, or seven times as much as in December 1938. Together with the deposits at banks and savings banks, the liquid funds of the Third Reich were 300 billion reichsmark when it collapsed. The real national income in 1946 is estimated at 50 billion reichsmark, or approximately 50% of the 1936 level.[588] It is clear that this imbalance between money supply and goods was bound to lead to inflation and hyperinflation if no serious measures were introduced to skim off surplus money.

The Reichsbank in the "Ostmark"

The organizational units of the Reichsbank in Austria had no monetary policy competences. According to a list from 1941, the Reichsbank operated the following offices in Austria, some of which were also responsible for offices outside the territory of present-day Austria: the Vienna Reichsbank head office with local branch offices in Eisenstadt and Znojmo, the regional branch office Graz with local branch offices in Celje, Klagenfurt, Kranj and Maribor as well as regional Reichsbank branch offices in Linz, Salzburg and Innsbruck (with the latter managing a local office in Bregenz).[589]

The vast majority of Reichsbank business was conducted in Berlin. The Vienna Reichsbank head office gained in importance over the years, likely due to its business ties to Eastern and Southeastern Europe, and had the highest turnover of all Reichsbank head offices in 1943 (table 8.1). The other Reichsbank branch offices in Austria, on the other hand, only had a relatively small turnover.

Table 8.1: **Turnover[I) of the German Reichsbank[590]

1940	Current account balances	Bills of exchange[II)]	Foreign exchange[III)]	Secured lending	Total
	in millions of reichsmark				
Berlin	1 108 422	142 066	4 541	622	1 255 651
Branch offices	561 707	2 536	1 272	3 196	568 711
Vienna	*29 451*	*37*	*73*	*5*	*29 566*
Graz, Linz, Salzburg, Innsbruck	*4 941*	*12*	*5*	*96*	*5 054*
Hamburg	*33 171*	*105*	*178*	*48*	*33 502*
Munich	*23 383*	*142*	*8*	*70*	*23 603*
1943					
Berlin	2 723 506	369 975	3 466	979	3 097 926
Branch offices	851 262	13 113	908	6 021	871 304
Vienna	*49 770*	*1 146*	*55*	*28*	*50 999*
Graz, Linz, Salzburg, Innsbruck	*15 852*	*22*	*21*	*83*	*15 978*
Hamburg	*48 464*	*794*	*108*	*161*	*49 526*
Munich	*37 403*	*1 109*	*14*	*91*	*38 616*

I) Revenues and expenditures.
II) Domestic bills and checks and treasury bills of the German Reich.
III) Foreign bills and checks, foreign exchange and transactions with foreign correspondents.

In 1943, the Vienna Reichsbank head office had more turnover (above all in transactions on current acccounts) than any other Reichsbank office. Most probably, the Vienna office also handled the transactions for the occupied countries in Southern and Eastern Europe.

By the end of the war, the economic situation in what had been Austria was no different from that of the rest of the German Reich: The production of goods not essential to the war effort had sunk, and only the price freeze, which was maintained until the last months of the war, prevented a sharp increase in prices. The Austrian Institute of Economic Research puts the amount of banknotes in circulation in Austria in December 1945 at 8 to 15 billion reichsmark. Even at 8 billion this would have been a more than twelvefold increase from the end of 1937. Add to this the purchasing power represented by increased bank deposits. In real terms, the GNP in 1945 was likely around 50% to 60% of the 1937 GNP.[591] One of the main priorities of the monetary policy of the Austrian Republic, which was reinstated in April 1945, was thus monetary reform, in particular measures to prevent another round of hyperinflation.

Schilling reinstatement and economic miracle (1945–1971)

"From the perspective of later crisis decades ... the boom of the 1950s and 1960s stands out from the 'history of advanced capitalism' like an erratic block."

Peter Berger, *Kurze Geschichte*, p. 276

The OeNB resumed operations soon after Soviet troops had taken control of Vienna. On April 14, 1945, Eugen Kaniak, deputy head of the cashier's division until 1938, was appointed OeNB Chairman pro tem. According to historian Siegfried Pressburger, "The Russians shared the Austrian view that the Nationalbank had never ceased to exist but merely suffered a hiatus under the German National Socialist rule."[592] Along with Kaniak, a Provisional General Council, including former OeNB President Kienböck, Creditanstalt CEO Joham and Secretary General of Erste österreichische Spar-Casse Thausing, temporarily ran the affairs of the OeNB. Similar to the actions of the provisional government formed on April 27, 1945, under Federal Chancellor Renner, the decisions adopted by the OeNB's management could be enforced initially only in the Soviet occupation zone. After October 20, 1945, the date of recognition by the Allied Council, the authority of Renner's government–and that of its agencies–extended throughout the whole of Austria.[593]

The schilling returns

One of the OeNB's first-order tasks was to determine the amount of currency in circulation throughout Austria and to relaunch an Austrian currency. Austria's post-war stock of banknotes consisted of reichsmark banknotes issued by the German Reichsbank as well as "Allied military schillings," notes that the United States had printed as a substitute currency for Allied troops entering Austrian territories, allegedly in the amount of 10 billion Austrian military schillings.[594] The bank intended to overprint the Reichsbank notes upon arrival of the Western powers in Vienna and launch concurrent efforts to print new schilling banknotes–a task that proceeded slowly due to frequent power cuts, the lack of banknote paper and limited transport capacities.[595] To create the legal foundation for the OeNB's operations, the Austrian government passed the Central Bank Transition Act on July 3, 1945, which stipulated that the OeNB's statutes from 1922 would remain in force and that amendments would be made only to the extent required to reflect current realities. The OeNB would take over the Reichsbank's notes circulating in Austria and the balances on its current accounts, which would be declared domestic legal tender, and post corresponding receivables from the German Reichsbank on the opposite side of its balance sheet. With regard to the OeNB's governance structure, the Central Bank Transition Act stipulated that the Federal Chancellor would appoint the OeNB president upon recommendation of the provisional government, and his deputy upon a proposal of the Federal Finance Office. The General Council of the OeNB, comprised originally of 13 members, was reduced to 9, all of whom were appointed by the Federal Chancellor upon recommendation of the government, "taking care of the representation of the most influential groups of the economy."[596]

Ultimately, Hans Rizzi, undersecretary of state in the finance ministry,[597] was appointed president of the OeNB. During the initial meeting of the newly inaugurated General Council on August 3, 1945, Rizzi provided a fundamental assessment of economic and monetary policy developments in the interwar years. Thus, the events that followed the outbreak of the Creditanstalt crisis indicated that accumulating even large gold and foreign exchange reserves was an inadequate approach to maintaining exchange rate parity as required under the OeNB's statutes. Clearly, monetary policy could not be pursued separately from economic policy. This tied in with the turn that the theoretical debate had taken in England and the United States, which represented a fundamental break with traditional central bank policy views. Having established these premises, Rizzi drew the following conclusions: "(1) Nations can no longer afford to allow domestic markets to be shaped by the unfettered dynamics of market forces. Economic planning and bank lending control have become manifest government responsibilities. (2) Likewise, international commodity and money markets need to be organized along supranational lines and with a common economic focus." According to President Rizzi, the ability to influence banks' investment policies and exercise control over the movement of capital were the essential tools needed to ensure appropriate and effective central bank policy.[598]

Back to normal one step at a time

When the Soviet forces arrived in Austria, the banks in the Russian occupation zone, whose currency supplies had already been disrupted during the war, were closed. Their reopening was delayed because the Red Army had seized all reichsmark supplies–some 519 million reichsmark–as war booty.[599] To get payment transactions moving again, the Soviet Union granted several loans, totaling 600 million reichsmark, to the Austrian government in May and June 1945. Following the Soviet infusion of reichsmark notes, public agencies and banks again had the cash they needed to resume operations. The Resumption of Payments Act, adopted on July 3, 1945,[600] permitted payment transactions to be restarted but also blocked a large part–60%–of the money supply held in the form of bank deposits, constituting a first attempt at addressing the problem of excess liquidity. Cash withdrawals of the remaining 40% were permitted subject to specified limits and for specified purposes. At the same time, the government appealed to the general public to deposit their cash savings with the banking system. In response to this appeal, the public indeed returned a substantial amount of hoarded notes to the banking system. In the months that followed, bank deposits far exceeded withdrawals, and banks' current account holdings with the OeNB surged from 588 million reichsmark in early April 1945 to 2,100 million reichsmark by 3 August.[601]

Ultimately, restoration of Austria's national currency was delayed until December 1945. The original agreement between the OeNB's management and the occupying forces had been to convert the reichsmark notes already in circulation into Austrian military schillings and then move to the schilling.[602] On October 7, 1945, however, the impending recognition of the Renner government by the Western allies prompted the Soviet Union to demand a direct conversion from reichsmark to schilling, which occurred in December 1945.[603] The Schilling Act of November 30, 1945, reinstated the Austrian schilling as the country's legal tender and sole unit of account, effective from December 21, 1945. During the third week of December 1945, reichsmark notes and military schillings in denominations greater than 10 reichsmark or Austrian military schillings were exchanged for Austrian schillings at a ratio of one-to-one. The per capita quota of the new currency was 150 Austrian schillings. Amounts beyond that threshold were transferred to limited access accounts.

The Schilling Act effectively blocked, but did not absorb the surplus money in the market. In the period that followed, the release of deposits held in blocked accounts and the financing of occupation costs through central bank loans caused a steady increase in the amount of money circulating in the economy. It soon became apparent that the measures introduced by the Resumption of Payments and Schilling Acts represented only the first steps toward creating a stable currency–steps that had to be supplemented by other monetary policy actions. By the end of 1947, 3.2 billion Austrian schillings had to be made available to offset occupation costs. In fact, support of the occupying forces is estimated to have consumed one-sixth of domestic output in 1946 and 6% the following year.[604] As of October 1946, occupation costs were financed by issuing treasury notes underwritten by the OeNB.[605] Austrian banks also subscribed to these instruments as a means to invest some of their central bank deposits, which would otherwise have been unremunerated, at an interest rate of 1.5%.[606]

The OeNB's first post-war weekly financial statements, published on October 7, 1946,[607] showed the currency in circulation at 5.1 billion Austrian schillings, of which 2.6 billion had been paid out for occupation costs. Unrestricted short-term liabilities stood at 3.1 billion Austrian schillings and blocked balances on current accounts at 4.3 billion Austrian schillings. These sums were counter-balanced on the assets side by 12.5 billion Austrian schillings in claims against the federal treasury, which, according to an amendment to the Central Bank Transition Act, replaced the receivables from the Reichsbank. The reserves in the form of gold (45,000 Austrian schillings) and foreign currency (9 million Austrian schillings) were negligible.

Following the collapse of the National Socialist regime, the rules issued by the Third Reich governing the possession and use of foreign currency continued in force until responsibility for foreign exchange control was transferred to the OeNB in October 1945.[608] The activities of the foreign exchange control agency established for that purpose were initially restricted to the purchase and sale of foreign notes, particularly as foreign postal correspondence only resumed in January 1946, followed by telegram correspondence the next month. In July 1946, the Foreign Exchange Control Act entered into force, and on October 26, 1946, provisional exchange rates, which initially equaled those prescribed by the occupying forces, were published in the official gazette.[609] According to a study by the Austrian Institute of Economic Research, at the rate of 10 schillings to 1 U.S. dollar, the Austrian currency was being undervalued by about 50%.[610]

While exports and imports of goods mostly relied on a system of bilateral barter during the initial post-war years, trade and payment agreements facilitating transactions on a clearing basis or in exchange for foreign currencies were concluded with a series of European countries in 1946.[611] The most immediate foreign trade policy challenge centered on procuring food for the urban population, which was suffering from hunger. Food reserves had been plundered or seized by the troops, the lack of transport was widespread, and the 1945 and 1946 crop yields for bread wheat hovered at about 50% of the 1934 to 1938 average.[612] The basic nutritional needs were met primarily by aid from the United Nations and the United States, as no foreign currency was available to pay for imports. The balance sheet for 1946 showed the OeNB's gold holdings at 132,000 Austrian schillings, and it was only upon restitution of some of the gold reserves stolen in 1938 that the value of the foreign exchange reserves in the OeNB's accounts increased.[613]

In 1945, 1,450 kilograms of gold were discovered in Salzburg, which the U.S. occupying forces turned over to the OeNB on February 19, 1947. The weekly financial statements dated February 23, 1947, reflected an increase in the bank's gold holdings equivalent to 47.4 million Austrian schillings, which Chief Executive Director Bartsch characterized as an important step toward accumulating the gold reserve needed to cover central bank money in circulation.[614] The Banca d'Italia later took action against the OeNB for restitution of the discovered gold, claiming that it had been seized from its reserves. Ultimately, the treasure was handed over to the Tripartite Gold Commission in Brussels (established in 1946 to facilitate the return of looted monetary gold to the claimant countries from which it originated), which released the "Salzburg gold" to the OeNB as an advance on the share Austria was to receive following the final decisions of the Tripartite Gold Commission.[615]

Marshall Plan aid and currency reform

Austria's economic situation deteriorated devastatingly during the catastrophic winter of 1946/47, when a large part of the population experienced acute hunger. Things only started to take a turn for the better when U.S. Secretary of State George C. Marshall announced a comprehensive system of recovery aid for Europe in June 1947. Austria's newly established "economic commission" (see below) attempted to set the price-wage structure on a new footing, and with the Currency Protection Act of December 1947, yet another step was taken toward consolidating the country's currency.

Under the Marshall Plan for the reconstruction of Western Europe (known officially as the European Recovery Program or ERP)–a program which, in the words of the Harriman Committee, would be in conformity with America's vital humanitarian, economic, strategic and political interests[616]–Austria received nonrepayable economic assistance equivalent to approximately 1.4 billion U.S. dollars from 1947 to 1953.[617] While much of the initial aid consisted of food supplies to improve the nutritional situation in Austria, it then turned to seed stock and fertilizer, energy resources and machinery, all of which were essential to bridging bottlenecks in the country's production structure. Given its lack of foreign currency, Austria would have been unable to import such goods, which were vital for its reconstruction effort. Measured at purchasing power parity, foreign aid accounted for more than 10% of domestic production in the early post-war years, and around 7% to 8% from 1948 to 1950.[618]

By 1947, real GDP had reached approximately 70% of the 1937 level and surpassed its pre-war figure in 1949.[619] The demand-pull fueled by the liquidity overhang in the market triggered a tremendous increase in the number of applications to the price control and central wage commissions, which remained responsible for authorizing price and wage changes (as they had been during the era of the Third Reich). In 1947, four key interest groups–the Federal Economic Chamber, the Chamber of Agriculture, the Chamber of Labor and the Federation of Trade Unions–joined forces to establish a permanent economic commission,[620] which negotiated a schedule of fixed prices for essential goods and services and adjusted wages and pensions to that schedule.[621] The first of these agreements, signed in August 1947, was sufficiently successful to lead to a series of renewals over the next four years. Although these measures relieved inflationary pressures to some extent, they ultimately proved unable to stabilize prices in the long term. The years from 1947 to 1951 were characterized as a period of "government controlled" inflation, which was the easiest way of "keeping ambitious economic and administrative investment plans to a reasonable level and broadly curtailing living standards" during the reconstruction phase.[622] The persistent liquidity overhang caused by a lack of consumer goods spurred a major surge in prices from 1947 onward and had to be sterilized before stability could be restored to the financial system. Furthermore, between 1938 and 1945, banks had invested most of their funds in German Reich debt instruments–which had become worthless once the Reich had ceased to exist–and were faced with the task of reducing their excess liabilities over assets.[623]

The 1947 currency reform

Austria's government and the OeNB originally intended to set currency reform aside until after the State Treaty had been concluded, but when negotiations broke down in May 1947, the reform of the schilling returned to the political agenda.[624] Agreement on the legal foundations was difficult to achieve due to differences of opinion among the government parties, particularly opposition from the industrial sector, banks and insurers. Industry representatives and–to the surprise of historians–Viktor Kienböck, who had advocated a deflationary monetary policy during the interwar years, challenged the existence of an inflationary surplus of money,[625] which delayed passage of the Currency Protection Act until November 1947. This act had three major objectives: decreasing note circulation, reducing bank deposits, and creating the prerequisites for an adjustment of bank balance sheets.[626] From December 10 to 27, 1947, banknotes and coins in circulation were exchanged for new schilling notes at a ratio of three to one. Only 150 schillings a person could go one-to-one. The accounts that had been blocked under the Resumption of Payments and Schilling Acts were written off the books entirely, and restricted accounts were converted into claims against the federal treasury. Public agency deposits were devalued by 25% and partially blocked for one year.

Chart 9.1: **Growth of consumer prices**[627]

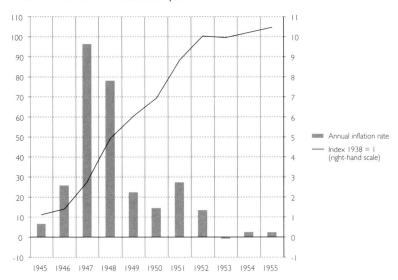

The official inflation rates hardly budged from 1838 to 1945. However, by 1945 the increase in the money supply was grossly out of proportion with the supply of goods, which had dropped sharply. In the absence of sweeping measures to mop up the excess money supply, this would have resulted in (open) inflation and hyperinflation. The five price-wage agreements signed between 1947 and 1951 led to a controlled adjustment of price levels in the face of excess liquidity generated by a scarcity of goods and thus arrested inflationary acceleration. The 1952/53 stabilization was achieved by implementing interest rate, lending and budget policies.

In the weeks preceding the currency reform, a "buying frenzy" took hold, and debts and tax liabilities were settled quickly to avoid cash accumulation. By November 1947, the amount of cash in circulation had dropped from 6.2 billion Austrian schillings to 2.9 billion. After the conversion period, 1.6 billion Austrian schillings in banknotes were in circulation and bank deposits were reduced by 10.7 billion to 5.4 billion Austrian schillings.[628] Holders of securities, insurance policies and physical assets came away without a haircut.[629]

The deposits pulled in under the Currency Protection Act were used to reduce federal debt to the central bank (3.7 billion Austrian schillings) and eliminate 6.5 billion Austrian schillings in credit institutions' worthless claims against the German Reich.[630] The currency reform had several positive effects:

the exchange rate between the schilling and the Swiss franc more than doubled, from 3.2 Swiss francs for 100 Austrian schillings to between 6 and 7 Swiss francs; black market rates for food declined; and stock prices, which had risen significantly in 1947, returned to more realistic levels.[631] The more optimistic expectations also led to a strong increase in economic output.

Real economic growth surged by almost 27% in 1948, supported in part by ERP funds, which totaled 280 million U.S. dollars that year. The revenue derived from selling commodities supplied by the United States under the ERP program was deposited in a counterpart account administered by the OeNB. During the first six months of the ERP, 1.45 billion Austrian schillings were earmarked to service government debt owed to the OeNB. Of that amount, 850 million Austrian schillings had to be used for achieving a permanent reduction in the volume of money in circulation and 600 million Austrian schillings for discounting trade bills to support investments in the production sector. The discount rate was 3.5% and the interest rate for ERP loans 5%.[632]

Current account deficits, lending controls and a new Central Bank Act

The primary goal of the investments made under the ERP program was to achieve a reasonable equilibrium in the balance of payments position over the medium term. In 1947, imports were three times as high as exports (chart 9.2), while in 1948, exports had reached only 54% of their 1937 level. The resultant foreign exchange gap was overcome in part by nonrepayable foreign aid. Business sector representatives blamed the low export volumes that followed the price adjustments of the first price-wage agreement on the supposedly inflated exchange rate and demanded that the Austrian currency be devalued. The OeNB opposed that stance because it believed such action would drive up import prices, causing a further increase in inflation, and argued that the weak exports were in fact the result of limited production capabilities.[633] Beyond those facts, some 50% of all exports were based on barter terms, which allowed exporters to retain between 10% and 90% of their export revenues and use them for imports of raw materials and intermediate goods. The OeNB preferred to promote this form of export support (termed "retention quotas") rather than devalue the national currency because it allowed for greater operational flexibility.[634] Foreign trade with Eastern European countries relied on bilateral clearing agreements that limited the amount of trade taking place under their terms—an approach that ran counter to the creation of a multilateral free trade system as envisaged by the Bretton Woods Agreement. For the European countries involved in the ERP, the Marshall Plan administration attempted several times to create a mechanism for multilateral settlements. Those efforts finally paid off in 1950 with the establishment of the European Payments Union.[635]

Chart 9.2: **Austrian exports and imports of goods and services** (in millions of U.S. dollars)[636]

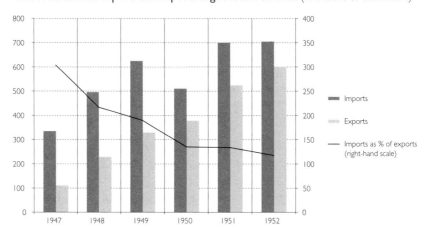

In 1947, the foreign exchange gap created by a threefold excess of imports over exports was closed by U.S. aid funds.

Multiple exchange rates

Under the system of retention quotas and bilateral clearing agreements, a large number of schilling exchange rates were in use, depending on the category of goods concerned and the country doing the importing and exporting. As an exception to its general stance, the International Monetary Fund (IMF), of which Austria became a member on October 27, 1948, accepted this exchange rate system for a limited period in lieu of establishing a fixed schilling-to-gold or schilling-to-U.S. dollar rate.[637] As 1949 progressed, however, the IMF piled pressure on Austria to adapt its exchange rate system, and the export industry continued to demand that the schilling's external value be reduced. When the British pound was devalued by approximately 30% in September 1949, the Nationalbank made preparations to restructure the schilling exchange rate system as well; however, the government did not stand ready to approve any currency policy measures prior to the elections scheduled for October 9, 1949.[638] That delay stoked mistrust of the schilling, which led to panic buying, a general flight to tangible assets and a surge in stock and gold prices, while cash holdings plunged. On November 22, 1949, the schilling was finally devalued by 30.6% against the U.S. dollar, and a less complex, if not uniform exchange rate regime was introduced, which replaced the official rate of 10 Austrian schillings for 1 U.S. dollar with a basic schilling/dollar rate of 14.4 and a premium schilling/dollar rate of 26. Additionally, exporters were forced to sell 40% of their foreign exchange earnings to the OeNB at the basic rate and were required to either use the 60% uniform retention quota for imports within 60 days or offer it to the OeNB at the premium rate. The effective exchange rate applied to all exports transacted in foreign exchange–the mean rate–thus came to 21.36 Austrian schillings per U.S. dollar.[639]

These exchange rate policy measures proved to be short-lived, however, as retention quotas were modified for various classes of transactions in January 1950.[640] Additionally, the fourth price-wage agreement of October 1950 introduced another adjustment in the schilling's exchange rate structure: a single rate of 21.36 Austrian schillings per U.S. dollar was established for all trade transactions while the premium rate was used for invisibles.[641] It was not until 1953 that Austria established a uniform exchange rate based on the prevailing premium rate.

Despite the monetary policy measures of 1949/50 and the consequent sharp devaluation of the schilling, Austria's current account deficit failed to shrink. In 1951 (as in the previous year), imports exceeded exports by one-third, although export activity had received a boost from international rearmament after the June 1950 outbreak of the Korean war. Nevertheless, the international "bull run" on commodities drove up prices for imports much faster than for exports. That deterioration in the terms of trade, coupled with the need to make advance payments for imports of commodities and capital goods, strained the foreign exchange balance.[642] As the 80 million units of account allocated to Austria as part of the European Payments Union had already been exhausted by March 1951, additional actions were required to trim the current account deficit, including measures to restrict the debt financing of imports. The OeNB had begun to explore intervention strategies to arrest the surge in lending growth in the final quarter of 1950. The credit volume more than quintupled between year-end 1947 and year-end 1950, and climbed by a further 42% in 1951 (table 9.1). The classical instrument of monetary policy–the discount rate–was the only tool available to the OeNB to influence lending by the banking sector since compulsory minimum reserves could be mandated only once the Nationalbank Act of 1955 was effective. Under the circumstances, however, the monetary committee of the OeNB's General Council opined that increasing the discount rate would exert only a minimal restraining effect.[643] On March 16, 1951, therefore, the OeNB reached an agreement with the Austrian Bankers' Association on qualitative credit control as a means to prevent the use of credit for speculative purposes or for economically unjustified increases in household consumption (such as using consumer credit to hoard goods).[644] With the OeNB's consent, the ministry of finance agreed in April 1951 on a quantitative lending limit with Austrian credit institutions, which required them to hold a certain proportion (initially 25%, to be increased to 30% by the end of 1951) of their lending in liquid assets with the OeNB or the Austrian Postsparkasse.[645]

Table 9.1: **Credit growth in Austria**[646]

Year-end	Commercial loans	Development loans	Total	Annual change
	in millions of schillings			in %
1947	2 146		2 146	–
1948	3 887	319	4 206	96.0
1949	5 954	1 057	7 011	66.7
1950	8 410	2 268	10 678	52.3
1951	11 116	4 074	15 190	42.3

The lending surge following on the heels of the 1947 currency reform was one reason for the high current account deficit. Accordingly, regulators had to take measures to curb credit expansion.

The March and April 1951 credit control agreements were stipulated by the European Payments Union (EPU) as a condition for its support of Austria's requests to the Marshall Plan authorities for allocation of additional funds. Both the Marshall Plan administration and the EPU also demanded a raise of the discount rate,[647] which was implemented in December 1951 (from 3.5% to 5%).[648] However, involving credit institutions more comprehensively in credit control agreements and curtailing lending to 70% of deposits did not have the hoped-for restrictive effect, and the credit volume expanded by a further 5.6% in the first quarter of 1952. Based on the outcomes achieved thus far, the Marshall Plan organizations did not consider Austria's corrective actions sufficient. As a result, they made the release of further counterpart funds and direct U.S. aid contingent upon a formal credit freeze, the introduction of refinancing ceilings for banks and another discount rate increase to 6%. These stabilization measures were also supported by an IMF delegation that was visiting Vienna at that time.[649] Thus, the OeNB's General Council decided in June 1952 to establish a ceiling for central bank refinancing at the prevailing level, which could only be exceeded in the event of a significant and unforeseen reduction of deposits. The discount rate was raised to 6% in an extraordinary meeting of the General Council on July 2, 1952–under the pressure of U.S. demands rather than in anticipation of any additional restrictive effect.[650]

The additional tightening measures soon yielded results: commercial lending shrunk by 7% in the second half of 1952, the cost of living and wholesale prices went down and the standard wage-rate index remained stable.[651] The downside of the stabilization policy, however, was a spike in unemployment by 97,000 between year-end 1951 and year-end 1952.[652] There is no doubt that the restrictive measures implemented by the OeNB–which, according to its chief executive director, was for the first time actively pursuing a monetary policy–played a part in ending post-war inflation. That outcome, however, was also aided by the voluntary price reduction campaigns mounted by the chambers of commerce in fall 1951, which essentially aimed to "pass on the savings created by the drop in international commodity prices to the consumer." This enabled the trade unions to exercise wage restraint, and at its Second General Assembly meeting in October 1951, the president of the Austrian Federation of Trade Unions recommended the omission of one wage round.[653]

While 1951 had still seen a 6.8% growth in real GDP, production stagnated in the wake of the stability measures enacted in 1951/52. This prompted businesses to focus their sales efforts with renewed vigor on foreign markets, resulting in a year-on-year increase in export revenues by almost 12% in 1952. Imports, and thus the trade deficit, decreased, and from August 1952 onward, the balance of payments with the EPU was positive. That same year, surpluses from tourism rose by 69% to 621 million Austrian schillings and foreign currency holdings within the OeNB grew by 1,627 million Austrian schillings, which made a positive impact on the schilling's standing in the international currency markets.[654] The increased confidence in the national currency also translated into an expansion of savings deposits by over 1 billion Austrian schillings (+45.5%) in 1952, which exceeded the previous three-year total and restored public trust in cash: notes in circulation rose by 1,016 million to 9,048 million Austrian schillings, and central bank balances increased by 1,313 million Austrian schillings or 7.6%. As the Bank for International Settlements expressed in its 1953 annual report, "The success achieved in Austria showed that it was possible for monetary and fiscal measures, properly applied, to be fully effective in a country occupied by four powers and, moreover, cut off from most of its former customers in the Danubian basin."[655]

In 1952, Austria also reached a satisfactory agreement on settlement of its pre-war debt, which was estimated at 1.6 billion Austrian schillings. During negotiations held in Rome in November and December 1952, Austria was granted a generous reduction in interest and principal payments due for the period from the end of the war to 1952. These arrears had to be repaid at just 28.5% of their nominal value in installments that ranged from 5 million to 8 million Austrian schillings over the period 1954 to 1978. The debt accumulated during the annexation period was assumed by the Federal Republic of Germany. Austria's remaining pre-war foreign debt was to be repaid from 1959 to 1980 at 4.5% interest. The charge for pre-war loans absorbed approximately 70 million Austrian schillings of Austria's annual budget. Of the volume of expenditure of the federal budget totaling 42 billion Austrian schillings in 1959 and 306 billion Austrian schillings in 1980, 0.17% and 0.02%, respectively, was spent on servicing pre-war foreign debt.[656]

Exchange rate unification

The unification of the schilling exchange rate essentially concluded the reconstruction period for the country's economy, and the 1954/55 Capital Market Acts brought its post-war economic consolidation process to a close. Immediately after the Raab government came into power on April 2, 1953, the schilling was devalued and the exchange rate standardized. Notably, the OeNB had long advocated such measures, but their implementation was delayed by the general elections and subsequent change in government.[657] The split exchange rate produced "premium losses" for the OeNB because it purchased foreign currency from exporters of invisibles at 26 Austrian schillings per U.S. dollar and sold it to importers at 21.36 schillings. For 1952 alone, those losses ran to 324 million schillings,[658] and with the rise in foreign trade volume, they could only continue to increase. Faced with the fact that the IMF had also been pushing for a unified exchange rate for several years, Austria finally adopted a standardized, single exchange rate of 26 Austrian schillings to 1 U.S. dollar on May 4, 1953.

The devaluation of the schilling in 1953 was expected to give a boost to foreign trade since it made exports cheaper, but also to push domestic prices higher. According to estimates by the Austrian Institute of Economic Research, if import price hikes were fully passed on to consumers, inflation would jump by 3.7%.[659] In an attempt to keep the cost of living as stable as possible, the government decided that bread wheat and imported animal feed should be sold at pre-unification (constant) prices. Since the budget did not include funding to cover the additional annual cost of approximately 400 million schillings for these subsidies, the OeNB provided the government with a total of 650 million Austrian schillings in 1953 and 1954 out of the revaluation gains in its gold and foreign exchange holdings. As Chief Executive Director Bartsch remarked, however, "from a monetary policy perspective, using revaluation gains in this manner is an exception and not really adequate."[660] In Bartsch's estimation, the revaluation gains totaled 1,270 million Austrian schillings, of which 469 million schillings were needed to cover premium losses up to and including April 1953.

The remaining 151 million schillings were left in the OeNB's books. When the IMF accepted the rate of 1 Austrian schilling equaling 0.0341796 grams of fine gold (which was based on the dollar-schilling exchange rate) as the schilling's parity, Austria was obliged to transfer its quota of 50 million U.S. dollars to the IMF within 30 days.[661]

The devaluation of the schilling and the aftereffects of the stabilization crisis triggered a sharp upswing in the trade balance. In commercial trade (i.e., not including ERP transactions), a surplus of 800 million Austrian schillings was achieved in 1953 against a deficit of 1,200 million Austrian schillings in 1952, while tourism revenue doubled year-on-year. Since price levels remained essentially unchanged in 1952/53, the head of the Austrian Institute of Economic Research attributed the disproportionate growth in foreign exchange revenue to the fact that "runaway capital returning to Austria was accounted for as spending by foreign travelers."[662]

The current account surplus necessitated a gradual liberalization of foreign trade, because as a "structural debtor nation," Austria had so far not been required to implement deregulation at the same pace as the other EPU members. On July 1, 1953, Austria became a full member of the EPU and concurrently implemented a 25% liberalization of imports (using 1952 as a reference year).[663] The foreign currency travel allowance for tourists was raised to 150 Austrian schillings in June 1953 and to 500 Austrian schillings in January 1954. For trips within OEEC countries, the tourist quota was set at 100 U.S. dollars per year, which had to be recorded in the traveler's passport.[664]

While foreign trade surpluses bolstered the OeNB's reserves, they also accelerated monetary growth and increased money market liquidity, which hampered the central bank's ability to enact effective intervention measures. Since the OeNB held that the interest rates on long-term investment loans were excessively high and thus deterred companies from borrowing, the discount rate was lowered from 5% to 4% in September 1953 despite the glut of money in the markets–the third successive cut in that year, following reductions of 0.5 percentage points in January and March which were intended as a "psychological" impetus to overcome the rise in unemployment.[665] Along with the September 1953 rate cut, the OeNB took additional measures to support banks' maturity transformations by extending refinancing commitments for long-term investment projects that met certain eligibility requirements. These commitments exceeded the applicable rediscount ceiling and were intended to eliminate potential liquidity problems in the future. At the same time, the central bank urgently appealed to the government to create the regulatory and legal framework necessary to ensure a well-functioning and effective capital market.[666]

Capital market legislation and the 1955 Nationalbank Act

After the end of World War II, the Austrian capital market had remained dormant until 1949, which saw its reactivation with the issuance of "reconstruction bonds" in the amount of 325 million Austrian schillings.[667] The issue volume had grown to 796 million Austrian schillings by 1953 and reached 2,156 million Austrian schillings by 1954.[668] A significant proportion of the government-guaranteed reconstruction bonds were purchased by banks during those two years, even though fiscal measures provided incentives for individuals and companies to commit their savings over the long term.[669] In 1954, several pieces of legislation were passed in an effort to secure adequate conditions for raising funds through the Austrian capital market. These included the Securities Settlement Act,[670] which established a process for determining the ownership status of securities held in collective custody, the Schilling Opening Balance Sheet Act,[671] which adjusted the valuation of assets and liabilities to the prevailing price and cost levels, and the Nationalization Compensation Act,[672] which regulated the compensation owed to former shareholders of nationalized industry and banking establishments. In a broader sense, capital market legislation also included the Bank Reconstruction Act,[673] the Insurance Reconstruction Act[674] and the 1955 Nationalbank Act.[675] These pieces of legislation gave Austrian banks and insurance companies the option of preparing annual financial statements for the period from 1945 to 1954. If the period-end balance of own assets fell short of the 1945 opening balance, they could enter the shortfall in their books as a claim against the federal treasury. However, that option was only used in a few cases, as Austrian banks had largely offset their total of 9 billion Austrian schillings in worthless claims against the Third Reich[676] by writing off blocked accounts and applying the earnings achieved since then.

The 1955 Nationalbank Act established the OeNB's legal framework and placed a range of modern monetary policy instruments at its disposal. At year-end 1954, the OeNB's balance sheet showed a well-poised picture (table 9.2). The federal debt, which in 1946 had been the OeNB's most important asset, had shrunk by 10.4 billion Austrian schillings, to one-sixth of its original value due to a combination of factors, namely restitutions of gold made to the Austrian government and transferred subsequently to the OeNB, the elimination of banknotes and deposits blocked previously by the Currency Protection Act from the books, and the use of counterpart funds. The stock in gold and foreign currency–including 1.2 billion Austrian schillings not separately disclosed–increased by more than 11 billion Austrian schillings between 1946 and 1954, and the value of banknotes in circulation roughly doubled. Since the nominal gross domestic product had quadrupled, the ratio of banknotes in circulation to the gross national product fell from approximately 25% in 1946 to 13% in 1954. Of note, the OeNB did not publish its 1954 balance sheet. In 1952, concerned "that the level of reserves shown on the books would excite demands both at home and abroad," the General Council decided not to publish year-end accounts until the new statutes had come into force.[677]

Table 9.2: **Selected items from the OeNB balance sheet**[678]

	Gold and foreign currency	Bills of exchange	Federal debt	Banknotes	Deposit liabilities	Total money supply
	in millions of schillings					
1946	19.2	0.0	12 547.2	5 656.5	2 598.4	8 254.9
1954	11 074.7	5 243.6	2 126.8	12 252.5	3 188.6	15 441.1
1954–1946	11 055.5	5 243.6	-10 420.4	6 596.0	590.2	7 186.2

In 1946, the OeNB's assets consisted almost entirely of claims against the federal treasury, which decreased by 10.4 billion Austrian schillings until 1954, while gold and foreign currency reserves rose by 11.1 billion Austrian schillings, and receivables from bills of exchange by 5.2 billion Austrian schillings.

The Central Bank Transition Act of 1945 affirmed that the OeNB, merely hindered in the exercise of its functions, had indeed remained in existence during the reign of the Third Reich. Hence, the central bank provisions that had applied until 1938 were reconfirmed apart from some clauses. Specifically, the

Central Bank Transition Act abrogated the requirement to back banknotes in circulation with gold and stable foreign exchange assets and the penalty tax in case of noncompliance. Moreover, the new requirement for weekly financial statements was to show only banknotes in circulation and short-term liabilities as well as the counterpart assets, but no other asset and liability positions. Compared to its predecessor legislation of 1922, the Nationalbank Act of 1955 introduced the following significant changes:

- Half the share capital of 150 million Austrian schillings was subscribed for by the Republic of Austria. The other half was made available to a range of eligible subscribers as determined by the federal government.
- The central objective of the OeNB was no longer the implementation of the gold standard but rather maintaining the value of the schilling with regard to both its domestic purchasing power and its international exchange value. Since the legislation was silent on priority, the OeNB would decide itself which approach to adopt in the event of a conflict of interest between the mandates for internal and external stability.
- While the OeNB was granted independence in policy-making, it was required to consider the economic policy of the federal government in the exercise of its monetary and credit policy.
- Minimum reserves were added to the OeNB's range of monetary policy instruments, and its operational framework was expanded to include open market operations in addition to its existing toolbox of discount and lending operations and foreign exchange transactions.
- Banks, insurance companies and other financial institutions were obliged to furnish the OeNB with all the information and data it required in the performance of its duties.[679]

In addition to introducing new capital market legislation, the government also intended at the same time to recast the legal framework for Austrian credit institutions. As a result, it agreed on July 16, 1955, on a bill called Austrian Banking Act. However, the parliament was unable to bridge the gaps between the divergent views of the coalition parties about the parliament's involvement in determining the level of liquidity reserves to be held by credit institutions, regulating the upper limit of individual loans, determining credit ceilings and negotiating agreements on credit and debit rates.[680] Because of those differences of opinion, Austria did not enact banking legislation reflective of current realities until 1979.

Dynamic catch-up process and stability risks

The State Treaty of May 1955 ended Austria's four-power occupation and restored its national sovereignty. It was preceded by the Moscow Memorandum of April 1955, which settled political issues and prescribed the economic obligations Austria would shoulder under the State Treaty. The costs associated with the State Treaty were estimated at 10 billion Austrian schillings for the decade after 1955,[681] which equates to about 0.6% of the GDP for that period. Historians believe that the burdens imposed by the State Treaty were more than offset by the benefits it brought to the Austrian economy.[682]

After achieving currency stabilization in 1953, Austria's economy embarked on a period of unparalleled growth. Indeed, within just 20 years, Austria was catapulted into the group of nations with the highest per capita income in the world (chart 9.3).

Of the countries shown in chart 9.3, only the Federal Republic of Germany recorded a larger gain in per capita income than Austria between 1950 and 1970. The income differential between the United States and Austria shrank from 66% to 7%, and Britain, which had posted an income level 22% higher than Austria's in 1950, ranked 24% below Austria in 1970. Between 1952 and 1970, Austria's real output grew at an average annual rate of 5.4%, and between 1952 and 1960 at even 6.7% per year. This exceptionally strong economic growth was driven by several factors. Because of the war and the shrinking of real production in the interwar period, in the early 1950s Austria lagged well behind other leading industrialized nations. By the second half of 1945, Austria's output and income levels were only 50% of those recorded in 1937 (which had already declined from their 1913 values). Against that bleak backdrop, a dynamic catch-up process was set in motion, supported comprehensively by measures taken to integrate Austria's domestic economy into the global market, investment-based tax incentives, cooperation

Chart 9.3: **Real GDP** per capita in an international comparison (Austria = 100)[683]

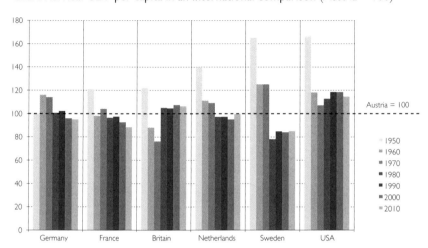

The comparatively strong economic growth Austria experienced in the two decades after 1950 narrowed its income gap relative to the most developed nations. Although the U.S. per capita income in 1950 was still 66% higher than Austria's, it exceeded the Austrian level by just 7% in 1970. In the decades that followed Austria could hold on to its position in the group of countries with the highest per capita income.

among organizations representing the interests of employers and employees (the social partnership) and a growth-supportive monetary policy.

Trade liberalization and export promotion

Austria's EPU membership committed the country to progressively liberalizing trade in goods and services. When the EPU was dissolved in December 1958 because the six-member European Economic Community (EEC) along with Britain, Denmark, Norway and Sweden made their currencies convertible for nonresidents, Austria followed suit by removing the foreign exchange control restrictions still in existence as of February 1959, coupled with a gradually relaxation of the foreign currency allowance for travel.[684] These liberalization steps, made possible because Austria's 1958 foreign exchange reserves of 12.3 billion Austrian schillings exceeded the 5-month volume of imports, had persistent effects on the current account, which since 1953 (with the exception of 1955) ran a surplus driven by higher exports as opposed to imports (chart 9.4).

Chart 9.4: **Exports and imports** (in % of nominal GDP)[685]

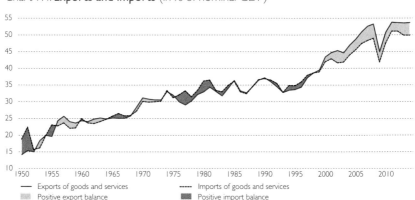

After the 1953 devaluation, the growth of foreign trade consistently outpaced the growth of domestic production. That condition was exacerbated by the discriminatory import policies applied by members of the newly established EEC against nonmember states. In Austria, efforts to boost exports included economic policy initiatives such as government-supported export credit funding or favorable OeNB rediscounting conditions for letters of credit used in foreign trade. From the second half of the 1970s onward, imports exceeded exports in some years. Since 2000, Austria's current account has closed with a surplus.

The devaluation-cum-unification of the schilling's exchange rate in 1953 was one factor that helped boost export activities by Austrian companies, even if (according to a study conducted by the Austrian Institute of Economic Research) export growth was driven largely by global economic trends rather than changes in export price levels.[686] Additional impetus was generated by export promotion measures including a refund regimen for turnover tax on exports,[687] export credit guarantees by the federal government and favorable export financing in the form of OeNB rediscount-eligible export letters of credit supported the gaining of market shares abroad. The 1950 Export Promotion Act[688] authorized the federal government to assume guarantees of up to 500 million Austrian schillings for export transactions, above all for exports against hard currencies–a ceiling raised consistently in tandem with the expansion of exports.[689] Under the Austrian export promotion scheme, the government assumed guarantees for export transactions, which could be refinanced through bank letters of credit at favorable interest rates and were eligible for rediscount with the OeNB on demand.[690]

The creation of the EEC in 1957 put a brake on Austria's export growth because customs duties imposed to favor imports from EEC members discriminated against trade with nonmember countries. The resultant decline in Austria's market share of EEC imports could only be recouped over time by exports to the European Free Trade Association (EFTA) during the 1960s.[691] Exports of goods and services as a proportion of GDP deteriorated and did not exceed the 1957 level (25.6%) until 1968.

High propensity to invest, strong expansion of lending

Beyond the expansion of exports, the rapid economic growth experienced in the 1950s and 1960s was also fueled by an increased propensity to invest. The ratio of investment to GDP, which hovered at 8.1% between 1924 and 1937, jumped to more than 21% during the decade from 1950 to 1960 and averaged just under 24% of GDP from 1950 to 1970 (chart 9.5).

Chart 9.5: **Investment** (in % of nominal GDP)[692]

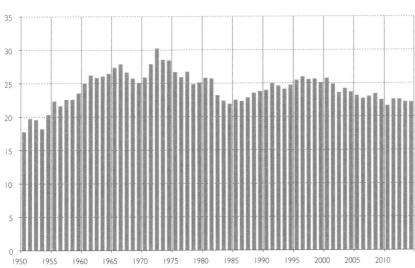

The high level of investment propensity was a key contributor to Austria's dynamic economic growth after 1945. Much of this momentum was spurred by favorable tax conditions and interest subsidies, and especially the virtually friction-free cooperation of the social partners, which boosted market and consumer sentiment.

The factors that stimulated investment propensity included Austria's favorable (and thus confidence-inspiring) socioeconomic conditions, a tax system that was conducive to investment, public-sector spending on infrastructure projects and a funding environment made especially favorable by subsidized loans.[693] If external financing was needed, loans from counterpart funds and other low-interest credit facilities were available. A 1965 OeNB survey showed that 41.3% of all schilling loans made by banks (other than savings and loan associations) to companies and households or public-sector institutions were subsidized.[694] The attainment of currency stabilization had an explosive impact on the lending volume of Austrian banks, which rose at an annual pace of 19.3% between 1953 and 1960 and at 16.4% per annum from 1953 to 1970. The changes in the discount rate and reserve requirements, implemented in conjunction with tightened credit control to contain inflation, only had a modest impact on credit expansion.

After currency stabilization was achieved in 1952, the discount rate was lowered in four consecutive stages from 6% in July 1952 to 3.5% in June 1954. In the period until 1970, the discount rate hovered in the range from 3.5% to 5%. All in all, it was reset nine times during that period, essentially with a view to signaling the central bank's monetary policy intentions, but the resulting effects were minimal. In view of the persistent upsurge in deposits, banks held back on central bank refinancing, while the numerous interest rate support schemes had a stabilizing effect on the general level of interest rates. Changes to the minimum reserves banks were required to hold with the OeNB[695]–introduced in December 1955 at a proportion of 5% of a bank's time and savings deposits and later determined on the basis of the maturity of deposits–likewise had little effect in controlling credit expansion.

From 1962 onward, the OeNB added open market operations to its set of monetary policy instruments. Contrary to the "classical" model of open market policy under which a central bank buys or sells securities on the secondary market to control liquidity and interest rate levels, the OeNB converted 560 million Austrian schillings of its claims against the federal government into treasury bills and sold them to credit institutions,[696] which, from their perspective, constituted interest-bearing minimum deposits with the OeNB.

The credit control agreements in existence since 1951 did not produce any significant restrictive effect, either. Although credit expansion was limited to a percentage of deposits, the strong concomitant growth in deposits gave banks sufficient leeway to augment their business volume. As a result, the volume of bank loans climbed by 163 billion Austrian schillings from 1953 to 1970, while their ratio relative to nominal GDP expanded from 16% to 47% during the same period. Although the availability of easy credit encouraged investment and growth, it also played an important role in the process of inflation.

Exchange rate and price developments

In the 1950s and 1960s, policy makers in most industrialized nations grappled with the problem of how to prevent creeping inflation from escalating into its runaway cousin. From an international perspective, Austria ranked among the countries with the best performance in matters of price stability,[697] despite some outliers such as the consumer price hikes of 1957 (4%) and 1962 (4.9%). The sharp acceleration of the inflation rate that took hold in 1957 prompted the creation of the Parity Commission for Wages and Prices. Before bargaining for price or wage increases started between the social partners, the commission deliberated with representatives of employees and employers on the general wage-price strategies, taking into account the macroeconomic situation of the country. In this manner it made a significant contribution to Austria's consensus-oriented wage and price policy.[698]

With the tools at its disposal, the OeNB was unable to achieve the objective stated in the Nationalbank Act, which was to "preserve the domestic purchasing power of the Austrian currency." Compared to most other countries, however, inflation in Austria was relatively low. This explains why maintaining its currency parity with the U.S. dollar, established in 1953, was never called into question. The favorable path of the current account, growth in foreign currency reserves and the liberalization of foreign trade created the conditions necessary for Austria's commitment to Article VIII of the IMF's Articles of Agreement on August 1, 1962. Accordingly, henceforward schilling amounts could be exchanged for other currencies without restriction–the schilling was convertible.[699] Article VI of the IMF Agreement also required Austria to ensure that the schilling exchange rate remained within a range of ±1% of its par value, expressed in gold or in U.S. dollars. As illustrated in table 9.3, that goal was achieved. Due to differences in dynamics across economies, however, the period until 1970 was characterized by substantial changes in exchange rates among major currencies. The Deutsche mark, for example, appreciated 14.5% against the schilling while the French franc fell by 37.1% and the British pound by almost 15%. Austria's economy was impacted predominantly by movements in the Deutsche mark because the Federal Republic of Germany was Austria's main trading partner–in 1968, for instance, Germany accounted for 41.5% of Austria's imports and 23.5% of its exports. The Deutsche mark had been adjusted upward by 4.75% in March 1961 and by 9.29% in October 1969 due to prolonged surpluses in the FRG's current account.[700] However, the Austrian government[701] and the OeNB decided jointly with the social partners to abstain from a revaluation of the schilling in 1969 since they believed that a weaker schilling rate against the Deutsche mark would spur economic growth, which had shrunk to just 2.8% (sic!) in 1967.

Table 9.3: **Mean foreign exchange rates**[702]

	USD	DEM	GBP	FRF	CHF
	ATS for 1 currency unit (USD and GBP) or 100 currency units (DEM, FRF and CHF)				
1954	26.0	619.1	72.8	743.0	594.6
1970	25.9	709.0	61.9	467.7	599.8
Change in %	*-0.6*	*14.5*	*-14.9*	*-37.1*	*0.9*

Between 1954 and 1970, following the currency unification, the schilling exchange rate remained stable against the U.S. dollar, declined by 14.5% against the Deutsche mark and became significantly stronger against the British pound and the French franc.

The exchange rate uncertainties of the 1960s gave rise to speculative capital movements since variations in growth and productivity dynamics across countries exacerbated external imbalances. As the international monetary system mandated the adjustment of fundamental imbalances by permanent changes to exchange rate parities, exchange rate movements were predictable and thus prone to speculation.

During the 1960s, the widening gap between U.S. gold reserves and its short-term liabilities to foreign central banks caused cracks in the monetary framework, which eventually led to the collapse of the system. In the 1944 Bretton Woods Agreement, the United States committed to backing central banks' U.S. dollar claims in gold at a rate of 35 U.S. dollars per fine ounce. At the end of the 1960s, the U.S. was no longer able to do so because its official gold reserves for 1968 stood at 10.9 billion U.S. dollars compared to a short-term foreign debt of 38.5 billion U.S. dollars.[703] The decision to end international convertibility of the U.S. dollar to gold announced by U.S. President Nixon as a "temporary" measure in August 1971 effectively dissolved the Bretton Woods system, which was based on fixed parities. As a result, Austria lost its monetary policy anchor and, like the other IMF members, was forced to adopt a new monetary policy strategy.

Austria's hard currency policy (1971–1999)

"There is little doubt that the systemic
disintegration would have occurred anyway
at some time. It required too much in terms
of the coordination of national policies.
Countries were more and more committed
to domestic growth."

Harold James, *Monetary cooperation*, p. 207

In the first two decades of its existence, the International Monetary Fund (IMF)–established at a UN conference held in Bretton Woods, New Hampshire, in 1944–had broadly succeeded in achieving the purposes defined in the first of its Articles of Agreement: promoting international monetary cooperation, facilitating the expansion of world trade and thereby promoting high levels of employment, promoting exchange rate stability and avoiding competitive exchange depreciations, eliminating foreign exchange restrictions on current account transactions, and supporting IMF member states in the correction of balance of payments deficits.[704] However, asymmetries in the economic development of individual IMF members dictated numerous exchange rate adjustments, including appreciation of the Deutsche mark (1961 and 1969) and depreciation of the British pound (1949 and 1967) and the French franc (1949, 1957, 1958 and 1969). In the 1960s, the U.S. dollar also came under downward pressure since the U.S. trade balance deteriorated in the face of increasing competitiveness in Europe and Japan. U.S. spending on social policy programs and its Vietnam War effort increased the supply of U.S. dollars, thus fueling skepticism about the United States' ability to meet all future claims by dollar holders in gold at the agreed upon rate of 35 U.S. dollars per troy ounce. That inherent flaw in the Bretton Woods system was identified as early as 1959 by Robert Triffin, a Belgian economist. Triffin argued that the continued growth of world trade would require central banks to pile up more foreign exchange reserves, which consisted chiefly of U.S. dollars. To provide the liquidity required, the United States had to run a persistent balance of payments deficit, which in turn undermined the credibility of the U.S. dollar's gold convertibility on which the system relied. To solve that dilemma, Triffin proposed the creation of a new reserve unit that would be linked neither to gold nor to the U.S. dollar.[705] The special drawing rights launched by the IMF on January 1, 1970, indeed essentially reflected his proposals.[706]

The crisis of the Bretton Woods system

In the 1960s, the easing of capital mobility restrictions and the emergence of the eurodollar market in London (the market for deposits and loans in U.S. dollars outside the United States) made short-term capital flows far more sensitive to interest rate differentials between financial centers. When the United States began to cut interest rates in 1970 to promote growth and the Federal Republic of Germany conversely raised interest rates to curb inflation, Europe was flooded with huge unwanted capital flows from the U.S. To comply with its intervention obligations, the Deutsche Bundesbank–Germany's central bank–was forced to buy 5.1 billion U.S. dollars in the first four months of 1971. After support purchases of an additional 2 billion U.S. dollars during just the first two trading days in May of that year, the Bundesbank took the drastic step of closing Germany's foreign exchange market. Notes in circulation and banks' deposits with the Bundesbank had already increased by almost 22% in 1970,[707] which accelerated the pace of inflation. The crisis of May 1971 essentially imposed the change to a floating exchange rate regime. Leading German economic research institutes and the German Council of Economic Experts had frequently advised before that time that such a change was needed to prevent imported inflation.[708]

When the foreign exchange market was reopened on May 10, 1971, Germany decided to float the Deutsche mark. The Netherlands followed suit, while the Swiss franc was revalued against the U.S. dollar by 7.07%. Following joint deliberations involving the federal government, the OeNB, the social partners, the opposition parties and banking sector representatives, the Austrian schilling was also revalued against the U.S. dollar by 5.5%.[709] As Federal Chancellor Kreisky pointed out in a parliamentary address, the notion of transitioning to a flexible exchange rate regime was considered "highly damaging" to the Austrian economy. Kreisky noted that a small country like Austria "is caught more strongly in the grip of intense international speculation when there are floating exchange rates, and it has fewer options to respond than a country like the Federal Republic of Germany." Furthermore, a system of flexible exchange rates would make it difficult for exporters and importers to be certain of foreign exchange prices, and the ensuing doubt would impede foreign trade.[710] The appreciation of the schilling would help combat inflation, and as Minister of Finance Androsch stressed, it would prevent further brain drain to neighboring countries.[711] Although the OeNB initially argued against a revaluation (reasoning that from a long-term perspective, the current account was balanced), it eventually consented to adjusting the schilling exchange rate.[712] From that point on, Austria used the exchange rate policy as an instrument to contain the risks of imported inflation rather than to maintain equilibrium in the balance of payments.

The exchange rate adjustments of May 1971 curbed the flight from the U.S. dollar for only a short while. President Nixon's announcement the following August to suspend dollar convertibility into gold effectively terminated the Bretton Woods Agreement. In December 1971, new currency parities were established after lengthy negotiations, which for the first time accommodated an effective depreciation of the dollar against gold (from 35 to 38 U.S. dollars per fine ounce).[713] Even before the U.S. Congress approved that agreement in spring 1972, however, a new wave of speculation emerged that was fueled by interest rate differentials operating against the USA. Following an announcement by President Nixon in January 1973 that he would lift the price and wage controls imposed after August 1971 and following publication of a high deficit in the 1972 balance of payments, the U.S. dollar was devalued by 10%. However, that action did nothing to stem the capital flight from the U.S. dollar to the Deutsche mark, the Swiss franc and the yen, which not only continued unabated, but even picked up steam. As a result, foreign exchange markets closed again in early March 1973 to avert a crisis. When they reopened, a return to fixed parities was not considered an option, and after a 3% revaluation of the Deutsche mark, the EEC countries decided to keep the exchange rates of their currencies within a fluctuation margin of 2.25% but float them jointly against the U.S. dollar (block floating). Norway and Sweden participated in that scheme, while the United Kingdom, Ireland, Italy, Japan, Canada and Switzerland maintained flexible exchange rates. Austria revalued the schilling by 2.25% and maintained its policy of keeping the external value of the Austrian currency stable against the currencies of its major trading partners.[714]

Exchange rate policy as an anti-inflation policy

In August 1971, the OeNB decided to base its exchange rate policy on an "indicator" first used after the foreign exchange market reopened on August 24, 1971.[715] That indicator was based on the currencies of several important trading partners that were gathered into a basket at the following weights: German mark 50.2%, Swiss franc 12.8%, Italian lira 12.3%, British pound 9.5%, Dutch guilder 6.9% and Swedish krona 8.3%.[716] The basket's composition was flexible enough to ensure overall exchange rate stability for the main trading partners. For example, the weak Italian lira was removed from the basket in March 1973 and the (overly) strong Swiss franc was replaced by the French franc, which was dropped in January 1974 because of its significant fluctuations against the other currencies. As of July 1976, the schilling exchange rate was based exclusively on the Deutsche mark.[717]

Although the May 1971 revaluation of the schilling and the December 1971 adjustment of exchange rate parities had been supported by a broad consensus of political parties and social partners, subsequent revaluations in March 1973 (2.25%) and June 1973 (4.8%) were criticized by the opposition parties for being too large despite the concurrent increases in the Deutsche mark's exchange rate by 3% and 5.5%.[718] Disagreement over the revaluation of the schilling triggered a fundamental debate within the OeNB's General Council over who actually held the authority for exchange rate decisions, since the law set no explicit guidelines. While the OeNB had effectively acted as the decision-making authority in preceding decades, it had always sought the consensus of the federal government via the minister of finance. As the debate failed to produce any concrete results,[719] all significant monetary and currency policy decisions continued to be made in close consultation between the minister of finance and the OeNB management.

Compared to the Federal Republic of Germany and Switzerland, Austria was only modestly affected by the speculative capital flows of the early 1970s. Still, the OeNB took preventive measures to "restrain inflows of dollars"[720] and entered into a gentlemen's agreement with the Austrian banks, which promised to maintain 40% of any increase in their schilling-denominated external liabilities as unremunerated deposits with the OeNB and refrain from importing foreign currency to improve their schilling liquidity. To mop up excess liquidity, the OeNB issued certificates of deposits totaling 2 billion Austrian schillings in August and September 1971, one of a number of measures taken to bring the "alarming"[721] pace of inflation under control. In early 1972, the following additional stabilization measures were agreed jointly with the ministry of finance:

- Central bank: increase of reserve requirements, lowering of credit ceiling in conjunction with tightened credit control measures, deposit of 75% of any increase in banks' schilling liabilities to nonresidents on nonremunerated accounts with the OeNB, and issue of certificates of deposits.
- Government: 15% reduction in "discretionary spending" (i.e., budgetary expenditures not mandated by law or contract), issue of schilling bonds and placement of the proceeds with the OeNB at zero interest, no foreign government borrowing and no federal guarantees for other debtors' foreign borrowing.[722]

In September 1972, Austria tightened its monetary policy even further and deliberalized international capital movements. Accordingly, Austrian banks agreed to restrict the granting and advertising of consumer loans, sales of domestic securities to foreigners were capped, the general authorization for nonresidents to purchase domestic property was revoked, the discount rate and minimum reserve requirements were raised, savings banks and credit cooperatives were included in the credit control agreements, and the ERP fund had to refrain from dealing in credits pending further notice.[723] Despite those measures, credit growth continued to accelerate, rising by 19.9% in 1971 and by 21% in 1972, which prompted a faster pace of inflation (chart 10.1). Although price growth in Austria outpaced that of Germany in most years, it remained significantly below the levels observed in the European OECD countries. The 1974 uptick in inflation (to above 9%) resulted primarily from the 1973 oil crisis. In the fall of 1973, Arab oil-producing nations proclaimed an oil embargo in response to the U.S. and other countries providing aid to Israel, which had been attacked by Egyptian and Syrian forces. The embargo triggered a drastic hike in oil prices, which in turn spurred inflation and dampened growth in oil importing countries–essentially because higher oil prices are tantamount to a tax levied by foreign countries that depresses GDP. In Austria, 1974 import prices for oil and oil products were 230% above their 1972 levels, which added a cost of 9 billion Austrian schillings to imports and equaled 6.5% of the entire import volume for 1973.[724]

Chart 10.1: **Growth of consumer prices**[725]

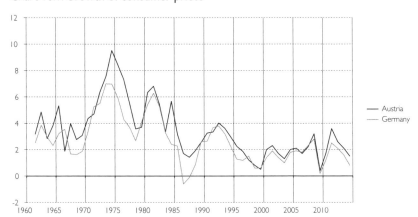

In the early 1970s, inflation skyrocketed due to globally high production growth rates and strong credit expansion. The tripling of oil prices in 1973 triggered a period of stagflation: sluggish real demand coupled with a high rate of inflation. Inflation rates were higher in Austria than in Germany, but because of a higher growth rate of productivity the competitiveness of Austrian firms did not change for the worse.

Economic slowdown and current account balance deficit

In the first half of the 1970s, soaring energy prices and increasing awareness of the limited supply of natural resources[726] gave rise to a global climate of skepticism about long-term growth prospects. As in other countries, Austria's economic growth faltered and declined to an average of 2.5% for the two decades following 1973, compared to an average of 5.4% in the period from 1953 to 1973 (chart 10.2). Unlike many other countries, however, Austria was largely able to cushion the unemployment that followed the economic setback by deploying a set of fiscal, monetary and income policy instruments, a tactic later dubbed "Austro-Keynesianism."[727] While the Austrian unemployment rate rose from 2% to 3.7% between 1975 and 1982, it stood at 10% in the European OECD countries in 1982, having increased by 5 percentage points since 1975.[728] In Austria, growth and employment were supported by an anticyclical budget policy, which led to a doubling of financial debt in proportion to GDP (24.8% in 1980).[729] The wage policy of the Austrian Federation of Trade Unions also yielded to economic needs and advocated a policy of wage restraint in 1977 when restrictive economic policy measures were prompted by a current account deficit that had widened to 3.7% of GDP (chart 10.3). The deterioration in the current account after 1973 was caused by surging energy import prices and the faster growth of Austria's economy compared to its major trading partners. While the Austrian growth edge over the European OECD countries in the years preceding the oil shock was mainly export driven (i.e., the result of gains in foreign market shares), the engine behind the higher rate of economic growth that occurred from 1975 onward was the comparatively higher growth rate of domestic demand, reflecting higher government spending motivated by economic policy considerations and increased consumer spending on the back of high wage settlements.[730] This expansionary path led to a substantial increase in the current account deficit during 1976 and 1977, which was contained in relatively short order by applying restrictive fiscal, monetary and income policies.

Chart 10.2: **Real economic growth in Austria**[731]

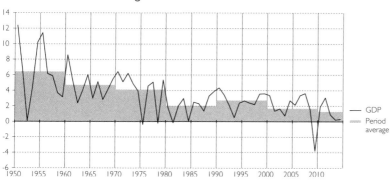

The years of exceptional growth ended with the massive surge in energy prices during the early 1970s. After 1973, the annual rise in real production was only about half of the rate achieved in the two preceding decades. The average growth rate of production was still lower after the turn of the century.

To curb credit expansion–a key contributor to the current account deficit–the OeNB cut banks' refinancing volumes.[732] In June 1977, central bank interest rates were increased by 1.5 percentage points and the availability of central bank refinancing was made contingent on a limitation of credit expansion to 1.1% per

month (limes). Consumer lending was treated more restrictively than investment lending, which was also reflected in an advertising ban on consumer
loans. At the same time, the OeNB furnished additional central bank funds to
Oesterreichische Kontrollbank AG for export financing and to Österreichische
Investitionskredit AG for investment project support.[733]

Chart 10.3: **Current account balance** (in % of nominal GDP)[734]

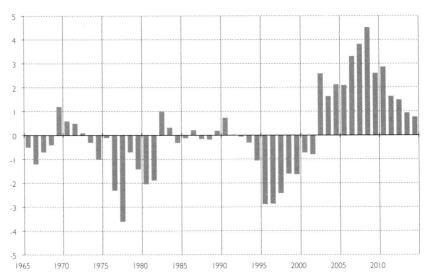

In 1976 and 1977, the current account balance deteriorated sharply because domestic demand played
a larger role in accelerating growth than in earlier years. The stabilization measures introduced in 1977
rapidly improved Austria's external balance. In the second half of the 1990s the current account showed
a deficit, since 2002 the balance of external transactions in goods and services has been in surplus.

The OeNB began supporting refinancing of claims against foreign costumers
through the purchase of export bills of exchange as early as 1950. It also made
central bank funds for export financing available to Österreichischer Export-
fonds GmbH and Oesterreichische Kontrollbank AG (Austria's government-ap-
pointed export credit agencies)[735] by purchasing certificates of deposit of those
institutions. As of 1976 (and on an even larger scale from 1983 onward), the
OeNB also provided refinancing facilities for investments.[736] This form of

"selective money creation" was equivalent to subsidization of exports and investment activities, as the central bank's lending rates were below market rates. Over time, the economic department of OeNB took an increasingly critical view of selective money creation in view of its potential to distort competition, its *de facto* long-term nature and the limited economic impact it had due to windfall gains.[737] Following Austria's entry into the European Monetary System, all forms of selective money creation had to be abandoned.

Criticism of Austria's hard currency policy

The mounting current account deficit also sparked debate over Austria's exchange rate policy. Demands by the export industry for a departure from the rigid peg to the Deutsche mark were supported by Federal Chancellor Kreisky, who in mid-1977 spoke out in favor of a more flexible exchange rate regime.[738] When the Scandinavian currencies were devalued in August 1977, some voices in the OeNB's board of management also began calling for a "more flexible exchange rate policy." University economists likewise recommended a downward revision of the exchange rate to improve the current account balance. Ultimately, however, the proponents for continuation of the hard currency policy prevailed. Their most important argument was that devaluation would only be effective if it reduced real domestic income to the point that it would cause a decline in domestic demand. Where economic policy was concerned, a wage and income policy that improved international competitiveness represented an easier approach compared to dampening wage increases to compensate for import price-induced inflation.[739] In terms of the schilling/mark exchange rate, however, the OeNB adopted a flexible stance (chart 10.4). For instance, when the Deutsche mark appreciated strongly against the U.S. dollar in late 1977, the OeNB decided against adhering firmly to the ceiling announced in July 1977 (7.19 schillings as the upper limit for 1 mark) and chose instead "to exceed that limit should circumstances warrant, without necessarily communicating such measures actively."[740] Although the schilling exchange rate depreciated by 2.4% between 1977 and 1979, this made virtually no impact on the current account balance. International competitiveness is influenced not only by the exchange rate, but also by the ratio of domestic and foreign price movements: If the trade-weighted bilateral exchange rate, the nominal effective exchange rate, rises more than the difference between the domestic and foreign inflation rates, then the competitiveness of the appreciating country is reduced (the real effective exchange rate rises).[741]

Chart 10.4: **Schilling/Deutsche mark exchange rates**[742]

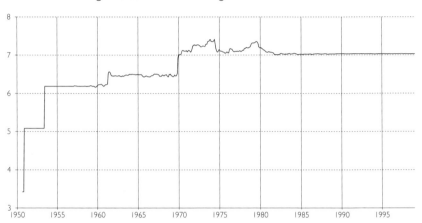

From the early 1960s to 1973, the schilling depreciated by almost 16% against the Deutsche mark. Although that trend reversed between 1971 and 1973 (when the schilling hardened from 7.33 to 7.08 Austrian schillings per 1 Deutsche mark), a renewed weakening trend followed soon after and persisted until 1979. In 1982, the exchange rate finally stabilized at 7.03 schillings per 1 Deutsche mark.

Following the collapse of the fixed exchange rate system, Austria embarked on an exchange rate policy that maintained a peg to the stable-valued Deutsche mark, which resulted in an appreciation in the schilling's real effective exchange rate during the 1970s (chart 10.5). As OeNB President Koren observed at the 1977 General Meeting, that factor, exacerbated by the accelerating pace of growth, was a primary contributor to the deterioration of the current account balance.[743] Yet, the OeNB retained the peg to the Deutsche mark as a means to prevent imported inflation as the primary objective of its exchange rate policy. In September 1979, a relatively lower inflation rate in Austria prompted an autonomous revaluation of the schilling–motivated in part by the need to cushion the impact of oil price hikes caused by the Iranian revolution[744]–which was accompanied by an increase in the OeNB's discount and lending rates by 1.5 percentage points in January 1980. In addition, a 1% surcharge was applied on credit use that exceeded 70% of a bank's refinancing quota.[745]

Chart 10.5: **Trade-weighted schilling exchange rates** (1970 = 100)[746]

Calculations of the schilling's effective exchange rates (trade-weighted measures summarizing the effects of schilling appreciation and depreciation against other currencies) performed by the Austrian Institute of Economic Research (WIFO) for the period from 1970 onwards show that the nominal effective exchange rate experienced a largely steady gain and peaked in 1995 at 179% of the 1970 value. The inflation-adjusted real effective exchange rate posted an 18% increase between 1970 and 1977, thereby contributing to the import surplus, and dropped by 3% from 1977 to 1985 before it climbed again, albeit to a lesser extent, in the years that followed.

The OeNB did not share concerns that this measure might dampen investment activity–a view supported by its Economic Analysis Division, which had concluded that the primary determinants of investment activity were profitability and capacity utilization, while interest rates played only a minor role due to companies' high level of internal financing.[747] Internationally, interest rate levels had risen significantly in the second half of 1979 because the leading central banks prioritized inflation control over supporting economic activity. By upholding its policy of low interest rates, the OeNB lost almost one-third of its foreign exchange reserves during that period.[748] That experience made it abundantly clear to all policy makers that an autonomous interest rate policy was incompatible with a fixed exchange rate and free capital movement. The schilling's peg to the Deutsche mark presupposed an essential similarity of both countries' fundamentals (i.e., interest rates, price levels and current account balances). As these conditions were met through Austria's use of fiscal, monetary and incomes policy instruments, Austria's exchange rate strategy gained credibility in the market, which enabled the OeNB to rebuff a speculative attack on the schilling in August 1993 in short order.[749]

Beginning in the 1980s, the OeNB followed the Deutsche Bundesbank's approach[750] of stepping up open market operations to influence interest rates in the money market. To control the supply of central bank money independently from movements in the current account balance, the scope of liquidity-providing open market operations was increased from 17 billion to 29 billion Austrian schillings in September 1982, and reached 55 billion Austrian schillings by 1993. Upon Austria's accession to the European Union and participation in the European Monetary System (EMS), the OeNB's refinancing instruments, including the components of selective money creation, had to be brought in line with EMS requirements.[751]

Financial market liberalization, EU accession and preparations for the euro

The restrictions on international capital movements introduced in 1971 to prevent speculative capital inflows were slackened in the second half of the 1970s and gradually eliminated in the 1980s. Full liberalization was achieved in November 1991.[752] The phased approach chosen for this reform process had a positive impact on economic development[753] and guarded against currency and banking crises, which–as practical experience has demonstrated–are more likely to occur in an environment of unfettered liberalization.[754] The elimination of administrative controls on international capital movements was accompanied by measures to liberalize the domestic capital market. The new Stock Market Act, passed in 1989, aligned Austria's national legislation with EC standards, improved investor protection and transferred tasks vested previously with government agencies to bodies of the stock exchange.[755] The 1992 Capital Market Act liberalized access to the Austrian bond market by removing the authorization requirement for bond issues by the minister of finance while tightening prospectus and reporting requirements to correspond with international standards.[756] Coupled with a move toward more market-based pricing, these measures triggered a foreign "buying frenzy"[757] for Austrian government bonds that boosted foreign currency reserves, yet also posed a potential threat to the hard currency policy. To counter the possibility of a massive sell-off of bonds triggered by a potential downgrade of Austria's sovereign credit rating (which would drive up long-term interest rates and depress foreign exchange reserves), the OeNB established a safety net for schilling securities and agreed to provide the banking sector with the required liquidity for market support operations.[758] Fortunately, the OeNB had no need to resort to this kind of market intervention until the schilling currency was replaced by the euro.

Austrian banks and the international debt crisis

As noted previously in this chapter, the early 1980s were marked by skyrocketing interest rates, largely because in the aftermath of the 1979/80 oil price shock, the central banks of the United States, the United Kingdom and the Federal Republic of Germany opted to prevent inflation rather than take measures to support economic activity. Since the U.S. dollar strengthened concurrently with the stagnation of economic growth, Latin American countries such as Brazil and Mexico could no longer service their foreign debts, which were denominated primarily in U.S. dollars. According to IMF calculations, the Latin American debt held by U.S. banks by the end of 1981 accounted for an average of 97.3% of their capital and reserves, and in many cases even exceeded 100%. This excessive concentration of risk not only threatened the solvability individual banks, but also jeopardized the macro stability of the financial system.[759] During the OeNB's April 1983 General Meeting, President Koren warned that the international financial sector was nowhere close to being prepared, institutionally or financially, for the impending collapse of the banking system.[760]

The Latin American debt crisis affected Austria to a far lesser extent than did the mounting debt burden of Eastern European countries, vis-à-vis Austrian banks, which represented about ten times that of its Latin American exposure. In March 1981, Poland defaulted on its external debt, and Hungary, the German Democratic Republic and Yugoslavia likewise had serious problems servicing their foreign debt.[761] In the years that followed, the two forums created to restructure international debt–the "London Club" for sovereign debt to commercial banks and the "Paris Club" for debt between national governments–negotiated a series of debt restructuring agreements. In 1991, Austria granted Poland[762] a 50% debt cut, which added a burden of 21 billion schillings to the federal budget. The debts of the German Democratic Republic were serviced by the Federal Republic of Germany following unification, and Hungary[763] and Yugoslavia[764] received bridge loans from the Bank for International Settlements and the IMF.

In the first half of the 1980s, the OeNB harbored serious doubts about whether the Austrian banking system could continue to function when faced with the insolvency of large debtors. In mid-1984, Austrian banks' non-government-backed foreign exposure totaled 116.7 billion Austrian schillings (which represented 4.1% of their aggregate total assets), of which Eastern European debt accounted for 77 billion Austrian schillings.[765] Aside from vastly insufficient risk provisions, the balance sheets of Austrian banks charted a risky maturity transformation structure: 122 billion Austrian schillings in short-term net liabilities and 136 billion Austrian schillings in long-term liabilities to foreign creditors stood against 240 billion Austrian schillings in long-term claims on foreign debtors denominated in schillings and foreign currency, of which 52% were payable by "problematic countries." A study by the OeNB's Economic Analysis Division described the situation among Austrian banks as "highly vulnerable" and explored actions the OeNB might take in response to a threat to the financial system.[766]

New Austrian banking legislation

The major source of the systemic problems being faced by the Austrian banking sector was the pronounced weakness of its capital base. That condition resulted from an overly expansive business policy (referred to by observers as "balance sheet fetishism") coupled with low profitability.[767] Between 1965 and 1985, total assets grew by an average of 15% per year, while the equity ratio declined from 5.7% to 2.5% of total assets.[768] Compounding these challenges, the legal framework for Austrian banks, established in 1979 by the Austrian Banking Act, was already outdated when it became law. According to a study by the Austrian Institute of Economic Research, "to get the key stakeholders to agree on legislation of this magnitude, requirements on minimum capital levels, large exposure caps, international operations and banking supervision were left unaddressed."[769] Therefore, soon after the 1979 Banking Act became effective, the OeNB pushed for more stringent rules on capital adequacy and risk limitation, an outcome that was achieved to some extent by the 1986 amendment to the Banking Act.[770] In an attempt to boost their profitability, Austrian banks established a target-rate cartel for lending and deposit rates.[771] However, that approach failed to yield the desired results, and even as Austria prepared for its EU accession at the beginning of the 1990s, the Austrian banking sector was still considered uncompetitive and incompatible with EU standards.[772] As part of the obligations that accompanied Austria's impending membership in the European Economic Area in 1994, a new Banking Act was passed in 1993 to harmonize national banking legislation with EU regulations.[773] Although that new legislation improved the organization and operation of Austrian banks, it failed to eliminate overbanking,[774] and thus did not deliver the "radical structural change" needed by the Austrian banking sector. In the years that followed, banks tried to avoid the necessity for downsizing by expanding progressively into the former Eastern bloc countries.

The 1993 Banking Act, crafted with far more OeNB involvement than prior banking sector-related legislation, also redefined the central bank's role in banking supervision since it acknowledged that concerns about the micro-level health and stability of the banking system were important factors influencing monetary policy-making.[775] The 1993 Banking Act established an Expert Commission charged with advising the minister of finance and the OeNB on general banking issues and matters of bank auditing. This clearly increased the

OeNB's involvement in supervisory activities, although primary responsibility for banking supervision remained with the minister of finance.[776]

Preparing for the single currency

The 1993 Banking Act, which aligned national banking legislation with EU law, was one part of the comprehensive efforts Austria made to prepare for its impending entry into the European Community. Austria formally applied for EC membership in July 1989. Before the end of the year, the OeNB and the Monetary Committee (whose role was to coordinate economy policy among EC[777] member states)[778] began initial consultations focused on exploring whether an association agreement with the European Monetary System would be advantageous for Austria.[779] The EMS had been established in March 1979 to stabilize foreign exchange rates among EC member states. Back in 1978, Austrian Chancellor Kreisky had suggested to the German ambassador in Vienna that he would appreciate Austria being invited to join the currency agreement under negotiation–a proposal also welcomed by German Chancellor Schmidt.[780] However, after further discussions at central bank governors' meetings in Washington and Basel, and following consultations between the OeNB and the ministry of finance, Austria had decided to retain the schilling peg to the Deutsche mark and not assume any further obligations to the EMS once it was clear that Austria would not be able to join the decision-making bodies of EMS for the time being.[781] Deliberations about a possible association with the EMS after Austria applied for EC membership led to the same conclusion. In a preliminary meeting of the Council of Ministers in February 1991 attended by OeNB President Schaumayer, it was decided, "that Austria would enter the European Monetary System and the European Central Bank *uno actu* with EC entry."[782]

Austria's accession to the EU on January 1, 1995, also obliged the country to join the EMS. Participation in the Exchange Rate Mechanism (ERM) of the EMS–the commitment to intervene in the foreign exchange market to maintain the fixed exchange rates prevailing under the ERM–was not mandatory. For example, Sweden and Finland, which joined the EC at the same time as Austria, did not participate in the ERM.[783] For Austria, ERM membership was essentially a matter of course, as the country had for some 20 years been following the policy of foregoing the use of the exchange rate as a tool to influence economic growth.

A federal law passed in December 1994 granted the minister of finance and the OeNB the requisite authority to make all declarations and announcements necessary for participation in the ERM.[784] On January 7, 1995, the EC's Monetary Committee accepted the central rate of 13.7167 Austrian schillings against 1 ECU (European currency unit) specified by Minister of Finance Lacina (as recommended by the OeNB), and Austria joined the EMS exchange rate and intervention mechanism on January 9, 1995.[785]

At the time Austria became a member of the EMS, the European Economic and Monetary Union (EMU) was in the second stage of the path leading to a single currency as outlined in the Maastricht Treaty. That stage had begun in 1994 with the establishment of the European Monetary Institute (EMI)[786] after completion of the first stage, which achieved total freedom for capital transactions and increased cooperation between central banks. The EMI was tasked with creating the legal, institutional and organizational framework for the European Central Bank and the European System of Central Banks. The Maastricht Treaty envisaged the introduction of a single European currency–the third and final stage of EMU–by 1999 in all EU member states that met the required convergence criteria. Specifically, those criteria were: annual government deficit below 3% of GDP; gross government debt below 60% of GDP; inflation rate no higher than 1.5 percentage points above the average of the three best performing EU member states; long-term interest rate no higher than 2 percentage points above the average of the three countries with the lowest inflation; and exchange rate stability, which required at least two consecutive years of participation in the ERM without devaluation and fluctuations that exceeded the ±15% fluctuation band of the national currency against the ECU.[787]

Institutional reform

The introduction of the single European currency was preceded by large-scale preparations involving the participation of many OeNB employees in EMI committees and national working groups. The primary central bank policy issues were addressed by EMI subcommittees that focused on monetary policy, foreign exchange policy and banking supervision, as well as working groups that concentrated on payment systems, banknotes, statistics, accounting issues, law and information systems.[788] To ensure effective implementation of the EMI's decisions, the OeNB developed a master plan comprising 60 projects that required the commitment of 292 OeNB employees, measured in full-time equivalents, until 1998.[789]

The preparatory steps for monetary policy integration also included a reform of the OeNB's organizational structure, which was launched soon after Austria applied for EU membership. In April 1993, OeNB President Schaumayer informed shareholder representatives that the recently completed reorganization included a redistribution of tasks, streamlining of decision-making processes, changes in the OeNB's Conditions of Service and a "substantial cut in the remuneration of board members."[790] Chief Executive Director Wala estimated the expected cost savings up to 1997 at 700 million Austrian schillings.[791] In 1997, a further pay cut for the OeNB's top senior executives was implemented because the Act on the Limitation of Remunerations for Public Officials,[792] which became effective on July 1, 1997, capped compensation for the "highest ranking official of the Oesterreichische Nationalbank" at 250% of the monthly salary of a National Council member. That cap formed the basis of the remuneration scale applicable to the members of the governing board.[793]

Nevertheless, the efforts made to streamline the OeNB's cost and organizational structures and to reform its remuneration system did not prevent political parties, particularly the right-wing populist Freedom Party (FPÖ), from attacking OeNB employees because of their "privileges" or criticizing OeNB policy in general. In April 1992, an extraordinary meeting of the General Council was convened when OeNB President Schaumayer and her deputies decided to address statements made by FPÖ party leader Jörg Haider, which they characterized as an "outright attack on the independence of a central bank." Haider had demanded the use of 60 billion schillings from central bank reserves for fiscal purposes and the abolition of the minimum reserve requirement in order to facilitate a reduction in the interest rate of working capital loans by 1 percentage point. The OeNB's General Council strongly objected to the FPÖ's proposals and denounced them as "a gross violation of the stability policy and independence of a central bank."[794] Ultimately, the OeNB made several changes to its Conditions of Service, which included substantial cuts to employee entitlements to a pension. Despite instituting these reforms, however, the OeNB's monetary policy and its staff remuneration system continued to face public criticism.

A single European currency—the OeNB as a Eurosystem central bank (1999–2016)

"The sheer frequency of events ... made it seem as if the wheels of time had suddenly begun to spin faster."

Klaus Liebscher, President's speech at the 1996 General Meeting[795]

The final, binding decision to change over to a common currency, which had been christened the "euro" at the European Council meeting in Madrid in 1995, was made by EU heads of state or government and ministers of finance in early May 1998. They also determined who would sit on the first Executive Board of the ECB (to be established on June 1, 1998), which countries would adopt the common currency from the outset, and the rate to be applied when converting national currencies into euros.[796] Having fulfilled the convergence criteria laid down in the Maastricht Treaty, Austria became part of the euro area along with ten other EU member states at the start of 1999. In the case of Austria, the changeover was based on a conversion rate of 13.7603 schillings per euro, as irrevocably fixed in December 1998. For the first three years, the euro remained an "invisible" currency, only used for accounting purposes and in electronic payments. The introduction of euro coins and notes did not start until January 1, 2002,[797] and the legacy currencies of the initial euro area members–Austria, Belgium, Finland, France, Germany, Ireland, Italy, Luxembourg, the Netherlands, Portugal and Spain–remained legal tender until June 2002. By 2015, another eight countries had joined the euro area: Greece (2001), Slovenia (2007), Malta and Cyprus (2008), Slovakia (2009), Estonia (2011), Latvia (2014) and Lithuania (2015).

Thus, the Oesterreichische Nationalbank is now a member of the Eurosystem, the central banking system of the euro area, which comprises the ECB and the national central banks of the euro area countries. In joining the Eurosystem, the OeNB essentially continued the stability-oriented monetary policy it had pursued in the previous decades. At the same time, however, joining the euro area brought about fundamental changes in the institutional framework in which monetary policy decisions were made, meaning that the OeNB also had to redefine its duties and its position in national and European economic policy-making. The monetary policy of the newly founded ECB operated smoothly, or at least it seemed that way until 2007. In reality, the formative years of the Eurosystem coincided with the accumulation of global macroeconomic imbalances and excessive risks in the international financial sector–a combination that in 2008 precipitated the most severe financial and economic crisis since the 1930s. The euro area was hit doubly by the crisis, as the liquidity problems of banks were followed by a sovereign debt crisis and doubts about the very viability of the monetary union in its current form. From 2008 onward, policy makers took a number of reform measures at the international and European level in order to strengthen the institutional base of the euro area and to prevent such a crisis from happening again. The new architecture of banking and financial market supervision significantly broadened the jurisdiction of the supervisory authorities and redefined supervisory roles at the national and European level. Although key competences were transferred to the ECB and other European bodies, these moves also gave national supervisory authorities–in the case of Austria, the Financial Market Authority and the OeNB–new responsibilities and significance. The quest for the adequate design and interaction of monetary and financial stability policies remains an unfinished chapter, even 200 years after the establishment of the Nationalbank.

Monetary policy may change, but the objective does not

The introduction of the euro was preceded by a long process in which the member states worked to agree on how they would handle monetary policy in the future. The framework ultimately selected for the common currency represented a compromise between various national traditions (which had often arisen from specific characteristics of national banking and financial systems) and the international consensus on optimal monetary policy as propagated in the 1990s.[798]

From stable exchange rates to stable prices

This consensus hinged on combining a price stability objective with an independent role for the central bank. Central bank independence was, of course, not a new idea–as the early history of note-issuing banks in Austria clearly shows–but it saw a revival in the economics discipline in the 1980s and 1990s, quickly attaining near-mythical status.[799] One important reason for this revival was the less-than-impressive record of monetary policy in the 1970s, which was characterized by high inflation and weak growth. Many economists concluded that the central bank had to be protected from the temptations of short-sighted cyclical economic policy and should only be given responsibility for maintaining stable prices. This division of tasks, in which the central bank was in charge of monetary policy but the government handled all other areas of economic policy, not only freed the central bank from influences that were harmful to the economy in the medium term, but also created advantages for the government. Once the financial markets had been liberated from the corset of post-war regulations, public confidence and the credibility of economic policy began to play an increasingly important role in keeping down the government's debt costs as well as in enhancing its ability to influence exchange rates in accordance with its desired policy. The hope was that an independent central bank with a mandate to contain inflation would be better able to build the necessary trust. Another advantage from the government's perspective was that the responsibility for necessary but potentially unpopular decisions such as interest-rate hikes was allocated to an independent institution. Besides an independent central bank, the second element of the aforementioned consensus on the design of monetary policy was the commitment to maintaining price stability. On the one hand, this reflected the view that in the long term monetary policy can only influence price levels, but not economic growth and employment.[800] On the other hand, it was also a way to secure the transfer of such an important policy area as monetary policy to an independent institution–which is not without its problems in a democracy–by defining a clear objective by which the central bank's policy could be measured, thus legitimizing the policy itself.[801]

This model was especially attractive in the European setting, as the institutional separation of central bank and treasury made it possible to establish a monetary union without immediately centralizing fiscal policy, which would not have been politically feasible. In addition, the commitment to a clearly defined objective made it easier to design monetary policy despite potentially conflicting ideas pursued by member states in other areas of economic policy. Last but not least, the objective of price stability and the independence of the ECB based on the model of the German Bundesbank also helped getting Germany on board as a member of monetary union.[802]

While central bank policies had always been geared toward maintaining monetary stability, the focus of policy-making shifted in the 1980s and 1990s. That period saw a trend toward defining price stability numerically in hopes of stabilizing inflation expectations, which are considered especially important for the economic decisions of households and businesses.[803] In many countries, central banks therefore shifted from intermediate objectives such as growth in the money supply or fixed exchange rates to a strategy of direct inflation targeting.[804] Central banks adhering to an inflation targeting strategy publish a numerical inflation target for a given policy horizon. If the forecast inflation rate is above the targeted level, the central bank will raise interest rates; if inflation is lower, monetary policy is eased. The newly founded ECB also opted for a numerical target in order to achieve the price stability objective laid down in the Treaty on European Union: as specified by the Governing Council of the ECB, the target for Eurosystem policy-making is to keep increases in the (harmonized) index of consumer prices in the euro area below 2% in the medium term. In 2003, the Governing Council specified the definition further by clarifying that the inflation rate should be below, but close to, 2% because the Eurosystem also wished to avoid excessively low inflation rates.[805]

In the early stages of the debate, it was not clear how the price stability target was to be attained in the euro area. In addition to inflation targeting, which at the time had only been employed in the EU by Finland, Sweden and the United Kingdom since the second half of the 1990s, various interim targets were also considered conceivable.[806] What was ruled out as impracticable for the euro area as a whole was an exchange-rate target such as the one used by Austria as well as the majority of EU countries first within the Bretton Woods framework and later under various European successor schemes.[807] The key alternative was therefore the strategy of the German Bundesbank, which applied a numerical target for growth in the money supply. After lengthy discussions, the EU countries decided in favor of a balanced approach in which the ECB would monitor a broad set of economic variables in addition to the money supply. The two-pillar strategy defined in 1999 and refined on multiple occasions time is based on two analytical perspectives:[808] Economic analysis largely focuses on assessing current economic and financial developments as well as the resulting risks to price stability in the short and medium term. For example, indicators include changes in economic output and demand, the development of unemployment rates, a broad range of price and cost indicators and exchange rate changes. Monetary analysis, on the other hand, focuses more on monitoring risks to price stability in the medium to long term, largely relying on the correlation between the money supply and price levels, which is stable from a medium- to long-term perspective. In addition to M3, the common broad measure of money supply which essentially includes cash as well as deposits with credit institutions with a maturity of up to two years, monetary analysis also considers credit growth and changes in asset prices.[809] The results of the analyses under both pillars and cross-checks thereof inform the decision-making of the ECB Governing Council. In light of the uncertainty as to what effect monetary policy would have in the newly established monetary union, this approach brought about obvious advantages and promised continuity given that "all EU central banks [used] a comprehensive and broadly similar selection of economic and financial indicators to determine their monetary policy course irrespective of the strategy they have opted for."[810] This also applied to the German Bundesbank, which in practice had repeatedly allowed deviations from its money supply targets when other indicators suggested that such deviations were justified.[811] This pragmatic approach also suited the OeNB, which had traditionally been concerned about supporting jobs.[812]

At least since the early 1980s, Austrian monetary policy was tied to the objective of keeping the schilling's exchange rate with the Deutsche mark stable. This general orientation toward stability did not change when the OeNB joined the Eurosystem. However, what certainly did change was the framework for monetary policy-making and the relevance of central bank independence, transparency and accountability.[813] Austria's hard currency policy of the 1980s and 1990s had been based on a broad political consensus and coordination between the central bank, the government and the social partners; this consensus was also reflected in the composition of the General Council, the OeNB's highest decision-making body.[814] In this participatory system, the *formal* independence of the central bank played only a secondary role–unlike in the multinational monetary union, where the institutional objectives and competences, including those of the new players, were yet to be defined.[815] At the same time, the *informal* ex ante accountability that in Austria had been guaranteed by the participation of all groups of society in the OeNB's General Council was replaced by the standards of *formal* ex post accountability and transparency defined for the ECB. Examples of this change include the press conferences after the meetings of the ECB Governing Council, regular hearings of the ECB president before the European Parliament, and the publication of accounts of the Governing Council meetings. Although monetary policy no longer forms part of an Austrian economic policy "consensus package," the distribution of roles between monetary policy and the other national areas of economic policy such as fiscal, structural and wage policy has changed little in practice: Monetary policy continues to serve as an anchor of stability policy, while the other areas of economic policy handle adjustments to shifts in economic demand or to the degree of competitiveness.[816] In this way, Austrian economic policy was well prepared for the requirements of the monetary union.

Implementing monetary policy

In line with the different monetary policy strategies pursued by the later euro area countries prior to 1999 as well as their differently structured financial systems and national economies, the central banks had used different tools before 1999 to influence the economy and thus attain their objectives.[817] In this area as well, the framework selected by the Eurosystem was based on an international consensus that had emerged in the 1980s and 1990s: the strong orientation of monetary policy instruments toward market mechanisms.[818] With the deregulation and internationalization of the financial markets, a process which accelerated in the 1980s, the previous set of instruments such as credit controls increasingly lost their effectiveness, while the prices determined on the financial markets gained importance for the economic decisions of households and businesses. In this way, the short-term interest rate–the financial market rate that the central bank can most effectively influence–became its most important policy tool. Essentially, the job of monetary policy makers in the 1990s and 2000s was as "simple" as setting the short-term interest rate to provide an adequate nudge for all variables that matter in the transmission mechanism of monetary policy, such as long-term interest rates, exchange rates, asset values, etc., which in turn affect the rate of inflation (as the objective of monetary policy).[819]

The operational framework that the ECB chose to implement its monetary policy reflects this consensus.[820] The ECB's main liquidity-providing transactions are open-market operations, in which the liquidity of the central bank is auctioned off to banks in a market-like procedure. Minimum reserves, which earlier were also used to control bank lending, now only serve to stabilize money market rates and increase demand for central bank liquidity, which makes it easier for the ECB to enforce its key interest rates on the market. Unlike earlier–and in order to prevent distortions of competition–minimum reserves are now remunerated. The two standing facilities–the deposit facility and the marginal lending facility–only serve to cushion extraordinary spikes in the need for, or supply of, liquidity and thus to stabilize the money market rate; they do not constitute the refinancing facilities of first resort. All of the ECB's credit operations are backed by collateral. The OeNB, which used to provide central bank liquidity through discounts and advances (i.e., standing facilities) and did not remunerate minimum reserves for many years, had begun to adapt its monetary policy tools to modern financial market conditions even before Austria decided to join the EU.[821] With the advent of the euro, the OeNB finally discontinued its time-honored discount operations–a line of business in which it had engaged since 1817.[822] At the end of 1998 the OeNB also stopped publishing weekly financial statements, which it had been disclosing almost without interruptions since 1848. Once the Eurosystem started publishing consolidated weekly statements for all euro area central banks, the OenB's own balance sheet was no longer relevant for interpreting monetary policy.[823]

In order to influence economic conditions in the euro area as a whole, the short-term interest rate set by the ECB must apply equally throughout the currency area. To facilitate the transmission of monetary policy, the Eurosystem enables a large number of banks to take part in monetary policy operations. In addition, a broad range of collateral has been defined as eligible for refinancing, with a view to effectively giving all credit institutions direct access to central bank liquidity. At the same time, another key priority was to promote the free flow of central bank liquidity within the monetary union. To this effect, it was necessary to integrate the national interbank markets to form a single European interbank market, based on a single payments system ("TARGET") which was launched in 1999 for all euro-denominated payments within the monetary union. In the absence of a comparable payments system for large-volume payments in Austria, the OeNB first launched a real-time gross settlement system for Austria in 1997 which was subsequently integrated into TARGET.[824]

The OeNB's role in the Eurosystem

In other words, the OeNB's participation in the Eurosystem led to changes, but not necessarily to a reduction in the tasks of the OeNB. In 1998, the Austrian Nationalbank Act was amended to reflect the new architecture of monetary policy.[825] First the formal independence of the central bank had to be bolstered. The role of the state commissioner, who had previously been responsible for ensuring that the bank acted in accordance with the law, was reduced to an advisory role in the OeNB's General Council and General Meeting. Lending to public-sector entities, which had in effect been eliminated with Austria's accession to the EU, was expressly prohibited. In addition, the federal government's share of profits was raised to 90%, and the accounting standards applicable to the OeNB were harmonized with the accounting rules under the Austrian Commercial Code. Finally, the duties of the OeNB were defined in line with those laid down in the ECB statutes.

The capital of the ECB comes from the national central banks of all EU countries, with the bulk of the capital coming from the central banks of the euro area countries. The OeNB's initial share in the capital key of the ECB in 1999 amounted to 2.36%, corresponding to the share of the Austrian population in the EU population and Austria's share in the EU's GDP. Likewise, the ECB's foreign reserve assets were established by means of a transfer of gold, U.S. dollar and Japanese yen assets from the euro area central banks. The key decision-making body on monetary and exchange-rate policy is the Governing Council of the ECB, which consists of the six members of the Executive Board appointed by the European Council and the governors of the national central banks. In this context, the governors of the national central banks make decisions as individuals and not as representatives of their respective countries, are not bound by the decisions of third parties and must not obtain or accept instructions from bodies or agencies of the EU, member states or other organizations. In order to ensure the independence of the governors, their term was set to at least five years, and precise rules were defined for dismissals. The OeNB General Council was relieved of its competence for monetary and exchange-rate policy and was given a status equivalent to that of the supervisory board of a stock corporation with regard to all matters other than those concerning monetary union.

Despite the *de jure* transfer of monetary sovereignty to the Eurosystem, the OeNB governor's participation in the decisions of the ECB Governing Council marked an effective increase in Austria's influence on European monetary policy.[826] The national central banks are responsible for preparing the positions of the central bank governors who participate in the Governing Council meetings. For the OeNB, this meant that it was necessary to significantly expand its analysis capacities. For example, macroeconomic projections for the euro area, which form an important basis for monetary policy decisions and for the efficient implementation of monetary policy strategy, required the OeNB to establish its own economic forecasting function. In order to ensure that members of the monetary union can rely on a similar basis of information, the requirements imposed on statistics in terms of precision, detail and timeliness have also grown, not least because of close international trade relations as well as the tightly interlinked financial markets. Statistical data collected by the national central banks include monetary statistics as the basis for money and credit aggregates, financial accounts and balance-of-payments statistics.[827] The financial crisis of 2008 further increased the need for adequate data to enable the ECB Governing Council to make informed decisions.

While monetary policy is decided at the ECB level, the national central banks are responsible for implementing those common policies. This means that important operational duties have remained in the hands of the OeNB, such as settling transactions with banks, intervening on the foreign exchange markets, managing foreign exchange reserves, putting banknotes into circulation, ensuring the supply of cash to the population and businesses, managing minimum reserve accounts for institutions subject to the relevant require-

The OeNB as a stock corporation—from dispersed shareholding to state ownership

When the Nationalbank was founded in 1816 as a stock corporation, its shares were issued in exchange for a combination of Vienna standard paper money and silver coins. This way the initial public offering (IPO) was part of the plans to withdraw the depreciated paper money from circulation. As a side effect, the Nationalbank achieved a relatively dispersed ownership structure: in 1822 the stock ledger included some 5,000 entries, many of which recorded holdings of just one or two shares.[828]

According to the initial charter, the entire profits of the bank—after allocating a fixed percentage to reserves—went to the shareholders.[829] The state received its share in seigniorage through loans, for which it paid below-market interest rates, rather than participating in the volatile earnings of the bank. Depending on economic conditions, the dividend could fluctuate heavily from one year to the next and would be particularly high during crisis years, when demand for central bank lending was particularly strong. The 1878 charter led to a fundamental reform of the profit-sharing arrangements. Now the state obtained a share of all profits in excess of a minimum return to shareholders. Over the years the minimum dividend was ultimately lowered to 4% while the share of the government in excess profits was increased gradually and based on a progressive scale. Even though this arrangement should in principle have isolated the private shareholders from fluctuations in earnings, strong and volatile earnings growth between 1900 and 1914 led to significant movements in dividends as well. When the Nationalbank was refounded in 1922 and new shares were issued, the minimum dividend was set at 8% in order to make the IPO attractive. As the Austro-Hungarian Bank before, the Nationalbank had a diverse ownership structure, even though credit institutions now dominated.[830]

Between 1945 and 1955 the Nationalbank operated within a provisional framework provided by the pre-1938 charter, without however reinstating the private shareholders. The 1955 Nationalbank Act reestablished the bank as a stock corporation. This time, however, the shares were not offered for public subscription but distributed among the state (which received 50%) as well as selected financial institutions and social partners like the Austrian Trade Union Federation and the chamber of commerce. The shares received a dividend of 6%. As the nominal capital after 1955 was much lower compared to previous periods, the dividend made up a smaller and declining share of total profits, even after having been raised to 10% in 1981. The remaining profits went to the treasury and to reserves in equal parts. In 1992 the OeNB was made liable to pay corporate income tax, and in 1998 the share of the treasury was increased to 90%.

The basic ownership structure remained unchanged until 2006. After the

Chart 11.1: Price of Nationalbank shares and dividends[831]

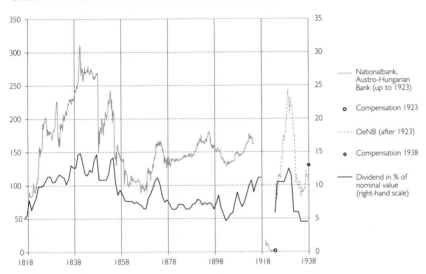

Legend:
- Nationalbank, Austro-Hungarian Bank (up to 1923)
- Compensation 1923
- OeNB (after 1923)
- Compensation 1938
- Dividend in % of nominal value (right-hand scale)

As dividends were high and the general level of interest rates declined, the share price increased strongly until 1848. In the mid-1850s the Nationalbank undertook two capital increases diluting existing shareholdings. Earnings per share declined and the share price, which had since recovered from the revolution of 1848, fell as well. Even though the 1900 charter increased the state's share in the bank's profits, dividends increased after 1900. During World War I, dividends were kept at the prewar level. After the war, the share price declined rapidly and when the bank was liquiditated in 1923 shareholders received barely anything. Until 1930, however, the share price of the newly founded OeNB rose spectacularly. The direct and indirect involvement in the rescue of the Creditanstalt 1931 lowered earnings and dividends significantly.[832] The share price fell accordingly. In 1938 the shareholders received a compensation slightly in excess of the current market price.

government had to step in to support the BAWAG P.S.K in 2005, both the bank and the Trade Union Federation, which had controlled the bank, had to transfer their share holdings to the treasury, bringing the share of the latter to 70%. The remaining institutional shareholders were bought out when the OeNB received considerable competences in banking supervision. Since 2010 the OeNB has been wholly owned by the state.

ment, exercising payments oversight, collecting statistical data, engaging in international exchange-rate policy cooperation, and participating in the activities of international financial institutions.[833] Another set of duties that initially remained at the national level were all activities related to supervising banks and financial markets, as the ECB was only assigned basic competences in this area.[834] Some of those tasks had previously not been handled by the OeNB or had to be restructured within the framework of the harmonized policies of the Eurosystem. The development of a real-time gross settlement system in preparation for joining the TARGET system was already mentioned above. In the field of cash operations, the OeNB–together with its newly established subsidiary Geldservice Austria–also took on a more prominent role, handling, among other things, the challenge of the exchange of schillings and the launch of euro notes and coins on January 1, 2002.[835]

The common monetary policy, 1999 to 2015

Looking back, the European Central Bank has largely managed to achieve its primary objective of keeping inflation below (but close to) the 2% mark since the introduction of the euro as an accounting currency in 1999 (chart 11.2). The average rate of inflation in the euro area came to 1.9% between 1999 and June 2015. Compared to realized inflation, which may temporarily deviate from the target value significantly due to shocks such as sharp increases or decreases in oil prices, the long-term inflation expectations relevant to economic decisions made by households and businesses are considered even more important from a monetary policy perspective. With a few exceptions, these expectations have also remained stable and close to the target level since 1999.[836]

Over this period of just over 15 years, key interest rates went through two cycles of increases and decreases (chart 11.2).[837] When the ECB assumed responsibility for monetary policy in 1999, inflation was low and growth prospects were moderate due to the crisis in Asia and Russia; as a result, the ECB lowered the key interest rate (its interest rate in main refinancing operations) to a minimum of 2.5%. By 2000, the key interest rate was back at a level of 4.75%, follow-

Chart 11.2: **Consumer prices and short-term interest rates in the euro area**[838]

The ECB has achieved its primary objective of keeping the inflation rate below (but close to) 2% in the medium term. The average rate of inflation came to 1.9% between 1999 and June 2015. The after-effects of the financial crisis pushed inflation to levels significantly below the target value in 2009 and between 2013 and 2015.

ing a series of rate increases in order to counter inflationary pressure in response to strong economic growth and an increasing money supply. The bursting of the dotcom bubble and the terrorist attacts in the USA in 2001 caused the outlook for the world economy to deteriorate rapidly, prompting a series of renewed key interest rate decreases in the euro area, like in the USA. Subsequently, key interest rates were kept at a low level until 2005 as the economy recovered only slowly. At the end of 2005, the ECB gradually began to roll back its accommodating monetary policy in order to ensure continued price stability in an environment of steady economic growth and rapid increases in money supply and lending. As the first signs of tension in the financial sector began to emerge in August 2007, the ECB responded with a number of changes in its liquidity supply operations. Since price pressures persisted, however, the key interest rates were again increased in the summer of 2008.

The worsening financial crisis after the collapse of the U.S. investment bank Lehman Brothers in September 2008 prompted the ECB as well as other major central banks around the world to reduce interest rates rapidly and to sharply expand refinancing volumes. The ECB's most important goal in this context was to restore the transmission of monetary policy, which had been placed in jeopardy due to the tensions on the financial markets and disorderly deleveraging. The nonstandard measures taken by the Eurosystem primarily addressed the banking sector, given the key role euro area banks play in the transmission of monetary policy as well as, unlike in the USA, in financial intermediation. The sovereign debt crisis that subsequently emerged in 2010 first hit Greece and then cascaded through Portugal, Ireland, Cyprus, Spain and Italy. Rising bond yields jeopardized the refinancing of the banking systems, which continue to be organized along national lines. The situation was exacerbated by speculations that individual countries might be forced to exit from the euro area on account of a sharp increase in credit risk premia. The ECB took action in 2010 by adopting a government bond purchase program with a view to limiting the rise in credit risk premia and announced in 2012 that it stood ready to buy unlimited quantities of government bonds. This was followed by a significant decline in risk premia. In 2014, monetary policy-making refocused on inflation. Given the sustained risk that inflation could remain substantially below the medium-term target despite the historically low level of interest rates, the ECB decided to carry out further purchases of securities issued by public and private sector agents across the euro area in order to facilitate the financing of investments and to bolster demand in the overall economy. In sum, banks' easier access to refinancing facilities in quantitative and qualitative terms as well as the purchase of private and public debt led to a sharp increase in the consolidated total assets of the Eurosystem and to a corresponding increase in the monetary base (chart 11.3). The inflation feared by some parties as a result did not arise because the funds made available by the Eurosystem primarily replaced the missing refinancing opportunities for banks on the money and capital markets. Due to their low own funds, banks were far more hesitant to grant new loans, and demand for loans was low due to the poor economic outlook. As a result, the M3 measure of money supply rose only very moderately after 2008.

Chart 11.3: **Eurosystem consolidated balance sheet** (in billion of euros)[839]

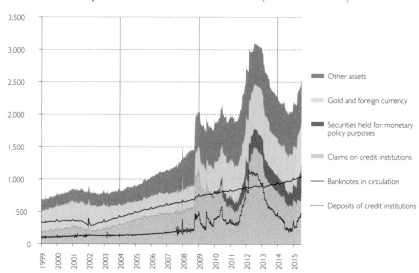

With a view to reducing uncertainty in the banking sector, the ECB has been providing unlimited quantities of central bank money at the discretion of its counterparties since 2008. As a result, the amount of central bank lending to the banking sector has increased and began to fluctuate sharply, reflecting the prevailing conditions in financial markets. The asset purchase programs adopted by the ECB fueled another round of significant increases in the amount of central bank money. This development was not accompanied by inflationary effects because of a stagnation in commercial bank lending.

New instruments to ensure financial stability

In addition to the unprecedented volume of liquidity provided by central banks, enormous amounts of public-sector funds were deployed in the form of equity investments and guarantees from the fourth quarter of 2008 onward in order to stabilize the international financial system. In order to prevent the future use of public funds wherever possible and to reduce the international financial system's vulnerability to crises, statutory own funds and liquidity requirements for financial institutions were tightened and new supervisory instruments were created.

The OeNB's long road to banking supervision, 1979 to 2008

According to the Austrian constitution, the supervision of banks and other financial institutions is the responsibility of the federal government. As mentioned in chapter 10, these supervisory activities were traditionally handled by the Austrian ministry of finance. The federal government issued banking licenses, defined the rules for the business activities of banks and acted as the authority that monitored their compliance with the law. Although the existence of a functioning financial system has always been a key prerequisite if the OeNB wanted to successfully implement its interest-rate and liquidity policy objectives, for a long time the OeNB was not directly involved in the supervision of banks. At the same time, however, the OeNB had access to information that was also relevant for the banking supervisors in the ministry of finance thanks to the central bank's regular contact with banks in refinancing operations, monthly reports of interim bank balance sheets to the OeNB and the Central Credit Register it maintains. Accordingly, the Austrian Banking Act of 1979 provided for the OeNB's involvement in banking supervision activities. On the basis of reports submitted to the OeNB, it examined whether banks were complying with Austrian regulations pertaining to own funds and liquidity requirements. In addition, the OeNB provided the ministry of finance with relevant information and had to be consulted before the ministry could take certain measures. The amendment to the Banking Act adopted in 1986 expanded these powers further.

In the wake of deregulation, the banking sector grew in relation to the overall economy and became increasingly complex.[840] The bankruptcy of the German Herstatt Bank in 1974 and the international debt crisis in the early 1980s were clear indicators of the sector's fragility. All over the world, supervisory authorities were given a more prominent role. In 1988, the Basel Committee for Banking Supervision, which was originally a body representing the central banks and supervisory authorities of the G10 nations, adopted uniform standards to define the minimum level of capital banks were required to hold. In Austria, the requirements of "Basel I" were implemented in the Austrian Banking Act of 1993, which also enabled OeNB staff to conduct on-site inspections of banks. However, those inspections were only conducted on an ad-hoc basis at the request of the Austrian finance ministry.[841] Finally, the Banking Act of 1993 also called for the deployment of an expert commission with two representatives each from the OeNB and the ministry of finance; the act also stipulated that all reports to the ministry from institutions subject to supervision were to be submitted to the OeNB at the same time.

Along with the introduction of new rules for the banking sector, in the 1990s economic policy makers also reconsidered the organization of banking supervision. As shown in the recommendations of the IMF at the time, the international consensus favored spinning off banking supervision to an authority that was independent of the ministry of finance and not subject to instructions from any authority. The main priority was to protect supervisors from political influence, not unlike assigning monetary policy to an independent central bank. This independence could be realized in different ways. Some countries created new authorities outside of the central bank to handle the supervision of banks as well as insurance companies and capital markets (integrated financial supervision), while others established banking supervision as a department within the independent central bank. All of these models have their advantages and disadvantages, which may matter more or less depending on the actual setup of the institution and the political and statutory conditions under which it operates.[842] One argument for an integrated financial supervision was the growing integration of banks, insurance companies, mutual funds and other financial institutions. Other arguments rested on a potential conflict of goals in the objectives of supervision and monetary policy, such as a central bank opting for a more accommodative monetary policy, in the interest of supporting ailing banks, than what would be justified by its price stability goal alone. Other concerns related to the fact that controversial decisions taken by a central bank in its supervisory capacity might damage its credibility as a monetary policy maker. In turn, advocates of entrusting the supervisory function to the central bank argued that dividing up supervisory responsibilities among two separate institutions in itself would not cause potentially conflicting goals to vanish. Much rather, a single institution has access to a broader range of information, will find it easier to balance different objectives when taking decisions and is in the end thus better placed to develop a coordinated crisis response. This is all the more true as problems at individual institutions may, on account of the increasing complexity of the financial sector, affect the functioning of payment systems and interbank markets that are of key relevance for the implementation of monetary policy. Until 2007 many countries preferred to keep monetary policy and banking supervison separate. This pattern has been reversed somewhat since the financial crisis. As a case in point, major tasks of the one-stop financial supervisor established in the UK in 2001 were reintegrated into the portfolio of the Bank of England in 2013. The repeated changes in the organization of financial market supervision in other countries as well indicate that no one model is clearly superior to the others and that successful supervision depends much rather on the political framework, the cooperation among authorities and not least the people involved.

In Austria, draft legislation in 1999 called for the creation of an independent banking supervisor as a subsidiary of the OeNB. Yet an ensuing change of government tipped the balance in favor of an integrated model of financial market supervision, leading to the establishment of a separate agency, the Austrian Financial Market Authority (FMA).[843] In a compromise between the government and the opposition that was necessary to pass a constitutional law defining the FMA's competences, the OeNB was made part of the supervisory framework to the extent that the FMA was obliged to delegate on-site inspections on market and credit risk to the OeNB. The FMA commenced operations in 2002. Supervisory practice after the outsourcing of supervisory activities to a separate agency showed, as the OeNB and FMA observed jointly in 2008, that "the new prudential structure featured some systemic weaknesses that could not be fully eliminated despite all cooperation efforts. For instance, there were overlaps and duplications in surveillance and analysis, and some gray areas regarding the scope of responsibilities."[844] In particular, the separation of on-site and off-site analysis proved to be especially unfavorable, as exposed by the parliamentary investigative committee on political responsibility after the federal government's assumption of guarantees for BAWAG P.S.K. and by reports of the Austrian Court of Audit. Similar problems also appeared in the supervision of Hypo Group Alpe Adria, which was nationalized at very high cost in 2009.[845] In response to this criticism, the supervisory reform in 2008 redefined the division of tasks between the OeNB and FMA. The OeNB's mandate, initially restricted to the inspection of credit and market risk, was broadened to include all business areas and all kinds of risks. Moreover, the OeNB was put in charge of the economic analysis and assessment of banks' internal risk management models. In principle, the OeNB was now in charge of independent fact-finding and assessment, while the FMA–as the competent legal authority–was responsible for legal evaluations and the imposition of any necessary sanctions or special requirements.[846] In the course of this reorganization, the OeNB was for the first time given the express mandate of ensuring financial stability.[847] In actual fact, the OeNB had taken action to this effect even earlier, for instance by providing guidance to the banking sector, as early as in 2003, on limiting foreign currency lending, which used to be rather popular in Austria but is, however, fraught with potential risks.[848] Another case in point is a joint OeNB and FMA initiative launched in 2012, requiring the subsidiaries of Austrian banks in Central, Eastern and Southeastern Europe to align their lending with local deposit-taking in the interest of strengthening their refinancing base.[849]

2008 financial crisis reveals weaknesses in supervision

The financial crisis of 2008 exposed a number of fundamental weaknesses in financial market regulation worldwide. The regulations in force up to that time had in part created wrong incentives and in part disregarded the rise of some significant risks. In the euro area, the shortcomings of *national* supervision and regulation exacerbated this situation in an *integrated* single market with a common currency. The ensuing reforms addressed three aspects: The reforms were designed, *first,* to increase the stability of individual financial institutions; *second,* to create mechanisms for reorganizing or winding down financial institutions in the event of failure that would not jeopardize the financial system and not require the use of taxpayer money, to the extent possible; and *third,* to ensure express consideration of the interaction between individual institutions and the financial system as a whole in supervisory decision-making. Moreover, competences were reshuffled at the EU level, with a view to adjusting the supervisory framework to the requirements of a single currency area.

In terms of microprudential supervision, which focuses on the safety and soundness of individual financial institutions, the new internationally applied "Basel III" rules require banks to hold more high-quality capital to absorb potential losses. New capital buffers as a backstop for unexpected losses are supposed to offset the procyclical elements of the preceding "Basel II" framework which were found to have exacerbated the crisis. Finally, a minimum leverage ratio, defined as disposable capital divided by total assets, should constrain the build-up of leverage in the banking sector. As another lesson from the crisis, banks will have to hold a higher amount of liquid assets in order to be able to deal with sudden liquidity outflows, and they have been encouraged to seek longer-term refinancing.

While banks will have to meet more stringent capital and liquidity requirements, the toolbox of supervisors has been broadened to enable them to take preemptive action once they have become aware of emerging problems. As evidenced by the case of Hypo Group Alpe-Adria, supervisors in Austria–very much like supervisors in other countries–had only limited possibilities, until the latest reforms, of intervening at an ailing bank before the situation became critical. The few available instruments, such as removing the bank's management, installing a state commissioner or revoking the banking license, were at the same time very radical measures that left little room for a differentiated response. The EU Capital Requirements Directive IV implemented in 2014 has given domestic supervisors new instruments, which may also be applied at earlier stages. Among other things, supervisors may now require the bank to sell business areas that constitute too high a risk, scale down its branch networks or reduce risk-taking in existing business areas.

In this context the question arose how to best reorganize or wind down banks that become distressed despite preventive measures. As the banking and financial crisis of 2008 and thereafter showed, failure may loom even for large and complex banks. In order to prevent a failure with possibly far-reaching consequences for the economy, public support might be unavoidable in such a case. To remedy this situation, which came to be widely known as "too big to fail," Austrian banks have been required to submit ex ante recovery and resolution plans since 2014 under the Austrian Banking Intervention and Restructuring Act, in anticipation of and in preparation for the Directive on Bank Recovery and Resolution that was being developed by EU legislators at the time and has since been been written into national law (Bank Recovery and Resolution Act, passed in 2015). Those two acts have given the supervisory authorities far-reaching powers of intervention at otherwise healthy banks which are meant to faciliate restructuring measures should they become necessary at some point. The rationale for these measures is to ensure that the cost of restructuring or winding down banks will be borne by the banks' owners and subordinate creditors in the first line, obviating the need for bail-out taxpayer money.[850] Recovery and resolution, just like supervision, has been defined as a joint responsiblity of the Financial Market Authority and the OeNB.

The second key area of reform was macroprudential supervision, i.e., supervision focusing on the safety and soundness of the financial system in the aggregate.[851] These reforms came in response to another key lesson from the financial crisis: left by its own devices, microprudential supervision, which focuses on the safety and soundness of individual financial institutions, and a monetary policy aimed at maintaining price stability do not suffice to safeguard the stability of the financial system. The reasons are manifold and include: The higher interdependence of financial institutions has significantly increased the potential for contagion and the pace of contagion. Moreover, the behavior of banks is inherently procyclical; they tend to take on too high a risk in good times, thus fueling a boom, and to act unreasonably cautiously in the event of crisis, thus deepening a bust. Finally, implicit government guarantees for "too big to fail banks" and the favorable tax treatment of debt may create wrong incentives and encourage excessive risk-taking. Evidence from the financial crises in recent decades has also shown that losses in output growth and jobs are the bigger the more the preceding booms were fueled by credit.[852] With regard to these aspects, too, the Capital Requirements Directive IV has likewise created new instruments and new possibilities: To limit the build-up of risks, capital requirements may now be raised in periods of strong credit growth but reduced in periods of weak credit growth. Systemically important banks whose insolvency would threaten to destabilize the entire financial system may now be required to hold additional capital. In addition, loan-to-value and loan-to-income ratios may be imposed to limit unhealthy credit growth in particular sectors. Examples would be upper limits for the use of loans in financing house purchases which may be defined in relation to household income or the value of the property. At the time of writing Austria had not yet passed corresponding legislation to introduce such instruments.

Last but not least the responsibilities for financial stability have been redefined at the EU level. The European Banking Authority, created by the EU in 2010, has been tasked with ensuring that EU countries indeed apply uniform supervisory standards and take action to close any national loopholes that may remain. However, the problems that the crisis of 2008 unmasked in the euro area had deeper roots. Notwithstanding the steps taken toward integration and the creation of European banking groups, individual banks continued to be perceived as national actors. Difficulties at individual banks quickly turned into a budgetary burden for the governments of the countries in which they were based, whereas the fiscal problems of some countries had a negative impact on the banks operating in those countries. The free movement of capital within the monetary union–which in itself was a great achievement in the European unification process–reinforced this vicious circle. As a consequence, deliberations at the European level led to the decision that it was necessary to break the link between banks and sovereigns and that supranational bodies should assume increased responsibility for a stable banking system, i.e., that a "banking union" should be established.[853]

The institutional framework for a banking union adopted in 2012 rests on three pillars: a single supervisory mechanism (SSM), a single resolution mechanism (SRM) and a system of harmonized deposit guarantee schemes. In this context, the European level was emphasized heavily in order to ensure the uniform, neutral monitoring of banking operations in all member states and adequately monitor the cross-border activities and structures of banking groups.[854] With regard to the single supervisory mechanism, this meant that the ECB generally assumed responsibility for all banks in the euro area. In practice, the ECB now directly supervises the most significant banks in the euro area–i.e., currently some 120 banks–with support from the national authorities, while the supervision of the other banks remained the responsibility of the national authorities (i.e., the FMA and the OeNB in the case of Austria), under the overall oversight of the ECB. The single resolution mechanism, the counterpart of the single supervisory mechanism, institutionalized the cooperation of the competent national authorities with a new European agency, the Single Resolution Board, which manages contributions from the banking sector designed to cofund any measures that may be required to restructure or wind down distressed banks. Together, these measures are supposed to help ensure that future banking crises will not jeopardize public households and that the systemically relevant services of banks–such as account transfers and cash withdrawals–will remain up and running in the event of a crisis.

Unlike in the case of microprudential supervision, the competences for macroprudential supervision remain largely within national jurisdictions, reflecting, among other things, the fact that financial cycles and macroprudential risks may vary significantly across countries. Cases in point are the credit-financed real estate booms in Spain or Ireland in the face of stable real estate prices in Germany before 2007. This gave rise to the decision to keep the responsibility for macroprudential measures essentially at the national level. In the case of Austria, the competent national body is the Financial Market Stability Board (FMSB), which can issue recommendations for further action by the FMA. FMSB members represent the finance ministry, the FMA, the Austrian Fiscal Advisory Council and the OeNB, which has been tasked with producing analyses as input for decision-making. As an ultimate safety net, the EU–specifically the European Systemic Risk Board–can intervene and overrule national decisions.

Policy in motion

Overall, the crisis thus led to a significant change in financial market supervision in two respects: *First,* the jurisdiction of supervisors and their toolbox were expanded substantially, and *second,* the national authorities–the federal government, the central bank and the independent supervisory authority– were complemented by counterparts at the European level. Even if some key competences were devolved to European institutions, the broadened scope of supervisory activity led to an expansion rather than a reduction of supervisory activities also at the national level. In addition, as in the case of monetary policy, the joint European financial stability forums such as EBA, SSM or SRM involve the national authorities in their decision-making processes, and it is clear these decisions have to be prepared.

These new tasks again raise questions on the assignment of responsibilities in this regard. One possible lesson from the financial crisis is that coordinated monetary and financial stability policies are often not just desirable but necessary, and that they can be best achieved by combining agendas in a single institution. Recently, there have been signs of changes in the institutional framework for national supervision toward a one-stop financial supervisor in some EU member states. However, different institutional models continue to exist across the EU. In any case, the highly invasive changes seen by the institutions responsible for the stability of the currency and the financial system at the international level in recent years show that any forecast of the future role of the Oesterreichische Nationalbank in the national and European context will certainly involve high uncertainty. In 2007, no one would have predicted that the ECB would assume responsibility for banking supervision less than ten years later, and no one would have guessed that OeNB staff would be responsible for developing concrete measures to prevent systemic financial crises, or measures for winding up and restructuring Austrian banks.

What is clear is that monetary and financial stability will remain important macroeconomic goals and that the duties associated with ensuring this stability will have to be performed. It is also clear that numerous such tasks should remain assigned to politically independent institutions and that while some should be handled by European institutions some might be better dealt with at the subsidiary national level, especially given that national institutions are closer to citizens and can therefore enjoy higher acceptance. Since its establishment in 1816, the OeNB has focused on issues related to the supply of cash, monetary policy, banking supervision, payment systems and statistics. Regardless of how and under what names these duties may be organized in the future, these issues–which the OeNB currently handles in part alone, in part jointly with other institutions–will remain at the heart of economic policy making.

Conclusion

The 200 years since the foundation of the Nationalbank in 1816 have been characterized by a series of fundamental changes in the realm in which the bank operates. Periods of yawning public sector deficits that required monetary financing, e.g., after 1848 and again during World War I, alternated with phases of balanced budgets. The Austrian economy, largely inward-directed and isolated from world markets through prohibitively high protective tariffs in the early 19th century, turned into a small, open economy with a high degree of international integration. The use of banknotes and bank accounts, for a long time limited to a very small proportion of society, is now commonplace. During the first 40 years of its life, the Nationalbank was by far the largest bank in Vienna and the only bank organized as a stock corporation. Its role evolved in the mid-19th century as the banking industry emerged and became increasingly diversified. Today, it has become a comparatively small economic agent in terms of balance sheet size but at the same time operates on a much larger scale in a very complex, internationally highly integrated financial system.

When the environment for central bank policy-making changed, so did the methods for achieving the two overarching goals of monetary and financial stability as well as the actual role that the bank played in achieving those goals. In the domain of financial stablity policy, issuing banking licenses and supervising banks' operations as a means of ensuring financial stability was for the longest time within the jurisdiction of the finance ministry. In this context, the Nationalbank had very few means to observe or influence the operations of individual banks, apart from insights derived from individual banks' recourse to its discount and lending operations and the power to restrict access to these instruments. Thus, the OeNB was confined to intervening only in the event of acute crises, such as after the stock market crash of 1873 or during the Creditanstalt crisis of 1931. The bank's management time and again tried to procure a wider range of confidential information about commercial banks and moreover to obtain control powers. When the OeNB attempted to learn more about the foreign liabilities of Austria's commercial banks during the interwar years, the banks quickly managed to ward off the initiative. Not until the banking supervision architecture was fundamentally reformed in 2008 were all significant powers in on-site and off-site banking analysis transferred to the Nationalbank. Looking at the 200 years, even important monetary policy-making powers were often exercised by the state rather than the Nationalbank, especially when the government monetized its debt, e.g., from 1848 until the 1870s, during and after World War I and again during World War II. In other words, the Nationalbank's authority to shape monetary and financial stability policy has been subject to continuous change and evolution.

But some key features remained constant and stable throughout these 200 years: The foundation of the Nationalbank permanently added a new economic agent to the Austrian institutional framework with a distinct role and a say–sometimes more, sometimes less–in economic policy-making. With the establishment of the Nationalbank, the state ceded some responsibilities and decision-making powers to an institution that was independent at least to the extent that other stakeholders had a voice in its operations in addition to the bank's governor, who was appointed by the emperor. During the first decades of the OeNB's existence, decision making was (partly) driven by stockholders' interests. As the stockholders were at the same time the public sector's main creditors, the OeNB was a forum in which different interests could be balanced–in a state otherwise ruled on absolutist principles. In the three decades leading up to World War I, the Austro-Hungarian Bank acted as a (partly) autonomous public agency, which was capable of representing common interests in an environment marked by constant struggles between and within Austria and Hungary over the distribution of power and resources within the dual monarchy. Finally, during the Second Republic after 1945, the OeNB was a key liaison between the government, the social partners and commercial banks and helped create the consensus needed to exercise a hard currency policy and to peg the Austrian schilling to the Deutsche mark. In fact, there were only two times during which the central bank was fully deprived of its autonomy: during the period of hyperinflation in the early 1920s, when the bank's operations essentially served to support the budget of the newly founded First Republic; and during the period from 1938 to 1945, when Austria and the OeNB had ceased to exist and the Nationalbank building at Otto-Wagner-Platz served as the Vienna Reichsbank head office.

Despite its proximity to the government, the OeNB largely succeeded in exercising control over monetary policy decisions in Austria at most times–unlike its predecessor institution from 1706, the Wiener Stadtbanco. Its history illustrates that the issue of central bank independence and the relationship with the state cannot be reduced to a simple formula. A closer look shows that periods of great stability during the OeNB's history did not necessarily coincide with the times at which central bank independence was on the soundest legal footing. As a case in point, the OeNB's autonomy after 1898, in years marked by stable exchange rates, was the result of the need for making decisions which the complex political system of the dual monarchy was unable to take. In this respect, the role of the Austro-Hungarian Bank, as the central bank was called from 1878, was not unlike that of the ECB, or the Eurosystem as a whole, during the financial crisis after 2008: The ECB and the Eurosystem also had to intervene repeatedly as the financial and government debt crisis unfolded from 2008 because the EU decision-making process took too long or because politics prevented a consensus from being reached. Thus, what counts is not so much independence as prescribed by law, but autonomy in practice as rooted in the institutional structure, the quality of the bank's management, the expert knowledge of its staff and the reputation the OeNB has built for itself on the basis of its successful track record.

The history of the OeNB also gives some insights into another disputed matter of central bank policy; that of rules versus discretion. The OeNB seems to always have had a certain leaning towards a flexible interpretation of rules. Both periods of successful fixed exchange rates, the peg to gold before 1914 and the peg to the Deutsche mark after the 1980s, were characterized by a rule that always retained a modicum of ambiguity: the central bank never explicitly committed to selling Deutsche mark or gold at a predetermined price. Much rather, in both periods, the system worked because investors were confident in the long-term stability of the peg and because the central bank had the power to control short-term developments thanks to a strong position in the foreign exchange market.

The financial and government debt crisis after 2008 has cast doubts on the consensus on central bank policy that had developed when inflation was low during the Great Moderation years. Focusing policy on an inflation target alone appears not to have been sufficient. Economic policy makers therefore forged new instruments, above all macroprudential regulations, and assigned part of the responsibility for supervising their implementation to central banks, which raised new issues about where policy-making institutions' responsibilities started and ended. The specific development of the crisis in the euro area launched a reassessment of the European unification project and the role of the single monetary policy.

All these recent experiences have been changing our own understanding of history. Once disregarded aspects have attracted researchers' interest. In recent years, new literature has been published on the history of currencies and monetary policy, some of it covering Austria, and it stands to be expected that this publishing trend will produce more new insights. Moreover, access to sources mapping the history of the Oesterreichische Nationalbank has improved markedly recently. The establishment of the OeNB History Archives in 1999 and the ongoing development and digitization of the archive have facilitated research based on the bank's internal records. The mass digitization of books, newspapers and magazines by the Austrian National Library in the past few years has not only made previously hard to access material internationally available but has also made content easily accessible using full-text optical character recognition (OCR) and full-text search, opening up new avenues for scientific research. Additional research opportunities still lie in expanding the collection of resources and in analyzing historical material using statistical methods. While using econometric methods to analyze economic history sources is not new, important parts of Austrian central bank history and policy have been examined only with qualitative methods; the data that have since become available would now be sufficiently numerous to allow econometric analysis as well.

Thus, the next chapter of Austrian monetary and financial history will be written not just as an account of the OeNB exercising monetary policy and financial supervision. Much rather, we can hope that in the near future, historiography will contribute to filling gaps in research, to challenging earlier conclusions, to introducing new assumptions and thus to putting new twists on the historiography of the Oesterreichische Nationalbank, keeping it up to date and full of informational value.

Currencies

	Currency unit	Currency coin (full-bodied coin)	Legal tender other than currency coins	Conversion
Before 1811	1 florin = 60 kreutzer	1 florin 14.03g silver (.833 fine)	after 1797/1800 paper florins (Bancozettel)[I)]	
1811	1 florin (Vienna standard) = 60 kreutzer	unchanged	Bancozettel (up to 1812), redemption certificates (Einlösungsscheine), anticipation certificates (Antizipationsscheine), from 1813	1 Vienna standard florin = 5 Bancozettel
1816	1 florin (Convention standard) = 60 kreutzer	unchanged	from 1848 banknotes, from 1849 state paper money[II)]	1 Convention standard florin = 2.5 Vienna standard florins
1857	1 florin (Austrian standard) = 100 (new) kreutzer	1 florin, 12,35g silver (.900 fine) major gold trading coin, minted from 1870: 4 florins = 10 francs, 3.225g gold (.900)	banknotes and state paper money	1.05 Austrian standard florins = 1 Convention standard florin
1892/1900[III)]	1 crown = 100 heller	10 crowns, 3.387g gold (.900 fine)	banknotes, state paper money (up to 1903) and 1-florin silver coins[IV)]	2 crowns = 1 Austrian standard florin

I) The legal tender status of Bancozettel was established by official decree in 1800 only but had been mandated from 1797 onward through various public regulations (Mensi, Geld, p. 673).
II) Bancozettel were retained in circulation in 1816 and continued to be accepted in payment under contracts based on Vienna standard florins. Officially the Vienna standard was demonetized in 1857 when Austrian standard florins were introduced. In practice, Bancozettel paper money was of minor relevance soon after 1816.
III) The crown was established as the new currency under the Currency Act of 1892, but crown accounting was introduced as late as 1900. Until then, the florin remained in use, at a fixed exchange rate of 2 crowns = 1 florin.

1925[V]	I schilling =100 groschen	100 schillings, 23.524g gold (.900 fine)	banknotes	I schilling = 10,000 crowns
1938	I reichsmark = 100 reichspfennigs	10 mark, 3.9825g gold (.900 fine)	banknotes	2 reichsmarks = 3 schillings
1945	I schilling = 100 groschen	–	banknotes are sole legal tender	I schilling = I reichsmark
1999	I euro = 100 cent	–	banknotes are sole legal tender	I euro = 13.7603 schillings

IV) While 2-florin coins and ¼-florin coins were demonetized in 1893, 1-florin coins remained legal tender. However, this rule applied only to the silver florin; acceptance of the new silver crowns for payment in private transactions was mandatory only up to an amount of 250 crowns. The legislation passed in 1892 put an end to the minting of new silver florins (Fellner, *Währungsreform*, pp. 104–113).

V) The first coins known as schilling were silver coins issued on the basis of legislation passed in December 1923. The gold content of the schilling was fixed by law in December 1924, and the changeover to schilling accounting was made in the course of 1925 (Kernbauer, *Währungspolitik*, pp. 163–171.)

CURRENCIES

Notes

Introduction

1 Capie et al., Development, p. 6.
2 Ultimately, the management functions of the *Wiener Stadtbanco* were moved to the treasury in 1816, and its cashier's office was closed in 1818. Fuchs, *Stadtbank*, pp. 112, 118.
3 See e.g. Goodhart, *Evolution*; or Grossman, *Unsettled account*, pp. 42–44.
4 On a functional perspective of central bank policy, see Ugolini, *What do we really know*. Historically, institutions other than central banks, such as commercial banks or the finance ministry, also performed central bank functions. Here, we apply an institutional focus and therefore concentrate on central banks proper.
5 See e.g. Good, *Economic rise*; Komlos, *Customs union*; and Rudolph, *Banking*.
6 Pressburger, *Noteninstitut*. Pressburger's chronological narrative, published in two parts with three and four volumes between 1959 and 1976, remains one of the major sources for research into OeNB history. As volumes 1 to 7 are numbered consecutively, page numbers in the references are preceded by an indication of either part I or II.
7 Raudnitz, *Staatspapiergeld*, was published in 1917; followed by Hofmann, *Devalvierung*, 1923; and Kraft, *Finanzreform*, 1927.
8 On the Habsburg monarchy as a monetary union, see e.g. Baltzarek, Österreichs Rolle; Flandreau, *The bank*; and Flandreau, Logic. On the dissolution of the monetary union, see Dornbusch, Monetary problems; Garber and Spencer, *Dissolution*; or Gross and Gummer, Ghosts of the Habsburg Empire.
9 Bachinger et al. (eds.), *Abschied vom Schilling*; Liebscher (ed.), *From the schilling to the euro*.
10 On the eve of the collapse of the Bretton Woods system, see Yeager, Fluctuating exchange rates; on the functioning of exchange rate bands, Flandreau and Komlos, Target zones; on monetary policy under a fixed exchange rate regime, Jobst, Market leader; Morys, *Classical gold standard*; on the choice between fixed and flexible exchange rates, Straumann, *Fixed ideas*.
11 Marcus, *Credibility, confidence and capital*; Flores and Decorzant, Going multilateral.

A first try at monetary autonomy—the Wiener Stadtbanco (1706–1816)

12 Cited by Raudnitz, *Staatspapiergeld*, p. 46.
13 Fuchs, *Stadtbank*, p. 25. Mensi, *Finanzen*, pp. 117, 179–181.
14 Roberds and Velde, Early public banks.
15 Denzel, *Nürnberger Banco Publico*, p. 29.
16 Roberds and Velde, Early public banks; Ugolini, *What do we really know*.
17 Sommer, *Kameralisten*, pp. 67–73, 99–104.
18 On the development of public finance in general, see Reinhard, *Staatsgewalt*, pp. 305–343. On Austria, Mensi, *Finanzen*, pp. 1–33; Vocelka, *Glanz und Untergang*, pp. 281–284; Winkelbauer, *Ständefreiheit*, I, pp. 465–470.
19 Winkelbauer, *Ständefreiheit*, I, pp. 487–493.
20 *Ibid.*, pp. 73–78.
21 Mensi, *Finanzen*, p. 43.
22 On the arbitrary treatment of creditors, see Eigner et al., Fi-

nanzplatz, pp. 914–915; Mensi, Staatsschuld, p. 1104; Mentschl and Otruba, *Österreichische Industrielle*, pp. 9, 14; Bidermann, Stadt-Bank, p. 348. Oppenheimer himself was jailed repeatedly and released only upon loaning the emperor large sums (Rauscher, Der Fall Oppenheimer, pp. 51–52).
23 Dickson, *Finance and government*, I, pp. 141–142.
24 Mensi, *Finanzen*, pp. 134, 765.
25 Dickson, *Finance and government*, I, pp. 140–178; Rauscher and Serles, Wiener Niederleger, pp. 163, 167. On court suppliers, see Schnee, *Hoffinanz*, III, pp. 231–249.
26 Dickson, *Finance and government*, I, p. 140.
27 Neal, How it all began; Dickson, *Financial revolution*.
28 Winkelbauer, *Ständefreiheit*, I, p. 525.
29 Hochedlinger, Problem der Kriegsfinanzierung, p. 119.
30 Dickson, *Finance and government*, I, pp. 146–147. Grunwald, *Oppenheimer*, pp. 150–170.
31 On the history of the *Banco del Giro*, see Mensi, *Finanzen*, pp. 179–206; Fuchs, *Stadtbank*, pp. 27–34; Holl, *Starhemberg*, pp. 103–111.
32 Mensi, *Finanzen*, pp. 194–197; Fuchs, *Stadtbank*, pp. 62–63, 68–70.
33 Holl, *Starhemberg*, pp. 112–114. The idea of securing broad-based support for the bank was also a core element of Johann Joachim Becher's blueprint for a "land bank." On the plans of Becher and Wilhelm Schröder, *ibid.*, pp. 101–102; Sommer, *Kameralisten*, pp. 100–104.
34 Holl, *Starhemberg*, pp. 239–241; on Paris, see Stasavage, *States of credit*, pp. 132–142.
35 The founding charter dated December 24, 1705, was published only once the corresponding agreement had

been reached with the City of Vienna on March 8, 1706 (Fuchs, *Stadtbank*, p. 36).

36 Moreover, the tax revenues were assigned irreversibly for a period of 15 years, and the *Wiener Stadtbanco* was given jurisdiction for managing the revenues (Fuchs, *Stadtbank*).

37 Mensi, *Finanzen*, p. 217.

38 The same policy was adopted temporarily from 1706 to 1708 (Fuchs, *Stadtbank*, pp. 45, 62).

39 *Ibid.*, p. 77.

40 Eigner et al., Finanzplatz, pp. 926–927.

41 Winkelbauer, *Ständefreiheit*, I, p. 528.

42 Beer, *Österreichische Finanzen*, p. 136; Mensi, *Finanzen*, p. 755.

43 For an overview, see Fuchs, *Stadtbank*, pp. 65–67, 87–91, 112–115.

44 On Bankalität, see Mensi, *Finanzen*, pp. 431–572; Fuchs, *Stadtbank*, pp. 119–126; Holl, *Starhemberg*, pp. 402–435.

45 Mensi, *Finanzen*, pp. 749–754.

46 Fuchs, *Stadtbank*, p. 83.

47 On the following, see Vocelka, *Glanz*, pp. 354–361.

48 Bidermann, Stadt-Bank, p. 442; Walter, Staatsbankprojekt, p. 447; Mensi, *Finanzen*, p. 716.

49 Fuchs, *Stadtbank*, p. 98; Walter, Staatsbankprojekt, p. 448; Dickson, *Finance and government*, I, pp. 241–243.

50 Walter, Staatsbankprojekt, p. 448.

51 *Ibid.*, p. 450.

52 Pressburger, *Noteninstitut*, I, pp. 77–78.

53 Baltzarek, *Wiener Börse*, pp. 21–28.

54 Beer, *Österreichische Finanzen*, p. 300.

55 Fuchs, *Stadtbank*, p. 112.

56 Raudnitz, *Staatspapiergeld*, p. 7.

57 *Ibid.*, pp. 2–3.

58 Pressburger, *Noteninstitut*, I, p. 48; Raudnitz, *Staatspapiergeld*, p. 4.

59 Mensi, *Papiergeld*, p. 672.

60 Raudnitz, *Staatspapiergeld*, p. 4.

61 *Ibid.*, p. 5.

62 *Ibid.*, p. 8.

63 Ernst, Geld, p. 661.

64 Raudnitz, *Staatspapiergeld*, p. 49. On lowering the coinage standard, see Stiassny, *Staatsbankrott*, p. 24; and Wagner, Kritik, pp. 594–596.

65 Becher, *Münzwesen*, p. 208.

66 Raudnitz, *Staatspapiergeld*, p. 26.

67 *Ibid.*, p. 29.

68 Source: Czörnig, *Handbüchlein*; Hauer, *Beiträge* (paper money), *Historical time series on interest rates* (price of silver), Pribram, *Materialien* (food prices). The consumer price index published by Mühlpeck et al., Index der Verbraucherpreise, starts in 1800, i.e., in the midst of the inflation period. To enable comparisons with the pre-war years, we used unweighted averages of 7 food prices in Vienna, from Pribram, *Materialien*. The index of Mühlpeck et al. is largely composed of food and broadly matches our food price averages after 1800. Note that the index of Mühlpeck et al. is based on silver prices, i.e., must be converted into paper money in line with the prevailing silver price to measure paper money inflation.

69 To ensure improved comparability over time, the different types of paper money have been converted into paper florins as used before the currency reform of 1811. Thus, banknotes in the amount of 100 florins as issued by the Nationalbank (after 1816, based on the Convention standard) = 250 Vienna standard florins as issued in the form of redemption or anticipation certificates (1811–1816) = 1,250 old paper florins (before 1811). Food prices were harmonized in the same way. Due to the lack of data for banknotes in circulation in 1816 and 1817, the actual amount of paper

money in circulation was somewhat higher in this period than indicated.

70 Raudnitz, *Staatspapiergeld*, pp. 30–33.

71 *Ibid.*, pp. 45–46, 56–57.

72 *Ibid.*, p. 63.

73 Unlike argued e.g. by Wagner, Kritik.

74 Raudnitz, *Staatspapiergeld*, pp. 38–43.

75 Brandt, *Neoabsolutismus*, p. 105. On government finance statistics, see Czörnig, *Handbüchlein*.

76 Stiassny, *Staatsbankerott*, p. 33; Wagner, Kritik, pp. 410–411.

77 Wagner, Kritik, S. 417–419.

78 Raudnitz, *Staatspapiergeld*, pp. 66–68. Wagner, Kritik, pp. 404–410.

79 Wagner, Kritik, p. 440.

80 Pressburger, *Noteninstitut*, I, pp. 66–73.

81 The *Vereinigte Einlösungs-und Tilgungsdeputation* established earlier with the silver decree was put in charge of handling the exchange.

82 A similar scale was used for the devaluation of the schilling in 1933. See chapter 8 ("transfer moratorium").

83 Cited by Pressburger, *Noteninstitut*, I, p. 66.

84 See also Tebeldi, *Geldangelegenheiten*, pp. 11, 47.

85 Raudnitz, *Staatspapiergeld*, pp. 80–96; Brandt, *Neoabsolutismus*, p. 106; for a positive view, see Stiassny, *Staatsbankerott*.

86 Brandt, *Neoabsolutismus*, pp. 105–106.

87 Freudenberger, *Lost momentum*, pp. 76–81.

88 Butschek, *Österreichs Wirtschaftsgeschichte*, pp. 97–102; Freudenberger, *Lost momentum*, p. 18; Komlos, *Customs union*, pp. 95–96.

89 This is a very rough estimate. In 1811, the nominal value of Austria's public debt (excluding paper money) totaled some 800 million florins (Czörnig, *Handbüchlein*, p. 124). Kausel put the nominal GDP of the later Austrian part

of the dual monarchy at an estimated 1,050 million florins in 1930. Taking into account growth between 1810 and 1830 and Hungarian economic output, we arrive at the figure of 80% indicated above. The data on Prussia are from Schremmer, *Steuern und Staatsfinanzen*, p. 163; the data on England from Mitchell, *British historical statistics*, pp. 600–603 and 822.

90 On this argument, see Brandt, *Neoabsolutismus*, pp. 114, 126–129.

91 Decree dated February 20, 1811, article 21.

92 Raudnitz, *Staatspapiergeld*, p. 106. On conversion into old paper florins, see endnote no. 69.

Fragile stability during the Nationalbank's formative years (1816–1848)

93 *Ibid.*, pp. 128–129; White, Making the French pay.

94 On earlier reforms proposed by Melchior Steiner in 1812 and anonymous plans dated 1813 and 1814, see Raudnitz, *Staatspapiergeld*, pp. 114–115.

95 Dickson, *Finance and government*, I, p. 309.

96 Lederer, *National-Bank*, p. 42.

97 The government did not want to delay the retirement of government paper money in exchange for banknotes until after completion of subscriptions for Nationalbank shares.

98 Pressburger, *Noteninstitut*, I, pp. 85–86.

99 *Ibid.*, I, pp. 121–122.

100 Lederer temporarily returned to the helm of the Nationalbank in 1848 because his successor, Franz Breyer Ritter von Breynau, passed away soon after having come into office.

101 Tschurn, *Verwaltungsorganismus*, pp. 27–28. The position of vice governor remained vacant from 1841 to 1849.

102 Other changes referred to the retirement of government paper money and the establishment of a reserve fund funded with the bank's income. For a reprint of the decrees of 1816, of the charter of 1817 and many other official documents, refer to Pressburger, *Noteninstitut*.

103 Urged by the finance ministry, the governing board nevertheless adopted an internal threshold, according to which at least one-sixth of banknotes in circulation had to be backed by silver reserves (Zuckerkandl, Austro-Hungarian Bank, p. 74).

104 Article 41.

105 Article 44.

106 Article 42.

107 Disputes regarding the charter were no longer settled by the supreme court but directly by the treasury. Compare article 57 of the charter of 1817 and article 59 of the charter of 1841.

108 Brandt, *Neoabsolutismus*, pp. 127–128.

109 Lederer, *National-Bank*, p. 49.

110 On interest rates from the 1830s onward, see also the *Historical time series on interest rates*.

111 Source: *Historical time series on the Nationalbank* (interest charged by the bank on receivables from the state, dividends), *Historical time series on interest rates* (government bond yields).

112 Not necessarily in comparison with other contemporary banks, though. See table 1 in Jobst and Ugolini, Coevolution.

113 Article 16.

114 Brandt, *Neoabsolutismus*, pp. 12–14.

115 Barany, Ungarns Verwaltung, pp. 312–328.

116 Brandt, *Neoabsolutismus*, p. 24.

117 Source: Author's illustration.

118 Good, *Economic rise*, pp. 21–24.

119 Cerman, Proto-industrielle Entwicklung; Sandgruber, *Ökonomie und Politik*, pp. 184–185.

120 Sandgruber, *Ökonomie und Politik*, p. 143.

121 Komlos, *Nutrition*, pp. 119–165.

122 Komlos, *Customs union*, p. 4.

123 Freudenberger, *Lost momentum*, p. 20; Komlos, *Nutrition*, p. 164.

124 Good, *Economic rise*, p. 45.

125 Komlos, *Customs union*, table no. 58.

126 Good, *Economic rise*, p. 65.

127 Matis, *Schwarzenberg-Bank*; Rager, *Wechselbank*.

128 Freudenberger, *Lost momentum*, pp. 167–205.

129 Brandt, *Neoabsolutismus*, p. 326; Brusatti, Unternehmensfinanzierung.

130 See the columns "Wechsler" (exchange offices) and "Großhändler" (merchants) in the *Tafeln zur Statistik* 1828 (table no. 74). While these figures must be taken with a grain of salt, they are likely to reflect the divide between Vienna and the other parts of the empire.

131 Blum, *Noble landowners*, pp. 113–126.

132 *Historical time series on credit institutions*.

133 Helleiner, *Territorial currencies*, pp. 19–31.

134 *Tabellen zur Währungsfrage*, p. 258; Kautz, *Nemzetgazdasági*, p. 194, puts the figure at 230 to 240 million florins.

135 *Tafeln zur Statistik* 1847/48 (table 36) put the daily wage of a Vienna-based worker at 24 crowns. Based on 25 workdays, this would sum up to 10 florins.

136 Blum, *Noble landowners*, pp. 171–202.

137 Weber, *Peasants into Frenchmen*, pp. 40.

138 Helleiner, *Territorial currencies*, pp. 34–35.

139 The figures for Germany roughly relate to the German empire as it existed in 1913. Source: *Historical time series on the Nationalbank* (Austrian paper money); *Tabellen zur Währungsfrage*, p. 258; Kautz, *Nemzetgazdasági*, p. 194; Fellner, *Währungsreform*, pp. 32–

33; Compass 1911 (Austrian coins), Huffman and Lothian, Money in the UK (England 1847, 1867), Capie and Webber, Total coin (England 1892, 1910); Sprenger, *Geldmengenänderungen* (Germany).

140 Changes of the price level can be neglected, as all prices are given in silver or gold units and as the general price level as expressed in gold, while subject to some volatility in the 19th century, did not show a particular trend. See Mühlpeck et al., Index der Verbraucherpreise.

141 See articles 13 to 20.

142 The charter of 1817 doubled the number of shares and halved the nominal amount. Thus, it actually took 1,000 Vienna standard florins and 100 Convention standard florins to obtain a single Nationalbank share.

143 Pressburger, *Noteninstitut*, I, p. 106.

144 By then, another 132 million florins had been withdrawn from circulation with a voluntary bond increase. By making an additional payment in the form of old (Vienna standard) paper money, holders of government bonds whose yield had been halved in the course of the 1811 sovereign default, were able to convert those bonds into new bonds with a 5% yield in the form of Convention standard florins.

145 Pressburger, *Noteninstitut*, I, p. 168.

146 Source: *Historical time series on the Nationalbank.*

147 Brandt, *Neoabsolutismus*, pp. 132–133; Beer, *Österreichische Finanzen*, pp. 162–163; Marx, *Wirtschaftliche Ursachen*, p. 90.

148 Lederer, *National-Bank*, p. 109.

149 *Historical time series on interest rates.*

150 For a list of the bank's executive directors, see Tschurn, *Verwaltungsorganismus.* On the composition of the discount committees, see the re-

spective annual reports.

151 Baltzarek, *Wiener Börse*, p. 45.

152 OeNB Archives, Governing Board meeting, September 21, 1820.

153 Lederer, *National-Bank*, pp. 140–141.

154 Apart from bills of exchange, the Nationalbank also discounted other securities with a short residual maturity, but the total volumes were much lower. See the notes to the *Historical time series on the Nationalbank.*

155 Discounted bills may, as a rule, be rediscounted, i.e., sold onward (e.g. to the central bank) to meet short-term liquidity needs. However, rediscounting has typically been an option for commercial banks only and is not part of the toolbox of central banks.

156 Article 65 of the Rules of procedure of 1817.

157 *Ibid.*, Article 60; collateral was accepted in lieu of the third signature.

158 For exceptions, see the notes to the *Historical time series on the Nationalbank.*

159 Sometimes also silver and gold coins or bullion.

160 See the *Historical time series on the Nationalbank.*

161 Pressburger, *Noteninstitut*, I, p. 176.

162 Lederer, *National-Bank*, pp. 152–153.

163 Pressburger, *Noteninstitut*, I, p. 179.

164 OeNB Archives, Governing Board meetings October 16, 1820; March 29, 1821; August 8, 1822; October 17, 1822; March 26, 1824; March 27, 1828; May 1, 1828; March 12, 1829.

165 Pressburger, *Noteninstitut*, I, p. 182.

166 Lederer, *National-Bank*, p. 269.

Turning from the treasury's banker to the banker's bank (1848–1878)

167 Tegoborski, *Des Finances*, first published in 1843 in Paris;

here p. 102 of the German translation published in 1845 in Vienna (edited and updated). Tebeldi, *Geldangelegenheiten*, p. 108. Actual circulation figures: *Historical time series on the Nationalbank.*

168 Reschauer, *1848*, pp. 87–90; Pressburger, *Noteninstitut*, I, p. 236.

169 Essentially, the bank published its complete balance sheet, yet without reporting its reserves on the liability side and the underlying investments on the asset side.

170 See e.g. *Wiener Zeitung.*

171 Zuckerkandl, *Austro-Hungarian Bank*, p. 77.

172 However, the bank was required to keep up the supply of silver to the treasury, which needed silver money to pay the troops in Italy. Pressburger, *Noteninstitut*, I, pp. 258, 260.

173 Kindleberger, *Manias*, p. 261.

174 Grossman and Rockoff, Fighting the last war; Ugolini, *What do we really know.*

175 Bordo, Lender of last resort; Goodhart, Myths; Grossman and Rockoff, Fighting the last war.

176 Bindseil, Central bank financial crisis management, p. 416–418.

177 On the differences between official and market interest rates as an indicator of discounting conditions see Bignon et al., Bagehot; and Jobst and Ugolini, Coevolution.

178 Pressburger, *Noteninstitut*, I, pp. 560–562.

179 Jobst, What drives, p. 20.

180 References cited in Brandt, *Neoabsolutismus*, p. 327. On the banking reform commission set up in 1850 see *ibid.*, pp. 641–645, and Pressburger, *Noteninstitut*, I, pp. 319–325.

181 The idea was above all to extend mortgage loans (envisaged as a monetary policy tool already by the charter of 1817) and to establish branch offices outside Vienna.

182 Brandt, *Neoabsolutismus*, pp. 305–306.
183 *Ibid.*, pp. 1001–1002.
184 Rumpler, *Chance*, p. 325.
185 Lucam, *Verhältnis*, table H.
186 *Tabellen zur Währungsstatistik* (table 152). Initially, the government issued interest-bearing treasury bills, which did not find enough investors, though, and therefore had to be discounted at the central bank in large quantities. Therefore, the state moved to issue unremunerated bills that were legal tender (Mensi, Geld, pp. 677–678).
187 Excluding liabilities accrued before 1848 stemming from the withdrawal of Vienna standard florins (Pressburger, *Noteninstitut*, I, pp. 404–406).
188 Brandt, *Neoabsolutismus*, pp. 696–697.
189 Source: *Historical time series on the Nationalbank*.
190 The data refer to Convention standard florins (up to 1858) or Austrian standard florins (after 1858). The time series on state paper money covers paper money in circulation, i.e., excludes central bank holdings as well as paper money in small denominations used in the place of coins.
191 Nationalbank balance sheet for March 27, 1855.
192 Pressburger, *Noteninstitut*, I, pp. 437–440.
193 Brandt, *Neoabsolutismus*, pp. 302–303. Charter as well as terms and conditions of the new division as in Pressburger, *Noteninstitut*, I, pp. 460–475.
194 Brandt, *Neoabsolutismus*, p. 310.
195 Pressburger, *Noteninstitut*, I, p. 384. On the restrictions in 1820 of the number of stocks issued, see page 44.
196 Or in banknotes with the premium reflecting the prevailing trading price of silver. The banknotes paid in were used to buy silver.
197 1 pound as defined by the customs union (500 g of fine silver) served to strike 30 thalers, 45 Austrian florins and 52.5 Southern German florins, respectively.
198 Source: *Historical time series on the Nationalbank*. The data refer to Convention standard florins (up to 1858) or to Austrian standard florins (after 1858).
199 The small denominations accounted for 149.5 million florins out of a total of 383.5 million florins at the end of 1857. On the related concerns of the governing board, see Pressburger, *Noteninstitut*, I, p. 524.
200 Source: *Historical time series on interest rates*.
201 Pressburger, *Noteninstitut*, I,, pp. 529–537, 539.
202 *Ibid.*, I, p. 553.
203 For a detailed description of the items in the OeNB's balance sheet, see the notes to the *Historical time series on the Nationalbank*.
204 This refers to the seigniorage for banknotes. Minting coins was the government's prerogative in Austria until the OeNB bought the state mint in 1989; until then, the government was also the direct beneficiary of the seigniorage for coins.
205 However, the treasury did assign securities from its portfolio to the bank, thus reducing the new liabilities from 133 million florins to 99 million florins. The bond issue that was supposed to raise 200 million florins (133 million florins of which the bank had provided in the form of advances) was not much of a success. Rather than redeeming the remaining 99 million florins, the treasury pledged the unissued quota as collateral (Zuckerkandl, *Austro-Hungarian Bank*, pp. 83f).
206 Kamitz, Geldpolitik, p. 137.
207 Exceptions included the statutory discount of bills of exchange and transactions carried out on commission, where any outstanding balance had to be settled at the end of month. Apart from the debate on the coverage system, the parliamentary debate focused on the term of the note issuance monopoly and the corresponding remuneration (Liese and Schulze, Geldpolitik, p. 516). On changes in the distribution of income, see below.
208 Pressburger, *Noteninstitut*, I, pp. 521–522.
209 The cause of the currency school was supported above all by Michaelis, Faucher and Knies. A key representative of the banking school was Adolph Wagner, who taught in Vienna between 1858 and 1863 and published a number of works on monetary reform in Austria.
210 The proposal to separate banknote issuance from banking business and to establish an upper threshold for banknotes in circulation in line with the British Bank Act of 1844 was already part of Governor Gravenegg's reform plan of 1849 (Pressburger, *Noteninstitut*, I, pp. 275–276).
211 A coverage ratio of one-third was based on convention rather than empirical analysis. Wagner, *Geld- und Credittheorie*, pp. 3–5, criticized the "caricature" interpretation of proportional coverage. On the Austrian statutes, see Neuwirth, *Bankacte*; Wagner, *Herstellung*.
212 Neuwirth, *Bankacte*, p. 52, considered the government bill to be based on Meyer, *Grundzüge*. On the position of the bank, see Lucam, *Beantragte Änderungen*.
213 In turn, the treasury promised a minimum dividend of 7%.
214 Beer, *Finanzen*, p. 338; Kamitz, Geldpolitik, p. 140; März, *Industrie- und Bankpolitik*, pp. 95–108.
215 Good, *Economic rise*, pp. 87–89; Liese and Schulze, Geldpolitik.

216 The discount limits of the branch offices were never actually used in full, to retain a buffer for ad hoc demand. However, after 1862, the use of discount loans (as a percentage of the limits) declined significantly. See Lucam, *Drittes Privilegium*, pp. 98–101, 114–117.

217 The provisions of the charter of 1863 which prohibited monetary financing of the treasury were suspended temporarily (Zuckerkandl, *Austro-Hungarian Bank*, p. 86).

218 Pressburger, *Noteninstitut*, I, p. 243.

219 *Ibid.*, I, p. 241. See the names in the financial statements published on July 5, 1849, reprinted in *ibid.*, I, p. 293.

220 Jobst, What drives. The business model of the support committees was revitalized in Brno in 1854 and used again in combating the crisis in Vienna in 1873. As to Brno, see Pressburger, *Noteninstitut*, I, pp. 401–402; as to the crisis in 1873, see below.

221 Lucam, *Verhältnis*, p. 35.

222 Exchange offices were located in Prague, Brno, Buda, Lviv, Linz, Graz, Trieste, Innsbruck, Timișoara and Sibiu. The exchange offices in Milan and Trento were closed again after a few years. By 1848, another outlet had been opened in Košice (Pressburger, *Noteninstitut*, I, pp. 168, 230).

223 Pressburger, *Noteninstitut*, I, p. 168; Lederer, *National-Bank*, pp. 43–44.

224 For details on information problems and the organizational setup of the branch network, see Jobst, Gouverner.

225 Pressburger, *Noteninstitut*, I, pp. 231–232.

226 The branch office rolled over an expiring emergency loan extended in 1848 (*ibid.* I, pp. 329, 349).

227 For a list of the branch offices and dates of establishment, see the annual reports. For details on the bank management's reluctant stance, see Pressburger, *Noteninstitut*, I, pp. 368–369. However, some initiatives to set up branch offices were also started by the bank, such as the inititiative led by Governor Gravenegg (*ibid.*, I, pp. 275–276). The bank commission convened by finance minister Krauss to work out plans to stabilize the currency likewise dealt with the geographical expansion of the bank's business activities. See Brandt, *Neoabsolutismus*, p. 244; Pressburger, *Noteninstitut*, I, pp. 319–324.

228 Brandt, *Neoabsolutismus*, p. 333.

229 Pressburger, *Noteninstitut*, I, p. 388.

230 *Ibid.*, I, p. 411.

231 Brandt, *Neoabsolutismus*: p. 337.

232 Lending by the branch offices was originally limited to loans provided in turn for subscription of *Nationalanlehen* bonds and was supposed to expire in 1859. Yet, in 1860, lending operations were institutionalized.

233 At the end of 1858 bonds with a nominal value of 57.7 million florins were posted as collateral at the bank, compared to a total outstanding 522 million in 1863 (*Historical time series on the National-bank*).

234 Lucam, *Drittes Privilegium*, pp. 10–11. Long-term loans were once again partly used in short-term operations: Jobst, What drives, p. 24.

235 Pressburger, *Noteninstitut*, I, pp. 476–479. For specifics on Hungarian property law, see Blum, *Noble landowners*, pp. 64–66; for details on the introduction of a land register, see Sarlós, Rechtswesen, p. 514, and Ogris, Rechtsentwicklung, pp. 584–585. The large landowners in Bohemia insisted on setting up a mortgage bank of their own, representing the Nationalbank for political reasons (Brandt, *Neoabsolutismus*, pp. 306–309).

236 Brandt, *Neoabsolutismus*, pp. 305–306; Bráf, Hypothekar-Credit, p. 592.

237 Pressburger, *Noteninstitut*, I, p. 451. This is not entirely correct. Before the mortgage bonds issued by the National-bank became a widely used instrument, the bank also extended loans backed by bank balances or banknotes. Also, the bank bought its own mortgage bonds on the stock exchange to support their price level. Over time, the relevance of such transactions diminished, however (Lucam, *Drittes Privilegium*, p. 139).

238 *Tafeln zur Statistik*, 1855–1857.

239 The establishment of the Creditanstalt was also linked to the reduction in government debt held with the Nationalbank (März, *Industrie- und Bankpolitik*, pp. 34–35).

240 Meanwhile, the National-bank's capital had risen considerably, to reach 110 million florins. As this amount was, however, invested in government debt, it was not available for discounting of commercial bills.

241 Only few reliable data on the composition of the National-bank's discount portfolio are available. The information on rediscounting is taken from an article published in *Die Presse* on July 6, 1855. The entire stock of bills (end-year values) held with the Nationalbank and the Escomptegesellschaft, as published in the *Tafeln zur Statistik*, 1855–1857.

242 Lecture given by the governor, as quoted in Pressburger, *Noteninstitut*, p. 492. Wirth, *Geschichte der Handelskrisen 1858*, p. 425.

243 *Ibid.* pp. 373–374; Flandreau, Central bank cooperation.

244 To prevent a run, the governor decided all by himself, even without consulting with

the other governing board members, and in violation of the statutes to grant Eskeles a loan collateralized with securities and mortgages. Yet renewed losses in 1859 following the war-related devaluation of the florin pushed Eskeles into default. Once the losses were disclosed, the secret extension of a loan was heavily criticized in the shareholder meeting. The governor defended himself by pointing out that "preserving one individual bank does not only help this bank alone but supports the livelihoods of thousands of people worth considering. To successfully carry out such rescue operations for the common good, it is imperative that the strictest confidentiality be maintained." (Pressburger, *Noteninstitut*, I, pp. 560–562.)

245 This autumnal drain is well documented especially for the USA. The resulting liquidity shortages repeatedly triggered crises in the financial hubs on the U.S. east coast and were among the main reasons why a U.S. central bank was set up in 1913. Similar monthly patters may also manifest themselves, for instance when wages and salaries or rents are regularly paid at the beginning or end of the month. Add to this payment conventions in the financial markets, such as the monthly or semi-monthly clearing of financial transactions. To keep current payments at a minimum, only one or two days per month were reserved for particular transactions on many stock exchanges in the 19th century. The same applied to the payment dates of bills. It was hence possible to net transactions, leaving only the difference to be settled by cash or via credit transfers. This practice reduced demand for cash during the month,

while pushing it up markedly at the payment dates.

246 In 1861, customers requesting advances of more than 100,000 florins accounted for 34 million florins (of which large landowners: 10.5 million florins) out of 52.7 million florins in secured loans (Lucam, *Verhältnis*, p. 36).

247 Lucam, *Drittes Privilegium*, pp. 21–22.

248 *Historical time series on interest rates.*

249 Articles 13 and 29 of the charter of 1863.

250 Under the charter of 1863, these dividends had to be topped up by the treasury. However, in 1868 the treasury refused to comply. The ensuing legal dispute was only settled when the charter was renewed in 1878.

251 Discount lending by the branch offices increased from 20 million florins in the period 1855–1867 to more than 60 million florins in the period 1872–1877 (*Historical time series on the National-bank*).

252 The bank successfully requested these statutory changes in compensation for violation by the treasury of its note-issuing monopoly (Zuckerkandl, *Austro-Hun-garian Bank*, p. 86).

253 Source: *Historical time series on interest rates.*

254 In the literature, the founding era was cited as a textbook example of a boom-bust cycle; see e.g. Kindleberger, *Manias.*

255 Good, *Economic rise*, pp. 164–165.

256 März, *Industrie- und Bankpolitik*, p. 140.

257 With a view to avoiding the political problem of state top-up payments, the objective was to achieve at least a dividend of 7% (see notes no. 213 and 250).

258 The crisis hit above all Hungary, and the Nationalbank was blamed accordingly. Neuwirth, *Bankacte*, chapter VI.

259 "I must reject the view that banks of issue address crisis events if address is meant to imply prevent. ... What major banks under sound management can do, notably so in periods of trade and credit crises, is to make an essential contribution to a softer resolution, by providing a safe backstop and helping to restore trust amid the general turmoil thanks to their strength and their strong creditworthiness." *Neue Freie Presse*, May 22, 1870, p. 14.

260 These figures include repurchase agreements in silver and gold, i.e., silver and gold sold by commercial banks to the Nationalbank subject to an agreement to buy these assets back at a predefined date at a predefined price. During the term of these transactions, the bank would count these holdings toward coverage of banknotes in circulation by specie and could, accordingly, raise the volume of banknotes in circulation. Likewise, asset portfolio shifts from long-term assets such as pfandbriefe to short-term assets such as discount and lending operations are likely to have had accommodative effects as well. While not increasing the volume of banknotes in circulation, these portfolio shifts might have dampened short-term market rates under certain conditions.

261 These treasury bills (short-term debt securities known as "Partialhypothekaran-weisungen," as they also granted creditors a mortgage on government salt mines) were linked to the volume of state paper money through two benchmarks, an upper limit for such treasury bills (100 million florins), and a combined upper limit for treasury bills and state paper money (400 million florins). (Mensi, Geld, p. 681).

262 Neuwirth, *Spekulationscrisis*, p. 61.

263 *Historical time series on credit institutions.*

264 The losses in stock prices relate to the period from end-March to End-October 1873. Neuwirth, *Spekulationscrisis*, p. 203.

265 This instrument was modeled after the suspension of the Bank Act in England, where the fixed quota for banknotes in circulation was also suspended in the crisis years of 1847, 1857 and 1866.

266 See the presentation made by Governor Pipitz at the General Meeting of 1874.

267 In Vienna, the Nationalbank paid 1 million florins into the operating fund, which amounted to 3.4 million florins. In Hungary, it contributed 200,000 florins (Pressburger, *Noteninstitut*, I, p. 1153).

268 Lucam, *Drittes Privilegium*, p. 85.

269 Support was provided for Eastern Hungarian Railways, whose bankruptcy would have endangered three Austrian banks (Pressburger, *Noteninstitut*, I, p. 1158). In October 1873, the Bankverein, a subsidiary of the Bodencreditanstalt, which in turn had close links with the monarch, came into trouble. The Nationalbank participated in the bail-out by rediscounting trade bills accepted by the support committee. The rescue operation lasted until 1875 (*ibid.*, I, p. 1165).

270 For a more detailed view of the bank's policies during the suspension of the Banking Act, see Lucam, *Drittes Privilegium*, pp. 79–88.

271 März, *Industrie- und Bankpolitik*, pp. 185–193; Matis, *Österreichs Wirtschaft*, pp. 13–21. For a summary, see Good, *Economic rise*, pp. 166–169.

272 Good, *Economic rise*, pp. 169–176. However, for a critical

view, see Schulze, *Machine-building industry*; and Schulze, *Patterns of growth*, p. 325.

273 Komlos, *Customs union*, pp. 162–163; Schulze, *Patterns of growth*, p. 324; Pammer, Austrian private investment.

274 *Historical time series on credit institutions.*

Two governments, one bank–the Austro-Hungarian monetary union (1878–1914)

275 Quoted by Pogány, Az Osztrák-Magyar Bank felszámolása, p. 19.

276 The first two charters expired after 25 years, the third after 14 years.

277 Kövér and Pogány, *Binationale Bank*, p. 27, footnote 42.

278 Weber, *Pester Ungarische Commerzialbank*, pp. 55–58. On Croatia see Rumpler, *Chance*, p. 302.

279 Dessewffy, *Schwebende Finanzfragen*, p. 91.

280 Brandt, *Neoabsolutismus*, pp. 332–333; Kövér and Pogány, *Binationale Bank*, pp. 26–28.

281 On the central bank's role in contributing to the formation of a nation state, see Helleiner, *Territorial currencies*; on Austria see Baltzarek, *Österreichs Rolle*, pp. 95–96.

282 On the Compromise of 1867, see e.g. Galantái, *Dualismus*; Katus, *Hungary in the dual monarchy.*

283 The Hungarian share of the state debt incurred before 1867 was governed by separate provisions.

284 On unclear passages in the final document and the genesis of the Compromise provisions, see Kövér and Pogány, *Binationale Bank*, pp. 28–33.

285 *Ibid.*, pp. 34–39.

286 Flandreau, *The bank.*

287 On interpreting this framework as a monetary union and the economic logic of negotiations, see Flandreau, Logic.

288 Stourzh, Dualismus, pp. 1177–1183.

289 On Austrian capital in Hungary, see Komlos, *Customs union*, pp. 162–206; and Pammer, Austrian private investment.

290 See Flandreau, Logic.

291 Kövér and Pogány, *Binationale Bank*, pp. 52–53; Neuwirth, *Bankacte*, pp. 456–457.

292 Pressburger, *Noteninstitut*, I, pp. 1334–1362.

293 The governors of the Austro-Hungarian Bank were Alois Moser (1878–1892, AT), Gyula Kautz (1892–1900, HU), Leon Ritter von Biliński (1900–1910, AT), Sándor Popovics (1910–1918, HU).

294 This concerned the establishment of contract offices. On the competences of contract offices, see this chapter below.

295 Concessions were made to Hungary with regard to cash payments, if introduced, and the expansion of Hungary's share of the bank's profit.

296 Kranister, *Geldmacher*.

297 Mises, Viertes Privilegium; May, *Hapsburg Monarchy*, p. 256; Komlos, *Customs union*, p. 195; Kolm, Spannungsfeld, p. 252.

298 Flandreau, Logic. On the loose link between long-term and short-term interest rates, see Flandreau and Jobst, Empirics.

299 Good, Financial integration.

300 The Austro-Hungarian Bank did not act as an intermediary in the sense of taking in deposits and channeling them into loans. Due to the disproportionate share of lending in regions with higher interest rates, however, the bank fulfilled an intermediary function in the end, which would have had to be carried out by private agents otherwise. The increase in demand for central bank liquidity in peripheral regions shows that private intermediaries, too, offered in-

termediation services, yet at higher costs.

301 Eddie, Economic Policy, p. 856

302 Flandreau, French crime.

303 Flandreau and Oosterlinck, Was the emergence.

304 Source: *Historical time series on interest rates*. Prices after 1900 are denominated in crowns and have been translated into florins for the chart to facilitate comparison.

305 Whereas silver parity was given through the statutory definition of the florin in silver, there was no equivalent definition of gold parity. While Austria began to strike florin coins in gold in 1870, those coins were not legal tender. Based on the coinage system of the Latin Monetary Union, according to which the gold franc was interchangeable with the silver franc based on an exchange rate of 1:15.5, the 8-florin gold coin was equivalent to 8.10 (Austrian standard) silver florins. Essentially, the minting of gold coins was only the first step toward alignment with Latin Monetary Union standards; in a second step, it would have been necessary to slightly adjust the silver content of the silver florin, similar to the changeover from Convention standard florins to Austrian standard florins in line with the Coinage Treaty of 1857. The chart was drawn on the assumption that this adjustment had already happened, meaning that the line for silver will correspond with the line for gold if, as was the case in 1873, the international gold/silver exchange rate was close to 1:15.5.

306 Flandreau and Eichengreen, Geography.

307 Einaudi, *Money and politics*.

308 At the time, gold was less expensive than silver, which started to change from the 1870s, though. Returning to convertibility based on a gold or bimetallic currency seemed to be an attractive option for Austria, not least for reasons of cost.

309 See also note 305 above.

310 Lesigang, Ursachen des Agio.

311 *Historical time series on interest rates*.

312 On the political economy, see Mises, Wirtschaftspolitische Motive; and Mises, Viertes Privilegium.

313 The gold standard was adopted even though experts were leaning toward the bimetallic standard. The latter, however, would have required international agreement, which could not be reached.

314 Fellner, *Währungsreform*, pp. 104–113.

315 *Ibid.* pp. 128–134.

316 The bank had held foreign bills of exchange before, but had traded them in exchange for coins only, not for banknotes, though. These transactions had therefore left the bank's total holdings of foreign assets unchanged. Jobst, Market leader; Spitzmüller, Währungsreform.

317 Zuckerkandl, Austro-Hungarian Bank, pp. 110, 118.

318 On the following, see Jobst, Market leader.

319 Flandreau and Komlos, Target zones.

320 Mises, Foreign exchange policy; Knapp, *The state theory of money*. On Belgium, see Ugolini, Origins of foreign exchange policy.

321 Mises, Viertes Privilegium, pp. 617–619.

322 Lucam, *Drittes Privilegium*, pp. 52–63; Tschurn, *Verwaltungsorganismus*, pp. 10, 19.

323 Jobst, Gouverner, p. 123.

324 On inspectors, see Tschurn, *Verwaltungsorganismus*.

325 Jobst, What drives, p. 26.

326 Jobst, Gouverner, pp. 15–17.

327 Source: Author's illustration.

328 Good, *Economic rise*; Good, Financial integration. On Hungary, see Pogány, Wirtschaftsnationalismus.

329 Mühlpeck et al., Index der Verbraucherpreise.

330 On Austria, see OeNB Archives, 283/1910; on Hungary, see Kövér and Pogány, *Binationale Bank*, p. 185.

331 Source: *Historical time series on the Nationalbank*.

332 *Historical time series on credit institutions*.

333 Komlos, *Financial innovation*.

334 Michel, *Banquiers*, pp. 143–149; Rudolph, *Banking*, pp. 70, 272.

335 Baltzarek, *Wiener Börse*, p. 161.

336 Lederer, *National-Bank*.

337 Kernbauer, *Beschleunigter Geldverkehr*.

338 Rauchberg, *Clearing- und Giro-Verkehr*, p. 180.

339 Source: *Historical time series on interest rates* (Austria); *NBER MacroHist* (Germany, England, France).

340 Flandreau and Komlos, Target zones.

World War I and the collapse of monetary union (1914–1919)

341 Popovics, *Geldwesen im Kriege*, pp. 30–38.

342 *Ibid.*, pp. 38–41.

343 Gold and foreign exchange reserves as disclosed do not include foreign exchange assets reported under "other assets."

344 Schulze, Austria-Hungary's economy, p. 105.

345 *Ibid.*, pp. 77–78.

346 *Ibid.*, p. 83.

347 The financial cost of World War I was also high for other nations, such as Germany; however, among the larger nations, only France had to suffer a similar decline in GDP as Austria did (Broadberry and Harrison, Economics of World War I, p. 12).

348 Broadberry and Harrison, Economics of World War I, pp. 14–15.

349 Pogány, Kriegskosten.

350 *Ibid.*

351 *Ibid.*

352 Popovics, *Geldwesen im Kriege*, p. 74.

353 *Ibid.*, S. 79. Hungary did not use the full amount of its share, because it required less central bank funding for various reasons. On the heated arguments between Austria and Hungary on this point, see Pogány, Kriegskosten.

354 Hardach, *Erster Weltkrieg*, p. 185.

355 Popovics, *Geldwesen im Kriege*, p. 164.

356 The Austro-Hungarian Bank's balance sheet does not support the widely held view that attractive credit conditions counteract the effects achieved by skimming off war loans, contributing to a rise in the supply of money. See, e.g., Butschek, *Österreichische Wirtschaftsgeschiche*, p. 177.

357 Popovics, *Geldwesen im Kriege*, p. 78.

358 Other items include foreign exchange assets and balances, valued at 372 million crowns at gold par, which is, however, overstated because of underlying losses (*ibid.*, pp. 133–134).

359 Source: *Historical time series on the Nationalbank*.

360 The Kingdom of Serbia was the center of the Kingdom of Serbs, Croats and Slovenes founded in 1918.

361 Sandgruber, *Ökonomie und Politik*, pp. 335ff.; Teichova and Matis (eds.), *Österreich und die Tschechoslowakei*; Berend and Ranki, *Economic development*, pp. 170ff.

362 Pressburger, *Notenbank 1816–1966*, pp. 324ff.

363 Pressburger, *Noteninstitut*, II, pp. 2022ff.

364 *Ibid.*, II, pp. 2040ff; Schubert, Emergence of national central banks, pp. 189ff.; Garber and Spencer, *Dissolution of the Austro-Hungarian empire*, pp. 9ff.

365 Pressburger, *Noteninstitut*, II, pp. 2077ff.

366 Zeuceanu, *La liquidation*, pp. 693–694; see also the Peace Treaty of Saint-Germain on the liquidation of the Austro-Hungarian Bank, Official Gazette, no. 852, December 5, 1922.

Hyperinflation and a new currency (1919–1931)

367 Historians date the "long 19th century" from the French revolution (1789) to World War I.

368 Kernbauer, *Währungspolitik in der Zwischenkriegszeit*, pp. 38–39. In the spring of 1919, foreign minister Otto Bauer conducted secret talks in Berlin with a view to introducing the German mark in Austria (Gulick, *Austria from Habsburg to Hitler*, I, p. 165). These plans met with opposition from the German Reichsbank. The Peace Treaty of Saint-Germain expressly prohibited Austria from forming a political union with Germany. As ruled later by the International Court of Justice in The Hague, this clause was construed to rule out economic union as well.

369 Gratz, Österreichische Finanzpolitik von 1848 bis 1948, p. 278.

370 Pressburger, *Noteninstitut*, II, p. 2303.

371 Federn, Die Kreditpolitik der Banken, pp. 59–60.

372 Kernbauer, *Währungspolitik in der Zwischenkriegszeit*, pp. 30ff.

373 März, *Joseph Schumpeter*, pp. 135ff; Ausch, *Als die Banken fielen*, pp. 16–17; *Neue Freie Presse*, March 16, 1919.

374 März, *Joseph Schumpeter*, p. 134.

375 Based on the financial statements as reprinted in Pressburger, *Noteninstitut*.

376 Author's calculations based on data from Walré de Bordes, *The Austrian crown*, pp. 82–83.

377 Author's calculations based on data from *ibid.*, pp. 114ff.

378 Source: Walré de Bordes, *The Austrian crown*, pp. 34–64, 65–106, 107–145. The data for banknotes in circulation refer to the Austrian entity of the Austro-Hungarian Bank after 1920 and were chained with banknotes in circulation across the monarchy before 1920.

379 Expectations that Austria would issue international bonds guaranteed by the League of Nations sufficed to stop the depreciation of the crown in foreign exchange markets. The crown bottomed out on August 25, 1922, even though the central bank continued to finance the budget deficit until November 18, 1922 (Dornbusch and Fischer, *Stopping hyperinflations*, pp. 16ff; Sargent, Four big inflations).

380 Ladner, *Seipel*, p. 87.

381 The further political development of the Danube region was above all in the interest of the German Reich and the Small Entente, a defensive alliance of Czechoslovakia, Yugoslavia and Romania under the auspices of France, as well as Italy, which had close ties with Hungary.

382 For verbatim information on the Geneva Protocols, see i.a. Pressburger, *Noteninstitut*, II, pp. 2299ff. See also Haas, Österreich im System der Pariser Vororteverträge, pp. 671–672.

383 Flores and Decorzant, *The League of Nations loans revisited*.

384 Ahamed, *Lords of finance*, p. 155. Montagu Norman was governor of the *Bank of England* from 1920 to 1940; Benjamin Strong was governor of the *Federal Reserve Bank of New York* from 1914 to 1928.

385 Berger, *Kurze Geschichte Österreichs*, pp. 22–23. In his autobiography, Ludwig von Mises, a leading liberal economist born in Austria, who worked for the Viennese Chamber of Trade in the interwar period and whose economic thinking was

broadly in line with that of the commissioner-general representing the League of Nations, called Zimmermann "an ignorant, tactless and arrogant Dutchman." (Mises, *Memoirs*, p. 69).

386 Karl, *Die österreichische Völkerbundanleihe* I; and Karl, *Die österreichische Völkerbundanleihe* II.

387 OeNB Archives, 1646/1923; Brauneis, *Entwicklung der Oesterreichischen Nationalbank*, p. 7.

388 OeNB Archives, 1600/1923.

389 Official Gazette, no. 490/1922.

390 The other 40 million Swiss francs were to be released at a later point. See Kernbauer, *Währungspolitik in der Zwischenkriegszeit*, pp. 68ff.

391 Clay, *Lord Norman*, p. 185.

392 Bundesgesetz vom 14. November 1922 betreffend die Abänderung und Ergänzung des Bundesgesetzes vom 24. Juli 1922, BGBl. Nr. 490 über die Errichtung einer Notenbank (Official Gazette, no. 823/1922).

393 The banking sector subscribed for 97% of the share capital of the OeNB. The share of proprietary subscriptions is not known. Bankhaus Rothschild deposited some 19% and other banks and bankers some 17% of the OeNB shares for the General Council meeting of 1923. Again, it is not known whether those shares were held for own account. (OeNB Archives, 1437/1930).

394 The Central Bank Transition Act (Official Gazette, no. 44/1923), which among other things provided for the dissolution of the Austrian entity of the Austro-Hungarian Bank, was not adopted until January 12, 1923, that is to say after the federal government had mandated the transition of operations to the bank's successor in an unconstitutional regulation on December 29, 1922. The journal *Der Österreichische Volkswirt*

considered this breach of the constitution to be evidence of "how badly the government neglected the law and the constitution, on the assumption that the commissioner-general would cover any arbitrariness." (*Der Österreichische Volkswirt*, January 13, 1923, p. 393).

395 Unless they were particularly volatile, foreign exchange assets could also be part of "precious metal."

396 Kernbauer, *Währungspolitik in der Zwischenkriegszeit*, pp. 79ff.

397 Reisch joined the finance ministry in 1891 and was promoted to the position of department head in 1910. From October 17, 1919, until November 20, 1920, he served as finance minister under the administrations of Renner III and Mayr I. In 1921 he was appointed vice president of the Bodencreditanstalt, where he had managed a division from 1918 to 1919 (*Österreichisches Biographisches Lexikon 1815–1950*, vol. 9, Vienna 1988, pp. 55–56); OeNB Archives, Governors and presidents of the Oesterreichische Nationalbank.

398 Rennhofer, *Ignaz Seipel*, p. 55.

399 Sayers, *The Bank of England 1891–1944*, I, pp. 167–168.

400 Ausch, *Als die Banken fielen*, p. 91, footnote 23.

401 OeNB Archives, 690/1923. The advisor, who had the rank of a co-president, was appointed by the Austrian President upon nomination by the federal government, which in turn acted on a binding proposal of the commissioner-general installed by the League of Nations.

402 Bundesgesetz vom 28. April 1923 über die zeitweilige Bestellung eines Beraters bei der Oesterreichischen Nationalbank (Official Gazette, no. 251/1923). See Kernbauer, *Währungspolitik in der Zwischenkriegszeit*, pp. 108ff.

403 *Ibid.*, p. 101.

404 *Ibid.*

405 Karl, *Die österreichische Völkerbundanleihe* I, p. 89. To finance the budget deficits until the League of Nations loan became available, the Austrian government had issued treasury bills in the amount of 5.5 million dollars (6% yield) in November 1922 and short-term gold bonds in the amount of 5.1 million dollars (8% yield) in December 1922. In December it took out swap loans from Austrian banks (7.2 million crowns = 1.4 million dollars): banks drew bills of exchange on the Kontrollbank, which submitted the bills for rediscount to the central bank, subject to the prevailing discount rate (9%). See Kernbauer, *Währungspolitik in der Zwischenkriegszeit*, pp. 106–107.

406 Layton and Rist, *The economic situation of Austria*, p. 131.

407 Statistische Nachrichten 1924, p. 268.

408 Spitzmüller, Die Geldwertpolitik der Oesterreichischen Nationalbank, pp. 81ff; and *Neue Freie Presse*, January 26, 1924.

409 *Die Industrie*, 5/1924.

410 Quoted from Zeissel, *Politik der Oesterreichischen Nationalbank*, p. 60.

411 Mises, Über Deflationspolitik, p. 16.

412 Calculated with data from Walré de Bordes, *The Austrian crown*, pp. 50, 83 and 133ff. Walré de Bordes assumes that banknotes worth 500 million crowns were circulating in the area of the Republic of Austria before the war. The price index excludes rents subject to rent control.

413 General Council member Neubauer argued in the General Council meeting of February 21, 1923, that medium-sized trade and industry operations faced an interest burden of between 6.5% and 7% on average per month.

This figure appears heavily overstated. Secured loans traded for an annual average rate of 65.8% at the stock exchange in 1923. In 1924, banks charged interest rates (including commission on turnover) in the range of 17% to 23% according to the Konjunkturforschungsinstitut. See ÖIfK-Monatsbericht 6/1938, p. 140.

414 OeNB Archives, 6th General Council meeting, April 26, 1923.

415 OeNB Archives, 2014/1923.

416 OeNB Archives, monthly report by the commissioner-general of the League of Nations, no. 4, October 10, 1923.

417 Statistische Nachrichten 1923, p. 7.

418 *Ibid.*

419 Baltzarek, *Wiener Börse*, pp. 119–124.

420 OeNB Archives, 11th General Council meeting, September 29, 1923. See also Brauneis, *Entwicklung der Oesterreichischen Nationalbank*, p. 14.

421 Brauneis, *Entwicklung der Oesterreichischen Nationalbank*, p. 6.

422 Layton and Rist, *The economic situation of Austria*, p. 131.

423 Bernholz, *Geldwertstabilität und Währungsordnung*, p. 70; Aldcroft, *From Versailles to Wall Street*, pp. 145–146.

424 Oestergaard, *Inflation und Stabilisierung*, p. 111.

425 *Mitteilungen*, 1924, pp. 36 and 44.

426 Brauneis, *Entwicklung der Oesterreichischen Nationalbank*, p. 12; Ausch, *Als die Banken fielen*, p. 139; OeNB Archives, monthly report by the commissioner-general of the League of Nations, no. 10, March 1924, pp. 24–25.

427 OeNB Archives, 662/1924; 14th Governing Board meeting, March 26, 1924.

428 OeNB Archives, monthly report by the commissioner-general of the League of Nations, no. 30, December 22, 1925; OeNB Archives, 1714/1925. The final instalment of this loan was redeemed in 1928.

429 Statistische Nachrichten 1925, p. 4.

430 Brauneis, *Entwicklung der Oesterreichischen Nationalbank*, pp. 20ff. On the rise and fall of banks outside Vienna, see Weber, *Der finanzielle Länderpartikularismus.*

431 Ausch, *Als die Banken fielen*, pp. 157–158.

432 Pressburger, *Notenbank*, p. 392.

433 OeNB Archives, 976/1925.

434 BoE, OV 27–27, Schnyder to Norman, February 6, 1924.

435 OeNB Archives, 976/1925.

436 Kernbauer, *Währungspolitik in der Zwischenkriegszeit*, pp. 133ff.

437 BoE, OV 28–28, Norman to Zimmermann, May 6, 1924.

438 Reisch, Aufgaben einer modernen Notenbank, pp. 193ff.

439 Compass 1925, vol. I, p. 170.

440 OeNB Archives, 23rd General Council meeting, September 12, 1924.

441 OeNB Archives, 25th General Council meeting, December 18, 1924.

442 *The Times*, December 22, 1924.

443 Compass 1925, vol. I, p. 170.

444 OeNB Archives, 19th Governing Board meeting, August 29, 1924.

445 Official Gazette, no. 461/1924.

446 Federal government regulation of April 29, 1926, Official Gazette, no. 108/1926, "Über die Rechnungsführung in Schillingen."

447 OeNB Archives, 20th Governing Board meeting, September 29 to October 1, 1924.

448 Official Gazette, no. 184/1925.

449 Repurchase agreements are financial transactions in which a party sells assets and simultaneously agrees to repurchase them at a future point in time, which may be prespecified or agreed later. For the period of the repurchase agreement, ownership of the assets is transferred to the buyer. There were heated discussions between the OeNB and the Bank of Eng-

land as to whether it was permissible to disclose foreign exchange assets acquired under repurchase agreements under cash currency reserves. At the request of the Bank of England, such assets were disclosed separately in the bank's financial statements from January 1925 onward. See Kernbauer, *Währungspolitik in der Zwischenkriegszeit*, pp. 147–148.

450 Kernbauer and Weber, Die Wiener Großbanken in der Zeit der Kriegs- und Nachkriegsinflation, p. 179.

451 *Mitteilungen*, 1926, pp. 234ff.

452 CA Archives, Bodencreditanstalt Board minutes, May 5, 1925.

453 CA Archives, Bankverein Board minutes, May 6, 1925; Bodencreditanstalt Board minutes, May 15, 1925; Sieghart, *Die letzten Jahrzehnte einer Großmacht*, p. 196.

454 In January 1923, French and Belgian troops invaded the Ruhr region with a view to enforcing the delivery of coal and steel in keeping with the reparation obligations laid down in the Treaty of Versaille. The Germans responded with a general strike and put up passive resistance. The ensuing production losses created export opportunities for Austrian and other companies.

455 Butschek, *Statistische Reihen zur österreichischen Wirtschaftsgeschichte*, table 5.1. With the exception of 1929, the investment ratio of the Austrian economy was consistently below 10% in the interwar years.

456 In 1929, 283,000 people were unemployed and 2,032,000 people were in paid employment. See *ibid.*, table 3.3.

457 Fibich, *Entwicklung der österreichischen Bundesausgaben*, pp. 170ff; Kernbauer, Österreichische Währungs-, Bank- und Budgetpolitik in der Zwischenkriegszeit, pp. 552ff.

458 Layton and Rist, *The economic situation of Austria*; Berger, *Kurze Geschichte Österreichs*, pp. 120–121.

459 OeNB Archives, 34th General Council meeting, October 7, 1925; act adopted on December 1, 1925, Official Gazette, no. 417/1925.

460 BoE, OV 28–31, Kay to Norman, February 11, 1926.

461 BoE, OV 28–31, Harvey to Franckenstein, November 7, 1925.

462 Official Gazette, nos. 169/1925 and 372/1926.

463 OeNB Archives, 2312/1923.

464 BoE, OV 28–30, memorandum dated April 22, 1925; OeNB Archives, 26th Governing Board meeting, March 27, 1925; OeNB Archives, 1138/1925, Reisch to Norman, March 22, 1926; BoE, OV 28–31, Norman to Kay, February 10, 1926.

465 Clarke, *Central bank cooperation 1924–1931*, p. 87. According to a memorandum of the Bank von England, "Sir Henry [Strakosch] and Dr. van Gijn were both of the opinion that a big margin of profit should be left for the foreign capitalists." BoE, OV 28–29, memorandum drafted by Osborne.

466 OeNB Archives, 522/1927.

467 OeNB Archives, 56th General Council meeting, September 23, 1927, and 58th General Council meeting, November 25, 1927.

468 Wärmer, Die Auslandsverschuldung Österreichs, p. 282.

469 OeNB Archives, 93rd General Council meeting, January 30, 1931. Deducting near-term nondomestic liabilities (66 million Austrian schillings) from foreign exchange reserves yields a coverage ratio of banknotes in circulation of 86%.

470 *Mitteilungen, passim.*

471 Berger, *Kurze Geschichte Österreichs*, pp. 108–109.

472 Ausch, *Als die Banken fielen*, pp. 307ff; Weber, *Vor dem großen Krach*, pp. 403ff;

Eigner and Melichar, Das Ende der Boden-Credit-Anstalt, pp. 56ff; Kernbauer, *Währungspolitik in der Zwischenkriegszeit*, pp. 276ff.

473 OeNB Archives, 363/1931.

474 Wärmer, *Das österreichische Kreditwesen*, p. 9.

475 *Ibid.*, p. 7.

476 *Ibid.*, p. 8.

477 Ausch, *Als die Banken fielen*, pp. 155ff; März, *Österreichische Bankpolitik 1913–1923*, pp. 465; Weber, *Vor dem großen Krach*, p. 192ff; Stiefel, *Camillo Castiglioni*, pp. 105ff and 161ff.

478 Kernbauer, *Währungspolitik in der Zwischenkriegszeit*, pp. 143–144.

479 *Ibid.*, pp. 257ff.

480 Wagner and Tomanek, *Bankiers und Beamte*, pp. 233–234; Ausch, *Als die Banken fielen*, pp. 147ff. President Reisch was appointed interim manager of PSK after the latter's losses became known; the institution was reorganized under his leadership.

481 März, *Bankpolitik 1913–1923*, pp. 459ff; Weber, *Vor dem großen Krach*, pp. 376ff; Natmeßnig, *Britische Finanzinteressen in Österreich*.

482 Kernbauer, *Währungspolitik in der Zwischenkriegszeit*, p. 280. The aforementioned receivables were booked under "other assets."

483 BoE, OV 28–34, Brauneis to Siepmann, October 12, 1929.

The Creditanstalt crisis, the Great Depression and World War II (1931–1945)

484 Ahamed, *Lords of finance*, p. 404.

485 *Ibid.*, p. 422.

486 Moggridge, *British monetary policy 1924–1931*.

487 Kindleberger, *The world in depression 1929–1939*, p. 40.

488 Irmler, Bankenkrise und Vollbeschäftigungspolitik, p. 291.

489 Hal, *The United States in the world economy*, p. 216; Lewis,

Economic survey 1919–1939, p. 61; Bernanke, The macroeconomics of the Great Depression, pp. 5ff; Friedman and Schwartz, *A monetary history*, pp. 299ff.

490 Kindleberger, *The world in depression 1929–1939*, p. 124.

491 Eichengreen, *Golden fetters*, pp. 12ff.

492 On the banking policy of Creditanstalt, see März and Weber, The antecedents of the Austrian financial crash, pp. 497ff; Ausch, *Als die Banken fielen*, pp. 335ff; Federn, Zusammenbruch der Österreichischen Kreditanstalt, pp. 414ff; Stiefel, *Finanzdiplomatie und Weltwirtschaftskrise.*

493 Schubert, *The Credit-Anstalt crisis of 1931*, p. 11.

494 Eichengreen, *Golden fetters*, p. 269.

495 Schubert, *The Credit-Anstalt crisis of 1931*, pp. 44 and 101ff.

496 Author's calculation, based on BIS, *2nd Annual Report*, p. 11.

497 CA Archives, Geschäftsbericht 1930, p. 15ff.

498 Stenographisches Protokoll, IVth legislature, 29th session, May 13, 1931; Austrian State Archives, Cabinet meeting minutes, no. 690, May 12, 1931.

499 BoE, OV 28–3, memorandum of May 17, 1931.

500 Judging from the rise in the number of 1,000 schilling notes in circulation. *Mitteilungen*, 1932, p. 16; OeNB Archives, 650/1932.

501 The OeNB's weekly financial statements underreported the increase in the bill portfolio and the decline in foreign exchange holdings in order to mask the extent of the decline in the reserve coverage ratio. To this effect, discounted bills were booked under "other assets" in exchange for foreign assets booked until then under "other assets". OeNB Archives, 16/1931.

502 *Mitteilungen*, 1/1932, p. 14–15.

503 BoE, OV 28–3, memorandum

of May 23, 1931. This amount acounted for 22% of Creditanstalt's short-term cross-border liabilities.

504 OeNB Archives, 1544/1931. The Second Creditanstalt Act, entitling the finance minister to assume liability as guarantor and debtor for deposits at CA, was adopted on May 28 (Official Gazette, no. 143/1931). Because of a dispute within the cabinet, finance minister Juch did not submit his guarantee statement until June 16. The Ender administration resigned after interior minister Winkler quit. A new cabinet led by Chancellor Buresch was sworn in on June 20, 1931. Austrian State Archives, Cabinet meeting minutes, no. 702, June 16, 1931, and no. 703, June 20, 1931.

505 OeNB Archives, 97th General Council meeting, Mai 13, 1931.

506 BoE, OV 28–3, Juch to Siepman (telegram), May 10, 1931; Siepman to Reisch, May 13, 1931.

507 OeNB Archives, 1550/1931.

508 OeNB Archives, 1531/1931.

509 OeNB Archives, 98th General Council meeting, May 29, 1931.

510 OeNB Archives, 1531/1931. BoE, OV 28–35, memorandum of May 30, 1931. The loan was due after three months, carried an interest rate of 5.25% plus a 0.25% commission charged by the BIS.

511 Berger, *Kurze Geschichte Österreichs*, p. 167; OeNB Archives, 99th General Council meeting, June 3, 1931. Gijsberg W. J. Bruins was university professor in Rotterdam and commissioner under the Dawes Plan at the Deutsche Reichsbank from 1924 to 1930.

512 Kindleberger, *The world in depression 1929–1939*, p. 151. Similar arguments have been put forth by Eichengreen, *Golden fetters*, p. 268.

513 OeNB Archives, 99th. General Council meeting, June 6, 1931,

and 100th General Council meeting, June 15, 1931.

514 OeNB Archives, 1555/1931.

515 OeNB Archives, 100th General Council meeting, June 15, 1931.

516 Brauneis announced this decision at the end of a cabinet meeting which was also joined by President Reisch, Vice President Thaa and the advisor, Bruins. Austrian State Archives, Cabinet meeting minutes, no. 703, June 22, 1931. Brauneis did not resume his position at the OeNB until September 1931, after the devaluation of the British pound had been announced.

517 Official Gazette, no. 309/1931.

518 OeNB Archives, 650/1932.

519 *Ibid.* The Bank of England demanded and received repayment of 50 million schillings in September 1931.

520 OeNB Archives, 110th General Council meeting, January 26, 1932.

521 Compass 1936, p. 162.

522 *Mitteilungen*, 1932, p. 15.

523 OeNB Archives, 4th meeting of the executive committee, November 30, 1931, and 109th General Council meeting, December 18, 1931.

524 Berger, *Kurze Geschichte Österreichs*, p. 187.

525 BoE, OV 28–69, Rost to Niemeyer, November 3, 1931.

526 OeNB Archives, 110th General Council meeting, January 26, 1932, and 373/1932.

527 OeNB Archives, 112nd General Council meeting, February 9, 1932.

528 Wärmer, *Das österreichische Kreditwesen*, p. 286.

529 OeNB Archives, 113rd General Council meeting, February 26, 1932.

530 OeNB Archives, 111st General Council meeting, February 4, 1932.

531 Kernbauer, *Währungspolitik in der Zwischenkriegszeit*, p. 337.

532 OeNB Archives, 116th General Council meeting, May 28, 1932.

533 Cabinet meeting minutes, First Republic, Abteilung VIII,

Kabinett Dr. Engelbert Dollfuss, vol. 1 (edited by Gertrude Enderle-Burcel), Vienna 1980, pp. 21ff.

534 Verordnung der Bundesregierung vom 11. Juli 1932, betreffend Übergangsbestimmungen für die Zeit der Devisensperre für Auslandsschulden (Official Gazette, no. 191/1932).

535 Joseph Avenol, from the staff of the French finance ministry, served as deputy secretary-general of the League of Nations from 1922 and as secretary general from 1933 to 1940. British economist Alexander Loveday worked in the League Secretariat from 1919 and was appointed director of the League's Financial Section and Economic Intelligence Service in 1931.

536 Berger, *Kurze Geschichte Österreichs*, pp. 159ff; Klingenstein, *Die Anleihe von Lausanne*, p. 126–127.

537 Bundesgesetz betreffend die Maßnahmen zur Sicherung des Gleichgewichts in den öffentlichen Haushalten vom 3. Oktober 1931 (Official Gazette, no. 294/1931).

538 *Mitteilungen*, 3/1934, p. 100.

539 OeNB Archives, 112nd General Council meeting, February 9, 1932, and 1354/1932.

540 Official Gazette, no. 73/1933.

541 OeNB Archives, 117th General Council meeting, July 27, 1932, and 1146/1932.

542 OeNB Archives, 117th General Council meeting, July 27, 1932.

543 BoE, OV 27–71 Abkommen zwischen der österreichischen Regierung, der Creditanstalt und dem Internationalen Gläubigerkomitee der Creditanstalt vom 11. Jänner und 27. April 1933, and BoE, OV 28–72, memorandum of December 3, 1934.

544 Fibich, *Entwicklung der österreichischen Bundesausgaben*, p. 159.

545 Spitzmüller, *... und hat auch Ursach, es zu lieben*, p. 370; CA Archives, Geschäftsbericht der Creditanstalt 1931 and

1932, p. 13; BoE, OV 28–73, memorandum of April 27, 1937.

546 Cabinet meeting minutes, First Republic, Abteilung VIII, Kabinett Dr. Engelbert Dollfuss, vol. 2, p. 492.

547 *Ibid.*, p. 494. Annex D to Cabinet meeting minutes, no. 860, outlines the adjustment program.

548 The OeNB ultimately contributed a total of 43.2 million schillings to the adjustment program. OeNB Archives, 123rd General Council meeting, May 23, 1931.

549 Verordnung der Bundesregierung vom 19. März 1933, betreffend die Erleichterung der Personallasten der Bankaktiengesellschaften (Bank Relief Regulation, Official Gazette, no. 68/1933). This regulation was based on the War Economy Enabling Act of July 24, 1917 (Official Gazette, no. 307). After March 3, 1933, parliament was prevented by the government from convening with military means. With this regulation, the government complied with one of the key conditions imposed by the Financial Committee of the League of Nations with regard to "structural" economic reforms. Berger, *Kurze Geschichte Österreichs*, p. 274.

550 OeNB Archives, 131st General Council meeting, April 23, 1934.

551 On the background of this solution and on the related debate, see Berger, *Im Schatten der Diktatur*, pp. 263ff and 325ff; Weber, *Die große Bankenfusion*, pp. 232ff.

552 OeNB Archives, 131st General Council meeting, April 23, 1934, and 1087/1934.

553 *Der Österreichische Volkswirt*, April 28, 1934.

554 Joham, Geld und Kreditwesen in Österreich, p. 67.

555 CA Archives, Geschäftsbericht 1936, p. 14.

556 Wärmer, *Das österreichische Kreditwesen*, pp. 56ff.

557 *Oesterreichische Nationalbank 1923–1948*, pp. 47–48;

OeNB Archives, 145th General Council meeting, February 7, 1936.

558 *Wirtschaftsstatistisches Jahrbuch* 1932/33, p. 340.

559 Bachinger and Matis, *Der österreichische Schilling*, p. 155.

560 Koren, Die Industrialisierung Österreichs, p. 242.

561 Fibich, *Entwicklung der österreichischen Bundesausgaben*, p. 143. Stiefel, *Finanzdiplomatie und Weltwirtschaftskrise*, p. 208, indicates somewhat higher investment spending for this period. In those years, the distinctions made between current expenditure and investment spending were rather "arbitrary."

562 OeNB Archives, 149th General Council meeting, October 13, 1936.

563 Bundesgesetz betreffend vorübergehende Maßnahmen zur Erhaltung heimischer Arbeitsgelegenheit (Devaluation Damages Compensation Act, Official Gazette, no. 426/1936).

564 Sokal, Der Währungsumbau des Goldblocks, p. 161.

565 Compass 1938, pp. 204ff.

566 Berger, *Kurze Geschichte Österreichs*, pp. 346ff, in particular p. 365.

567 Kausel et al., *Österreichs Volkseinkommen 1913–1963*. The balance of payments records for the 1930s are incomplete. Attempts by the Ministry of Finance to construct a balance of foreign transactions failed according to Kieböck. OeNB Archives, 148th General Council meeting, July 10, 1936.

568 OeNB Archives, Reports of the chief executive director on the annual financial statements, *passim*.

569 OeNB Archives, *Mitteilungen*, *passim*.

570 Kausel et al., *Österreichs Volkseinkommen 1913–1963*.

571 Butschek, *Statistische Reihen zur österreichischen Wirtschaftsgeschichte*, table 3.3.

572 Schausberger, *Griff nach Österreich*, p. 580.

573 On February 12, 1938, Chancellor Schuschnigg had made major concessions to Hitler at a meeting in Berchtesgaden as a tradeoff in the hope of preventing a National Socialist coup in Austria (Schausberger, Der Anschluss, pp. 524ff).

574 Goldinger, Der geschichtliche Ablauf, p. 261; Stuhlpfarrer, Der deutsche Plan einer Währungsunion mit Österreich, p. 293; Koblenz Archives, R2/14.599.

575 On National Socialist agitation at the OeNB from 1930 to 1938 and staff cleansings after the "takeover," see Rathkolb and Venus, *Reichsbankanstalten 1938–1945*.

576 OeNB Archives, 392/1938. The major statutory changes affecting the Nationalbank that were enacted after the Anschluss are: Gesetz über die Deutsche Reichsbank vom 15. Juni 1939 (Law Gazette of the German Reich, I, p. 1015; Verordnung zur Übernahme der Österreichischen Nationalbank durch die Deutsche Reichsbank vom 17. März 1938 (Law Gazette of the German Reich, I, p. 254); Durchführungsverordnung über die Einführung der Reichsmark im Lande Österreich und zur Übernahme der Österreichischen Nationalbank durch die Reichsbank vom 23. April 1938 (Law Gazette of the German Reich, I, p. 405); and 2. Durchführungsverordnung zur Übernahme der Österreichischen Nationalbank durch die Reichsbank vom 12. Oktober 1938 (Law Gazette of the German Reich, I, p. 1419).

577 OeNB Archives, 1336/1938; Butschek, *Die österreichische Wirtschaft im 20. Jahrhundert*, p. 60; Bachinger and Matis, *Der österreichische Schilling*, p. 167, consider the schilling to have been undervalued.

578 Gabriel, Österreich in der großdeutschen Wirtschaft, pp. 648ff.

579 Koblenz Archives, R2/13.694 and R2/13.692.
580 Butschek, *Statistische Reihen zur österreichischen Wirtschaftsgeschichte,* table 5.1.
581 Butschek, *Österreichs Wirtschaft 1938 bis 1945,* p. 56.
582 Hansmeyer and Caesar, Kriegswirtschaft und Inflation (1936–1948), p. 370.
583 *Ibid.,* p. 375.
584 *Ibid.,* p. 374; and Speyerer, *Die Reichsbankverfassung unter dem Bankgesetz vom 30. August 1924,* pp. 45ff.
585 Hansmeyer and Caesar, Kriegswirtschaft und Inflation (1936–1948), pp. 380ff.
586 *Ibid.,* p. 388. As a case in point for the minor relevance of Funk, and hence the Reichsbank, the authors cite the fact that the Nuremberg Military Court did not count them among the key agents of economic warfare.
587 Veit, *Grundriss der Währungspolitik,* pp. 594–595.
588 Hansmeyer and Caesar, Kriegswirtschaft und Inflation (1936–1948), pp. 416ff.
589 Verwaltungsbericht der Deutschen Reichsbank (for 1941), pp. 32ff.
590 Source: Verwaltungsbericht der Deutschen Reichsbank (for 1940, 1943).
591 *WIFO-Monatsberichte,* no. 1/2 (1945), p. 5. Butschek puts the real GNP of 1946 at 64% of the level of 1937. See Butschek, *Vom Staatsvertrag zur Europäischen Union,* p. 219.

Schilling reinstatement and economic miracle (1945–1970)

592 Pressburger, *Notenbank,* p. 486.
593 Weinzierl and Skalnik (eds.), *Das neue Österreich,* timeline, p. 395.
594 OeNB Archives, 1st General Council meeting, August 3, 1945.
595 OeNB Archives, minutes of all 11 provisional General Council meetings, May 14 to July 24, 1945.

596 Gesetz vom 3. Juli, 1945 über die einstweilige Neuordnung der Oesterreichischen Nationalbank (Central Bank Transition Act, Official Gazette, no. 45).
597 Hans Rizzi (1880–1968) worked in the finance ministry from 1919 to 1938, ultimately as director of the credit department, and also served as OeNB state commissioner. In 1940 he had been sent into retirement for political reasons.
598 OeNB Archives, 1st General Council meeting, August 3, 1945.
599 Seidel, *Österreichs Wirtschaft und Wirtschaftspolitik,* p. 112.
600 Gesetz vom 3. Juli 1945 über die Wiederaufnahme der Zahlungen der Kreditunternehmungen (Resumption of Payments Act, Official Gazette, no. 44).
601 OeNB Archives, 1st General Council meeting, August 3, 1945.
602 OeNB Archives, 2nd General Council meeting, September 21, 1945.
603 Seidel, *Österreichs Wirtschaft und Wirtschaftspolitik,* p. 124.
604 *Ibid.,* p. 130.
605 Bundesgesetz vom 13. Juni 1946, womit Bestimmungen des Notenbank-Überleitungsgesetzes und der Notenbanksatzungen abgeändert werden (amendment to the Central Bank Transition Act, Official Gazette, no. 122/1946); OeNB Archives, 11th General Council meeting, September 27, 1946.
606 OeNB Archives, 66/1947. These treasury notes had a maturity of 3 months, yielded 1.5% in interest and were eligible for discounting at the OeNB.
607 OeNB Archives, 10th General Council meeting, July 11, 1946, and 12th General Council meeting, October 25, 1946.
608 OeNB Archives, 3rd General Council meeting, October 26, 1945.
609 *Mitteilungen,* 1/1947, p. 4.

610 WIFO, "Gesamtschau der österreichischen Wirtschaft im Jahre 1946," in: *WIFO-Monatsberichte,* no. 1–3/1947, p. 38.
611 OeNB Archives, 8th General Council meeting, April 16, and 13rd General Council meeting, November 22, 1946.
612 Seidel, *Österreichs Wirtschaft und Wirtschaftspolitik,* pp. 176ff.
613 OeNB Archives, 15th General Council meeting, January 30, 1947.
614 OeNB Archives, 16th General Council meeting, February 27, 1947.
615 OeNB Archives, 92nd General Council meeting, December 16, 1953.
616 *Zehn Jahre ERP in Österreich, 1948/1958,* p. 45; Loth, *Die Teilung der Welt,* p. 167.
617 Seidel, *Österreichs Wirtschaft und Wirtschaftspolitik,* p. 303. This figure includes congressional and interim aid in the amount of USD 156.1 million that Austria received in 1947, between the announcement of the Marshall plan and its endorsement by Congress (Sandgruber, *Ökonomie und Politik,* p. 452).
618 Seidel, *Österreichs Wirtschaft und Wirtschaftspolitik,* p. 306.
619 Butschek, *Statistische Reihen zur österreichischen Wirtschaftsgeschichte,* table 5.1.
620 *Wiener Zeitung,* July 26, 1947.
621 *Mitteilungen,* 10/1947, p. 5; WIFO, *Die österreichische Lohnpolitik seit Kriegsende,* in: *WIFO-Monatsberichte,* no. 8/1949, p. 4.
622 Nemschak, *Zehn Jahre österreichische Wirtschaft,* p. 72.
623 To prevent deposit balances from rising further, remunerating deposits was prohibited by law in 1946 and 1947. See Bundesgesetz vom 19. Februar 1946 über die Untersagung der Auszahlung von Dividenden für das Geschäftsjahr 1944 und die Vergütung von Einlagezinsen für das Kalenderjahr 1945 (Ban on

Interest Payments Act, Official Gazette, no. 87/1946). Two amendments to this act extended the ban until the end of 1947.

624 OeNB Archives, 19th General Council meeting, May 22, 1947.

625 *Die Industrie,* vol. 47 (1947), July 5, 1947, pp. 3ff, and November 8, 1947, pp. 1–2; Kienböck, *Währung und Wirtschaft,* p. 20; Seidel, *Österreichs Wirtschaft und Wirtschaftspolitik,* p. 157; Kindleberger, *The German economy, 1945–1947,* p. 80. Peter Krauland, ÖVP minister for economic planning and protection of property, who advocated in favor of mopping up liquidity, was therefore considered to be "mad" by Kienböck (as reported by Krauland). See Schärf, *Österreichs Erneuerung,* p. 281.

626 *Mitteilungen,* 1/1948, p. 3.

627 Source: *Historical time series on macroeconomic indicators.*

628 OeNB Archives, 27th General Council meeting, February 19, 1947.

629 Bachinger and Matis, *Der österreichische Schilling,* p. 193.

630 Seidel, *Österreichs Wirtschaft und Wirtschaftspolitik,* p. 162.

631 OeNB Archives, 25th General Council meeting, December 18, 1947; 26th General Council meeting, January 22, 1947; 27th General Council meeting, February 19, 1947.

632 OeNB Archives, 31st General Council meeting, July 8, 1948, and 32nd General Council meeting, September 16, 1948.

633 OeNB Archives, 22nd General Council meeting, September 25, 1947.

634 OeNB Archives, 36th General Council meeting, December 16, 1948.

635 Tew, *International monetary co-operation, 1945–1952,* p. 96; Der Weg zur Europäischen Zahlungsunion, ECA memorandum to the U.S. Congress of February 23,

1950, in: *Österreichisches ERP-Handbuch,* p. 305.

636 Source: *Mitteilungen.*

637 *Mitteilungen,* 10/1948, pp. 3–4; Article XX of the Articles of Agreement of the International Monetary Fund, Official Gazette, no. 105/1949.

638 OeNB Archives, 42nd General Council meeting, July 7, 1949, 43rd General Council meeting, September 1, 1949 and extraordinary General Council meeting, September 29, 1949; WIFO, "Die österreichische Wirtschaft und die internationalen Währungsabwertungen," in: *WIFO-Monatsberichte,* no. 9/1949, pp. 345ff.

639 *Mitteilungen,* 12/1949, pp. 3ff, and *WIFO-Monatsberichte,* no. 11/1949, pp. 441ff.

640 OeNB Archives, 47th General Council meeting, January 23, 1950; *Wiener Zeitung,* January 29, 1950.

641 OeNB Archives, 54th General Council meeting, September 28, 1950, and 55th General Council meeting, October 26, 1950.

642 WIFO, "Die wirtschaftliche Lage", in: *WIFO-Monatsberichte,* no. 3/1951, pp. 113ff.

643 OeNB Archives, 58th General Council meeting, January 18, 1951.

644 OeNB Archives, 59th General Council meeting, February 22, 1951.

645 *Mitteilungen,* 4/1951, pp. 178ff.

646 Source: *Mitteilungen.*

647 *Mitteilungen,* 4/1951, pp. 178ff.

648 OeNB Archives, extraordinary General Council meeting, December 5, 1951.

649 OeNB Archives, 74th General Council meeting, April 16, 1952, and 76th General Council meeting, June 26, 1952.

650 OeNB Archives, extraordinary General Council meeting, July 2, 1952.

651 WIFO, "Die Entwicklung der österreichischen Wirtschaft auf einzelnen Gebieten im Jahre 1952," in: *WIFO-Monatsberichte,* no. 2/1953, p. 38.

652 WIFO, "Rückblick auf das Jahr

1952," in: *WIFO-Monatsberichte,* no. 12/1952, p. 348.

653 Seidel, *Österreichs Wirtschaft und Wirtschaftspolitik,* p. 499.

654 OeNB Archives, 82nd General Council meeting, January 21, 1953; OeNB Archives, *Mitteilungen* 1954, p. 110; WIFO, "Die Entwicklung der österreichischen Wirtschaft auf einzelnen Gebieten im Jahre 1952," in: *WIFO-Monatsberichte,* no. 2/1953, pp. 31ff.

655 BIS, 23rd Annual report, p. 30.

656 WIFO, "Der Bundeshaushalt im Jahr 1953," in: *WIFO-Monatsberichte,* no. 4/1654, pp. 138ff; Compass 1954, pp. 118ff.

657 OeNB Archives, 78th General Council meeting, September 24, 1952, and 79th General Council meeting, October 22 , 1952.

658 OeNB Archives, extraordinary General Council meeting, April 30, 1953.

659 WIFO, "Zur Vereinheitlichung der Wechselkurse," in: *WIFO-Monatsberichte,* no. 4/1953, pp. 107ff.

660 OeNB Archives, 86th General Council meeting, May 27, 1953.

661 OeNB Archives, meeting of the executive committee, May 30, 1953. The national IMF member is the Republic of Austria. OeNB participation in international organizations which foster monetary cooperation was based on Article 57 of its charter.

662 Nemschak, *Zehn Jahre österreichische Wirtschaft,* p. 56.

663 *Mitteilungen,* 7/1953, p. 359.

664 OeNB Archives, announcements no. 62, 6/1953, no. 65, 11/1953 and no. 70, 12/1953.

665 OeNB Archives, 82nd General Council meeting, January 21, 1953, and 89th General Council meeting, September 23, 1953.

666 OeNB Archives, 90th General Council meeting, October 23, 1953.

667 Bundesgesetz vom 19. Mai 1949 über die Aufnahme

einer Bundesanleihe (Reconstruction Bonds Act, Official Gazette no. 135/1949). This act defined neither the issuance volume nor the interest rate, which is problematic from a constitutional perspective.

668 WIFO, "Gesamtschau der österreichischen Wirtschaft im Jahre 1954," in: *WIFO-Monatsberichte*, no. 2/1955, p. 50.

669 Bundesgesetz vom 24. April 1953 über Begünstigungen einer Anleihe der Verbundgesellschaft (Energy Bond Act 1953, Official Gazette, no. 50/1953) and Bundesgesetz vom 24. April 1953 über die Begünstigung des Sparens (Savings Promotion Act, Official Gazette, no. 51/1953).

670 Bundesgesetz vom 7. Juli 1954 zur Bereinigung des Wertpapierwesens (Securities Settlement Act, Official Gazette, no. 188/1954).

671 Bundesgesetz vom 7. Juli 1954 über die Aufstellung von Schillingeröffnungsbilanzen und über die Umstellung (Schilling Opening Balance Sheet Act, Official Gazette, no. 190/1954).

672 Bundesgesetz vom 7. Juli 1954 über Entschädigungen für verstaatlichte Anteilsrechte (First Nationalization Compensation Act, Official Gazette, no. 189/1954). See Langer, *Verstaatlichungen in Österreich*, pp. 86ff.

673 Bundesgesetz vom 8. September 1955 zur Ordnung der wirtschaftlichen und finanziellen Lage der Kreditunternehmungen (Bank Reconstruction Act, Official Gazette, no. 183/1955).

674 Bundesgesetz vom 8. September 1955 über den Wiederaufbau der Vertragsversicherung (Insurance Reconstruction Act, Official Gazette, no. 185/1955).

675 Bundesgesetz vom 8. September 1955 zur Neuordnung der Rechtsverhältnisse der Oesterreichischen National-bank (Nationalbank Act, Official Gazette, no. 184/1955).

676 Seidel, *Österreichs Wirtschaft und Wirtschaftspolitik*, pp. 542–543.

677 OeNB Archives, 72nd General Council meeting, February 13, 1952.

678 Source: OeNB Archives, 15th General Council meeting, January 30, 1947, and 104th General Council meeting, February 23, 1955.

679 Schwarzer et al., *Das österreichische Währungs- und Devisenrecht*, pp. 147ff.

680 Bronold, Die Bestrebungen zu einer Neufassung des KWG seit 1949, pp. 51ff; Heller, Der dritte Anlauf, p. 16.

681 Matis, Vom Nachkriegselend zum Wirtschaftswunder, p. 222.

682 Seidel, *Österreichs Wirtschaft und Wirtschaftspolitik*, p. 468.

683 Source: Butschek, *Vom Staatsvertrag*, p. 16 (1950–1970, at 1995 prices and exchange rates); IMF (from 1980, GDP at purchasing power parity).

684 *Mitteilungen*, 2/1959, p. 70.

685 Source: Butschek, *Statistische Reihen zur österreichischen Wirtschaftsgeschichte*, table 6.1., 1954–1975 SNA 68; 1976–1994 ESA 95; from 1995 ESA 2000.

686 WIFO, "Preis- und Einkommenselastizität des österreichischen Exportes," in: *WIFO-Monatsberichte*, no. 9/1956, pp. 314ff.

687 Bundesgesetz vom 20. Juli 1951, über Änderungen auf dem Gebiete der direkten Steuern und der Umsatzsteuer (Tax Adjustment Act, Official Gazette, no. 191/1951).

688 Bundesgesetz vom 14. Juli 1950 über die Förderung der österreichischen Ausfuhr (Export Promotion Act, Official Gazette, no. 149/1950).

689 Official Gazette, no. 192/1969.

690 OeNB Archives, 53rd General Council meeting, July 26, 1950.

691 Butschek, *Vom Staatsvertrag zur Europäischen Union*, pp. 58–59.

692 Source: Butschek, *Statistische Reihen zur österreichischen Wirtschaftsgeschichte*, table 5.4., 1954–1975 SNA 68; 1976–1994 ESA 95; from 1995 ESA 2000.

693 Tax incentives for investments were initiated by Reinhard Kamitz, minister of finance from 1952 to 1960. Investments in infrastructure were pushed by Karl Waldbrunner, minister for transport and nationalized industry from 1946 to 1956 and minister for transport and power industry from 1956 to 1962.

694 *Mitteilungen*, 8/1966, pp. 492–496.

695 OeNB Archives, 112nd General Council meeting, November 16, 1955.

696 *Mitteilungen*, 1/1962, p. 2.

697 BIZ, 33rd Annual report, 1962/63, pp. 76–77.

698 Butschek, *Vom Staatsvertrag zur Europäischen Union*, pp. 46–47.

699 *Mitteilungen*, 8/1962, p. 467. For Article VIII of the statutes of the Monetary Fund, see: International Monetary Fund, Articles of Agreement, Washington 2011, pp. 22ff.

700 *Mitteilungen*, 3/1961, p. 136. WIFO, "Die Aufwertung der D-Mark und die Folgen für Österreich," in: *WIFO-Monatsberichte*, no. 11/1969, pp. 450ff.

701 Finance minister Koren, the latter OeNB President, was in favor of increasing the exchange rate of the Austrian schilling broadly (but not fully) in line with the appreciation of the Deutsche mark, but he failed to convince the social partners.

702 Source: Butschek, *Statistische Reihen zur österreichischen Wirtschaftsgeschichte*, table 1.10.3.

703 McKinnon, *Money in international exchange*, p. 260.

Austria's hard currency policy (1971–1999)

704 James, *International monetary cooperation*, pp. 50–51.
705 Triffin, The return to convertibility, pp. 3ff.
706 Van der Wee, *Der gebremste Wohlstand*, pp. 476ff.
707 Deutsche Bundesbank, *Annual report 1970*, pp. 97 and 126.
708 German Council of Economic Experts, *Jahresgutachten 1964/65*, pp. 131ff.
709 Matis, Vom Nachkriegselend zum Wirtschaftswunder, pp. 261ff.
710 Stenographisches Protokoll, XIInd legislature, May 12, 1971, pp. 3162ff.
711 Androsch, Entscheidung für den Schilling, in: *Arbeiter-Zeitung*, May 11, 1971.
712 OeNB Archives, 754th Governing Board meeting, February 3, 1971.
713 James, *International monetary cooperation*, p. 236.
714 BIS, *Annual report 1973*, pp. 25ff.
715 Following the speech of President Nixon of August 15, 1971, announcing the suspension of dollar convertibility into gold, the foreign exchange market remained closed from August 16 to August 23, 1971.
716 OeNB Archives, 781st Governing Board meeting, August 25, 1971. The Dutch weight should be representative of Belgium, and the Swedish exchange rate should be representative of the exchange rates of Norway and Denmark.
717 Mooslechner et al., From Bretton Woods to the euro, pp. 25ff.
718 OeNB Archives, 861st Governing Board meeting, July 2, 1973.
719 OeNB Archives, 296th General Council meeting, July 17, 1973.
720 OeNB Archives, extraordinary General Council meeting, May 10, 1971.
721 OeNB Archives, Annual report 1971, pp. 7f.

722 OeNB Archives, 798th Governing Board meeting, January 31, 1972. These decisions requiring approval by the General Council were reached in its meeting on February 23, 1972. OeNB Archives, 281st General Council meeting, February 23, 1972.
723 OeNB Archives, Chronik der Währungspolitik, pp. 152ff.
724 Stankovsky, "Die österreichische Erdölrechnung 1974," in: *WIFO-Monatsberichte*, no. 3/1975, pp. 139ff.
725 Source: Butschek, *Statistische Reihen zur österreichischen Wirtschaftsgeschichte*, table 8.1; OECD, Eurostat, Statistics Austria.
726 Meadows et al., *The limits to growth*.
727 Seidel, Austro-Keynesianismus, pp. 11ff.; Weber and Venus (eds.), *Austro-Keynesianismus in Theorie und Praxis*.
728 OeNB Archives, Geschäftsbericht 1982, p. 89.
729 Staatsschuldenausschuss, Jahresbericht 2012, Annex, table A 3.
730 Smeral and Walterskirchen, "Der Einfluß von Wirtschaftswachstum und Wettbewerbsfähigkeit auf die Leistungsbilanz," in: *WIFO-Monatsberichte*, no. 7/1981, pp. 373ff.
731 Source: Butschek, *Vom Staatsvertrag*, p. 221; Statistics Austria.
732 OeNB Archives, 1025th Governing Board meeting, January 7, 1977.
733 OeNB Archives, 1048th Governing Board meeting, June 8, 1977, and 336th General Council meeting, June 22, 1977.
734 Source: Butschek, *Statistische Reihen zur österreichischen Wirtschaftsgeschichte*, tables 5.1 and 6.1; OeNB, Statistics Austria, 1979–1994: ESA 95, from 1995: ESA 2000.
735 Haschek, *Exportförderung*; Roßmann, Exportförderung in Österreich, pp. 57–77;

Mastalier, "Exportförderung durch erleichterte Kreditbeschaffung," in: *WIFO-Monatsberichte*, no. 8/1968, pp. 319–328; Stankovsky, "Grundlagen der Exportförderung in Österreich," in: *WIFO-Monatsberichte*, no. 7/1983, pp. 459–474.
736 OeNB Archives, 321st General Council meeting, February 19, 1976; OeNB Archives, 391st General Council meeting, March 23, 1983; Aiginger and Bayer, "Die Top-Aktion," in: *WIFO-Monatsberichte*, no. 10/1982, p. 594.
737 OeNB Archives, Pech records, 1982, "Zur Bedeutung der Notenbankrefinanzierung für die Österreichische Investitionskredit AG"; OeNB Archives, Pech records, 1986, "Anmerkungen zur Frage der selektiven Geldschöpfung der Notenbank."
738 *Neue Zürcher Zeitung*, August 9, 1977.
739 OeNB Archives, 1060th Governing Board meeting, August 29, 1977; OeNB Archives, 1086th Governing Board meeting, February 8, 1978.
740 OeNB Archives, 1075th Governing Board meeting, December 21, 1977.
741 Seidel, "Der effektive Wechselkurs des Schillings," in: *WIFO-Monatsberichte*, no. 8/1978, pp. 384–396; Mooslechner, "Neuberechnung der WIFO-Wechselkursindizes," in: *WIFO-Monatsberichte*, no. 7/1982, pp. 424–433.
742 Source: *Historical time series on interest rates*.
743 OeNB Archives, President's Speech, in: *Mitteilungen*, 4/1978, Annex I.
744 OeNB Archives, Annual report 1979, p. 35.
745 OeNB Archives, 360th General Council meeting, January 23, 1980.
746 Source: WIFO. Up to 1999 effective exchange rates of the schilling, after 1999 real-effective and nominal-effective exchange rates of the euro

based on Austrian foreign trade.

747 OeNB Archives, 1206th Governing Board meeting, October 22, 1980.

748 OeNB Archives, 1169th Governing Board meeting, January 16, 1980.

749 OeNB Archives, 1860th Governing Board meeting, August 12, 1993, 1861st Governing Board meeting, August 19, 1993, 1863rd Governing Board meeting, September 2, 1993, and 1864th Governing Board meeting, September 9, 1993.

750 Baltensperger, Geldpolitik bei wachsender Integration (1979–1996), p. 489.

751 OeNB Archives, 518th General Council meeting, September 21, 1995.

752 Lachs, Devisenliberalisierung ab 1. November 1986, pp. 610ff.; Lachs, Devisenliberalisierung der OeNB, pp. 339ff.; Lachs, Devisenliberalisierung zum 1. Jänner 1990, pp. 3ff.; Brandner, Liberalisierung der österreichischen Devisenbestimmungen, pp. 608ff.

753 Nowotny, Die Hartwährungspolitik, p. 65.

754 Kaminsky and Reinhart, The twin crisis, pp. 473–500.

755 Stenographisches Protokoll, XVIIth legislature, 116th parliamentary session, November 8, 1989, p. 13789.

756 Stenographisches Protokoll, annex no. 271, XVIIIth legislature, p. 1.

757 OeNB Archives, 1849th Governing Board meeting, June 17, 1993.

758 OeNB Archives, 1896th Governing Board meeting, March 24, 1994, and OeNB Archives, 1900th Governing Board meeting, April 20, 1994.

759 James, International monetary cooperation, pp. 347ff.

760 OeNB Archives, President's speech, in: Mitteilungen, 4/1983.

761 Stankovsky, "Verschuldung der Oststaaten in Österreich," in: WIFO-Monatsberichte, no. 4/1981, pp. 228ff.; OeNB Archives, 1271st Governing Board meeting, February 17,

1982, and 1308th Governing Board meeting, November 11, 1982.

762 OeNB Archives, 1734th Governing Board meeting, April 4, 1991.

763 BIS, Annual Report 1983, p. 184; OeNB Archives, 1280th Governing Board meeting, April 21, 1982, and 1302nd Governing Board meeting, September 29, 1982.

764 OeNB Archives, 1339th Governing Board meeting, July 7, 1983.

765 OeNB Archives, Pech records, "Aufstellung des Obligos diverser Länder bzw. Ländergruppen gegenüber Österreich." In 1984, Austrian banks' capital amounted to around 75 billion Austrian schillings.

766 OeNB Archives, Pech records, "Mögliche Auswirkungen einer akuten internationalen Verschuldungskrise auf Österreich."

767 Revell, Costs and margins in banking: An international survey; Revell, Costs and margins in banking: Statistical supplement 1978–1982.

768 Handler and Mooslechner, "Hintergründe und ökonomische Aspekte der Novellierung des Kreditwesengesetzes 1986," in: WIFO-Monatsberichte, no. 12/1986, pp. 762ff.

769 Ibid., p. 765.

770 Vranitzky, Gedanken zu einer leistungsstarken Kreditwirtschaft; Handler and Mooslechner, "Hintergründe und ökonomische Aspekte der Novellierung des Kreditwesengesetzes 1986," in: WIFO-Monatsberichte, no. 12/1986, pp. 777ff.

771 OeNB Archives, Pech records, "Ergebnis einer Aussprache zu 'Ordnungspolitische Richtlinien im Bankgeschäft' am 18.2.1984"; OeNB Archives, Chronik der Währungspolitik, pp. 252–253.

772 OeNB Archives, 465th General Council meeting, Sep-

tember 19, 1990; Kramer, "Strukturprobleme Österreichs aus der Sicht des Avis der EG-Kommission," in: WIFO-Monatsberichte, no. 9/1991, pp. 519ff.

773 Würz, The new Austrian Banking Act, pp. 27–33 Spranz, Das Bankwesengesetz aus der Sicht der Notenbank, p. 21.

774 Nowotny, Volkswirtschaftliche Aspekte des Bankwesengesetzes, p. 10.

775 Spranz, Das Bankwesengesetz aus der Sicht der Notenbank, p. 21.

776 Bundesgesetz über das Bankwesen (Banking Act, Official Gazette, no. 532/1993).

777 Abbreviations: The European Economic Community (EEC) was founded concurrently with the European Atomic Energy Community (Euratom) in 1957, following the creation of the European Coal and Steel Community (ECSC) in 1952. The Treaty of Brussels, adopted on April 8, 1965, provided for the merger of those three institutions (EEC, Euratom, ECSC) on July 1, 1967, as well as for the creation of the European Communities (EC). The EC have since been replaced by the European Union (EU), which was established by the Treaty on the European Union (TEU), signed in Maastricht on February 7, 1992, and became operational on November 1, 1993. Euratom and ECSC were dissolved in 2003, leaving in place the EU as the sole European institution.

778 Kees, Der Währungsausschuss, pp. 135–136.

779 OeNB Archives, 458th General Council meeting, December 20, 1989.

780 Deutsche Bundesbank Archives, B 330/42773. Vienna Embassy to Federal Foreign Office in Bonn, Germany, September 21, 1978; Austrian Central Statistical Office, Austrian State Archives, 002800/9–V/79.

781 OeNB Archives, 1119th Governing Board meeting, December 13, 1978; OeNB Archives, 1128th Governing Board meeting, March 14, 1979; OeNB Archives, President's speech, in: *Mitteilungen*, 4/1979.

782 OeNB Archives, 470th General Council meeting, February 21, 1991.

783 OeNB Archives, 1930th Governing Board meeting, November 24, 1994 (Finland), and 1931st Governing Board meeting, December 1, 1994 (Sweden).

784 Bundesgesetz über die Teilnahme Österreichs am Wechselkursmechanismus des Europäischen Währungssystems (Official Gazette, no. 1059/1994).

785 OeNB Archives, Statistisches Monatsheft, 1/1995, p. 4.

786 European Monetary Institute, *Annual report 1994*, pp. 62ff.

787 European Monetary Institute, *Convergence report*, pp. 3ff.

788 OeNB Archives, Annual report 1995, p. 40.

789 OeNB Archives, 2035th Governing Board meeting, November 20, 1996, and 528th General Council meeting, September 26, 1996.

790 OeNB Archives, President's speech at the 1992 General Meeting.

791 OeNB Archives, 490th General Council meeting, December 17, 1992.

792 Bundesverfassungsgesetz über die Begrenzung von Bezügen öffentlicher Funktionäre (Official Gazette, I, no. 64/1997).

793 OeNB Archives, 536th General Council meeting, May 15, 1997.

794 OeNB Archives, extraordinary General Council meeting, April 8, 1992.

A single European currency–the OeNB as a Eurosystem central bank (1999–2016)

795 April 18, 1996.

796 OeNB Annual Report 1998, p. 22.

797 Lachs and Ritzberger, *Der Euro*.

798 James, *Making the European Monetary Union*.

799 Singleton, Central banking, pp. 204–220.

800 ECB, *Monetary policy*, pp. 55ff.

801 Singleton, *Central banking*, p. 272.

802 De Grauwe, *Economics of monetary union*, pp. 153–156; James, *Making the European Monetary Union*, pp. 322f.

803 ECB, *Monetary policy*, p. 64.

804 Singleton, *Central banking*, p. 249.

805 ECB, *Monetary policy*, pp. 64–69.

806 Galvenius and Mercier, Story of the Eurosystem framework, p. 129.

807 OeNB Annual Report 1997, pp. 42f.

808 Papademos and Stark, *Enhancing monetary analysis*.

809 ECB, *Monetary policy*, pp. 69–83.

810 OeNB Annual Report 1997, p. 42.

811 Richter, Geldpolitik im Spiegel der wissenschaftlichen Diskussion.

812 Gartner and Schuberth, Monetary policy strategy; OeNB Annual Report 1997, p. 43.

813 For further information, see Gnan et al., Monetary policy regime change.

814 Pech, Entstehung währungspolitischer Strategien. The roles of the social partners had already begun to change before Austria joined the EU; see e.g. Lauber, Wirtschafts- und Finanzpolitik.

815 However, studies on the independence of the central bank arrived at the conclusion that the OeNB was also very independent in the past by international comparison. See e.g.

Cukierman et al., Measuring independence.

816 Mooslechner, 10 years of Austrian EU membership, p. 34.

817 Galvenius and Mercier, Story of the Eurosystem framework, pp. 128f.

818 Borio, *Implementation of monetary policy*.

819 ECB, *Monetary policy*, pp. 58–62.

820 For more information, *see ibid.*, pp. 93–116.

821 Pech and Weninger, Comments on the policy instruments. For a comparative perspective, see Forssbæck and Oxelheim, Interplay.

822 However, trade bills were retained as loan collateral, supplemented by corporate debt/bonds and bank receivables; see OeNB Annual Report 1998, p. 34.

823 In 2013 the OeNB resumed the publication of monthly financial statements, releasing historic data for the period from 1999 at the same time. See also the *Historical time series of the Nationalbank*.

824 ARTIS (Austrian Real Time Interbank Settlement System). See OeNB Annual Report 1997, pp. 61–62.

825 Official Gazette, no. 60/1998. The essential provisions of the new Nationalbank Act are explained in the OeNB's Annual Report 1998, pp. 39–40. For more on the parts of the old Nationalbank Act that were not compatible with EU law, see European Monetary Institute, *Progress towards convergence*, p. 134.

826 Dvorsky and Lindner, 10 years of EU membership.

827 OeNB Annual Report 1998, pp. 44f.

828 OeNB Archives, Annex to the financial statements for 1822.

829 On the following, see also the comments in the *Historical time series on the Nationalbank*.

830 In 1938, some 10% of the shares were in public hands. Savings banks and banks and bankers held slightly above

30%, respectively. The finance ministry was a key stakeholder with 13%, with insurance companies, associations, companies and nonresidents accounting for the remainder (Kernbauer, *Währungspolitik*, p. 420).

831 Source: *Historical time series on the Nationalbank, Historical time series on interest rates*. To be able to compare stock prices over time, the listed prices are shown in relation to the paid-in nominal amounts, as adjusted for payments to or from shareholders. The nominal amount of an OeNB share, 600 florins up to 1855, was increased in 1855 and 1856, when new shares were issued with a capital add-on, and subsequently reduced in 1869, with shareholders receiving money back. 1900 saw another increase in the nominal capital, technically in the form of a transfer from reserves to capital. Since this operation came without payments to or from shareholders, it is not shown in the chart. The same holds true for the increase in the share capital resulting from the devaluation of the schilling vis-à-vis gold in 1934, which did not trigger any payments to or from shareholders either. The adjusted nominal value was also taken as the basis for calculating the nominal yield of the share capital. Prices between 1919 and 1923 were calculated in U.S. dollars.

832 Kernbauer, *Währungspolitik*, pp. 369, 376–377.

833 OeNB Annual Report 1998, p. 36.

834 OeNB Annual Report 1997, p. 57.

835 OeNB Annual Report 1999, p. 45. For more on the establishment of Geldservice Austria, see OeNB Annual Report 2000, p. 51.

836 ECB, *Monetary policy*, p. 122. Survey-based measures of longer-term inflation expectations declined somewhat in the course of 2014 but did not drop below 1.8%. ECB, *Economic Bulletin*, 4/2015, p. 23.

837 *Ibid.*, pp. 117–129.

838 Source: ECB and Eurostat.

839 Source: ECB, weekly financial statements.

840 Grossman, *Unsettled account*, pp. 251–265.

841 Würz, The new Austrian Banking Act.

842 ECB, Role of central banks.

843 Bundesgesetz über die Errichtung und Organisation der Finanzmarktaufsichtsbehörde (Financial Market Authority Act), Official Gazette, I, no. 97/2001.

844 FMA and OeNB, *Banking Supervision in Austria*, pp. 10–11.

845 Ammann et al., *Bericht*.

846 FMA and OeNB, *Banking Supervision in Austria*, pp. 11–12.

847 "Die Oesterreichische Nationalbank hat im öffentlichen Interesse das Vorliegen aller jener Umstände zu beobachten, die für die Sicherung der Finanzmarktstabilität in Österreich von Bedeutung sind." ["In the public interest, the OeNB shall monitor all conditions that are relevant for maintaining financial stability in Austria."] (Bundesgesetz, mit dem das Bankwesengesetz, das Sparkassengesetz, das Finanzmarktaufsichtsgesetz und das Nationalbankgesetz 1984 geändert werden. Official Gazette, no. 108/2007).

848 OeNB, Financial Stability Report, 6 (2003), p. 32.

849 OeNB, Financial Stability Report, 23 (2012), pp. 38f.

850 Huber and Merc, Banking recovery and resolution directive.

851 On the following, see Eidenberger et al., Macroprudential supervision.

852 Borio, Financial cycle and macroeconomics.

853 When the ECB was established, the idea of putting it in charge of banking supervision had been discussed, but ultimately it was not given any supervisory competence apart from the role of observer. Padoa-Schioppa, *EMU and banking supervision.*

854 ECB, *Guide to banking supervision*, September 2014.

References

Abele, Hans and Ewald Nowotny (ed.) (³1989), *Handbuch der österreichischen Wirtschaftspolitik*, Vienna.

Ahamed, Liaquat (2009), *Lords of finance. The bankers who broke the world*, London/New York.

Ahrens, Gerhard (1986), *Krisenmanagement 1857: Staat und Kaufmannschaft in Hamburg während der ersten Weltwirtschaftskrise*, Hamburg.

Aiginger, Karl and Kurt Bayer (1982), "Die Top-Aktion. Eine neue Form der Investitionsförderung," in: *WIFO-Monatsberichte*, no. 10, pp. 594–605.

Aldcroft, Derek H. (1977), *From Versailles to Wall Street, 1919–1929*, Berkeley/Los Angeles.

Ammann, Manuel, Carl Baudenbacher, Ernst Wilhelm Contzen, Irmgard Griss and Claus-Peter Weber (2014), *Bericht der unabhängigen Untersuchungskommission zur transparenten Aufklärung der Vorkommnisse rund um die Hypo Group Alpe Adria*, Vienna.

Androsch, Hannes (1971), "Entscheidung für den Schilling," in: *Arbeiter-Zeitung*, May 11, 1971.

Androsch, Hannes (1985), *Die politische Ökonomie der österreichischen Währung: Ein Überblick über die österreichische Währungspolitik von 1760 bis 1984 vor dem Hintergrund der internationalen Entwicklung*, Vienna.

Aulinger, Barbara (2000), *Vom Gulden zum Euro: Geschichte der österreichischen Banknoten*, Vienna.

Ausch, Karl (1968), *Als die Banken fielen. Zur Soziologie der politischen Korruption*, Vienna.

Bachinger, Karl (1981), *Umbruch und Desintegration nach dem Ersten Weltkrieg. Österreichs wirtschaftliche und soziale Ausgangssituation in ihren Folgewirkungen auf die Erste Republik*, 2 volumes, Vienna.

Bachinger, Karl, Felix Butschek, Herbert Matis and Dieter Stiefel (eds.) (2001), *Abschied vom Schilling. Eine österreichische Wirtschaftsgeschichte*, Graz/Vienna/Cologne.

Bachinger, Karl and Herbert Matis (1974), *Der österreichische Schilling. Geschichte einer Währung*, Graz.

Bachinger, Karl and Dieter Stiefel (eds.) (2001), *Auf Heller und Cent. Beiträge zur Finanz- und Währungsgeschichte*, Vienna.

Bachmayer, Othmar (1960), *Die Geschichte der österreichischen Währungspolitik*, Vienna.

Baltensperger, Ernst (1998), "Geldpolitik bei wachsender Integration (1979–1996)," in: *Fünfzig Jahre Deutsche Mark*, pp. 475–559.

Baltzarek, Franz (1973), *Die Geschichte der Wiener Börse*, Vienna.

Baltzarek, Franz (1980), "Finanzplatz Wien – die innerstaatliche und internationale Stellung in historischer Perspektive," in: *Quartalshefte der Girozentrale*, no. 4, pp. 11–63.

Baltzarek, Franz (2014), "Österreichs Rolle bei der Integration und Desintegration von Währungsräumen in Mitteleuropa von der Mitte des 18. Jahrhunderts bis zur Mitte des 20. Jahrhunderts," in: *Jahrbuch für Wirtschaftsgeschichte*, no. 1, pp. 93–127.

Bank for International Settlements (1963/1973/1983), *Annual report*, Basel.

Bank for International Settlements (2011), *Basel III: A global regulatory framework for more resilient banks and banking systems*, revised version June 2011, Basel.

Barany, George (1975), "Ungarns Verwaltung 1848–1918," in: Adam Wandruszka and Peter Urbanitsch (eds.), *Verwaltung*, pp. 306–468.

Becher, Siegfried (1838), *Das österreichische Münzwesen vom Jahre 1524 bis 1838*, Vienna.

Beer, Adolf (1877), *Die österreichischen Finanzen im XIX. Jahrhundert*, Prague.

Berend, Ivan and Georgy Ranki (1974), *Economic development in East-Central Europe in the 19th and 20th centuries*, New York.

Bérenger, Jean (1975), *Finances et absolutisme autrichien dans la seconde moitié du XVIIème siècle*, Paris.

Berger, Peter (2000), *Im Schatten der Diktatur. Die Finanzdiplomatie des Vertreters des Völkerbundes in Österreich, Meinoud Marinus Rost van Tonningen 1931–1936*, Vienna.

Berger, Peter (2007), *Kurze Geschichte Österreichs im 20. Jahrhundert*, Vienna.

Bernanke, Ben (2000), "The macroeconomics of the Great Depression: a comparative approach," in: Ben Bernanke, *Essays on the Great Depression*, Princeton, pp. 5–37.

Bernholz, Peter (1989), *Geldwertstabilität und Währungsordnung*, Tübingen.

Bidermann, Ignaz (1858), "Die Wiener Stadt-Bank," in: *Archiv für Kunde österreichischer Geschichts-Quellen*, pp. 341–446.

Bignon, Vincent, Marc Flandreau and Stefano Ugolini (2012), "Bagehot for beginners. The making of lender-of-last-resort operations in the mid-nineteenth century," in: *Economic History Review*, no. 2, pp. 580–608.

Bindseil, Ulrich (2004), *Monetary policy implementation: theory, past, present*, Oxford.

Bindseil, Ulrich (2014), *Monetary policy operations and the financial system*, Oxford.

Bischof, Günter (1999), *Austria in the first cold war, 1945–1955*, Basingstoke.

Blum, Jerôme (1948), *Noble landowners and agriculture in Austria, 1815–1848. A study in the origin of the peasant emancipation of 1848*, Baltimore.

Bond, Niall (2014), "La monnaie en Allemagne et en Autriche au dix-huitième siècle: réflexions et recompositions," in: Jérôme Blanc and Ludovic Desmedt (eds.), *Les pensées monétaires dans l'histoire*, Paris, pp. 861–896.

Bordo, Michael (1990), "The lender of last resort: alternative views and historical experience," in: *Federal Reserve Bank of Richmond Economic Review* 76, 1, pp. 18–29.

Bordo, Michael, Øyvind Eitrheim, Marc Flandreau and Jan Qvigstad (eds.) (2015/16), *Central banks at a crossroads: What can we learn from history?* Cambridge (forthcoming).

Bordo, Michael and Anna J. Schwartz (1999), "Under what circumstances, past and present, have international rescues of countries in financial distress been successful?", in: *Journal of International Money and Finance*, pp. 683–708.

Borio, Claudio (1997), "The Implementation of monetary policy in industrial countries: a survey," in: *Bank for International Settlements Economic Papers*, no. 47.

Bráf, Albin (1899), "Der landwirtschaftliche Hypothekar-Credit während der letzten 50 Jahre," in: *Geschichte der österreichischen Land- und Forstwirtschaft und ihrer Industrien 1848–1898*, vol. 1, Vienna, pp. 579–677.

Bráf, Albin (1905), "Banken," in: Ernst Mischler and Josef Ulbrich (eds.), *Österreichisches Staatswörterbuch. Handbuch des gesammten österreichischen öffentlichen Rechtes*, vol. 1, Vienna, pp. 391–396.

Brandner, Peter (1991), "Liberalisierung der österreichischen Devisenbestimmungen," in: *WIFO-Monatsberichte*, no. 11, pp. 608–613.

Brandt, Harm-Hinrich (1978), *Der österreichische Neoabsolutismus: Staatsfinanzen und Politik 1848–1860*, Göttingen.

Brauneis, Viktor (1924), *Die Entwicklung der Oesterreichischen Nationalbank. Memorandum verfaßt zur Information der Delegierten des Völkerbundes*, Vienna.

Broadberry, Stephen and Mark Harrison (2005), "The economics of World War I: an overview," in: Stephen Broadberry and Mark Harrison (eds.), *The economics of World War I*, Cambridge, pp. 3–40.

Bronold, Kurt (1979), "Die Bestrebungen zu einer Neufassung des KWG seit 1949," in: *Österreichisches Bankarchiv*, Nr. 11, pp. 51–67.

Brusatti, Alois (1960), "Unternehmensfinanzierung und Privatkredit im österreichischen Vormärz," in: *Mitteilungen des österreichischen Staatsarchivs*, pp. 331–379.

Brusatti, Alois (1965), "Graf Philipp Stadion als Finanzminister," in: *Österreich und Europa. Festgabe für Hugo Hantsch zum 70. Geburtstag*, Graz, pp. 281–294.

Butschek, Felix (1985), *Die österreichische Wirtschaft im 20. Jahrhundert*, Vienna.

Butschek, Felix (1999), *Statistische Reihen zur österreichischen Wirtschaftsgeschichte. Die österreichische Wirtschaft seit der industriellen Revolution*, Vienna.

Butschek, Felix (2004), *Vom Staatsvertrag zur Europäischen Union. Österreichs Wirtschaftsgeschichte von 1955 bis zur Gegenwart*, Vienna.

Butschek, Felix (2011), *Österreichische Wirtschaftsgeschichte. Von der Antike bis zur Gegenwart*, Vienna.

Capie, Forrest, Charles Goodhart and Norbert Schnadt (1994), "The development of central banking," in: Forrest Capie, Stanley Fisher, Charles Goodhart and Norbert Schnadt (eds.), *The future of central banking: the tercentenary symposium of the Bank of England*, Cambridge, pp. 1–112.

Capie, Forrest and Alan Webber (1983), "Total coin and coin in circulation in the United Kingdom, 1868–1914," in: *Journal of Money, Credit and Banking*, no. 1, pp. 24–39.

Carsten, Francis L. (1988), *Die erste österreichische Republik im Spiegel zeitgenössischer Quellen*, Vienna.

Cassel, Gustav (1922), *Money and foreign exchange after 1914*, New York.

Cassel, Gustav (1928), *Post-War Monetary Stabilisation*, New York.

Cerman, Markus (1994), "Proto-industrielle Entwicklung in Österreich," in: Markus Cerman (ed.), *Proto-Industrialisierung in Europa: Industrielle Produktion vor dem Fabrikszeitalter*, Vienna, pp. 161–176.

Chaloupek, Günther, Dionys Lehner, Herbert Matis and Roman Sandgruber (2003), *Österreichische Industriegeschichte 1700–1848: Die vorhandene Chance*, Vienna.

Clarke, Stephen (1967), *Central bank cooperation 1924–1931*, published by the Federal Reserve Bank of New York, New York.

Clay, Henry (1957), *Lord Norman*, London.

Clement, Werner et al. (ed.) (1989), *Stephan Koren 1919–1988. Wirtschaftsforscher und Wirtschaftspolitiker in Österreich*, Vienna.

Cukierman, Alex, Steven Webb and Bilin Neyapti. 1992. "Measuring the independence of central banks and its effect on policy outcomes," in: *The World Bank Economic Review* 6, no. 3, pp. 353–398.

Czörnig, Carl (1861), *Statistisches Handbüchlein für die österreichische Monarchie*, Vienna.

De Grauwe, Paul (^{9}2012), *Economics of monetary union*, Oxford.

Denzel, Markus (2012), *Der Nürnberger Banco Publico, seine Kaufleute und ihr Zahlungsverkehr (1621–1827)*, Stuttgart.

"Der Weg zur Europäischen Zahlungsunion, Memorandum der ECA an den US-Kongreß vom 23.2.1950," in: *Österreichisches ERP-Handbuch*, Vienna 1950, pp. 303–309.

Dessewffy, Emil (1856), *Über die schwebenden österreichischen Finanzfragen*, Pest/Vienna.

Deutsche Bundesbank (1970). *Annual report 1970*, Frankfurt am Main.

Dickson, Peter (1967), *The financial revolution in England: A study in the development of public credit 1688–1756*, London.

Dickson, Peter (1987), *Finance and government under Maria Theresia: 1740–1780*, 2 volumes, Oxford.

Dornbusch, Rudiger and Stanley Fischer (1986), *Stopping hyperinflations, past and present*, Cambridge (Mass.) (NBER Working Paper 1810).

Dornbusch, Rudiger (1992), "Monetary problems of post-communism: Lessons from the end of the Austro-Hungarian Empire," in: *Weltwirtschaftliches Archiv*, no. 3, pp. 391–424.

Dvorsky, Sandra and Isabella Lindner (2005), "10 years of EU membership–the OeNB in a changing environment," in: *Monetary Policy & the Economy*, Q2/2005, pp. 42–52.

Eddie, Scott (1982), "Limits on the fiscal independence of sovereign states in customs union: tax union aspects of the Austro-Hungarian monarchy, 1868–1911," in: *Hungarian Studies Review*, no. 2, pp. 7–29.

Eddie, Scott (1989), "Economic policy and economic development in Austria-Hungary 1867–1914," in: *Cambridge Economic History of Europe*, vol. VIII, Cambridge, pp. 814–886.

Eichengreen, Barry (1992), *Golden Fetters. The Gold Standard and the Great Depression, 1919–1939*, New York/Oxford.

Eidenberger, Julia, David Liebeg, Stefan Schmitz, Reinhard Seliger, Michael Sigmund, Katharina Steiner, Peter Strobl and Eva Ubl (2014), "Macroprudential supervision: A key lesson from the financial crisis," in: *Financial Stability Review 27*, pp. 83–94.

Eigner, Peter and Andrea Helige (eds.) (1999), *Österreichische Wirtschafts- und Sozialgeschichte im 19. und 20. Jahrhundert. 175 Jahre Wiener Städtische Versicherung*, Vienna.

Eigner, Peter and Peter Melichar (2008), "Das Ende der Boden-Credit-Anstalt und die Rolle Rudolf Siegharts," in: *Österreichische Zeitschrift für Geschichtswissenschaften*, no. 3, S. 56–114.

Eigner, Peter, Michael Wagner and Andreas Weigl (1991), "Finanzplatz: Wien als Geld- und Kapitalmarkt," in: Günther Chaloupek, Peter Eigner and Michael Wagner (eds.), *Wien. Wirtschaftsgeschichte 1740–1938*, Vienna, pp. 909–997.

Einaudi, Luca (2001), *Money and politics. European monetary unification and the international gold standard (1865–1873)*, Oxford.

Ernst, Karl v. (1895), "Geld (A. Geschichte des Münzwesens bis zum Jahre 1857)," in: Ernst Mischler and Josef Ulbrich (eds.), *Österreichisches Staatswörterbuch. Handbuch des gesammten österreichischen öffentlichen Rechtes*, vol. I, Vienna, pp. 649–665.

European Central Bank (1999), "The institutional framework of the European System of Central Banks," in: *Monthly Bulletin July*, pp. 55–63.

European Central Bank (n.d.), *The role of central banks in prudential supervision*, Frankfurt am Main. www.ecb.europa.eu/pub/pdf/other/prudentialsupcbrole_en.pdf

European Central Bank (³2011), *The monetary policy of the ECB*, Frankfurt am Main.

European Central Bank (2014), *Guide to banking supervision*, Frankfurt am Main.

European Monetary Institute (1995), *Annual Report 1994*, Frankfurt am Main.

European Monetary Institute (1996), *Progress toward convergence*. Frankfurt am Main.

European Monetary Institute (1997), *The European Monetary Institute*, Frankfurt am Main.

European Monetary Institute (1998), *Convergence report*, Frankfurt am Main.

Federn, Walther (1925), "Die Kreditpolitik der Banken," in: Julius Bunzel (ed.), *Geldentwertung und Stabilisierung in ihren Einflüssen auf die soziale Entwicklung in Österreich*, Munich, pp. 54–74.

Federn, Walther (1932), "Der Zusammenbruch der Österreichischen Creditanstalt," in: *Archiv für Sozialwissenschaft und Sozialpolitik*, pp. 403–465.

Fellner, Friedrich (1911), *Die Währungsreform in Ungarn. Mit besonderer Rücksicht auf die Aufnahme der Barzahlungen*, Vienna.

Fellner, Friedrich (1916), "Das Volkseinkommen Österreichs und Ungarns," in: K. K. Statistische Zentral-Kommission (ed.), *Statistische Monatsschrift*, Brno, pp. 485–625.

Fibich, Alexander (1977), *Die Entwicklung der österreichischen Bundesausgaben in der Ersten Republik (1918–1938)*, doctoral thesis, Vienna.

Fischer, Erich (1914), "Der Staatsbankrott von 1816 und die Sanierung der österreichischen Finanzen nach den Napoleonischen Kriegen," in: *Zeitschrift für Volkswirtschaft und Sozialpolitik*, pp. 252–317.

Flandreau, Marc (1996), "The French crime of 1873: An essay on the emergence of the international gold standard, 1870–1880," in: *Journal of Economic History* 56, no. 4, pp. 862–897.

Flandreau, Marc (1997), "Central bank cooperation in historical perspective: a skeptical view," in: *Economic History Review*, no. 4, pp. 735–763.

Flandreau, Marc (2001), *The Bank, the states, and the market: An Austro-Hungarian tale for Euroland,*

1867–1914, Vienna (Oesterreichische National-bank Working Papers 43).

Flandreau, Marc (2006), "The logic of compromise: Monetary bargaining in Austria-Hungary," 1867–1913, in: *European Review of Economic History* 10, no. 1, pp. 3–33.

Flandreau, Marc and Barry Eichengreen (1996), *"The geography of the gold standard,"* in: Jorge Braga de Macedo, Barry Eichengreen and Jaime Reis (eds.), *Currency Convertibility: The Gold Standard and Beyond*, London, pp. 113–143.

Flandreau, Marc and Clemens Jobst (2009), "The empirics of international currencies: Networks, history and persistence," in: *Economic Journal*, no. 119 (April), pp. 643–664.

Flandreau, Marc and John Komlos (2001), "Core or periphery? The credibility of the Austro-Hungarian currency 1867–1913," in: Bachinger and Stiefel (eds.), *Auf Heller und Cent*, pp. 163–183.

Flandreau, Marc and John Komlos (2006), "Target zones in theory and history: Credibility, efficiency, and policy autonomy," in: *Journal of Monetary Economics* 53, no. 8, pp. 1979–1995.

Flandreau, Marc and Kim Oosterlinck (2012), "Was the emergence of the international gold standard expected? Evidence from Indian Government securities," in: *Journal of Monetary Economics* 59, no. 7, pp. 649–669.

Flores, Juan and Yann Decorzant (2012), Public borrowing in harsh times: The League of Nations Loans Revisited (Departamento de historia economia e institutions, Universidad Carlos III de Madrid Working Paper WP 12-07, September 2012)

Flores, Juan and Yann Decorzant (2015/16), "Going multilateral? Financial markets' access and the League of Nations Loans, 1923–1928," in: *Economic History Review* (forthcoming).

FMA and OeNB (2009), *Banking Supervision in Austria*. Vienna.

Forssbæck, Jens and Lars Oxelheim (2007), "The interplay between money market development and changes in monetary policy operations in small European countries, 1980-2000," in: David Mayes und Jan Toporowski (eds.), *Open market operations and financial markets*, London, pp. 120–152.

Frank, Otto (2002), *Die Entstehung nationalen Geldes: Integrationsprozesse der deutschen Währungen im 19. Jahrhundert*, Berlin.

Freudenberger, Herman (2003), *Lost Momentum: Austrian Economic Development 1750s–1830s*. Vienna.

Friedman, Milton and Anna Schwartz (1963), *A monetary history of the United States 1867–1960*, Princeton.

Fuchs, Konrad and Max Scheithauer (1983), *Das Kreditwesen in Österreich*, Vienna.

Fuchs, Rudolf (1998), *Die Wiener Stadtbank: Ein Beitrag zur österreichischen Finanzgeschichte des 18. Jahrhunderts*, Frankfurt am Main.

Gabriel, S. L. (1938), "Österreich in der großdeutschen Wirtschaft," in: *Jahrbücher für Nationalökonomie und Statistik* 138, no. 6, pp. 641–694.

Galántai, József (1990), *Der österreichisch-ungarische Dualismus: 1867–1918*, Vienna.

Galvenius, Mats und Paul Mercier (2011), "The story of the Eurosystem framework," in: Paul Mercier und Francesco Papadia (eds.), *The concrete euro. Implementing monetary policy in the Euro area*. Oxford, p. 115–214.

Garber, Peter and Michael Spencer (1994), *The Dissolution of the Austro-Hungarian Empire: Lessons for Currency Reform*, Princeton.

Gartner, Christine and Helene Schuberth (1996), "The monetary policy strategy of the European Central Bank," in: *Reports and Summaries*, no. 3, pp. 58–70.

Gnan, Ernest, Claudia Kwapil and Maria Teresa Valderrama (2005), "EU and EMU entry: a monetary policy regime change for Austria?" in: *Monetary policy & the economy*, Q2/2005, pp. 53–68.

Goldinger, Walter (1954), "Der geschichtliche Ablauf der Ereignisse in Österreich von 1918 bis 1945," in: Heinrich Benedikt (ed.), *Geschichte der Republik Österreich*, Vienna, pp. 15–288.

Good, David (1977), "Financial Integration in the Late Nineteenth-Century Austria," in: *The Journal of Economic History 34(4)*, pp. 890–910.

Good, David (1977), "National bias in the Austrian capital market before World War I," in: *Explorations in Economic History 14*, pp. 141–166.

Good, David (1984), *The economic rise of the Habsburg Empire, 1750–1914*, Berkeley/Los Angeles.

Goodhart, Charles (1988), *The evolution of central banking*, Cambridge (Mass.).

Goodhart, Charles (1999), "Myths about the lender of last resort," in: *International Finance* 2, no. 3, pp. 339–360.

Granichstaedten-Czerva, Rudolf (1954), "Die Entstehung der Oesterreichischen Nationalbank," in: *Österreichisches Bankarchiv* 2, no. 3, pp. 86–95.

Gratz, Alois (1949), "Österreichische Finanzpolitik von 1848 bis 1948," in: Mayer (ed.), *Hundert Jahre*, pp. 222–309.

Gratz, Gustav and Richard Schüller (1930), *Der wirtschaftliche Zusammenbruch Österreich-Ungarns*, Vienna.

Gross, Stephen and S. Chase Gummer (2014), "Ghosts of the Habsburg Empire: Collapsing currency union and lessons for the Eurozone," in: *East European politics and societies and cultures* 28, no. 1, pp. 252–265.

Grossman, Richard (2010), *Unsettled account: The evolution of banking in the industrialized world since 1800*, Princeton.

Grossman, Richard and Hugh Rockoff (2015/16), "Fighting the last war: Economists on the lender of last resort," in: Bordo et al. (ed.), *Central banks at a crossroads*, forthcoming; available as an NBER working paper at www.nber.org/papers/w20832.

Grunwald, Max (1913), *Samuel Oppenheimer und sein Kreis*, Vienna.

Guger, A. (1998), "Economic policy and social democracy: The Austrian experience," in: Oxford Review of Economic Policy 14, no. 1, pp. 40–58.

Gulick, Charles (1948), *Austria from Habsburg to Hitler*, Berkeley/Los Angeles.

Gutkas, Karl (1970), "Die politische Entwicklung," in: *Österreich 1945–1970. 25 Jahre Zweite Republik*, Vienna, pp. 1–191.

Haas, Hans (1995), "Österreich im System der Pariser Vororteverträge," in: Emmerich Talos et al. (ed.), *Handbuch des politischen Systems Österreichs. Erste Republik 1918–1933*, Vienna, pp. 665–693.

Haas, Karl (1978), "Industrielle Interessenpolitik in Österreich zur Zeit der Weltwirtschaftskrise," in: *Jahrbuch für Zeitgeschichte*, no. 1, pp. 97–126.

Hal, Lary B. (1943), *The United States in the World Economy*, Washington.

Handler, Heinz (1989), *Grundlagen der österreichischen Hartwährungspolitik. Geldwertstabilisierung, Phillipskurve, Unsicherheit*, Vienna.

Handler, Heinz and Peter Mooslechner (1986), "Hintergründe und ökonomische Aspekte der Novellierung des Kreditwesengesetzes 1986," in: *WIFO-Monatsberichte*, no. 12, pp. 762–781.

Hanisch, Eva (1995), "The OeNB's minimum reserve policy," in: *Reports and Summaries*, no. 4, pp. 25–28.

Hansmeyer, Karl-Heinrich and Rolf Caesar (1976), "Kriegswirtschaft und Inflation (1936–1948)," in: Deutsche Bundesbank (ed.), *Währung und Wirtschaft in Deutschland 1876–1975*, Frankfurt am Main, pp. 367–429.

Hardach, Gerd (1973), *Der Erste Weltkrieg 1914–1918*, Munich.

Haschek, Helmut (1967), *Exportförderung durch Kreditgewährung und Übernahme von Haftungen*, Vienna.

Hauer, Joseph von (1848), *Beiträge zur Geschichte der österreichischen Finanzen*, Vienna.

Helleiner, Eric (2004), *The making of national money: Territorial currencies in historical perspective*, Ithaca.

Heller, Hans (1978), "Der dritte Anlauf," in: Helmuth Slaik et al. (ed.), *Aktuelle Probleme zum Recht des Kreditwesens*, Vienna, pp. 14–50.

Hertz, Friedrich (1903a), *Die Diskont- und Devisenpolitik der Oesterreichisch-ungarischen Bank*, Vienna.

Hertz, Friedrich (1903b), *Die Oesterreichisch-ungarische Bank und der Ausgleich*, Vienna.

Hestermann, J. K. (1818), *Eine Akzie der österreichischen Nazional-Bank. Betrachtungen über die Vortheile, welche die Theilnehmer an diesem Institute von ihrer Einlage erwarten dürfen*, Vienna.

Hochedlinger, Michael (2010), "'Onus Militare.' Zum Problem der Kriegsfinanzierung in der frühneuzeitlichen Habsburgermonarchie 1500–1750," in: Peter Rauscher (ed.), *Kriegführung und Staatsfinanzen. Die Habsburgermonarchie und das Heilige Römische Reich vom Dreißigjährigen Krieg bis zum Ende des habsburgischen Kaisertums*, Münster, pp. 81–136.

Hochreiter, Eduard and Georg Winckler (1995), "The advantages of tying Austria's hands: The success of the hard currency strategy," in: *European Journal of Political Economy* 11, no. 1, pp. 83–111.

Hochreiter, Eduard (2000), "The Role of National Central Banks (NCBs) in the Eurosystem: Current State of Play," in: *Atlantic Economic Journal*, Vol. 28, no. 3, September, pp. 300–308.

Hock, Carl von (1879), *Der österreichische Staatsrat 1760–1848*, Vienna.

Hofmann, Victor (1923), *Die Devalvierung des österreichischen Papiergelds im Jahre 1811*, Vienna.

Holl, Brigitte (1976), *Hofkammerpräsident Gundaker Thomas Graf Starhemberg und die österreichische Finanzpolitik der Barockzeit (1703–1715)*, Vienna.

Hollerer, Siegfried (1974), *Verstaatlichung und Wirtschaftsplanung in Österreich 1946–1949*, Vienna.

Huber, Dieter and Georg Merc (2014), "The banking recovery and resolution directive and the EU's crisis management framework: principles, interplay with the comprehensive assessment and the consequences for recapitalizing credit institutions in crisis situations," in: *Financial Stability Report 28*, pp. 75–90.

Huffman, Wallace and James R. Lothian (1980), "Money in the United Kingdom, 1833–1880," in: *Journal of Money, Credit and Banking* 12, no. 2, pp. 155–174.

International Monetary Fund (2011), *Articles of Agreement*, Washington.

Irmler, Heinrich (1976), "Bankenkrise und Vollbeschäftigungspolitik (1931–1936)," in: Deutsche Bundesbank (ed.), *Währung und Wirtschaft in Deutschland 1876–1975*, Frankfurt am Main, pp. 283–329.

James, Harold (1996), *International monetary cooperation since Bretton Woods*, New York/Oxford.

James, Harold (2012), *Making the European Monetary Union*, Cambridge, Massachusetts.

Jobst, Clemens (2009), "Market leader: The Austro-Hungarian Bank and the making of foreign exchange intervention, 1896–1913," in: *European Review of Economic History* 13, no. 3, pp. 287–318.

Jobst, Clemens (2010). "Gouverner une banque centrale décentralisée: l'exemple austro-hongrois,

1847–1914," in: Olivier Feiertag and Michel Margairaz (ed.), *Gouverner une banque centrale*, Paris, pp. 113–140.

Jobst, Clemens (2014), "What drives central bank branching? The government, the Austrian National Bank and local lending in the territory of present-day Slovakia 1845–1880," in: František Chudják, Ľudovít Hallon and Andrea Leková (eds.), *Centralbanking in Central Europe*, Bratislava, pp. 14–27.

Jobst, Clemens und Thomas Scheiber (2014), "Austria-Hungary," in: Bank of Greece, Bulgarian National Bank, National Bank of Romania, Oesterreichische Nationalbank (eds.), *South-Eastern European monetary and economic statistics from the nineteenth century to World War II*, Athens/Sophia/Bucharest/Vienna.

Jobst, Clemens and Stefano Ugolini (2016), "The co-evolution of money markets and central banks, 1815–2008," in: Bordo et al., *Central banks at a crossroads* (forthcoming).

Joham, Josef (1937), *Geld und Kreditwesen in Österreich*, Vienna.

Kalkmann, Philipp (1899), *Die Entwertung der österreichischen Valuta im Jahre 1893 und ihre Ursachen*, Freiburg im Breisgau.

Kaminsky, Graciela and Carmen Reinhart (1999), "The twin crisis: the causes of banking and balance-of-payments problems," in: *American Economic Review* 89, no. 3, pp. 473–500.

Kamitz, Reinhard (1949), "Die österreichische Geld- und Währungspolitik von 1848 bis 1948," in: Mayer (ed.), *Hundert Jahre*, pp. 127–221.

Karl, Rudolf (1925), *Die österreichische Völkerbundanleihe*, Vienna.

Karl, Rudolf (1929), *Die österreichische Völkerbundanleihe*, vol. II, Vienna.

Katus, László (2008), *Hungary in the Dual Monarchy, 1867–1914*, Boulder (Colorado).

Kausel, Anton, Hans Seidel and Nandor Nemeth (1965), "Österreichs Volkseinkommen 1913–1963," in: *14. Sonderheft des WIFO- Monatsberichte*, Vienna.

Kautz, Gyula (1868), *A nemzetgazdasági eszmek fejlődési törtenéte és befolyása a közviszonyokra Magyarországon* (History and impact of economic theories on public life in Hungary), Pest.

Kautz, Gyula (1892), *Vorschläge zur Erneuerung des Privilegiums der Oesterreichisch-ungarischen Bank / Oesterreichisch-ungarischen Bank*, Vienna.

Kees, Andreas (1981), "Der Währungsausschuss," in: *Jahrbuch der Europäischen Integration*, pp. 135–144.

Kernbauer, Hans (1987), "Beschleunigter Geldverkehr. Die Veränderung der Zahlungsgewohnheiten durch die Einführung des Postscheckverkehrs im österreichischen

Raum," in: Bernhard Heiller and Michael Wagner (eds.), *Im kurzen Wege. 100 Jahre Postscheckverkehr*, Vienna, pp. 43–61.

Kernbauer, Hans (1991), *Währungspolitik in der Zwischenkriegszeit. Geschichte der Oesterreichischen Nationalbank von 1923 bis 1938*, Vienna.

Kernbauer, Hans (1995), "Österreichische Währungs-, Bank- und Budgetpolitik in der Zwischenkriegszeit, in: Emmerich Talos (ed.), *Handbuch des politischen Systems Österreichs. Erste Republik 1918–1933*, Vienna, pp. 552–569.

Kernbauer, Hans (2016), *Die Oesterreichische Nationalbank von 1969 bis 1999*, Vienna (forthcoming).

Kernbauer, Hans and Fritz Weber (1984), "Die Wiener Großbanken in der Zeit der Kriegs- und Nachkriegsinflation," in: Gerald D. Feldman et al. (eds.), *Die Erfahrungen der Inflation im internationalen Zusammenhang und Vergleich*, Berlin, pp. 142–187.

Keynes, John Maynard (1920), *The economic consequences of the peace*, London.

Kienböck, Viktor (1947), *Währung und Wirtschaft*, Vienna.

Kienzl, Heinz (ed.) (n.d.), *Österreichs Wirtschafts- und Währungspolitik auf dem Weg nach Europa. Festschrift für Maria Schaumayer*, Vienna.

Kindleberger, Charles (1973), *The world in depression, 1929-1939*, London.

Kindleberger, Charles (1989), *The German economy, 1945–1947*, London.

Kindleberger, Charles (⁶2011), *Manias, panics and crashes: a history of financial crises*, Basingstoke.

Klausinger, Hansjörg (2002), *The Austrian School of economics and the gold standard mentality in Austrian economic policy in the 1930s*, Vienna (Department of Economics, Vienna University of Economics and Business Administration Working Paper, December 2002).

Klingenstein, Grete (1965), *Die Anleihe von Lausanne*, Vienna/Graz.

Knapp, Georg Friedrich (1924), *The state theory of money*, London.

Kolm, Evelyn (2001), "Die Oesterreichisch-ungarische Bank im Spannungsfeld der Nationalitätenkonflikte," in: Bachinger and Stiefel (eds.), *Auf Heller und Cent*, pp. 221–252.

Komlos, John (1983), "The diffusion of financial technology into the Austro-Hungarian monarchy towards the end of the nineteenth century," in: John Komlos (ed.), *Economic Development in the Habsburg Monarchy in the Nineteenth Century, Essays*. New York, S. 137–163.

Komlos, John (1983), *The Habsburg monarchy as a customs union*, Princeton.

Komlos, John (1987), "Financial innovation and the demand for money in Austria-Hungary, 1867–1913," in: *Journal of European Economic History (16)*, pp. 587–605.

Komlos, John (1989), *Nutrition and economic development in the eighteenth-century Habsburg monarchy: An anthropometric history*, Princeton.

Koren, Stephan (1961), "Die Industrialisierung Österreichs," in: Wilhelm Weber (ed.), *Österreichs Wirtschaftsstruktur gestern–heute– morgen*, vol. I, Berlin, pp. 223–550.

Kövér, György (1988), "The London Stock exchange and the credit of Austria-Hungary 1867–1871," in: *Acta Historica Academiae Scientiarum Hungaricae* 34, pp. 159–170.

Kövér, György and Ágnes Pogány (2002), *Binationale Bank. Die binationale Bank einer multinationalen Monarchie: Die Österreichisch-Ungarische Bank (1878–1922)*, Wiesbaden.

Kraft, Johanna (1927), *Die Finanzreform des Grafen Wallis und der Staatsbankrott von 1811*, Graz.

Kramar, Karl (1886), *Das Papiergeld in Österreich seit 1848*, Leipzig.

Kramer, Helmut (1991), "Strukturprobleme Österreichs aus der Sicht des Avis der EG-Kommission," in: *WIFO-Monatsberichte*, no. 9, pp. 519–521.

Kranister, Willibald (³1988), *Die Geldmacher: vom Gulden zum Schilling*, Vienna.

Lachs, Thomas (1986), "Die Liberalisierung der Devisenbestimmungen ab 1. November 1986," in: *Österreichisches Bankarchiv*, no. 12, pp. 608–612.

Lachs, Thomas (1989), "Die Devisenliberalisierung der OeNB im Kontext der Wirtschafts- und Währungspolitik," in: *Österreichisches Bankarchiv*, no. 4, pp. 339–343.

Lachs, Thomas (1991), "Die letzte Etappe der Devisenliberalisierung," in: *Österreichisches Bankarchiv*, no. 10, pp. 700f.

Lachs, Thomas and Doris Ritzberger-Grünwald (1998), *Der Euro: Europas neue Währung*, Vienna.

Langer, Edmond (1966), *Die Verstaatlichungen in Österreich*, Vienna.

Lauber, Volkmar (³1997) "Wirtschafts- und Finanzpolitik," in: Herbert Dachs et al. (eds.), *Handbuch des politischen Systems Österreichs. Die Zweite Republik*, Vienna, pp. 545–556.

Layton, Walter and Charles Rist (1925), *The economic situation of Austria*, Geneva.

Lederer, Carl (1847), *Die privilegirte österreichische National-Bank, ihre Gründung, ihre Entwicklung und ihr Wirken*, Vienna.

Leonhart, Gustav (1886), *Die Verwaltung der Oesterreichisch-ungarischen Bank 1878–1885*, Vienna.

Lesigang, Wilhelm (1876), "Die Ursachen des Agio und seiner Schwankungen in Österreich," in: *Jahrbuch für Nationalökonomie und Statistik* no. 27, pp. 209–245 and no. 28, pp. 205–293.

Lewis, Arthur W. (1949), *Economic survey 1919–1939*, London.

Lichter, Jörg (1999), *Preußische Notenbankpolitik in der Formationsphase des Zentralbanksystems 1844 bis 1857*, Berlin.

Liebscher, Klaus (ed.) (2002), *Vom Schilling zum Euro. Beiträge zur Zeitgeschichte der österreichischen Wirtschaftspolitik und der Oesterreichischen Nationalbank. Festschrift für Adolf Wala zum 65. Geburtstag*, Vienna.

Liebscher, Klaus and Wilfried Seipel (eds.) (2002), *From the schilling to the euro. Continuity and stability*, Vienna.

Liese, Joachim and Max-Stephan Schulze (1993), "Geldpolitik und Konjunktur in Österreich: Die 'Plener'sche Stagnation' 1862 bis 1866," in: *Vierteljahrschrift für Sozial- und Wirtschaftsgeschichte* 80, no. 4, pp. 510–530.

Lónyai, Menyhért (1875), *Die Bankfrage*, Budapest.

Lopuszanski, Eugen (1907), *Das Bankwesen Österreichs*, Vienna.

Loth, Wilfried (1982), *Die Teilung der Welt. Geschichte des Kalten Krieges 1941–1955*, Munich.

Lucam, Wilhelm (1861a), *Die Oesterreichische Nationalbank und ihr Verhältnis zu dem Staate*, Vienna.

Lucam, Wilhelm (1861b), *Zur österreichischen Bank- und Finanzfrage*, Vienna.

Lucam, Wilhelm (1862), *Die beantragten Änderungen des Übereinkommens zwischen dem Staate und der österreichischen National-Bank*, Vienna.

Lucam, Wilhelm (1876), *Die Oesterreichische Nationalbank während der Dauer des dritten Privilegiums*, Vienna.

Lucam, Wilhelm (1897), *Parität und Regierungseinfluß in der künftigen Oesterreichisch-Ungarischen Bank*, Vienna.

Lucam, Wilhelm (1898), *Die künftigen Statuten der Oesterreichisch-Ungarischen Bank*, Vienna.

Marcus, Nathan (2013), *Foreign advisors to the Austrian National Bank 1923–1929: control or cooperation?* Unpublished conference paper ("Central Banks as Organizations" at the Banque de France on October 9, 2013).

Marcus, Nathan (2015/16), *Credibility, confidence and capital: Austrian reconstruction and the collapse of global finance, 1921-1931*. Cambridge (Mass.) (forthcoming).

Marperger, Paul Jacob (1717), *Beschreibung der Banquen und deroselben wie auch der Banquiers in ihrem Recht*, Serre.

Marx, Julius (1965), *Die wirtschaftlichen Ursachen der Revolution von 1848 in Österreich*, Graz.

März, Eduard (1968), *Österreichische Industrie- und Bankpolitik in der Zeit Franz Josephs I.*, Vienna.

März, Eduard (1984), *Austrian banking and financial policy: Creditanstalt at a turning point, 1913–1923*, London.

März, Eduard and Fritz Weber (1983), "The antecedents of the Austrian financial crash," in: *Zeitschrift für Wirtschafts- und Sozialwissenschaften* 103, pp. 497–519.

Mastalier, Volker (1968), "Exportförderung durch erleichterte Kreditbeschaffung," in: *WIFO-Monatsberichte*, no. 8, pp. 319–328.

Matis, Herbert (1972), *Österreichs Wirtschaft 1848–
1913: Konjunkturelle Dynamik und
gesellschaftlicher Wandel im Zeitalter Franz
Josephs I.*, Berlin.

Matis, Herbert (2001), "Vom Nachkriegselend zum
Wirtschaftswunder – der Schilling im 'goldenen
Zeitalter'," in: Karl Bachinger (ed.), *Abschied vom
Schilling: Eine österreichische Wirtschafts-
geschichte*, Graz, pp. 155–285.

Matis, Herbert (2005), *Die Schwarzenberg-Bank. Kapi-
talbildung und Industriefinanzierung in den
habsburgischen Erblanden*, Vienna.

May, Arthur (1951), *The Hapsburg Monarchy 1867–
1914*, Cambridge (Mass.).

Mayer, Hans (ed.) (1949), *Hundert Jahre österreichischer Wirtschaftsentwicklung 1848–1948*, Vienna.

McKinnon, Ronald I. (1979), *Money in international
exchange. The convertible currency system*, New
York.

Meadows, Dennis L., Donella H. Meadows, Jørgen
Rander and William W. Behrens (1972), *The
limits to growth. A report for the Club of Rome's
report on the predicament of mankind*, New
York.

Mecenseffy, Emil (1894), *Werth und Preis des Privilegiums der Oesterreichisch-ungarischen Bank*,
Vienna.

Mecenseffy, Emil (1896), *Die Verwaltung der Oesterreichisch-ungarischen Bank 1886–1895*, Vienna.

Mecenseffy, Emil (1897), *Bericht über den Goldbesitz
der Oesterreichisch-ungarischen Bank*, Vienna.

Mensi, Franz Freiherr von (1890), *Die Finanzen
Oesterreichs von 1701–1740. Nach archivalischen
Quellen dargestellt*, mit Unterstützung der
kaiserlichen Akademie der Wissenschaften in
Vienna, Vienna.

Mensi, Franz Freiherr von (1906), "Finanzpatent vom
20. Februar 1811," in: Ernst Mischler and Josef Ulbrich (eds.), *Österreichisches Staatswörterbuch.
Handbuch des gesammten österreichischen öffentlichen Rechtes*, vol. 2, Vienna, pp. 62–65.

Mensi, Franz Freiherr von (1909), "Staatsschuld," in:
Ernst Mischler and Josef Ulbrich (eds.), *Österreichisches Staatswörterbuch. Handbuch des
gesammten österreichischen öffentlichen Rechtes*,
vol. 4, Vienna, pp. 399–465.

Mensi, Franz Freiherr von (1895), "Geld (C. Papiergeld)," in: Ernst Mischler and Josef Ulbrich
(eds.), *Österreichisches Staatswörterbuch. Handbuch des gesammten österreichischen öffentlichen Rechtes*, vol. 1, Vienna, pp. 672–686.

Mentschl, Josef and Gustav Otruba (1965), *Österreichische Industrielle und Bankiers*, Vienna.

Meyer, Carl von (1861), *Grundzüge für die Herstellung
und Erhaltung einer convertiblen Papier-
währung in Oesterreich mit besonderer Rücksicht
auf die englische Bankacte vom Jahr 1844 und
deren Anwendbarkeit auf die hiesigen Verhältnisse*, Vienna.

Michel, Bernard (1976), *Banques & banquiers en
Autriche au début du 20e siècle*, Paris.

Mikoletzky, Hanns Leo (1965), "Schweizer Händler
und Bankiers in Österreich vom 17. bis zur Mitte
des 19. Jahrhunderts," in: Institut für Österreichische Geschichtsforschung/Wiener Katholische
Akademie (ed.), *Festgabe für Hugo Hantsch zum
70. Geburtstag*, Graz, pp. 149–181.

Mises, Ludwig von (1907), "Die wirtschaftspolitischen
Motive der österreichischen Valutaregulierung,"
in: *Zeitschrift für Volkswirtschaft, Sozialpolitik
und Verwaltung*, no. 16, pp. 561–582.

Mises, Ludwig von (1909), "The Foreign Exchange
Policy of the Austro-Hungarian Bank," in: *The
Economic Journal* 19, no. 74, pp. 201–211.

Mises, Ludwig von (1912), "Das vierte Privilegium der
Österreichisch-Ungarischen Bank," in: *Zeitschrift
für Volkswirtschaft, Sozialpolitik und Verwaltung*, no. 21, pp. 611–624.

Mises, Ludwig von (1924), "Über Deflationspolitik," in:
*Mitteilungen des Verbandes österreichischer
Banken und Bankiers*, pp. 13–18.

Mises, Ludwig von (2009), *Memoirs*, Auburn, Ala-
bama.

Mitchell, Brian (1988), *British Historical Statistics*,
Cambridge.

Moggridge, Donald E. (1972), *British Monetary Policy
1924–1931: The Norman conquest of $4.86*. Cam-
bridge.

Mooslechner, Peter (1982), "Neuberechnung der
WIFO-Wechselkursindizes," in: *WIFO-Monatsberichte*, No. 7, pp. 424–433.

Mooslechner, Peter (2005), "10 years of Austrian EU
membership: elements of an overall economic
assessment," in: *Monetary Policy & the Economy*,
Q2/2005, pp. 28–41.

Mooslechner, Peter, Stefan Schmitz and Helene Schuberth (2007), "From Bretton Woods to the euro:
the evolution of Austrian monetary policy from
1969 to 1999," in: Oesterreichische Nationalbank
(ed.), *From Bretton Woods to the euro–Austria on
the road to European integration. Workshop in
memoriam Karl Waldbrunner 1906–1980*, Vienna (Proceedings of OeNB Workshops, vol. 11),
pp. 21–44.

Morys, Matthias (2006), *The classical gold standard
in the European periphery: a case study of Austria-Hungary and Italy, 1870–1913*, unpublished
doctoral thesis, London School of Economics.

Mühlpeck, Vera, Roman Sandgruber and Hannelore
Woitek (1994), "The consumer price index from
1800 to 1914. A calculation in retrospective for
Vienna and the contemporary territory of Austria," in: Herbert Matis (ed.), *The economic devel-*

opment of Austria since 1870, Aldershot, pp. 199–229.

Nationalbank (1862a), *Die beantragten Änderungen an den Statuten und dem Reglement Oesterreichischen Nationalbank*, Vienna.

Nationalbank (1862b), *Die beantragten Änderungen des Übereinkommens zwischen dem Staat und der Oesterreichischen Nationalbank*, Vienna.

Natmeßnig, Charlotte (1998), *Britische Finanzinteressen in Österreich. Die Anglo-Österreichische Bank*, Vienna.

Nautz, Jürgen (1999), *Ethnische Konfliktlagen und monetäre Integration*, Vienna.

Nautz, Jürgen (2006), "Kommunikationsstruktur und Bankgeschäft der Notenbank der Habsburgermonarchie," in: *Scripta mercaturae* 40, pp. 241–264.

Neal, Larry (2000), "How it all began: the monetary and financial architecture of Europe during the first global capital markets, 1648–1815," in: *Financial History Review* 7, no. 2, pp. 117–140.

Nemec, Ciril (1924), *La Banque austro-hongroise et sa liquiditation*, Paris.

Nemschak, Franz (1955), *Ten years of Austrian economic development, 1945–1955*, Vienna.

Nemschak, Franz (1970), *Österreichs Wirtschaft in den sechziger und siebziger Jahren. Rückschau und Ausblick*, Vienna.

Neuwirth, Joseph (1873), *Bankacte und Bankstreit in Österreich-Ungarn 1862–1873*, Leipzig.

Neuwirth, Joseph (1874), *Bank und Valuta in Oesterreich-Ungarn. 2. Die Speculationskrisis von 1873*, Leipzig.

Nötel, Rudolf (1984), "Money, Banking and Industry in Interwar Austria and Hungary," in: *Journal of European Economic History* 13, pp. 137–202.

Nowotny, Ewald (2006), "Die Hartwährungspolitik und die Liberalisierung des Kapitalverkehrs sowie des Finanzsektors," in: Oesterreichische Nationalbank (ed.), *From Bretton Woods to the euro–Austria on the road to European integration. Workshop in memoriam Karl Waldbrunner 1906–1980*, Wien (Proceedings of OeNB Workshops, vol. 11), pp. 45–68.

Nowotny, Ewald (1993), "Volkswirtschaftliche Aspekte des Bankwesengesetzes," in: Bank Austria, *Bankwesengesetz. Textausgabe mit ausgewählten Beiträgen*, Vienna, pp. 7–20.

Oestergaard, Peter (1928), *Inflation und Stabilisierung des französischen Francs*, Jena.

Oesterreichische Nationalbank (1991), *Striking a balance–175 Years of Austrian National Bank*, Vienna.

Oesterreichische Nationalbank (1996), *Die Oesterreichische Nationalbank als Unternehmen*, Vienna.

Ogris, Werner (1975), "Die Rechtsentwicklung in Cisleithanien 1848–1918," in: Wandruszka and Urbanitsch (eds.), *Verwaltung*, pp. 538–662.

Österreichisches Biographisches Lexikon 1815–1950, vol. 9, Vienna 1988.

Österreichs Volkseinkommen 1913 bis 1963, Vienna 1965.

Ostersetzer, Alfred (1892), Währungswechsel und Aufnahme der Baarzahlungen: Übersichtliche Darstellung der Valutafrage, Vienna.

Otruba, Gustav (1968), *Österreichs Wirtschaft im 20. Jahrhundert*, Vienna.

Otruba, Gustav (1981), "Die Einführung des Goldstandards in Österreich-Ungarn und seine Auswirkungen auf die Preis- und Lohnentwicklung," in: Hermann Kellenbenz (ed.), *Weltwirtschaftliche und währungspolitische Probleme seit dem Ausgang des Mittelalters*, Stuttgart, pp. 123-162.

Otto, Frank (2004), "Der Diskurs um die deutsche Währungsvereinheitlichung im 19. Jahrhundert: Die Konstruktion der Ideologie des nationalen Geldes," in: *Jahrbuch für Wirtschaftsgeschichte/Economic History Yearbook* 45, no. 1, pp. 197–220.

Padoa-Schioppa, Tommaso (1999), *EMU and banking supervision*, Lecture at the London School of Economics on February 24, 1999. www.ecb.europa.eu/press/key/date/1999/html/sp990224.en.html

Pammer, Michael (1998), "Austrian private investment in Hungary, 1850–1914," in: *European Review of Economic History*, no. 2, pp. 141–170.

Pammer, Michael (2002), *Entwicklung und Ungleichheit: Österreich im 19. Jahrhundert*, Stuttgart.

Papademos, Lucas und Jürgen Stark (eds.) (2010), *Enhancing monetary analysis*. Frankfurt am Main.

Pauley, Bruce F. (1988), *Der Weg in den Nationalsozialismus. Ursprünge und Entwicklung in Österreich*, Vienna.

Pech, Helmut and Franz Weninger (1990), "Comments on the policy instruments of the Austrian National Bank," in: *Reports and summaries* 1990(3), pp. 21–25.

Pech, Helmut (2002), "Zur Entstehung währungspolitischer Strategien," in: Liebscher, Klaus (ed.), Vom *Schilling zum Euro*, pp. 111–123.

Perz, Helmuth (1989), *Aspekte der Kriegsfinanzierung: Die österreichischen Kriegsanleihen 1914–1918*, unpublished master's thesis, University of Vienna.

Pichler, Rupert (1996), *Die Wirtschaft der Lombardei als Teil Österreichs. Wirtschaftspolitik, Außenhandel und industrielle Interessen 1815–1859*, Berlin.

Pogány, Ágnes (1992), "Az Osztrák-Magyar Bank felszámolása" [The liquidation of the Austro-Hungarian Bank], in: *Ætas*, no. 4, pp. 19–33.

Pogány, Ágnes (2006), »Wirtschaftsnationalismus in Ungarn im 19. und 20. Jahrhundert«, in: Ágnes Pogány, Eduard Kubů und Jan Kofman (Hg.),

Für eine nationale Wirtschaft: Ungarn, die Tschechoslowakei und Polen vom Ausgang des UJ. Jahrhunderts bis zum Zweiten Weltkrieg, Berlin, S. 11–71.

Pogány, Ágnes (2016), "Kriegskosten und Kriegsfinanzierung: Die Finanzgebarung der österreichisch-ungarischen Monarchie während des Ersten Weltkriegs," in: Helmut Rumpler (ed.), *Die Habsburgermonarchie 1848–1918. Bd. XI: Die Habsburgermonarchie und der Erste Weltkrieg. Vol. I: Der Kampf um die Neuordnung Mitteleuropas*, Vienna (forthcoming).

Popovics, Alexander (1925), *Das Geldwesen im Kriege*, Vienna–New Haven.

Pressburger, Siegfried (1966), *Oesterreichische Notenbank 1816–1966. Geschichte des Oesterreichischen Noteninstituts*, Wien.

Pressburger, Siegfried (1969–1976), *Das österreichische Noteninstitut 1816–1966*, part I, volumes 1–3 (1703–1878) and part II, volumes 1–4 (1878–1922), Vienna.

Pribram, Alfred (1938), *Materialien zur Geschichte der Preise und Löhne in Österreich*, Vienna.

Probszt, Günther (1973), *Österreichische Münz- und Geldgeschichte. Von den Anfängen bis 1918*, Vienna.

Protokolle des Ministerrates der Ersten Republik, Abteilung VIII, Kabinett Dr. Engelbert Dollfuss, vol. 1, edited by Gertrude Enderle-Burcel, Vienna 1980.

Protokolle des Ministerrates der Ersten Republik, Abteilung VIII, Kabinett Dr. Engelbert Dollfuss, vol. 2, edited by Gertrude Enderle-Burcel, Vienna 1982.

Rager, Fritz (1918), *Die Wiener Commerzial-, Leih- und Wechselbank (1787–1830). Beitrag zur Geschichte des österreichischen Aktienbankwesen*, Vienna.

Rathkolb, Oliver and Theodor Venus (2013), *Reichsbank offices 1938–1945 in focus: the Vienna Reichsbank head office*, Vienna.

Rauchberg, Heinrich (1897), *Der Clearing-und Giro-Verkehr in Österreich-Ungarn und im Auslande*, Vienna.

Raudnitz, Josef (1917), *Das österreichische Staatspapiergeld und die privilegierte Nationalbank*, Erster Teil: *1762 bis 1820*, Vienna.

Rauscher, Peter (2013), "Der Fall Oppenheimer und Gomperz 1697. Hofjuden und die Finanzierung des deutschen Fürstenstaats im 17. und 18. Jahrhundert," in: Dieter Lindenlaub, Carsten Burhop and Joachim Scholtyseck (eds.), *Schlüsselereignisse der deutschen Bankengeschichte*, Stuttgart, pp. 51–62.

Rauscher, Peter and Andrea Serles (2015), "Die Wiener Niederleger um 1700. Eine kaufmännische Elite zwischen Handel, Staatsfinanzen und Gewerbe," in: *Österreichische Zeitschrift für Geschichtswissenschaften*, no. 1, pp. 154–182.

Reinhard, Wolfgang (1999), *Geschichte der Staatsgewalt. Eine vergleichende Verfassungsgeschichte Europas von den Anfängen bis zur Gegenwart*, Munich.

Reisch, Richard (1925), "Die höheren Aufgaben einer modernen Notenbank, insbesondere in Krisenzeiten," in: *Mitteilungen des Verbandes österreichischer Banken und Bankiers*, pp. 193–207.

Rennhofer, Friedrich (1978), *Ignaz Seipel, Mensch und Staatsmann: Eine biographische Dokumentation*, Vienna/Cologne/Graz.

Reschauer, Heinrich (1872), *1848. Geschichte der Wiener Revolution*, vol. 1, Vienna.

Revell, Jack (1980), *Costs and margins in banking: an international survey*, Paris.

Revell, Jack (1986), *Costs and margins in banking: statistical supplement 1978–1982*, Paris.

Richter, Rudolf (1998), "Die Geldpolitik im Spiegel der wissenschaftlichen Diskussion," in: Deutsche Bundesbank, *50 Jahre Deutsche Mark*, Munich, pp. 561–606.

Rittmann, Herbert (1975), *Deutsche Geldgeschichte 1484–1914*, Munich.

Roberds, William and Francois Velde (2015/16), "Early public banks," in: Michael Bordo, Øyvind Eitrheim, Marc Flandreau and Jan Qvigstad (eds.), *Central banks at a crossroads: What we learn from history?*, Cambridge (forthcoming).

Rosenberg, H. (1939), "The struggle for a German-Austrian customs-union 1815–1939," in: *The Slavonic and East European Review* 14, pp. 332–342.

Rossmann, Bruno (1982), "Exportförderung in Österreich," in: *Wirtschaft und Gesellschaft*, no. 1, pp. 57–77.

Rothschild, Kurt W. (1947), *Austria's economic development between the two wars*, London.

Rudolph, Richard (1976), *Banking and industrialization in Austria-Hungary*, Cambridge.

Rumpler, Helmut (1997), *Eine Chance für Mitteleuropa: bürgerliche Emanzipation und Staatsverfall in der Habsburgermonarchie 1804–1914*, Vienna.

Rumpler, Helmut and Anatol Schmied-Kowarzik (eds.) (2014), *Die Habsburgermonarchie 1848-1918. Band XI: Die Habsburgermonarchie und der Erste Weltkrieg. 2. Teilband: Weltkriegsstatistik Österreich-Ungarn 1914-1918. Bevölkerungsbewegung, Kriegstote, Kriegswirtschaft*, Vienna.

Sachverständigenrat zur Begutachtung der gesamtwirtschaftlichen Entwicklung (1965), *Jahresgutachten 1964/65*, Stuttgart/Mainz.

Sandgruber, Roman (1982), *Die Anfänge der Konsumgesellschaft. Konsumgüterverbrauch, Lebensstandard und Alltagskultur in Österreich im 18. und 19. Jahrhundert*, Vienna.

Sandgruber, Roman (1995), *Ökonomie und Politik. Österreichische Wirtschaftsgeschichte vom Mittelalter bis zur Gegenwart*, Vienna.

Sargent, Thomas (1982), "The ends of four big inflations," in: Robert Hall (ed.), *Inflation: causes and effects*. Chicago–London, pp. 41–97.

Sargent, Thomas (2013), *Rational Expectations and Inflation*, Princeton.

Sarlós, Béla (1975), "Das Rechtswesen in Ungarn," in: Wandruszka and Urbanitsch (eds.), *Verwaltung*, pp. 499–537.

Saul, Samuel Berrick (1969), *The myth of the Great Depression 1873-1896*, London.

Sax, Emil (ed.) (1875). *Bericht über die Verhandlungen des ersten Kongresses österreichischer Volkswirte*, Vienna.

Sayers, Richard S. (1976), *The Bank of England 1891–1944*, vol. I, Cambridge.

Schärf, Adolf ([7]1960), *Österreichs Erneuerung 1945-1955. Das erste Jahrzehnt der zweiten Republik*, Vienna.

Schasching, Johannes (1954), *Staatsbildung und Finanzentwicklung. Ein Beitrag zur Geschichte des österreichischen Staatskredits in der 2. Hälfte des 18. Jahrhunderts*, Innsbruck.

Schausberger, Norbert (1978), *Der Griff nach Österreich. Der Anschluß*. Vienna-Munich.

Schausberger, Norbert (1983), "Der Anschluß," in: Erika Weinzirl and Kurt Skalnik (eds.), *Österreich 1918-1938. Geschichte der Ersten Republik*, vol. I, Vienna, pp. 517–552.

Schebek, Edmund (1873), *Collectiv-Ausstellung von Beitägen zur Geschichte der Preise: veranstaltet zur Weltausstellung 1873 in Wien von der Handels- und Gewerbekammer in Prag*, Prague.

Schelle, Karel (2010), *Staat und Recht in der Zeit Metternichs*, Diplomarbeit, University of Munich.

Schmitz, Wolfgang (1970), *Geldwertstabilität und Wirtschaftswachstum. Währungspolitik im Spannungsfeld des Konjunkturverlaufs. Festschrift für Andreas Korp*, Vienna/New York.

Schnee, Heinrich (1953–1955), *Die Hoffinanz und der moderne Staat*, 6 Bde., Berlin.

Schremmer, Eckart (1994), *Steuern und Staatsfinanzen während der Industrialisierung Europas: England, Frankreich, Preußen und das Deutsche Reich 1800 bis 1914*, Berlin.

Schubert, Aurel (1992), *The Credit-Anstalt crisis of 1931*, New York.

Schubert, Aurel (1999), "The emergence of national central banks in central Europe after the breakup of the Austro-Hungarian monarchy," in: Carl-Ludwig Holtfrerich, Jaime Reis and Gianni Toniolo (eds.), *The emergence of modern central banking from 1918 to the present*, Aldershot, pp. 186–230.

Schulze, Max-Stephan (1997), "The machine-building industry and Austria's great depression after 1873," in: *Economic History Review*, no. 2, pp. 282–304.

Schulze, Max-Stephan (2000), "Patterns of growth and stagnation in the late nineteenth century Habsburg economy," in: *European Review of Economic History*, no. 4, pp. 311–340.

Schulze, Max-Stephan (2005), "Austria-Hungary's economy in World War I," in: Stephen Broadberry and Mark Harrison (eds.), *The economics of World War I*, Cambridge, pp. 77–111.

Schwarzer, Alfred et al. (1987), *Das österreichische Währungs- und Devisenrecht*, Vienna.

Seidel, Hans (1978), "Der effektive Wechselkurs des Schillings," in: *WIFO-Monatsberichte*, no. 8, pp. 384–396.

Seidel, Hans (1982), "Austro-Keynesianismus," in: *Wirtschaftspolitische Blätter*, no. 3, pp. 11–15.

Seidel, Hans (2005), *Österreichs Wirtschaft und Wirtschaftspolitik nach dem Zweiten Weltkrieg*, Vienna.

Sieghart, Rudolf (1932), *Die letzten Jahrzehnte einer Großmacht. Menschen, Völker, Probleme des Habsburger-Reichs*, Berlin.

Singleton, John (2011), *Central banking in the twentieth century*, Cambridge.

Smeral, Egon and Ewald Walterskirchen (1981), "Der Einfluß von Wirtschaftswachstum und Wettbewerbsfähigkeit auf die Leistungsbilanz," in: *WIFO-Monatsberichte*, no. 7, pp. 373–384.

Sokal, Max (1936), "Der Währungsumbau des Goldblocks," in: *Österreichische Zeitschrift für Bankwesen*, Nr. 5/6, pp. 121–165.

Sommer, Louise (1920/1925), *Die österreichischen Kameralisten in dogmengeschichtlicher Darstellung. Erschienen in 2 Teilen*, Vienna.

Speyerer, Siegmund (1940), *Die Reichsbankverfassung unter dem Bankgesetz vom 30. August 1924 und unter dem Gesetz über die Deutsche Reichsbank vom 15. Juni 1939*, doctoral dissertation, Erlangen.

Spitzmüller, Alexander (1900), "Die österreichisch-ungarische Währungsreform," in: *Zeitschrift für Volkswirtschaft, Sozialpolitik und Verwaltung*, Nr. 11, pp. 338–393, 497–559.

Spitzmüller, Alexander (1924), "Die Geldwertpolitik der Oesterreichischen Nationalbank," in: *Mitteilungen des Verbandes österreichischer Banken und Bankiers*, pp. 81–92.

Spitzmüller, Alexander (1955), "… und hat auch Ursach, es zu lieben," Vienna.

Spranz, Dietmar (1993), "Das Bankwesengesetz aus der Sicht der Notenbank," in: Bank Austria, *Bankwesengesetz. Textausgabe mit ausgewählten Beiträgen*, Vienna, pp. 21–29.

Sprenger, Bernd (1982), *Geldmengenänderungen in Deutschland im Zeitalter der Industrialisierung (1835–1913)*, Cologne.

Staatsschuldenausschuss (2013), *Bericht über die öffentlichen Finanzen 2012*, Vienna.

Stankovsky, Jan (1975), "Die österreichische Erdöl-rechnung 1974," in: *WIFO-Monatsberichte*, no. 3, pp. 139–141.

Stankovsky, Jan (1981), "Verschuldung der Oststaaten in Österreich," in: *WIFO-Monatsberichte*, no. 4, pp. 228–230.

Stankovsky, Jan (1983), "Grundlagen der Export-förderung in Österreich," in: *WIFO-Monats-berichte*, no. 7, pp. 459–474.

Stasavage, David (2011), *States of credit: Size, power, and the development of European polities*, Princeton.

Steeb, Christian (1999), *Die Grafen von Fries. Eine Schweizer Familie und ihre wirtschaftspolitische und kulturhistorische Bedeutung für Österreich zwischen 1750 und 1830*, Leobersdorf.

Stein, Lorenz von (1855), *Die neue Gestaltung der Geld- und Credit-Verhältnisse in Österreich*, Vienna.

Steiner, Fritz (1913), *Die Entwicklung des Mobil-bankwesens in Österreich. Von den Anfängen bis zur Krise 1873*, Vienna.

Stiassny, Paul (1912), *Der österreichische Staats-bankerott von 1811*, Vienna.

Stiefel, Dieter (1988), *Finanzdiplomatie und Weltwirtschaftskrise – die Krise der Credit-Anstalt und ihre wirtschaftlich-politische Bewäl-tigung*, Frankfurt am Main.

Stiefel, Dieter (2012), *Camillo Castiglioni oder die Metaphysik der Haifische*, Vienna.

Stourzh, Gerald (2000), "Der Dualismus 1867–1918: Zur staatsrechtlichen und völkerrechtlichen Problematik der Doppelmonarchie," in: Helmut Rumpler and Peter Urbanitsch (eds.), *Die Habs-burgermonarchie. Bd. VII: Verfassung und Parla-mentarismus. 1 Teilband: Verfassungsrecht, Ver-fassungswirklichkeit, zentrale Repräsentativkör-perschaften*, Vienna, pp. 1177–1230.

Straumann, Tobias (2010), *Fixed ideas of money. Small states and exchange rate regimes in twenti-eth-century Europe*, Cambridge.

Stuhlpfarrer, Karl (1981), "Der deutsche Plan einer Währungsunion mit Österreich," in: *Anschluß 1938. Protokoll eines Symposiums in Wien vom 14./15.3.1978*, Munich, pp. 271-294.

Szechenyi, Stephan (1830), *Ueber den Kredit*, Leipzig.

Talos, Emmerich (1981), *Staatliche Sozialpolitik in Österreich. Rekonstruktion und Analyse*, Vienna.

Tebeldi, Albrecht [d. i. Karl Beidtel] (1847), *Die Geld-angelegenheiten Österreichs*, Leipzig.

Tegoborski, L. (1845), *Über die Finanzen, den Staats-credit, die Staatsschuld, die finanziellen Hülfs-quellen und das Steuersystem Österreichs*, Vienna.

Teichova, Alice and Herbert Matis (eds.) (1996), *Öster-reich und die Tschechoslowakei 1918–1938. Die wirtschaftliche Neuordnung in Zentraleuropa in der Zwischenkriegszeit*, Vienna.

Tew, Brian (1952), *International monetary co-opera-tion, 1945–1952*, London.

Triffin, Robert (1959), "The return to convertibility. 1926–1931 and 1958–? or Convertibility and the morning after," in: *Banca Nazionale del Lavoro, Quarterly Review 48* (March), pp. 3–57.

Triffin, Robert (1960), *Gold and the dollar crisis: the future of convertibility*, New Haven.

Tschurn, Karl (1908), *Die Entwicklung des Verwal-tungsorganismus der Oesterreichisch-un-garischen Bank, vormals privilegierte oester-reichische Nationalbank*, Vienna.

Turnheim, Georg (ed.) (2009), *Österreichs Ver-staatlichte. Die Rolle des Staates bei der Entwick-lung der österreichischen Industrie von 1918 bis 2008*, Vienna.

Ugolini, Stefano (2011), *What do we really know about the long-term evolution of central banking? Evi-dence from the past, insights for the present*, Oslo (Norges Bank Working Paper 2011/15).

Ugolini, Stefano (2012), "The origins of foreign ex-change policy: the National Bank of Belgium and the quest for monetary independence in the 1850s," in: *European Review of Economic History* no. 1, pp. 51–73.

Van der Wee, Herman and G. Kurgan-Van Hentenryk (2000), *Die Bank in Europa*, Antwerp.

Van der Wee, Herman (1984), *Der gebremste Wohl-stand. Wiederaufbau, Wachstum, Strukturwan-del 1945–1980*, Munich (Geschichte der Weltwirtschaft im 20. Jahrhundert, vol. 6).

Van Dillen, J. G. (ed.) (1934), *History of the principal public banks*, The Hague.

Veit, Otto (1961), *Grundriss der Währungspolitik*, Frankfurt am Main.

Vocelka, Karl (2001), *Glanz und Untergang der höfi-schen Welt. Repräsentation, Reform und Reak-tion im habsburgischen Vielvölkerstaat*, Vienna.

Vranitzky, Franz (1986), "Gedanken zu einer leis-tungsstarken Kreditwirtschaft," in: *Vortragsreihe des Verbandes österreichischer Banken und Bankiers*, no. 1, pp. 5–18.

Wagner, Adolph (1861/1863), "Zur Geschichte und Kri-tik der österreichischen Bankozettelperiode," in: *Zeitschrift für die gesamte Staatswissenschaft 17*, pp. 577–635, and *ibid*. 19, pp. 392–488.

Wagner, Adolph (1862a), *Die Geld- und Credittheorie der Peel'schen Bankacte*, Wien.

Wagner, Adolph (1862b), *Die Herstellung der Nation-albank mit besonderer Rücksicht auf den Bank-plan von Finanzminister von Plener*, Vienna.

Wagner, Gertrude (1990), "Großhändler, Bankiers und Industrielle – Juden in der ersten Hälfte des 19. Jahrhunderts," in: *Österreichisch-jüdisches Geistes- und Kulturleben*, pp. 1–16.

Wagner, Michael and Peter Tomanek (1983), *Bankiers und Beamte. Hundert Jahre Österreichische Postsparkasse*, Vienna.

Wala, Adolf (ed.) (1994), *Der Schilling. Ein Spiegel der Zeiten*, Vienna.

Walré de Bordes, Jan (1924), *The Austrian crown. Its depreciation and stabilization*, London.

Walter, Friedrich (1937), "Die Wiener Stadtbank und das Staatsbankprojekt des Grafen Kaunitz aus dem Jahre 1761," in: *Zeitschrift für Nationalökonomie* 8, no. 4, pp. 444–460.

Wandruszka, Adam and Peter Urbanitsch (eds.) (1975a), *Die Habsburgermonarchie 1848–1918. Die wirtschaftliche Entwicklung*, Vienna.

Wandruszka, Adam and Peter Urbanitsch (eds.) (1975b), *Die Habsburgermonarchie 1848–1918. Verwaltung und Rechtswesen*, Vienna.

Wärmer, Gustav (1934), "Die Auslandsverschuldung Österreichs," in: *Mitteilungen des Verbandes österreichischer Banken und Bankiers*, no. 10, pp. 227–291.

Wärmer, Gustav (1936), *Das österreichische Kreditwesen*, Vienna.

Weber, Eugen (1977), *Peasants into Frenchmen: the modernization of rural France 1870–1914*, London.

Weber, Fritz (1981), *Der finanzielle Länderpartikularismus. Aufstieg und Fall der Provinzbanken in der Ersten Republik*. Tagung der "Wissenschaftlichen Kommission zur Erforschung der österreichischen Geschichte der Jahre 1918–1938, Vienna.

Weber, Fritz (1987), "Österreichs Wirtschaft in der Rekonstruktionsperiode nach 1945," in: *Zeitgeschichte* 17, April, pp. 167–298.

Weber, Fritz (1991), *Vor dem großen Krach. Die Krise des österreichischen Bankwesens in den zwanziger Jahren*, Habilitationsschrift an der Universität Salzburg.

Weber, Fritz (2011), "Die große Bankenfusion des Jahres 1934," in: Peter Berger, Peter Eigner and Andreas Resch (eds.): Die vielen Gesichter des wirtschaftlichen Wandels (kursiv), Wien, pp. 223–258.

Weber, Fritz (2016), *Die Geschichte der Oesterreichischen Nationalbank 1938 bis 1979*, Vienna (forthcoming).

Weber, Fritz and Theodor Venus (eds.) (1993), *Austro-Keynesianismus in Theorie und Praxis*, Vienna.

Weber, Gustav (1938), *Die Pester Ungarische Commerzialbank und die Oesterreichisch-ungarische Bank in der zweiten Hälfte des 19. Jahrhunderts*, doctoral dissertation, Munich.

Weinzierl, Erika and Kurt Skalnik (eds.) (1975), *Das neue Österreich. Geschichte der Zweiten Republik*, Graz/Vienna/Cologne.

Welzl, Lucia (1989), *Die Familie Geymüller: Über die politische, wirtschaftliche und gesellschaftliche Situation in Österreich in der ersten Hälfte des 19. Jahrhunderts und die Bedeutung der Familie Geymüller in dieser Zeit*, doctoral dissertation, Vienna.

White, Eugene (2001), "Making the French pay. The costs and consequences of the Napoleonic reparations, in: *European Review of Economic History*, no. 3, pp. 337–365.

Wieser, Friedrich (1893), "Resumption of specie payments in Austria-Hungary," in: *Journal of Political Economy* 1, no. 3, pp. 380–405.

WIFO (1947), "Gesamtschau der österreichischen Wirtschaft im Jahre 1946," in: *WIFO-Monatsberichte*, no. 1–3, pp. 1–40.

WIFO (1949a), "Die österreichische Lohnpolitik seit Kriegsende," in: WIFO-Monatsberichte (kursiv), no. 8, attachment, pp. 1–15.

WIFO (1949b), "Die österreichische Wirtschaft und die internationalen Währungsabwertungen," in: *WIFO-Monatsberichte*, no. 9, pp. 346–350.

WIFO (1949c), "Die Neuordnung der österreichischen Devisenbewirtschaftung," in: *WIFO-Monatsberichte*, no. 11, pp. 443–448.

WIFO (1951), "Die wirtschaftliche Lage," in: *WIFO-Monatsberichte*, no. 3, pp. 113–138.

WIFO (1953a), "Die Entwicklung der österreichischen Wirtschaft auf einzelnen Gebieten im Jahre 1952," in: *WIFO-Monatsberichte*, no. 2, pp. 31–75.

WIFO (1953b), "Zur Vereinheitlichung der Wechselkurse," in: *WIFO-Monatsberichte*, no. 4, pp. 107–116.

WIFO (1954), "Der Bundeshaushalt im Jahr 1953, in: *WIFO-Monatsberichte*, no. 4, pp. 133–140.

WIFO (1955), "Gesamtschau der österreichischen Wirtschaft im Jahre 1954," in: *WIFO-Monatsberichte*, no. 2, pp. 44–96.

WIFO (1956), "Preis- und Einkommenselastizität des österreichischen Exportes," in: *WIFO-Monatsberichte*, no. 9, pp. 314–321.

WIFO (1969), "Die Aufwertung der D-Mark und die Folgen für Österreich," in: *WIFO-Monatsberichte*, no. 11, pp. 450–457.

Winkelbauer, Thomas (2003), *Ständefreiheit und Fürstenmacht. Länder und Untertanen des Hauses Habsburg im konfessionellen Zeitalter*, 2 volumes, Vienna.

Wirth, Max (1858), *Geschichte der Handelskrisen*, Frankfurt am Main.

Wirth, Max (1874), *Geschichte der Handelskrisen*, Frankfurt am Main.

Wirth, Max (1875), *Die österreichisch-ungarische Bankfrage*, Vienna.

Wirth, Max (1894), *Die Notenbank-Frage in Beziehung zur Währungsreform in Österreich-Ungarn*, Frankfurt am Main.

Würz, Michael (1993), "The new Austrian Banking Act," in: *Reports and Summaries*, No. 4, pp. 27–33.

Yeager, Leland (1969), "Fluctuating exchange rates in the nineteenth century: the experience of Austria and Russia," in: Robert Mundell and Alexander Swoboda (eds.), *Monetary Problems of the International Economy*, Chicago/London, pp. 61–89.

Zehn Jahre ERP in Österreich 1948/1958, (1958), Vienna.

Zeissel, Stephan (1928), *Die Politik der Oesterreichischen Nationalbank*, Vienna/Kiel.

Zeuceanu, Alexandre (1924), *La liquidation de la banque d'Autriche-Hongrie*, Vienna.

Zich, Wilhelm (2009), *Der Wiener Münzvertrag vom 24. Januar 1857 und Carl Ludwig von Bruck*, doctoral dissertation, Vienna.

Zipser, Wolfgang (1997), *Auf der Suche nach Stabilität: Das Zentralbankgeldangebot der österreichischen Nationalbank 1923 bis 1937*, Frankfurt am Main.

Zuckerkandl, Robert (1911), "The Austro-Hungarian Bank," in: National Monetary Commission (ed.), *Banking in Russia, Austro-Hungary, The Netherlands and Japan*, Washington, pp. 55–118.

Zugschwerdt, Johann Baptist (1855), *Das Bankwesen und die privilegirte österreichische Nationalbank*, Vienna.

Archives

OeNB Archives: Bank History Archives of the Oesterreichische Nationalbank
  Minutes of the meetings of the Governing Board (Direktion): no./date
  Minutes of the meetings of the General Council (Generalrat): no./date
  File: no./year
Austrian State Archives

BoE: Bank of England archives
CA Archives: Historical archives of the Creditanstalt, now Unicredit
Deutsche Bundesbank Archives
Koblenz Archives

Periodical publications of the Nationalbank

Vortrag des Gouverneurs an den löblichen Bank-Ausschuß (1819–1863)

General-Versammlung der priv. österreichischen Nationalbank (1864–1878)

Jahressitzung der Generalversammlung der Oesterreichisch-ungarischen Bank (1879–1914, 1918, for subsequent years only balance sheets were published)

Jahresbericht und Vorlagen zur Jahressitzung der Generalversammlung der Oesterreichischen Nationalbank (1924–1938)

Bericht über das Geschäftsjahr mit Jahresabschluss (1957–), also available in English

Mitteilungen des Direktoriums der Oesterreichischen Nationalbank (1923–1938, 1946–1989)

Reports and Summaries; renamed Focus on Austria in 1997 [Berichte und Studien] (1990–2003)

Financial Stability Report [Finanzmarktstabilitätsbericht] (2001–)

Monetary Policy & the Economy [Geldpolitik und Wirtschaft] (2004–)

Statistical sources

Historical time series compiled on the occasion of the OeNB's bicentennial, available at www.oenb.at.
  Volume 1: Nationalbank: balance sheet and profit and loss statements
  Volume 2: Credit institutions: balance sheet, profit and loss, structural data
  Volume 3: Interest rates, yields, exchange rates
  Volume 4: Macroeconomic indicators
Statistische Nachrichten, edited by the Bundesamt für Statistik (1923–1937)

Statistische Tabellen zur Währungsfrage der Österreichisch-ungarischen Monarchie, edited by the k.k. Finanzministerium (1892).

Tabellen zur Währungsstatistik, edited by the k.k. Finanzministerium (1893, 1896–99, 1903–1906).

Tafeln zur Statistik der oesterreichischen Monarchie (1828–1871)

Wirtschaftsstatistisches Jahrbuch, edited by the Vienna Chamber of Labour (1925–1937)

Tables

Charts and maps

Photo credits

Index

advances 52, 61, 62f., 68f., 79f., 135f., 150, 249
  development of 46, 57, 59, 84f., 87f., 90, 94f., 144,
    147f., 167, 188, 193
  eligible counterparties and collateral 43, 45, 61, 57,
    84f., 92
  interest rate on 43, 88, 92, 163, 233
Allgemeine Depositenbank 165–166
allied military schilling 195
Alpine lands 49
Androsch, Hannes 224
Anglo-Austrian Bank 159, 172
Antizipationsscheine (anticipation certificates) *see*
    paper money
Arnstein & Eskeles, banking house 48, 69, 87
Austrian State Treaty (1955) 214
Austro-Hungarian Bank *see* Nationalbank
Austro-Keynesianism 228
Avenol, Joseph Louis Anne 182
Banco del Giro 13, 17f.
Bancozettel *see* paper money
banking union 264f.
Bank for International Settlements (BIS) 178f., 208
Bank of England 22, 157, 159f., 165f., 169f., 172, 175, 178f.,
    180, 260; (Peel's Act) 78f.
bank of issue, regional 115
banknotes *see* paper money
banknote tax 137, 159, 182, 228
banks
  development of 49, 85–87, 91–94, 137f., 171–173,
    183–186, 201, 236f.
  legislation 213, 237, 258f.
  lending and deposit rates, cartel for 237
  public 13–15
  relationship with the central bank 81f., 86f., 135f.,
    183–186, 252
  resolution of 263
  supervision 238, 257–266
  see also private banks
Banque de France 51
Bankverein, Wiener 184
Barbier, Adrian Nikolaus 41
Bark, Peter 176
barter trade 199, 203
Bartsch, Franz 209
Basel capital rules 258, 262
BAWAG P.S.K. 69, 260
Biliński, Leon 99, 122
bills of exchange 60
  supply of 56, 87, 131, 134
  see also discount operations
bimetallic standard 124f.
block floating 225
Bodencreditanstalt 69, 160, 171, 173
Bohemian lands 18, 21, 46–50, 102, 122, 133f.
Bosel, Siegmund 172

branch offices of the Nationalbank
  contract offices 132f.
  establishment of 56f., 83f., 115, 120, 131, 133
  exchange offices 47, 54
  services of 83f., 87, 94, 118, 119, 121, 131–136, 145
Brauneis, Viktor 164, 173, 178f., 187
Bretton Woods 204, 221, 223, 225, 246
Brno 47, 51, 82
Bruck, Karl Ludwig 73, 115
Bruins, Gijsbert 179
Budapest 47, 51, 82f., 95, 115, 119f., 121, 131, 134f., 148
Bundesbank, Deutsche 224, 234, 245–247
capital flight 155, 158, 210, 224f.
capital market legislation (1954) 211
Castiglioni, Camillo 165
certificates of deposit 148
Charles VI 20
Chotek, Rudolf 22
clearing agreements 183, 204
coin 24
  hoarding of 25f.
  in circulation 50f., 130
coinage standard *see* florin, Wiener Münzkon-
    vention
Compromise, Austro-Hungarian *see* Hungary
convergence criteria 239
convertibility 219
  see also foreign exchange control; on the convert-
    ibility of paper money into coin *see* paper money,
    silver or gold convertibility
coverage of banknotes in circulation
  actual 55, 56, 59, 62, 65f., 71, 87, 92f., 129, 143f., 167, 182
  statutory rules 42, 58, 70f., 79f., 136f., 140f., 159f., 212
  suspension of statutory rules 94, 144, 146
  see also banknote tax
Creditanstalt(-Bankverein) 69, 86f., 139, 171ff., 176ff.,
    184, 186
crown 128
  issuance of gold crowns 130
currency basket 225
currency reform, *see* florin, crown, schilling
currency separation 122, 150
current account 188, 203, 205, 229
debt crisis, international 235f.
deflation *see* price developments
Dessewffy, Emil 115
devaluation (change of silver or gold parity) (1811)
    29f; (1892) 128; (1933) 183; (1936) 187
Devisenzentrale (central office of payments to and from
    foreign countries) *see* foreign exchange control
Dietrichstein, Josef 41
discount committee 60, 56, 131
discount operations 52, 60f., 68, 247
  counterparties in 43, 45, 56, 69, 82, 86f., 135f.
  development of 43, 56, 86f., 90, 92, 94f., 134f., 144,

Acknowledgments

This book has benefited from the knowledge and helpfulness of many people. Our special thanks go to:

Walter Antonowicz, Axel Aspetsberger, Franz Baltzarek, Peter Berger, Vincent Bignon, Alexander Dallinger, Elisabeth Dutz, Sandra Dvorsky, Marc Flandreau, Anna Gehmacher, Ernest Gnan, Michael Grundner, Martin Handig, Walpurga Köhler-Töglhofer, Claudia Köpf, Lisa Kothmayr, György Kövér, Börries Kuzmany, Claudia Kwapil, Peter Mooslechner, Ágnes Pogány, Vanessa Redak, Ronald Reepel, Beate Resch, Kilian Rieder, Doris Ritzberger-Grünwald, William Roberds, Stefan Schmitz, Aurel Schubert, Dietmar Spranz, Dominik Stelzeneder, Martin Summer, Karin Turner-Hrdlicka, Stefano Ugolini, Heinrich Wicke, Michael Würz.

The Quest for Stable Money

Central Banking in Austria, 1816–2016

Project management: Manfred Fluch, Clemens Jobst, Ingeborg Schuch, Jürgen Hotz, Joachim Fischer
Editorial office: Maren Barton, Ingeborg Schuch
Translations: Christopher J. Anderson, Michaela Beichtbuchner, Ingrid Haussteiner, Rena Mühldorf, Sylvi Rennert, Ingeborg Schuch, Susan Starling, Susanne Steinacher
Layout, typesetting and cover design: Fuhrer, Wien
Cover illustration: Oesterreichische Nationalbank at Vienna © Oesterreichische Nationalbank
Printing office and book binder: Beltz Bad Langensalza
Printed on acid free paper
Printed in Germany
Bibliographic Information published by the Deutsche Nationalbibliothek.
This publication has been catalogued by the Deutsche Nationalbibliothek in the Deutsche Nationalbibliografie; detailed bibliographic data are available at http://dnb.d-nb.de

ISBN 978-3-593-50535-0

Distribution throughout the world except Germany, Austria and Switzerland by
The University of Chicago Press
1427 East 60th Street
Chicago, IL 60637

For further information:
www.campus.de
www.press.uchicago.edu

Published with support from